MINORITY RIGHTS IN THE PACIFIC REGION

Minority Rights in the Pacific Region

A Comparative Analysis

JOSHUA CASTELLINO
and
DAVID KEANE

OXFORD
UNIVERSITY PRESS

Great Clarendon Street, Oxford OX2 6DP

Oxford University Press is a department of the University of Oxford.
It furthers the University's objective of excellence in research, scholarship,
and education by publishing worldwide in

Oxford New York

Auckland Cape Town Dar es Salaam Hong Kong Karachi
Kuala Lumpur Madrid Melbourne Mexico City Nairobi
New Delhi Shanghai Taipei Toronto

With offices in

Argentina Austria Brazil Chile Czech Republic France Greece
Guatemala Hungary Italy Japan Poland Portugal Singapore
South Korea Switzerland Thailand Turkey Ukraine Vietnam

Oxford is a registered trade mark of Oxford University Press
in the UK and in certain other countries

Published in the United States
by Oxford University Press Inc., New York

© J. Castellino and D. Keane, 2009

First published 2009

British Library Cataloguing in Publication Data

Data available

Library of Congress Cataloging in Publication Data
Castellino, Joshua.
Minority rights in the pacific region : a comparative analysis /
Joshua Castellino and David Keane.
p. cm.
Includes bibliographical references and index.
ISBN 978–0–19–957482–7
1. Minorities—Legal status, laws, etc.—Oceania. 2. Human
rights—Oceania. I. Keane, David, 1978– II. Title.
KVC145.I64C37   2009
342.9508'5—dc22   2009020757

Typeset by Newgen Imaging Systems (P) Ltd., Chennai, India
Printed in Great Britain
on acid-free paper by the
MPG Books Group, Bodmin and King's Lynn

ISBN 978–0–19–957482–7

1 3 5 7 9 10 8 6 4 2

Contents

Abbreviations

AALR	Anglo-American Law Review
AC	Appeal Cases
A Crim R	Australian Criminal Reports
AILR	Australian Indigenous Law Reporter
AJHR	Australian Journal of Human Rights
AJIA	Australian Journal of International Affairs
AJIL	American Journal of International Law
ALB	Aboriginal Law Bulletin
ALJR	Australian Law Journal Reports
ALR	Australian Law Reports
APV	Asia Pacific Viewpoint
ARA	Annual Review of Anthropology
AS	Asian Survey
ASILN	American Society of International Law Newsletter
ASILP	American Society of International Law Proceedings
AUILR	American University International Law Review
AULR	Auckland University Law Review
AYIL	Australian Yearbook of International Law
BCEALR	British Columbia Environmental Affairs Law Review
BJIL	Brooklyn Journal of International Law
BKJIL	Berkeley Journal of International Law
BRNZS	British Review of New Zealand Studies
BYIL	British Yearbook of International Law
BYULR	Brigham Young University Law Review
CA	Current Anthropology
CERD	Committee for the Elimination of Racial Discrimination
CILJ	Cornell International Law Journal
CLB	Commonwealth Law Bulletin
CLR	Commonwealth Law Reports
DLJ	Dalhousie Law Journal
DULJ	Dublin University Law Journal
EIPR	European Intellectual Property Review
EPL	European Public Law
EPLJ	Environmental and Planning Law Journal
FCA	Federal Court of Australia
FCR	Federal Court Reports (Australia)
FLR	Federal Law Reports (Australia)
FOLR	Fordham Law Review

GIELR	Georgetown International Environmental Law Review
GJ	The Geographical Journal
GJICL	Georgia Journal of International & Comparative Law
GLR	Griffith Law Review
GR	Geographical Review
HC	History Compass
HELR	Harvard Environmental Law Review
HHRJ	Harvard Human Rights Journal
HICLR	Hastings International & Comparative Law Review
HILJ	Harvard International Law Journal
HRLR	Human Rights Law Review
HRQ	Human Rights Quarterly
IAHCR	Inter-American Court of Human Rights
ICCPR	International Covenant on Civil and Political Rights
ICJR	International Criminal Justice Review
ICJ Rep	International Court of Justice Reports
ICLQ	International & Comparative Law Quarterly
ILB	Indigenous Law Bulletin
ILO	International Labour Organization
IMR	International Migration Review
IS	International Security
IUCN	International Union for the Conservation of Nature
JAAR	Journal of the American Academy of Religion
JEH	Journal of Environmental Health
JLP	Journal of Law & Policy
JPH	Journal of Pacific History
JPS	Journal of the Polynesian Society
JSPL	Journal of South Pacific Law
KJLPP	Kansas Journal of Law and Public Policy
LIJ	Law Institute Journal
LSF	Legal Studies Forum
LSR	Law & Society Review
MGLJ	McGill Law Journal
MJICEL	Macquarie Journal of International and Comparative Environmental Law
MJIL	Melbourne Journal of International Law
MLJ	Melanesian Law Journal
MQLJ	Macquarie Law Journal
MULR	Melbourne University Law Review
NDL	Notre Dame Lawyer
NSWLR	New South Wales Law Reports
NYUJILP	New York University Journal of International Law & Politics
NZAR	New Zealand Administrative Reports

NZEP	New Zealand Economic Papers
NZIR	New Zealand International Review
NZJEL	New Zealand Journal of Environmental Law
NZJH	New Zealand Journal of History
NZLJ	New Zealand Law Journal
NZJP	New Zealand Journal of Psychology
NZJPIL	New Zealand Journal of Public International Law
NZLR	New Zealand Law Reports
NZPCC	New Zealand Privy Council Cases
NZ Rec LR	New Zealand Recent Law Review
NZTPA	New Zealand Town Planning Appeals
OC	Oceans Connect
OJLS	Oxford Journal of Legal Studies
PA	Pacific Affairs
PNASUSA	Proceedings of the National Academy of Sciences of the United States of America
PRLPJ	Pacific Rim Law & Policy Journal
PS	Pacific Studies
RIDH	Revista Iberoamericana de Derechos Humanos
SJIL	Standford Journal of International Law
SJILC	Syracuse Journal of International Law & Commerce
SLR	Stellenbosch Law Review
SPPC	Social and Personality Psychology Compass
STLR	St Thomas Law Review
SYLR	Sydney Law Review
TICLJ	Temple International & Comparative Law Journal
TJIL	Texas Journal of International Law
TL	Transnational Law
TPQ	Town Planning Quarterly
UMJLR	University of Michigan Journal of Law Reform
UNDP	United Nations Development Programme
UNESCO	United Nations Educational, Scientific, and Cultural Organization
UNSWLJ	University of New South Wales Law Journal
UTLJ	University of Toronto Law Journal
VJTL	Vanderbilt Journal of Transnational Law
VLR	Vanderbilt Law Review
VUWLR	Victoria University of Wellington Law Review
WA	World Archaeology
WLR	Washington Law Review
WUJLP	Washington University Journal of Law & Policy
YHRDLJ	Yale Human Rights and Development Law Journal
YLJ	Yale Law Journal

Table of Cases

Table of UN Documents, International Treaties and Declarations, and Other International Documents

UN DOCUMENTS

INTERNATIONAL TREATIES AND DECLARATIONS

OTHER INTERNATIONAL DOCUMENTS

Table of Domestic Legislation and Special Reports

AUSTRALIA

NEW ZEALAND

Waitangi Tribunal Reports (in numerical order)

FIJI

PAPUA NEW GUINEA

TABLE OF OFFICIAL AND NON-GOVERNMENTAL REPORTS

Australia

Papua New Guinea

Introduction

The states in the Pacific Basin have received very little attention in international law and politics. While Australia and New Zealand have always been considered part of international society, the numerous smaller states that make up the region seem to be isolated as much metaphorically as physically. Yet in the United Nations General Assembly each of these sovereign states has a single equal vote, and to that extent, in theory at least, the views of Fiji are as important as those of France. In addition, the Pacific states raise very important fundamental questions of international law in general, concerning the nature of the sovereignty of states, the law of the sea over boundaries and territorial seas, the testing of nuclear weapons, and 'planted populations' and their rights.

This volume is offered from the perspective of human rights and comparative constitutional law. It is underpinned by a simple idea—to be able to test the efficacy of the human rights promise of the equal dignity and worth of every human being; it is important to examine the extent to which states provide for vulnerable groups within their domestic legal setting. Studying this issue in the Pacific context is fascinating: the region is rife with complexities concerning the migration of human populations; determinations of what constitutes 'indigenous' and 'settler'; the means through which territory can be acquired in law; the manner in which a modern state can emerge from layers of different identities; and how these states can play a full role in international society.

The region is also characterized by a high proportion of indigenous populations, who form majority populations, in many of the Pacific Island states, or who are seeing increased protection and alleviating standards, such as the Maori in New Zealand, or who remain relatively vulnerable, such as the Aborigines and Torres Strait Islanders in Australia.

The question of new migrant populations is of growing importance in the region. While a large proportion of this migration consists of Asian migration to Australia and New Zealand, it is important to note the movement and settlement of Pacific Islander populations to various states in the region. This migration can sit uncomfortably with established notions of unicultural or bicultural national identity prevalent in the states in the region.

In addition several of the states within this region have 'associate' status or are 'unincorporated territories' of the United States of America, France,

New Zealand, or Australia.[1] Thus problems associated with decolonization and independence remain. Other aspects of public international law relevant to the region are: a) sea-level rise that is threatening some islands altogether;[2] b) the use of many of the islands as US military bases;[3] and c) fall-out on the region from the previous Australian government's immigration policy.[4] It is against this backdrop that many of the states are framing their indigenous peoples and minority rights policy, which has received inadequate attention in international society.

As with the comparative model established in a previous book that forms part of this series, *Minority Rights in Asia: A Comparative Legal Analysis*,[5] the objective of this book can be summarized as follows: (a) to foster a greater understanding of the legal and political climate of the states in the Pacific; (b) to understand the extent to which the Pacific states seek to implement international human rights standards; (c) to generate further research and debate about a region largely marginalized in international discourse; and (d) to test the veracity of the human rights project through an examination of its impact on the more vulnerable populations of the state.

For the purpose of this volume the following states will be considered to be part of the 'Pacific': Australia, New Zealand, American Samoa, Federated States of Micronesia, Guam, Nauru, Niue, Papua New Guinea, Solomon Islands,[6] Tuvalu, Fiji, Kiribati, New Caledonia, Northern Mariana Islands, Pitcairn Islands, Tokelau, Vanuatu, Cook Islands, French Polynesia, Marshall Islands, Palau, Samoa, Tonga, Wallis and Futuna.

The idea of creating a regime for the protection of the vulnerable few from the tyranny of the many has been a fundamental axis along which international law has evolved. As Thornberry has detailed,[7] minority rights law has a rich history and arguably is a crucial component of constitutional law in nearly every state in the world. However, the discourse remains dominated by ideas and models that derive primarily from the western liberal state. While protecting minorities is always challenging, other states that do not form part of the western legal tradition face difficulties in being able to understand the very basis through

---

[1] For general reading on the notion of 'Associate States' in public international law and international relations, see Robert Jackson, *The Global Covenant: Human Conduct in a World of States* (Oxford: Oxford University Press, 2003).

[2] For a general reading on the subject, see Bruce C. Douglas, Michael S. Kearney, and Stephen P. Leatherman (eds), *Sea-Level Rise: History & Consequences* (San Diego: Academic Press, 2001).

[3] See John Bellamy Foster, *Naked Imperialism: The US Pursuit of Global Dominance* (New York: Monthly Review Press, 2006).

[4] For a general reading, see John Vrachnas *et al*, *Migration and Refugee law: Principles and Practice in Australia* (Cambridge: Cambridge University Press, 2005).

[5] Joshua Castellino and Elvira Domínguez Redondo, *Minority Rights in Asia: A Comparative Legal Analysis* (Oxford: Oxford University Press, 2006).

[6] The name of this state is sometimes spelt Soloman Islands.

[7] Patrick Thornberry, *International Law and the Rights of Minorities* (Oxford: Clarendon Press, 1991) 27. Thornberry traces the origins of minority rights law to the thirteenth century.

which to grant rights to all their citizens and groups. The human rights agenda is held up as a moral panacea: states are expected to make the administrative, legislative, and judicial changes necessary to their systems to enable the protection and promotion of the civil, political, economic, social, and cultural rights of their citizens, and to a lesser extent, others within their territorial jurisdiction.

The opening chapter of this volume engages the complexities of the region by providing a historical overview of the peopling of the Pacific. In addition it discusses the particular nature of the challenges that the Pacific states face and provides a broad-brush picture of the difficulties that indigenous peoples and minorities face within them. There is no regional human rights body in the Pacific. Attempts to create one are discussed in some detail in this chapter.

This book offers a detailed view of four states in the subsequent chapters, namely Australia, New Zealand, Fiji, and Papua New Guinea. This analysis is broken down into four main sections: an historical overview, identification of the relevant groups, the rights of indigenous peoples, and minority rights enshrined in law and the remedies available. Common issues that arise across the four chapters include land and resource rights, political participation, education, religion and language, and the role of customary law.

The concluding chapter seeks to reiterate some of the main arguments presented, and to comment, from a comparative perspective, on how minority rights regimes are evolving in the specific settings selected. Rather than arriving at a definitive insight into a unifying theory for the protection of minority and indigenous rights in the region, it aims to identify nuances and principles that have emerged from state practice. Towards this end the book concludes with a series of concrete recommendations and suggestions with a view to enhancing regional and international cooperation, with a special emphasis on models for indigenous and minority protection.

NB: This book was completed prior to April 2009 when Frank Bainimarama's interim military government in Fiji, declared illegal, was reinstated by the president who abrogated the 1997 Constitution and sacked the judiciary. The conclusions emphasize the fragile nature of Fiji's democracy, and this is borne out by these events. Fiji is now firmly under military control with a view to holding elections in 2014. The 1997 Constitution discussed herein is as close as Fiji has come to offering a fair deal to all its minority and indigenous groups. It was a blueprint for reconciliation, and in the authors' opinion its recent abrogation is a disaster for the state and its neighbours.

January 2009

1

An Overview of Indigenous Peoples and Minority Rights in the Pacific

1.1 History of the Pacific Islands

The Pacific is by far the largest ocean covering one-third of the earth's surface, and at 165,384,000 square kilometres, more than twice the size of the Atlantic Ocean.[1] The Pacific waters are characterized by vast expanses, dotted with over 5,000 islands, more than those scattered about the rest of the world combined.[2] For human history, the most important variable has been distance, and it is the last marine basin to be brought into the reach of a world system.[3] The term 'Pacific' as a geographic and subject delineator is a European construct, and although the change in name from 'Mar del Sur' (and other similar names) to 'Pacific Ocean' occurred in 1520, the former name persisted for about two centuries before yielding.[4] 'Mar del Sur' or 'South Sea' applied initially only to the Bay of Panama, but continued to be used, apparently because European mariners had to sail far to the south to enter its waters. The term 'Pacific' came into usage as shifting nineteenth-century trade patterns made the northern Pacific an important area of global commerce.[5] 'South Sea' faded as a descriptive term only after World War II.[6]

Inter-island exchange and marriage became important factors in creating regional sub-zones, which were further cemented through mythological and genealogical ties. These interaction zones reveal important long distance

---

[1] Gerard Segal, *Rethinking the Pacific* (Oxford: Clarendon Press, 1990) 6.

[2] Segal (n 1) 7.

[3] Paul Blank, 'The Pacific: A Mediterranean in the Making?' (1999) 89 (2) *OC* 265–77, 267, and 275.

[4] O.H.K. Spate, ' "South Sea" to "Pacific Ocean": A Note on Nomenclature', (1977) 12 (4) *JPH* 205–11, cited in K.R. Howe, *Nature, Culture and History: The 'Knowing' of Oceania* (Honolulu: University of Hawaii Press, 2000) 60.

[5] O.H.K. Spate, ' "South Sea" to "Pacific Ocean": A Note on Nomenclature' (1977) 12 (4) *JPH* 205–11, cited in Martin Lewis, 'Dividing the Ocean Sea' (1999) 89 *GR*188–214 at 199 and 208.

[6] ibid 208. Micronesia, lying almost wholly north of the equator, is still often popularly located in the 'South Pacific', perhaps a reflection of the continuing influence of the 'South Sea' concept.

inter-connections prior to Magellan's arrival.[7] The 'Pacific Island Countries' (PIC), one of six distinct zones in the Pacific basin, is located in the south and centre of the ocean. Almost all the people, plants, and animals in the Pacific originated from Asia, with the first people arriving about 50,000 years ago, moving from what is now Indonesia and into western New Guinea.[8] The Pacific region is ethnically diverse, with nations made up of numerous minority groups and indigenous peoples, as well as resettled peoples and internal migrants from different parts of far-flung groups of islands.[9]

Islands are more than dots of land; and the surrounding seas, with their resources and mythological associations, form part of an islander's consciousness of 'territory'. When modern two-hundred mile economic zones are taken into account, island nation-states are far bigger than many countries in Europe, and when undersea minerals are considered, potentially as wealthy.[10] The islands fall into three categories, based on human rather than physical geography: Melanesians, Polynesians, and Micronesians.[11] The terms were coined by the French explorer Dumont d'Urville to describe the perceived racial differences between the peoples of the Pacific Islands in 1832, with Melanesia meaning 'dark islands', Polynesia 'many islands', and Micronesia 'little islands'.[12]

Melanesia is by far the largest area, and contains 97 per cent of the land and 75 per cent of the population of the Pacific Islands. It is composed of New Guinea, including Papua New Guinea and Irian Jaya, the Solomon Islands, Vanuatu, and New Caledonia.[13] Diversity is the essential characteristic of Melanesia, and it displays a remarkable array of ethnic groups, social organization, topography, and languages. Most of the 1,200 or so Melanesian languages belong to the Austronesian language family, with non-Austronesian languages found in New Guinea and some in the Solomon Islands.[14] Papua New Guinea, with around 840 distinct living languages, is the most ethnically diverse state in the world, while Vanuatu, with approximately 109 languages but with a far smaller population, has the highest number of languages per capita in the world.[15]

Polynesia occupies the eastern part of the ocean, including Hawaii in the north, Easter Island, the Marquesas Islands, Society Islands, Tuamotu and Austral Islands in the east, New Zealand in the south, the Cook Islands in the centre,

[7] Rainer Buschmann, 'Oceans of World History: Delineating Aquacentric Notions in the Global Past' (2004) 2 (1) *History Compass* 1–10 at 2.

[8] Ron Crocombe, *The South Pacific: An Introduction* (Auckland: Longman Paul, 1987) 3.

[9] Jon Fraenkel, 'Minority Rights in Fiji and the Solomon Islands' UN doc E/CN.4/Sub.2/AC.5/2003/WP.5, UN Sub-Commission on Promotion and Protection of Human Rights, Working Group on Minorities, 5 May 2003, Executive Summary.

[10] Howe (n 4) 61.   [11] Segal (n 1) 8.

[12] Ann Gibbons, 'The Peopling of the Pacific' (2001) *Science* Vol 291 No 5509, 1735–7 at 1735.

[13] Crocombe (n 8) 17.

[14] I.C. Campbell, *A History of the Pacific Islands* (Christchurch: University of Canterbury Press, 1989) 18 and 23.

[15] Fraenkel (n 9) 3.

Tonga and Samoa in the west, and Tokelau and Tuvalu in the north-west.[16] Thus the points of the 'Polynesian triangle' are New Zealand at the bottom, Hawaii at the top, and Easter Island in the far-east.[17] The languages spoken by these peoples are closely related, and form one group within the vast Austronesian language family.[18] Polynesian peoples retain the idea of hierarchical social and political distinctions and rank, manifest in ruling chiefs. The state of Fiji can be regarded as part of Melanesia or Polynesia or both.[19]

Micronesia is a series of small islands lying mainly to the north of the equator, including Kiribati, Nauru, the Marshall Islands, the Federated States of Micronesia (formerly the Caroline Islands, comprising Yap, Truk, Pohnpei, and Kosrae), Paulau, Guam, and the Mariana Islands.[20] In terms of languages, Micronesia is more diverse than Polynesia and less diverse than Melanesia, representing one or more branches of the Austronesian language family.[21] By contrast with Melanesia, the smaller islands of Polynesia and Micronesia are mostly relatively ethnically homogenous, with small migrant or settler communities.[22]

The 'apparent neatness' with which the Pacific populations fall into the three categories belies the intricate network of divisions and continuities between and within them.[23] Generations of anthropologists have been drawn to the Pacific Islands and as a result there are manifold studies of the cultures and peoples of this most heterogenous collection of cultures and languages in the world.[24] Perplexing questions have been asked, as outlined by Campbell:

'Where did they come from?' was the question asked by the first European explorers, a question asked often and answered in many different ways ever since. The crux of the problem, as it was usually posed, was the Polynesian distribution. Accounting for the settlement of Melanesia seemed comparatively straight-forward: the Melanesians had occupied a chain of elongated islands which seemed to point across the narrow ocean passages to the next land. The Micronesians on their innumerable, tiny specks of land also seemed to have quite readily flowed from the adjacent Asian mainland. Explaining how they actually got to their island homes was a difficulty, but only a technical one. The Polynesians presented the real problem. The relative homogeneity of their cultures and languages implied that their geographical dispersal was fairly recent, and that it had taken place fairly quickly. But the most obvious migration route, out of Asia, via the Melanesian islands which seem to point the way, was occupied by a population whose extreme diversity implied an enormous antiquity...In other words, the most likely route between the Polynesian homeland and their islands was blocked by a tenacious people who were there first.[25]

Recognizing the undercurrent behind the investigation into the so-called 'Polynesian problem', archaeologist Golson framed the issue bluntly, as one of:

[16] Campbell (n 14) 14.   [17] Crocombe (n 8) 17.   [18] Campbell (n 14) 14.
[19] Crocombe (n 8) 18.   [20] ibid 17.   [21] Campbell (n 14) 26.
[22] Fraenkel (n 9) 3.   [23] Campbell (n 14) 26.   [24] ibid 27.
[25] Campbell (n 14) 28.

How to get the linguistically and culturally homogenous Polynesians into the central Pacific without racial contamination from the more diversified and presumably longer-established Melanesians to the west.[26]

Polynesia is the last area of the world to have been settled by people.[27] Many geneticists and linguists have proposed an 'express train to Polynesia' model of migration,[28] in which the ancestors of Polynesia came from Taiwan, where farmers speaking Austronesian languages set sail 3,600–6,000 years ago, largely bypassing the indigenous Papuan-speaking people of Melanesia.[29] Thus Diamond notes that when Polynesians got to Hawaii and New Zealand, 'ancient China's occupation of the Pacific was complete'.[30] The archaeological evidence was a trail of distinctive pottery and shell ornaments known as the 'Lapita' culture that first appeared 3,500 years ago in the Bismarck Archipelago in Papua New Guinea, spreading eastwards to arrive in Fiji some 3,000 years ago.[31] From there they continued east leaving distinctive red-slipped pottery, using the islands as stepping-stones to Tonga and Samoa.[32] Similarly, a recent genetic analysis of Pacific rats supports the theory that Lapita mariners from South-east Asia moved across the region in a series of migrations, from 6,000 to 3,000 years ago.[33]

Convincing rebuttals have since been made against the archaeological case for Taiwan being the original homeland,[34] with many genetic studies revealing a gross genetic dissimilarity between Taiwan and Polynesia at multiple loci, in type, specificity, and proportion.[35] A consequent 'slow boat' model has been proposed:

The ancestors of Polynesians were Austronesians who moved out of Southeast Asia—not necessarily Taiwan—whose population expanded along the coast of New Guinea, inter-mingled, and then moved out into Polynesia. But it was not an express train, because as they moved through Melanesia, they moved slowly enough to mix extensively with Melanesians.[36]

---

[26] Quoted in John Terrell, Terry Hunt, and Chris Gosden, 'The Dimensions of Social Life in the Pacific: Human Diversity and the Myth of the Primitive Isolate' (1997) 38 (2) *CA* 155–95 at 171.

[27] Gibbons (n 12) 1735. This statement excludes Antarctica.

[28] The 'express train' metaphor is attributed to Jared Diamond in a 1988 article in *Nature* magazine (ibid 1736). See also Diamond and Bellwood, 'Farmers and their Languages: The First Expansions' (2003) 300 *Science* 597–603.

[29] Gibbons (n 12) 1735.   [30] Terrell, Hunt, and Gosden (n 26) 172.

[31] Gibbons (n 12) 1735.   [32] ibid.

[33] Society for Science and the Public, 'Rat DNA Points to Pacific Migrations' (2004) *Science News* Vol 166 No 2. The research obtained mitochondrial DNA from 100 Pacific rats. The DNA exhibited three geographically distinct patterns, one of which appears only on islands just off the Asian coast, reflecting interaction among people who probably didn't migrate elsewhere. A second pattern extends from the islands into Oceania's western half, probably mirroring human migration along that path. (n 39 below).

[34] Stephen Oppenheimer, 'The Express Train from Taiwan to Polynesia: On the Congruence of Proxy Lines of Evidence', (2004) 36(4) *WA* 591–600 at 593.

[35] ibid 596.

[36] Mark Stoneking, Max Planck Institute for Evolutionary Anthropology, quoted in Gibbons (n 12) 1737.

Genetics, archaeology, and linguistics are slowly synthesizing in line with this conclusion. Forensic linguistic studies still point to Taiwan as the source of the Austronesian languages, while genetics and archaeology rule it out as the place of origin for genes and Lapita culture.[37] Gibbons concludes:

> ... although Captain Cook was right in spotting the cohesiveness of Polynesians from Hawaii to New Zealand, he was wrong about what he saw as their profound differences from Melanesians: the groups have a common genetic heritage and their differences are only skin deep.[38]

Where the Lapita originally came from and how they occupied Polynesia remains contested, and evidently, 'simplistic models that constrain the history of language, biology and culture with a single explanation are clearly inappropriate for understanding the human settlement of the Pacific'.[39] Molecular biology has uncovered the significant presence of 'Melanesian markers' in the 'Polynesian' gene pool, with the conclusion that 'the most parsimonious interpretation of the genetic data was that the Polynesians were derived from Austronesian-speaking paleo-populations of Melanesian Near Oceania'.[40] They cannot be derived, biologically speaking, directly from Asia, and must have emerged out of an earlier Melanesian population matrix.[41]

Terrell, Hunt, and Gosden chart the development of Pacific anthropology, and question the research agenda that has accompanied investigations into the region. In 1961, at the tenth Pacific Science Congress, anthropologist Andrew Vayda remarked that the isolation of Pacific Island populations made them 'convenient laboratories for us'.[42] Indeed, Howe considers anthropology to have been 'an integral part of the colonizing processes' in the Pacific.[43] New perspectives since the 1950s and early 1960s have shifted the view of the Pacific as a remote and undeveloped 'laboratory' to a notable sphere of human accomplishments, on land and sea, with the ocean considered more an avenue for interchange than a barrier to human affairs.[44] Pacific anthropology has revised its framework, and classification of human diversity in the Pacific into Melanesia, Polynesia, and Micronesia is considered 'fundamentally misleading'.[45] There is a requisite need for a shift in focus:

> Why have biologists and geneticists continued to embrace the fallacy of seeing the Polynesian story as the main line of biological and cultural history of the Pacific? Why has Melanesia's diversity seemed less problematic? ... how did this diversity evolve in the absence of isolation?[46]

---

[37] ibid.   [38] ibid.

[39] E. Matoo-Smith, J.H. Robins, and R.C. Green, 'Origins and Dispersals of Pacific Peoples: Evidence from mtDNA Phylogenies of the Pacific Rat' (2004) Vol 101 No 24, *PNAS USA* 9167–72 at 9172.

[40] Terrell, Hunt, and Gosden (n 26) 172.   [41] ibid 172.

[42] ibid 155.   [43] Howe (n 4) 53.

[44] Terrell, Hunt, and Gosden (n 26) 156.   [45] ibid 163.

[46] ibid 172 and 174.

Pacific trade in early modern times was significant, with for example trans-Pacific silver flows to China equalling or exceeding those that passed across the Atlantic and the Eurasian land mass.[47] During the sixteenth century, the expanding reach of Europe began to weave the Pacific basin into an emerging global economy. Although Pacific trade fell in relative terms with the Industrial Revolution and integration of the Atlantic economy, trans-Pacific flows caught up again with the 'opening' of Japan, the settlement of Australia and New Zealand, the opium trade, and the colonization of South-east Asia.[48] The mastery of distance means that the Pacific basin could be on the threshold of cultural and economic harmonization and integration, in effect becoming 'another Mediterranean',[49] closing in on the prediction by Marx and Engels that the Pacific will replace the Atlantic as the centre of gravity of world commerce.[50]

European cultures have been important influences during the last 200 years, a short period relative to the 50,000 years of Pacific history.[51] The beachcombers were the first Europeans to settle on the Pacific Islands, followed by traders, missionaries, and administrators associated with the formal establishment of colonies.[52] By 1900, all Pacific Islands had fallen under the authority of foreign powers.[53] Prolonged and intense influences have not led to Pacific Island cultures becoming like those of the majority settler populations in New Zealand or Australia, and they are unlikely to do so.[54] Crocombe estimates that the waning of European influence will be accompanied by a resurgence of some aspects of Pacific cultures, followed by a major cultural dominance from Asia.[55]

Religious denominations were introduced into the Pacific Island Countries from churches in Britain or Germany, or from the Roman Catholic Church, from 1796.[56] During the 1830s, the London Missionary Society (LMS) moved from Tahiti westward across the Pacific to Samoa, Tonga, and the New Hebrides (Vanuatu), northward to the Gilbert (Kiribati) and Ellice (Tuvalu) Islands, and in the 1870s, LMS missionaries entered Papua, or southern New Guinea.[57] Wesleyan Methodists were able to establish a mission in Tonga where they were successful in converting several very prominent chiefs and from there they moved northwest to Fiji.[58] Presbyterianism was introduced into New South Wales in the early 1800s and into the far south of New Zealand, Otago, and South-land in the 1840s.[59] As the nineteenth century progressed, a number of denominations that had evolved in the United States of America also made their entry into the South

---

[47] Blank (n 3) 267.   [48] ibid 267.   [49] ibid 276.
[50] Quoted in Ravi Palat, 'Pacific Century: Myth or Reality?' (1996) 25(3) *Theory and Society* 303–47 at 303.
[51] Crocombe (n 8) 22.
[52] Patrick Nunn, 'Recent Environmental Changes on Pacific Islands' (1990) 156 (2) *GJ* 125–40 at 127.
[53] Campbell (n 14) 136.   [54] Crocombe (n 8) 23.   [55] ibid 22.
[56] Don Paterson, 'New Impulses in the Interaction of Law and Religion: A South Pacific Perspective' (2003) *BYULR* 593–623 at 595.
[57] ibid 595.   [58] ibid 596.   [59] ibid.

Pacific, the first of these probably being the Latter-day Saints ('Mormons').[60] By the middle of the twentieth century, the island countries of the Pacific had been largely evangelized by introduced religious denominations.[61] Presently, a Christian ethos pervades the Pacific Islands.[62]

Indentured labourers, who were recruited from Fiji by colonial authorities in Fiji in the late nineteenth and early twentieth centuries, brought with them their Hindu and Muslim religions. Those who remained in Fiji, and their descendants, have not proselytized, so these religions have largely remained confined to the Indians of Fiji.[63]

Presently the Pacific Islands range from fully independent nations to incorporated territories. LAWASIA, in its 1989 proposal for a Pacific Charter of Human Rights, divided the region into eight groupings on the basis of suitability for inclusion in its proposed regional body. The division is an interesting benchmark for assessing the political status of the Pacific Islands, and highlights the legacy of colonization.

The first group to be considered are the fully independent Pacific Island nations, all of which have constitutionally entrenched and enforceable human rights. They are: Fiji, Kiribati, Nauru, Papua New Guinea, Solomon Islands, Tonga, Tuvalu, Vanuatu, and Western Samoa. There is no question but that they should be approached for inclusion.[64]

The second group, Australia and New Zealand, are sited in the south-western reaches of the Pacific. They see themselves as Pacific nations and maintain strong and positive links with the nations of the region. The cause of human rights in both these countries would be advanced if they joined in the proposed charter.[65]

There are a growing number of almost independent countries in the region. The UN trusteeship held by the USA over Micronesia is coming to an end. Compacts of free association have been concluded, under which these countries are responsible for their own foreign policy. They are: the Federated States of Micronesia, the Marshall Islands, Palau.[66]

Theoretically, New Zealand is responsible for the defence and foreign affairs of the Cook Islands, Niue, and Tokelau. In practice, in regional matters at least, the Cook Islands manages its own interests. The situation is not clear in relation

---

[60] ibid 598. Although only established in the United States in the 1830s, Mormon missionaries appeared in eastern Polynesia in 1846, in New Zealand in 1854, and later in other island countries.

[61] ibid 600.

[62] Jane Kelsey, 'World Trade and Small Nations in the South Pacific Region' (2005) 14 *KJLPP* 247–89 at 288.

[63] Paterson (n 56) 600.

[64] 'Report on a Proposed Pacific Charter of Human Rights, prepared under the auspices of LAWASIA, May 1989' (1992) 22 *VUWLR* 103.

[65] ibid 104.   [66] ibid.

to Niue and Tokelau; however, all three countries should be approached to join the Charter.[67]

The Commonwealth of the Northern Mariana Islands, although a part of Micronesia, has chosen to be a self-governing commonwealth with the USA responsible for its defence and foreign aid and assisting significantly with economic development. For it to become a party to the Charter, the USA would have to ratify the Charter on its behalf.[68]

Guam in Micronesia in the north-west Pacific and American Samoa in the central-west pacific, are unincorporated territories of the USA, administered through the country's Department of the Interior. American Samoa has not made any serious attempt to change its status. In Guam, the position is less clear, with the question of indigenous rights arising. Some interest in the question of a proposed charter has been shown in Guam and both territories should be approached.[69]

Wallis and Futuna, New Caledonia, and French Polynesia are incorporated into the French Republic as *territoires d'outre mer*, and are governed by civil law systems.[70] Conflict in French Caledonia is evident, where French settlers who wish to remain part of France outnumber the indigenous population. In French Polynesia, the French settlers hold a similar view, but are a minority. Approaches should be made to these territories.[71]

Four political entities remain for consideration. Norfolk Island in the south-west Pacific is a part of Australia. Hawaii is a state of the USA and fully integrated into that country. There are substantial Samoan, Tongan, and Micronesian communities there as well as the large indigenous Hawaiian population, and many citizens of Hawaii desire to identify more closely with the Pacific.[72] The question of Rapanui or Easter Island, which is a province of Chile, was considered by the working party, as well as the British dependency, the Pitcairn Islands. It was decided to leave the question of whether these three entities might be approached for future membership of a regional entity unresolved.[73]

---

[67] ibid.   [68] ibid.   [69] ibid.

[70] Catherine Giraud-Kinley, 'The Effectiveness of International Law: Sustainable Development in the South Pacific Region' (1999) 12 *GIELR*125–76 at 129 and fn 7: In New Caledonia, the 'Accords de Noumea' of 5 May 1998 replaced the 'Accords de Matignon' of 1988, after a majority of New Caledonians voted in favour of the former in a referendum held on 8 November 1998. They provide for the progressive transfer of jurisdiction from France to New Caledonia, such as jurisdiction over its Exclusive Economic Zone. See Law No 7302 of 5 May 1988, J.O., 11 June 1998 (New Caledonia) or Noumea Accords. A referendum on the independence of New Caledonia, however, was postponed for another fifteen to twenty years.

[71] 'Report on a Proposed Pacific Charter of Human Rights, prepared under the auspices of LAWASIA, May 1989' (n 64) 104.

[72] For instance, at the meeting of the United Nations Human Rights Council in June 2008, an organization called *Oceania Human Rights Network* was launched by Hawaiian academic and indigenous activist, Professor Joshua Cooper. See further Hawaii Institute for Human Rights <http://www.humanrightshawaii.org/> [last accessed 25 March 2009)].

[73] 'Report on a Proposed Pacific Charter of Human Rights, prepared under the auspices of LAWASIA, May 1989' (n 64) 103–5.

Regional cooperation in the Pacific began in the aftermath of the Second World War. In 1947 the South Pacific Commission was established to offer advice, coordinate development projects, and conduct research. All territories in the Pacific eventually joined the South Pacific Conference, which reviews the work of the Commission.[74] A further regional advance was the founding of the University of the South Pacific in Suva, Fiji, in 1966.[75] In 1981, the *Pacific Islanders' Producers Association* was reconstituted as the *South Pacific Forum*, which provides a means for heads of Pacific governments, including Australia and New Zealand, to arrange matters of common economic interest.[76] The agreements establishing the *South Pacific Forum* did not allow the admission of dependent territories as members of the organization.[77] The Forum established a structure for continuing economic consultation, the *South Pacific Economic Cooperation*, which was replaced by a 1991 agreement establishing the *South Pacific Forum Secretariat*. In 2000, the body was renamed the Pacific Islands Forum.[78] The regional activity did not have an initial strong impact. By the early 1980s, trade within the Pacific Islands region amounted to only about 1 per cent of total trade conducted by Pacific nations, with the South Pacific Commission estimating that it could only ever grow as high as 5 per cent. The regional bodies themselves continued to be funded largely by foreign governments.[79]

Environmental protection became an important catalyst for greater regional cooperation in the Pacific, intensified by common opposition to nuclear testing by France and the United States in their respective Pacific territories since the 1960s.[80] According to Carew-Reid:

The view expressed by island countries on such crucial regional concerns as nuclear weapons testing, disposal of radioactive wastes and the management and conservation of fisheries continues to be strongly coloured by what they perceive as continuing colonial and imperial motives of the metropolitan powers. These forces and a recognition of the mutual benefits to be gained by pooling resources have led to a distinctive regional cohesion.[81]

French testing of nuclear weapons at Mururoa in the Tuamotu group began in 1966. Many United States of America and United Kingdom tests had taken place in the Pacific since the first nuclear test by the US in 1945.[82] Pressure from the Forum along with international environmental organizations forced the French to adopt underground rather than atmospheric tests in 1975.[83] The International

---

[74] Campbell (n 14) 215.   [75] ibid 216.
[76] ibid.   [77] Giraud-Kinley (n 70) 137.
[78] Pacific Islands Forum Secretariat <http://www.forumsec.org.fj/pages.cfm/about-us/> [last accessed 25 March 2009].
[79] Campbell (n 14) 217.   [80] Giraud-Kinley (n 70) 127.
[81] Jeremy Carew-Reid, *Environment, Aid and Regionalism in the South Pacific* (Canberra: Australian National University Press, 1989) quoted in Giraud-Kinley (n 70) 127–8.
[82] Law of the Sea Institute, 'Oceans in the Nuclear Age' (University of California, Berkeley) <http://www.law.berkeley.edu/centers/ilr/ona/pages/testing.htm> [last accessed 25 March 2009].
[83] Campbell (n 14) 218.

Court of Justice 1974 judgment in the *Nuclear Tests Case (New Zealand v France)* had found that New Zealand's claim that France had violated international law by carrying out atmospheric tests causing the deposit of radio active fall-out on New Zealand territory was devoid of any object, after France had announced, while the case was pending, that it would cease the conduct of such tests.[84] In 1985, the *South Pacific Nuclear Free Zone Treaty* was drawn up, a multilateral agreement among the nations of the South Pacific which prohibits the test-ing, manufacture, and stationing of nuclear explosive devices, and the dump-ing of nuclear waste, within the zone. The area covered reaches the west coast of Australia to the South American Nuclear Free Zone, from the equator to 60 degrees South (the northern boundary of the 1959 Antarctic Treaty).

French underground testing generated a renewed appeal to the international court. On 22 September 1995, the International Court of Justice (ICJ) issued an order in reply to the filing by New Zealand of a 'Request for an Examination of the Situation' in accordance with paragraph 63 of the court's 1974 judgment in the *Nuclear Tests Case (New Zealand v France)*.[85] Dismissing New Zealand's request to re-open the suspended 1974 case, the ICJ concluded that the subject-matter of the 1974 judgment concerned exclusively atmospheric tests and not any other form of testing. The basis of the 1974 judgment was found to be France's undertaking not to conduct any further atmospheric nuclear tests, preventing the court from taking into consideration questions relating to underground nuclear tests. Only in the event of a resumption of nuclear tests in the atmosphere would the basis of the 1974 judgment have been affected.[86] In 1996, the United States, France, and the United Kingdom joined China and the Commonwealth of Independent States in signing the *South Pacific Nuclear Free Zone Treaty*. Bello examines the dissenting opinions in the ICJ's 1995 order:

The dissenting judges found, however, that New Zealand had made a *prima facie* case that the dangers that had precipitated its Application in 1973 were present in 1995 by reason of the French underground nuclear tests, and thus affected the basis of the Judgment of 1974. In their view, this factor in turn entitled New Zealand to a substan-tive determination, at a subsequent stage of the proceedings, of the situation arising from French underground nuclear testing. The dissents seem to imply a fear that the Court's dismissal might be interpreted as a tacit endorsement of radioactive contamination by underground tests. This interpretation, however, is not warranted by the texts of the Judgment of 1974 or the Order of 1995, which merely concern atmospheric nuclear test-ing and simply do not apply to underground testing.[87]

---

[84] *Nuclear Tests (Australia v France)* (Interim Protection) ICJ Rep 1973, 99; *Nuclear Tests (New Zealand v France)* (Interim Protection), ICJ 1973, 135; *Nuclear Tests (New Zealand v France)* Judgment, ICJ Rep 1974, 457.

[85] Peter Bekker, 'Recent Developments at the World Court: ICJ Dismisses New Zealand's Request to Reopen Nuclear Tests Case' (1995) *ASILN*.

[86] ibid.

[87] Judith Bello, 'International Decision: New Zealand Challenge to Underground Testing by France in South Pacific', (1996) 90 *AJIL* 280–6 at 285.

Environmental protection continues to foster regional cooperation in the Pacific. The *South Pacific Regional Environment Programme* (SPREP) came into existence as one of the United Nations Environment Programme's (UNEP) *Regional Seas Programmes* with the endorsement and active participation of members of the South Pacific Commission. In 1991, a decision of the inter-governmental SPREP meeting announced the beginning of negotiations to establish SPREP as an independent regional organization. A consensus was finally reached in June 1993 with the signing of the SPREP Agreement, which entered into force on 31 August 1995.[88]

Regional environmental protection treaties in the Pacific Islands, including those that established SPREP and the Pacific Islands Forum, manifest an explicit and strong commitment to the goal of sustainable development, with the result that the concept has crystallized as a regional rule of customary international law.[89] Further examples of environmental protection at the regional level are illustrated by recent steps towards ensuring the sustainable use of native forests by the heads of state of the Melanesian countries. In 1995, the Forum adopted a regional Code of Conduct for Logging, following which the government of Vanuatu reinstated regulations prohibiting the export of logs and flitches.[90] Yet Grove warns against the portrayal of Pacific Island governments as environmentalist:

In the post colonial period, many 'independent' governments, many of them actually run by isolated social elites, have tended to repeat, sometimes even more crudely and brutally, the arrogant environmental mistakes made by their predecessors. Frequently they have displayed the same disdain and disrespect for indigenous and traditional knowledge. Large-scale prestige projects for dam-building, irrigation, land development and aforestation or deforestation have proved just as seductive to post-colonial as to colonial governments, and past mistakes have simply been re-run on much larger scales.[91]

For example, a satellite survey of Papua New Guinea's forests found that 'half of its trees could be lost by 2021'.[92] Papua New Guinea is a founder of the Rainforest Coalition group of tropical states that argue developed countries should pay them to protect their forests as a means of combating climate change. Yet the study's author, Phil Shearman, emphasizes the 'passive complicity of government authorities' in the state in the loss of at least 15 per cent of its rainforest since independence.[93]

---

[88] Giraud-Kinley (n 70) 135–6.   [89] ibid 138 and 170.
[90] ibid 173.
[91] Richard Grove, *Ecology, Climate and Empire* (Cambridge: White Horse Press, 1997) 3, quoted in Howe (n 4) 76.
[92] David Adam, 'Third Largest Tropical Forest Could Be Halved by 2021' *The Guardian* (London) 3 June 2008.
[93] ibid.

The Pacific Islands remain heavily dependent on Australia and New Zealand and former colonial powers, especially the United Kingdom and the United States of America, for export markets, imports, investment, and aid.[94] A number of preferential and non-reciprocal agreements that accompanied the colonies' transition to political independence provide a lifeline for their commodity exports. A new trade-led development strategy, beginning with the 'stepping stone' approach of a free trade area among themselves—the *Pacific Island Countries Trade Agreement* (PICTA)—came into effect in April 2003.[95]

1.2 Pacific and International Law

1.2.1 Pacific and International Human Rights Bodies

Regional cooperation in the area of human rights in the Pacific has not been forthright. In October 2005, the sixteen leaders of the Pacific Islands Forum adopted a *Pacific Plan of Action for Strengthening Regional Cooperation and Integration*. This plan incorporated references to human rights, including the following: 'where appropriate, the ratification and implementation of international and regional human rights conventions and agreements and support for meeting reporting and other requirements'. Human rights treaty ratification has been identified by members of the Forum as a regional priority for immediate implementation.[96]

The fundamental challenge to the effectiveness of international human rights in the Pacific is the non-ratification of UN human rights treaties and non-compliance with reporting obligations.[97] The Pacific region has by far the lowest ratification of the seven core international human rights treaties in the world.[98] Of the fourteen Pacific Island Forum member states,[99] and excluding Australia and New Zealand, three have ratified at least three of the international treaties, nine have ratified two (on women's rights and child rights), and two have ratified

[94] Kelsey (n 62) 249.   [95] ibid 250.

[96] OHCHR, *Advancing the Implementation of Human Rights in the Pacific* (Suva: OHCHR Publications, 2007) vii <http://pacific.ohchr.org/docs/Compilation%20Book.pdf>.

[97] Dejo Olowu, 'The United Nations Human Rights Treaty System and the Challenges of Commitment and Compliance in the South Pacific' (2006) 7 *MJIL*155–84 at 180.

[98] P. Imrana Jalal, 4. Two further international human rights treaties have been drafted but are not yet in force—the Convention on the Rights of Persons with Disabilities, adopted by General Assembly Resolution 61/106 of 13 December 2006 and the International Convention for the Protection of All Persons from Enforced Disappearance, adopted by General Assembly Resolution 61/177 of 20 December 2006 <http://www.rrrt.org/assets/Pacific%20Culture%20and%20 Human%20Rights.pdf> [last accessed 25 March 2009].

[99] ibid 4 fn 1. Cook Islands, Fiji, Kiribati, Marshall Islands, Micronesia (Federated States of), Nauru, Niue, Palau, Papua New Guinea, Samoa, Solomon Islands, Tonga, Tuvalu, and Vanuatu. Jalal notes that this information may not be definitive as the OHCHR website has conflicting information.

one (on child rights).[100] By treaty, the ratification record for Pacific Island
Countries is as follows:

*International Convention for the Elimination of All Forms of Racial
Discrimination* (ICERD): Australia (1975), Fiji (1973), Nauru (signed
2001), New Zealand (1972), Papua New Guinea (1982), Solomon Islands
(1982), Tonga (1972);

International Covenant on Economic, Social, and Cultural Rights: Australia (1975),
New Zealand (1978), Solomon Islands (1982);

International Covenant on Civil and Political Rights (ICCPR): Australia (1980),
Nauru (signed 2001), New Zealand (1978);

*International Convention for the Elimination of All Forms of Discrimination
Against Women* (CEDAW): Australia (1983), Cook Islands (2006), Fiji (1995),
Kiribati (2004), Marshall Islands (2006), Micronesia, Federated States of
(2004), New Zealand (1985), Papua New Guinea (1995), Samoa (1992),
Solomon Islands (2002), Tuvalu (1999), Vanuatu (1995);

International Convention Against Torture: Australia (1989), Nauru (signed 2001),
New Zealand 1989;

Convention on the Rights of the Child (CRC): Australia (1990), Cook Islands
(1997), Fiji (1993), Kiribati (1995), Marshall Islands (1993), Micronesia,
Federated States of (1993), Nauru (1994), New Zealand (1993), Niue (1995),
Palau (1995), Papua New Guinea (1993), Samoa (1994), Solomon Islands
(1995), Tonga (1995), Tuvalu (1995), Vanuatu (1993);[101]

International Convention on Migrant Workers and their Families: none.

Pacific Island Countries have entered reservations and declarations to their
treaty obligations that give cause for concern.[102] Fiji has entered extensive reservations to Articles 2, 3, and 5 ICERD,[103] resulting in repeated calls from the
Committee on the Elimination of Racial Discrimination to withdraw them,
or at least indicate their duration.[104] The result of the reservations is that Fiji
defines its obligation to prevent and eradicate all forms of racial discrimination
as a matter of its political convenience.[105] For Papua New Guinea:

> … acceptance of this Convention [ICERD] does not therefore indicate the acceptance of
> obligations by the Government of Papua New Guinea which go beyond those provided

---

[100] ibid.
[101] UNDP Pacific Sub-regional Centre, Status of Ratifications and Reservations of the
International Instruments by the Pacific Island Countries <http://www.undp.org.fj/index.
cfm?si=main> [last accessed 25 March 2009].
[102] Olowu (n 97) 173.
[103] OHCHR, Status of ICERD ratifications <http://treaties.un.org/Pages/ViewDetails.aspx?
src=TREATY&id=319&chapter=4&lang=en> [last accessed 25 March 2009]. See further ch 5.
[104] CERD/C/SR.553.   [105] Olowu (n 97) 175.

by the Constitution, nor does it indicate the acceptance of any obligation to introduce judicial process beyond that provided by the Constitution.[106]

As a result, the Convention appears not to confer any rights beyond those accorded in domestic legislation. Similarly, Tonga's reservation to ICERD reads:

To the extent [...], that any law relating to land in Tonga which prohibits or restricts the alienation of land by the indigenous inhabitants may not fulfil the obligations referred to in article 5 (d) (v), [...], the Kingdom of Tonga reserves the right not to apply the Convention to Tonga.[107]

The CRC, the most successful global and Pacific Island human rights treaty in terms of ratification, has also been limited through reservations. The Cook Islands' total of four reservations and two declarations[108] confines the treaty's application to its nationals, and denies the automatic conferral of nationality on displaced children.[109] Kiribati's reservation to Articles 24, 26, and 28 of the CRC, together with its declaration to render the rights stipulated in Articles 12–16 subject to Kiribati's traditional practice,[110] '...effectively deny human rights protection to children'.[111] Samoa too has a reservation, to Article 28 of the CRC, excluding its obligation to provide free primary education to children.[112]

The Federated States of Micronesia has entered a reservation to CEDAW, which asserts that the federation is 'not at present in a position to take the measures either required by Article 11(1)(d) of the Convention to enact comparable worth legislation, or by Article 11(2)(b) to enact maternity leave with pay or with comparable social benefits throughout the nation'.[113] The federation also reserves the right

...not to apply the provisions of Articles 2(f), 5, and 16 to the succession of certain well-established traditional titles, and to marital customs that divide tasks or decision-making in purely voluntary or consensual private conduct.[114]

Oloku notes that the Committee on the Elimination of Discrimination against Women considers all reservations to Article 16 to be incompatible with the Convention and therefore impermissible.[115] Further investigation into the extensive reservations and declarations by Pacific Island Countries is required.[116]

While reservations limit the applicability and weaken the reach of international human rights law in the Pacific, the region's failure to comply with its reporting obligations is as problematic. There appears to be a 'pervasive

---

[106] OHCHR, Status of ICERD ratifications (n 103).   [107] ibid.
[108] OHCHR, Status of CRC ratifications <http://treaties.un.org/Pages/ViewDetails.aspx?src=TREATY&id=133&chapter=4&lang=en> [last accessed 25 March 2009].
[109] Olowu (n 97) 173.   [110] ibid.
[111] ibid 175.   [112] ibid.
[113] OHCHR, Status of CEDAW ratifications <http://www2.ohchr.org/english/bodies/ratification/8.htm> [last accessed 25 March 2009].
[114] ibid.   [115] Olowu (n 97) 176.   [116] ibid.

reluctance' among Pacific Island states to submit obligatory state reports when they are due.[117] In relation to the ICERD, Papua New Guinea and the Solomon Islands rank among the nations with the highest number of overdue reports, while Tonga is overdue on its 15th, 16th 17th, and 18th reports.[118] Under CRC, the majority of Pacific Island states have at least one report overdue, and under CEDAW, Samoa and Vanuatu submitted their initial reports almost ten years late.[119] Although erratic submission of reports is rife within the UN treaty-monitoring system,[120] it is a particularly significant problem in the Pacific Islands given the absence of any regional machinery.[121] This is only partly offset by the UN treaty-bodies' willingness to review states that persistently refuse to submit a report. For example, the Committee on Economic, Social, and Cultural Rights reviewed the performance of the Solomon Islands in the continued absence of a state report.[122] This requires an effective civil society contribution usually through the form of a 'shadow report'. However, while the examination of shadow reports sounds promising this has to be countered by the relatively low level of civil society activity in the region.[123]

Non-ratification and non-compliance are fundamental challenges to an effective international human rights regime in the Pacific. Respect for, promotion, and protection of human rights is linked to all of the strategic objectives in the Pacific Plan of Action: in particular reduced poverty (4); improved health (6); improved education and training (7); improved gender equality (8); recognized and protected cultural values, identities, and traditional knowledge (11); improved transparency (12); improved political and social conditions for stability (13); and increased commitment to regional approaches and policies. All but the last of these strategic objectives is directly connected to provisions contained in the core human rights conventions, with the advantage of the imposition of a legal obligation for compliance.[124] According to Jalal, there are five reasons for the low levels of ratification: resources; substantive obstacles, including cultural, political, economic, and legal; the role of non-governmental organizations (NGOs); strategic positioning of the UN; and lack of national human rights bodies.[125]

Only Vanuatu requires ratification of a treaty through Parliament, and previously Pacific Island Countries simply ratified a convention without much consultation with government departments or civil society.[126] The process preceding ratification is now far more complex, with greater awareness from government departments and citizens on the need for effective consultation, and internal protocols requiring a broad range of contributions from stakeholders.

---

[117] ibid 177.   [118] ibid 178.   [119] ibid.
[120] For a general reading on the treaty system and challenges for the future, see Philip Alston and James Crawford (eds), *The Future of UN Human Rights Treaty-monitoring* (Cambridge: Cambridge University Press, 2000).
[121] Olowu (n 97) 178.   [122] ibid 178–9.
[123] ibid 179.   [124] Imrana Jalal (n 98) 6.
[125] ibid 7.   [126] ibid.

For example, it took ten years of advocacy from CEDAW to get the convention ratified in Fiji, and even longer in the Solomon Islands. It is doubtful if the process would have been successful without additional financial and technical resources from a variety of women's groups, such as UNIFEM and the *Pacific Regional Rights Resource Team* (RRRT).[127] Reporting requirements are considered to be the most practical constraint to ratification, involving further intensive levels of consultations and the potential need for outside consultants, with very few Pacific Island Countries having the internal capacity to write their own reports.[128] The dialogue with the treaty bodies is costly and time-consuming and requires significant resources to facilitate a team of civil servants to attend the process, in Geneva or New York. Smaller Pacific Island Countries cannot release officials from domestic responsibilities for the periods required. Finally the compliance process needs political will, considerable technical capacity, and financial resources. Again Fiji provides an example, whereby the *Family Law Act 2003*, implemented to conform to CEDAW requirements, took several years to pass into law and to implement in the form of the setting up of the Family Division of the existing courts.[129]

Although there is no homogenous Pacific Island Countries human rights culture,[130] some PIC governments and communities believe that Pacific Island culture is incompatible with human rights. While Pacific culture focuses on the good of the community as a whole, human rights focus on individual rights at the supposed expense of the collective good.[131] There is a perceived conflict between convention standards and unwritten customary law, as discussed later in the context of indigenous custom.[132] More particularly, human rights treaties, with their emphasis on equality and access to resources for all, are perceived to be threatening to indigenous communal land systems.[133] Political barriers exist, with human rights perceived as obstacles to economic growth. Legal and political tolerance has been shown towards interruptions of democracy by the military or police, resulting in conflict in Fiji, Solomon Islands, and Vanuatu.[134] Key donors in the Pacific, notably AusAID and NZAID, appear to be concentrating on poverty elimination, while increasingly linking this goal to human rights protection. For instance, human rights-based approaches are integrated into NZAID's organizational culture as well as into all of its policies, strategies, programmes, and processes.[135] Legally, most PICs are of the incorrect view that they need to amend all their laws to make them compliant with conventions *before* ratification. It is poorly understood that ratification can precede the process of amendment and is a means by which assistance in compliance can be

[127]　ibid 8.　　[128]　ibid 9–10.　　[129]　ibid 11.

[130]　For a parallel discussion in the Asian context about the existence of 'Asian Values', see Joshua Castellino and Elvira Domínguez Redondo, *Minority Rights in Asia: A Comparative Legal Analysis* (Oxford: Oxford University Press, 2006), 11–26.

[131]　ibid.　　[132]　See e.g. 55–56.　　[133]　Castellino and Domínguez Redondo (n 130) 17.

[134]　ibid 15–16.　　[135]　ibid 16.

sought from the UN. Many PICs consider that there are sufficient human rights in their domestic legal frameworks.[136]

In most PICs civil society NGOs are the driving force behind ratification of international treaties. Many NGOs have a limited capacity because PICs lack a proper legal framework for robust civil society organizations, and NGOs do not display sophisticated rights-based strategies. Well-organized and well-funded local NGOs are '... the most significant critical factor in determining whether a convention gets ratified or not'.[137] There have been specific local groups mobilizing around the ratification of CEDAW and CRC, but no groups dedicated to the other five conventions. In Fiji, the Citizens' Constitutional Forum filed a 'shadow' report to Fiji's state report to CERD, but was not involved in the ratification process.[138] CEDAW has found support for ratification from government ministries, departments, and influential officials throughout the Pacific, and joint partnerships between governments and NGOs have facilitated its implementation.[139]

The presence of UN bodies can have an important effect. Until recently, United Nations Development Programme (UNDP) Pacific Offices in Fiji, Papua New Guinea, and Samoa did not see themselves as having a specific 'human rights mandate'.[140] The RRRT is the only regional project with a specific and broad mandate on human rights and has been involved with ratification, reporting and implementation of ICERD, CEDAW and CRC in Fiji, Solomon Islands, Cook Islands, Tuvalu, Federated States of Micronesia, Samoa, Kiribati, and Vanuatu. UNDP's association with this project began only in 2002, and the UNDP Pacific Sub-regional Centre, set up in 2005, now has a human rights specialist with a mandate to advocate for ratification.[141] Importantly, the Office of the High Commissioner for Human Rights (OHCHR) has just opened a regional office in Suva, Fiji, which will have a critical role in supporting the other five core treaties.[142]

Human rights commissions can promote the ratification of conventions and nationalization of their provisions. Besides Australia and New Zealand, only Fiji has a human rights commission, and it is critical that all PICs develop national human rights mechanisms and grant them appropriate powers in concordance with the 'Paris Principles'. For very small countries, national commissions may not be viable and other options, including a regional mechanism, could be considered.[143]

1.2.2 Pacific Charter of Human Rights

Van Dyke observes that the Pacific Island area shows the 'greatest promise of forming a cohesive sub-region for the purpose of developing a human rights

---

[136] ibid 18.   [137] ibid 20.
[138] ibid. In fact, the United Kingdom ratified ICERD on Fiji's behalf.
[139] ibid 20–1.   [140] ibid 21.   [141] ibid.
[142] ibid.   [143] ibid 22.

organisation' within Asia and the Pacific.[144] In 1980 Patrick Downey, then Human Rights Commissioner for New Zealand, mooted the idea of a human rights commission for the Pacific, and various discussions and initiatives resulted.[145] Following the example of the *International Commission of Jurists* in beginning the process which led to the *African Charter of Human and Peoples' Rights*, the *Human Rights Committee* of LAWASIA, a non-governmental organization, conducted a conference in Fiji in 1985 entitled *Prospects for the Establishment of an Intergovernmental Human Rights Commission in the South Pacific*.[146] The conference resulted in the formation of two working committees termed the Working Party, and in 1986 three recommendations were made: first, that the African 'Banjul Charter' be used as a model for the Pacific; second, that a human rights officer be attached to a regional organization as an interim measure; and third, that the Pacific region be defined.[147]

By August 1986, a model treaty was proposed, which set down civil, political, economic, social, cultural, and peoples' rights based on the *Banjul Charter*, and suggested a supervisory body charged with compliance and technical assistance to governments.[148] The recommendations called for a commission with the power to receive complaints, conduct investigations, and issue recommendations, rather than a court that could issue binding decisions on states.[149] On 15–17 May 1989, a seminar held in Apia, Western Samoa, of twenty delegates from Micronesia, Melanesia, Polynesia, New Zealand, and Australia, considered the report of the Working Party, including the draft 'Pacific Charter of Human Rights'.[150] The seminar resolved to encourage the governments of the Pacific to begin the process of drafting a treaty based on the proposed charter.

Van Dyke noted in 1988 that while these efforts were at non-governmental level, they '…can be expected ultimately to be successful', reflecting the momentum generated by the 1985 conference and subsequent draft charter.[151] There was considerable optimism that the setting up of such a sub-regional commission would be viewed as a positive first step towards the eventual establishment of a commission of human rights for the entire Asian

---

[144] Jon Van Dyke, 'Prospects for the Development of Inter-governmental Human Rights Bodies in Asia and the Pacific' (1988) 16 *MLR* 28–33 at 29.

[145] Olowu (n 97) 170.

[146] 'Report on a Proposed Pacific Charter of Human Rights, prepared under the auspices of LAWASIA, May 1989' (n 64) 99.

[147] Report of the Working Party on a Proposed Pacific Charter of Human Rights (December 1986), cited in Tony Deklin, 'Strogim Hiumen Raits: A Proposal for a Regional Human Rights Charter and Commission for the Pacific' (1992) 20 *MLR* 93–106 at 99.

[148] 'Report on a Proposed Pacific Charter of Human Rights, prepared under the auspices of LAWASIA, May 1989' (n 64) 99.

[149] Van Dyke (n 144) 30.

[150] 'Report on a Proposed Pacific Charter of Human Rights, prepared under the auspices of LAWASIA, May 1989' (n 64) 100. This report gives the full text of the draft charter. Draft art 14A provides for the rights of minorities, and is a reproduction of art 27 ICCPR.

[151] Van Dyke (n 144) 33.

region.[152] However no state was willing to oversee the project, and Deklin complained in 1992:

There is a need for some country to take leadership in organizing the regional support for human rights, and it might naturally be expected that both Australia and New Zealand would rise to the occasion. But this seems unlikely, largely because both of these countries have human rights problems arising from their own respective minority groups.[153]

Consequently:

... the task is to identify those Pacific Island countries whose governments have a good human rights record and who support these rights, to take the lead in organizing the setting up of the proposed Pacific Human Rights Commission. If this can be done it will at least pave the way toward the establishment of a truly intergovernmental human rights commission which is what we all want to see for the peoples of the Pacific.[154]

There was no concordance between Pacific governments and civil society in the pursuance of a regional mechanism, and no further advances were made. Wilde calls the draft charter '...an agreed text around which NGOs can campaign', and surmises that until inter-governmental meetings seriously begin the task of considering regional machinery, such a regime remains '...largely in the realm of human rights activism'.[155] Nevertheless LAWASIA is currently considering the rejuvenation of the draft Pacific Charter of Human Rights, seeking the agreement of governments of all Pacific countries to adhere to a set of basic human rights principles.[156] A University of the South Pacific/Fiji Human Rights Commission Working Group, which began its review in late 2005, is also pursuing the idea of a regional system for the Pacific.[157]

Commentators largely agree that a Pacific Human Rights Commission would be a valuable regional mechanism. They are divided as to its possible role and whether pursuing it would be beneficial given the resources and diversion of energy that would be required. As noted, the Pacific region has by far the lowest ratification rates worldwide of the seven core international human rights treaties.[158] Jalal supports the creation of a regional mechanism, but argues that such a body should be oriented towards providing technical and financial assistance to Pacific Island states for ratification, implementation, and reporting under existing international human rights treaties.[159] This ought not to be confused

[152] 'Report on a Proposed Pacific Charter of Human Rights, prepared under the auspices of LAWASIA, May 1989' (n 64) 167.
  [153] Deklin (n 147) 205. Deklin was a member of the Working Party.
  [154] ibid 105–6.
  [155] Ralph Wilde, 'NGO Proposals for an Asia-Pacific Human Rights System' (1999) 1 *YHRDLJ* 137–42 at 142.
  [156] LAWASIA, 'Human Rights Activities' <http://lawasia.asn.au/content/cms/Human+Rights+Activities/151/> cited in Olowu (n 97) 171 fn 76.
  [157] ibid.   [158] Imrana Jalal (n 98) 4.   [159] ibid 42.

with a regional court, which she considers would be 'a severe and further drain on Pacific resources'.[160]

The mechanism LAWASIA envisions also distinguishes itself from a regional court, but the role of its proposed commission is decidedly different to that proposed by Jalal; clearly, the LAWASIA commission would oversee an agreed binding regional treaty and would monitor its implementation in a quasi-judicial manner. Jalal views the role of a regional commission as providing technical assistance in ratifying and implementing the UN human rights treaties, which could come under an OHCHR-initiated and sponsored regional fund.[161]

Olowu calls the renewal of discussions on the prospects of a regional human rights treaty 'commendable', but asks whether these developments should come at the exclusion of the UN human rights treaty system.[162] He writes:

...apart from being a desire that remains not immediately feasible, the prospect of a regional human rights system cannot be a tenable reason for South Pacific countries to shun well-established normative and institutional mechanisms of the UN human rights system.[163]

More importantly, there is a lack of consensus on the conceptual, institutional, and geopolitical parameters of any regional system.[164] Some have called for an 'Asian' or 'Asia-Pacific' approach (encompassing the broader Pacific), while others favour a more limited 'South Pacific' or 'Pacific Island Countries' system.[165]

A further criticism levelled at the proposal is its focus on collective rights as an essential aspect of the Pacific interpretation of human rights protection. For example, Deklin states that the exclusion of the rights of groups from international human rights treaties 'does not quite fit into the Pacific context', as collective group rights 'characterise the Pacific communities as a matter of social and cultural principle'.[166] Wickliffe speculates that the reason Pacific governments have been slow to accede to international instruments is due to the lack of attention given to collective rights and duties, '...concepts that fit easily within Pacific cultures'.[167] He employs the term *'Pacific Charter of Human and Peoples' Rights and Duties'* to describe a proposed regional mechanism, in a direct reference to the African system, with the view that it would invoke a regional philosophy of rights and responsibilities.[168] LAWASIA believes the African process is a useful platform upon which to build a charter of rights for the Pacific region.[169]

---

[160] ibid.   [161] ibid.   [162] Olowu (n 97) 171–2.

[163] ibid 172.   [164] ibid 171.

[165] ibid 157, fn 10. Olowu notes that the phrases 'South Pacific' and 'Pacific Island Countries' have been used by various writers in different contexts with varying meanings.

[166] Deklin (n 147) 95.

[167] C. Wickliffe, 'Human Rights Education in the Pacific' (1999) 3 *JSPL*, Working Paper 1 <http://www.vanuatu.usp.ac.fj/journal_splaw/working_papers/wickliffe1.htm> [last accessed 25 March 2009].

[168] ibid.

[169] 'Report on a Proposed Pacific Charter of Human Rights, prepared under the auspices of LAWASIA, May 1989' (n 64) 107.

Powles also focuses on the concept of 'duties' in the African Charter, and their relevance to the Pacific context.[170] Oluwa is unconvinced by these parallels:

...since the notion of 'collective rights' and 'duties' surfaced in the African Charter in 1981, there has been no pronouncement or definition of the scope of these concepts by the African Commission on Human and Peoples' Rights...In fact, the uncertainty over what constitutes 'peoples' within the context of 'collective rights' in the African Charter has ensured that the concept of collective rights remains one of the weakest aspects of that regional treaty...time has proven that they are merely cosmetic moral code...why should scholars writing on human rights in the Pacific be interested in strengthening the orientation of South Pacific human rights towards such conceptually problematic ideas?...no appeal to cultural relativism must be allowed to insulate the South Pacific from the ever-widening promise of international human rights.[171]

Peebles accepts that the fear of 'undue deference to regional norms' has been an obstacle to the development of a regional mechanism.[172] This fear is considered a reaction to cultural relativists, and an expression of the belief that a regional interpretation of rights in the Pacific would 'corrupt the global law'.[173] He sketches a proposal for an *Oceania Human Rights Commission*, governed by an *Oceania Human Rights Charter*, and engendering a companion court. Fears of a relativist agenda would be assuaged by UN involvement in the process, which would ensure that the Oceania human rights order would remain connected with, and responsive to, the global system.[174] LAWASIA also emphasized that the UN needs to take an active role in encouraging the achievement of its policy objectives in the Pacific region by supporting the initiative to establish a regional human rights treaty.[175]

The problem with the UN approach is that is has concentrated on promoting a regional system for the 'Asia Pacific' region, which it defines as including Middle Eastern and Central Asian states in an area which covers half the world, and which 'just happens to include Pacific states'.[176] Since 1990, the UN has held a series of workshops in attempts to provide an impetus towards the establishment of a regional commission for 'Asia Pacific', which have all failed. This is not surprising given that some forty countries have attended the various workshops, as diverse and removed as Afghanistan, Yemen, Bhutan, Fiji, and Palestine.[177]

A sub-regional focus in the Pacific would:

...cure the UN's pursuit of inappropriate regional human rights organisations, covering countries from the Middle East to the Pacific, in an unsuitable definition of the

---

[170] Guy Powles, 'Duties of Individuals: Some Implications for the Pacific Including "Duties" in "Human Rights" Documents' (1992) 22 (3) *VUWLR*, 49.

[171] Olowu (n 97) 168–9.

[172] Dave Peebles, *Pacific Regional Order* (Canberra: Australian National University, 2005) 198.

[173] ibid.   [174] ibid 199.

[175] 'Report on a Proposed Pacific Charter of Human Rights, prepared under the auspices of LAWASIA, May 1989' (n 64) 107.

[176] Peebles (n 172) 194.   [177] ibid 196.

Asia Pacific which can add little value to the global system's efforts to promote human rights.[178]

The benefits to the Pacific are evident, and even Oluwo, perhaps the strongest critic of the process thus far, acknowledges that the proposed Pacific regional human rights system is a significant advancement that would strengthen the profile of human rights in the South Pacific region.[179]

The proposal for a regional Pacific human rights mechanism must resolve two outstanding problems: the geopolitical understanding of the parameters of the Pacific region or sub-region; and the failure of Pacific states to engage with the international human rights bodies. The first problem involves the UN understanding of the term 'Asia Pacific' as including, but not being limited to, the Pacific states. Thus UN support for a regional system in 'Asia Pacific' is far too general to have any meaning, given that it includes Central Asia, South Asia, South-east Asia, and the Middle East, as well as the Pacific.[180] The second problem directly affects the proposed role of the Pacific regional mechanism. Should it be principally a facilitator for Pacific states to engage with the international process, or should it be a *sui generis* branch of international law akin to the African, European, and Inter-American systems? Allied to this issue is the question of a Pacific interpretation of human rights standards, including collective rights, and the danger that a Pacific regional mechanism would just be a substitute for, rather than a complement to, the international system.

The apparent absence of political will overshadows the entire process. Again, the failure to engage with the international system prompts the question as to why Pacific governments would engage with a regional system; and indeed whether such a system would utilize concepts of collective rights and duties to whittle down accepted international standards. In 1992, Deklin thought it unlikely that Australia or New Zealand would take a lead in organizing regional support for human rights. Is this still the case? It seems that the impetus for the project is now with two groups, LAWASIA and the University of the South Pacific in Fiji, which, significantly, is one of only three states in the region that has a national human rights commission.[181] Current political instability in Fiji may render it unsuitable for leading such a project.

The concept of a Pacific regional system is generally attributed to former New Zealand Human Rights Commissioner, Patrick Downey. New Zealand could facilitate a forum for the development of a regional system, in support of the University of the South Pacific and LAWASIA initiative. The difficulties around the definition of the Pacific region seem to arise only in the international context,

---

[178] ibid 211.   [179] Olowu (n 97) 183.

[180] This attitude also pervades among international NGOs. For instance, see the annual report of Minority Rights Group International 'State of the World's Minorities', which amalgamates several of these regions together in reporting on their minority rights provisions, despite their obvious differences and sizes.

[181] Imrana Jalal (n 98) 42.

and there is a relative consensus around what states should be included and what states should not. The proposed commission could have a dual role in providing technical assistance to Pacific states to engage with the international procedures, while supervising the implementation of a binding charter. A *Pacific Human Rights Charter* and Commission would be the first 'sub-regional' human rights mechanism, and would be a remarkable contribution to the growth of international human rights institutions.

1.3 Minority Rights in the Pacific: An Overview

Having examined the history of the region, its performance in terms of the global human rights regime, and the attempts to form a sub-regional or regional focal point for human rights protection, this final section offers a brief glimpse of the issues that emerge in each of the Pacific nations. The countries will be divided by sub-region along the lines described in section 1.1. The book uses four case-studies, Australia, New Zealand, Fiji, and Papua New Guinea, to examine the challenges to the protection of indigenous peoples and minority rights in the region. It is important to acknowledge the state of minority rights and indigenous peoples in the other countries that form this region. Detailed examination of each state is beyond the scope of the present volume; the following sections offer a brief overview of some of the problems they experience.

The complex governance structure of the *Federated States of Micronesia* (due to the vast spread between the different islands that constitute the state) provides an interesting model through which to examine the protection of human rights, with the Polynesian minority and Outer Islanders facing rising levels of discrimination in terms of access to resources and employment.

Guam, an unincorporated territory of the USA, provides a backdrop (as with some of the French dependencies) for the extent to which the discourse of self-determination is a realistic option for states that are so small. In addition, in the context of Guam, this genuine claim has to be balanced against the relatively large proportion of US-born settlers in the state. The notion of 'planted populations' is well-developed in international law, but usually dominated by discussions around entities like Palestine or Northern Ireland.[182] A focus on this question in such a different background is likely to make an important contribution to the academic literature on the subject. Against this, Guam has fostered US aid-dependency that makes the prospect of independence

---

[182] For an analysis of such application in other settings, see Charles E. Ehrlich, 'Democratic Alternatives to Ethnic Conflict: Consociationalism and Neo-Separatism' (2000–2001) 26 *BJIL* 447; David Wippman, 'Powersharing as a Response to Cultural Dominance' (1996) 90 *ASILP* 206; Bede Harris, 'Constitutional Mechanisms for the Protection of Group Rights' (1991) 2 *SLR* (1991) 49.

difficult, challenging the notion of 'sovereignty' and its implications. The high proportions of Filipinos, Europeans, Koreans, and Micronesians whose rights are not always adequately protected within the state engage the notion of multiculturalism.[183]

The discourse of statehood and sovereignty is also challenged by the extent to which the state of *Nauru*, which recently ratified the *Geneva Conventions on the Laws of Armed Conflict*,[184] is in fact a true state. Nauru has become a 'failed' state following the collapse of the phosphate mining industry, which has led to the population dynamic of the state being dramatically altered, with many migrant workers being repatriated. The physical distance of Nauru from Australia and its desperate need for an income has led to it becoming a processing house for those seeking asylum in Australia.

The *Solomon Islands* bears some resemblance to Papua New Guinea especially in its linguistic diversity, with over ninety indigenous languages spoken on the Islands. There has been a growth of ethnic-identity oriented violence between migrant Malaitans and the indigenous Guadalcanese.[185] While the United Nations Regional Assistance Mission to the Solomon Islands (RAMSI)[186] remains in place, its military component has been reduced, an indicator of the lowering of tension between these communities. The end of hostilities has finally enabled the state to give its full attention to the ailing Solomon economy, with some debate over whether or not to privatize various state monopolies.

New Caledonia remains the most troubled of the French overseas territories in the region. Sustained European immigration over the last century has left

---

[183] While the most authoritative writing on the subject remains the work of Will Kymlicka, *The Rights of Minority Cultures* (Oxford: Oxford University Press, 1995), the application of the concept is interesting in other contexts. Among these are Geoffrey Brahm Levey, 'The Political Theories of Australian Multiculturalism' (2001) 24 *UNSWLJ* 869; Arthur Glass, 'Multiculturalism, Law and the Right of Culture' (2001) 24 *UNSWLJ* 862; Tamir Yael, 'A Note on Multiculturalism and Cultural Dominance' (1996) 90 *ASILP* 200 and Denise Meyerson, 'Multiculturalism, Religion and Equality' (2001) *Acta Juridica* 104.

[184] Nauru became the 194th state to ratify the Geneva Conventions of 12 August 1949, when it lodged its documents on 27 June 2006. The new state of Montenegro (2 August 2006) is the only state to have ratified the Conventions after that date [accurate as of July 2007]. For the latest ratification information, see <http://www.cicr.org/ihl.nsf/WebSign?ReadForm&id=375&ps=P> [accessed 18 July 2007].

[185] For a general reading on Solomon Islands in the context of its governance, see Sandra Tarte and Tarcisus Tara Kabutaulaka, 'Rethinking Security in the South Pacific: Fiji and the Solomon Islands' in Bruce Vaughn (ed), *The Unravelling of Island Asia? Governmental, Communal and Regional Instability* (Westport, CT: Praeger, 2002) 61–82.

[186] The Regional Assistance Mission to the Solomon Islands (RAMSI) is a partnership between the government and people of the Solomon Islands and the contributing countries of the Pacific region. It is a long-term exercise aimed at helping create the conditions necessary for a return to stability, peace, and a growing economy. RAMSI first arrived in the Solomon Islands on 24 July 2003, at the invitation of the Solomon Islands government. Its deployment was facilitated by *The Facilitation of International Assistance Act* (No 1 of 2003) passed by the government of the Solomon Islands.

the indigenous Melanesian population as a large minority (44 per cent) with their ethnic cousins the Polynesians accounting for a further 12 per cent.[187] The central cause for conflict is the issue of land rights, and the manner in which indigenous territory was acquired by settlers.[188] The implementation of the *Noumea Accords of 1998*[189] devolves considerable authority to New Caledonia, with a vote on independence set to take place in 2014.[190] Partly in deference to this process tensions have dampened with the *Front de Libération Nationale Kanak et Socialiste* (who advocated an armed struggle for independence) now more keen to make a success of the form of autonomy currently offered to them.[191] The Wallisians and Futunan minorities nonetheless remain vulnerable within the state, with high rates of unemployment and violent disputes in recent years over land ownership.[192] Like the other states in this region, there is grow-ing resentment against Asian immigration. This resentment is also echoed in France's other overseas territories in the region. In *French Polynesia*, unlike in New Caledonia, the movement for independence in the state has not taken on the same level of intensity, with autonomy rather than outright independence appearing the favoured option.[193] This is also the preferred option in *Wallis and Futuna*, where the relatively small number of French settlers are not viewed with as much resentment as in the other territories. The Futunans who constitute 33 per cent of the population do desire greater autonomy from the Wallisians rather than the French.[194]

Wallisians and Futunans, along with i-Kiribati, are the chief minorities in *Vanuatu*.[195] These in-groups, along with other Melanesian populations

---

[187] For a general reading of the history of New Caledonia, see Cyril S. Belshaw, *Island Administration In The South West Pacific: Government And Reconstruction In New Caledonia, The New Hebrides, And The British Solomon Islands* (London: Royal Institute Of International Affairs, 1950).

[188] See D. Custos, 'New Caledonia, a Case of Shared Sovereignty within the French Republic: Appearance or Reality?' (2007) 13(1) *EPL* 97–132.

[189] For a discussion about the contents of this treaty and its significance for Kanak independ-ence, see Alan Berman, '1998 and Beyond in New Caledonia: At Freedom's Gate?' (1998) 7(1) *PRLPJ* 1–76; Alan Berman, 'Future Kanak Independence in New Caledonia: Illusion or Reality?' (1998) 34 *SJIL* 287–346.

[190] See esp Alan Berman, 'The Noumea Accords: Emancipation or Colonial Harness?' (2001) 36 *TILJ* 277–97.

[191] ibid.   [192] ibid.

[193] Bernard Gille and Yves-Louis Sage, 'The Territory of French Polynesia' (1993) 23 (1) *VUWLR* 1–14. For a more general reading of the background of this society, see Nicholas Thomas, *Marquesan Societies: Inequality and Political Transformation in Eastern Polynesia* (Oxford: Clarendon Press, 1990).

[194] For a general reading in the context of the development of this State, see Giraud-Kinley (n 70) 125–76.

[195] For a general reading on two very important issues in Vanuatu i.e. land tenure and linguistic rights, see Margaret Critchlow Rodman, *Masters of Tradition: Consequences of Customary Land Tenure in Longana, Vanuatu* (Vancouver: University Of British Columbia Press, 1987); Terry Crowley, *Beach-la-Mar to Bislama: The Emergence of a National Language in Vanuatu* (Oxford: Clarendon Press, 1990) respectively. Other analyses of the type of

contribute to the linguistic diversity of the state, which while adopting Bislama as its national language, sees usage of over 105 other languages. The tensions *vis-à-vis* minority and indigenous issues exist in the form of difficulties facing many of the non-local populations in gaining citizenship rights, and in some intermittent tensions between Anglophone and Francophone areas. While the state is a Less Developed Country its financial situation is likely to improve as it has had access to *Millennium Challenge Funds* since 2006.

The *Northern Mariana Islands* and *Palau* have significant Filipino populations who live within the states as minorities. Of the two, Northern Mariana Islands has been the more diverse, with Chinese and Micronesians working alongside Filipinos in the textile industry. More recently, however, the industry has been destroyed by US trading regulations causing many of the minority groups to leave.[196] This has increased dependence on the US remittances gained from serving as a military base, raising further questions over the nature of the application of the doctrine of state sovereignty in this particular context. The Chamoros and Carolinians alone have citizenship rights that are denied to migrants.[197] In Palau, the previous alarms over the increasing Filipino population appear to have diminished with the migrant population stabilizing at 15 per cent.[198]

In addition to a discussion of the minority and indigenous peoples oriented issues in the states mentioned above, a brief mention needs to be made of the situation in several other states in the region that are relatively homogenous. These include states such as *American Samoa, Niue, Tuvalu* (which is facing a significant

customary law in operation in Vanuatu are available in Jennifer Corrin Care, 'Bedrock and Steel Blues: Finding the Law Applicable in Vanuatu' (1998) 24 *CLB* 594–612; Reid Mortensen, 'Comity and Jurisdictional Restraint in Vanuatu' (2002) 33*VUWLR* 95–116; Tess Newton Cain, 'Convergence or Clash—The Recognition of Customary Law and Practice in Sentencing Decisions of the Courts of the Pacific Island Region' (2001) 2 *MJIL* 48–68; Sue Farran, 'Family Law and French Law in Vanuatu: An Opportunity Missed' (2004) 35 *VUWLR* 367–84; Miranda Forsyth, 'Beyond Case Law: Kastom and Courts in Vanuatu' (2004) 35 *VUWLR* 427–46; Guy Powles (n 170); Guy Powles, 'Changing Pacific Island Constitutions: Methods and Philosophies' (1992) 22 *VUWLR* 63–83; George D. Westermark, 'Reflections on Customary Law: The Mirror of Pacific Kastom' (1993–1994) 17 *LSF* 269–73. For an interesting survey of women's rights across the Melanesian states, see Kenneth Brown and Jennifer Corrin Care, 'Conflict in Melanesia: Customary Law and the Rights of Women' (1998) 24 *CLB*1334–55. Also see Don Paterson (n 56).

196 For a consideration of trade issues and its impact in the region, see Jane Kelsey (n 62). Also see Daniel Orlow, 'Of Nations Small: The Small State in International Law' (1995) 9 *TICLJ* 115–40.

197 This discussion remains important in the context of several Pacific Island states, see (in the context of Vanuatu) Erika J. Techera, 'Protected Area Management in Vanuatu' (2005) 2 *MJICEL*107–19.

198 This alarm has occasionally been provoked by the threat of real violence all across the region. For literature that discusses this, see Roger S. Clark, 'Humanitarian Intervention: Help to Your Friends and State Practice' (1983) 13 *Georgia J of Intl & Comparative L* 211–16; Fergus Hanson, 'Promoting a Pacific Pacific: A Functional Proposal for Regional Security in the Pacific Islands' (2003) 4 *MJIL* 254–98.

sea-level threat which is likely to see a re-location of its population in the near future), *Kiribati*, the *Pitcairn Islands*, *Tokelau* (a non-self governing territory of New Zealand), the *Cook Islands*, the *Marshall Islands*, *Samoa*, and *Tonga*. Many of these states have minority populations consisting of nationals of the other states, and there are hints of a rise in tension towards newer, mainly Chinese immigrants.[199]

---

[199] For a general reading of issues within these states and the region (including a history of external interference) in the Pacific, see Aiko Watanabe, 'Japan, the United States, and the Pacific since 1945: An Overview' (1989) 16 *Ecology LQ* 9–21. Also see Austin Ranney and Howard R. Penniman, *Democracy in the Islands: The Micronesian Plebiscites of 1983* (Washington DC: American Enterprise Institute for Public Policy Research, 1985). For an interesting comment on an island that has a particularly interesting history, see A.H. Angelo and Andrew Townsend, 'Pitcairn: A Contemporary Comment' (2003) *1 NZJPIL* 233–51.

2

Australia

Introduction

By far the most influential state in the region, Australian history is rife with difficult periods in its relations with its indigenous populations. The newly elected government of Kevin Rudd finds itself once again confronting a discussion that had arisen in the early 1990s and looked like it was close to resolution—namely how a modern state is to reconcile itself with the indigenous populations in its midst, against whom the state in previous guises has perpetrated egregious crimes underwritten by a racist ideology, including (in the context of the Stolen Generations) the 'crime of crimes', genocide. These policies linked to 'Social Darwinism', and adopted through programmes such as 'Smoothing the Dying Pillow' of an inferior civilization, have left a deep legacy of distrust among the Australian polity.[1] The hope of reconciliation raised by the famous *Mabo* judgment in 1992 quickly dissipated as fear-mongering among rival stakeholders resulted in a policy reversal. Instead, relations between the indigenous community and the Australian state deteriorated during the governments of John Howard,[2] a nadir from which hope has only recently begun to emerge after the government's apology to its aboriginal peoples.[3]

---

[1] For a book that provides a general picture of the kind of discussion that has shaped the country, see Gillian Cowlishaw, *Rednecks, Eggheads, and Blackfellas: A Study of Racial Power and Intimacy in Australia* (Sydney: Allen and Unwin, 1999). A different perspective is provided by the edited collection Rod Kemp, Marion Stanton, and Geoffrey Blainey (eds), *Speaking for Australia: Parliamentary Speeches That Shaped Our Nation* (Crow's Nest, NSW: Allen and Unwin, 2004). For a particularly compelling view that takes a particular aboriginal focus, see Bain Attwood, *Telling the Truth about Aboriginal History* (Crow's Nest, NSW: Allen and Unwin, 2005). For other books that discuss similar subject material to that addressed here, though from perspectives other than law, see John Docker and Gerhard Fischer (eds), *Race, Colour and Identity in Australia and New Zealand* (Sydney: University of New South Wales Press, 2000); and Elaine Thompson, *Fair Enough: Egalitarianism in Australia* (Sydney: University of New South Wales Press, 1994).

[2] A general (though not complete) picture of this is provided by Judith Brett, *The Australian Liberals and the Moral Middle Class: From Alfred Deakin to John Howard* (Cambridge: Cambridge University Press, 2003). One particularly offensive episode that nonetheless captures the mood of Howard's politics on the indigenous issue was the decision to impose a drink and pornography ban on aboriginals in Northern Territory. See Joshua Castellino, 'Drink Ban for Australian Aboriginals: Paternalistic Determinations for a "Sub-Human Race"?' (2007) *American Chronicle* <http://www.americanchronicle.com/articles/30579> [accessed 2 April 2008].

[3] The incoming Australian government's apology to aboriginal Australians, delivered in the speech of Prime Minister Kevin Rudd at the federal Parliament on 13 February 2008, captures

The previous government's active stance in the so-called 'War against Terror' and its unquestioning endorsement of the policies of the United States of America and the United Kingdom raised tensions at home and attracted waves of violence against newer immigrants, especially Asians and Muslims. The hardening of attitudes against new immigrants (ironic for a state built on immigration) further raised tensions against the 'Other' in Australian life. The governmental decision to abandon 'multiculturalism' for a stronger emphasis on 'Australian-ness' inevitably perpetrated a 'white' rather than composite national identity.

The dismantling of the elected *Aboriginal and Torres Straight Islander Commission* amidst great acrimony, and its replacement by the government-appointed *National Indigenous Council*, further challenged the articulation of indigenous rights in society during the Howard period. In fact, ever since the effective reversal of the *Mabo* decision concerning land rights, Australia had been going backwards in terms of the recognition of native title.[4]

It is clear that the key to reconciliation between settlers in Australia and its indigenous peoples lies in the resolution of land rights issues. Meanwhile aboriginal life expectancy remains twenty years lower than that of other Australians,[5] and the communities are over-represented in an array of social problems besetting the state.[6] The threat to indigenous culture is reflected in the disappearance of some aboriginal languages,[7] and the previous government's intransigence in the face of sustained criticism of its policies by international human rights bodies.[8] Australia has also attracted adverse attention for its 'Pacific Solution' anti-refugee policy which saw a re-interpretation of its territorial waters to avoid

a sentiment that lies at the heart of relations between 'victims' and 'perpetrators' and the way in which mechanisms for restorative justice could be used to ease past wrongs. See Prime Minister Kevin Rudd, *Australian Parliament, Canberra, 13 February 2008.*

[4] There were sporadic sparks of hope such as the decision by a Perth court to accept a native title claim over urban land in the city in 2006. The Tasmanian government's apology in 2006, for its role in the Stolen Generations scheme is to be particularly commended. The apology was announced alongside a compensation scheme of Aus $4 million, providing a useful model for other states to adopt. Failing this it would appear that the outlook for Australia's indigenous peoples has been bleaker than for its new in-groups who, while facing increased hostility, are nonetheless better placed to advance economically and socially, thus creating a buffer between them and sustained discrimination.

[5] For general population decisions in Australia and the discrepancy between vulnerable populations and others, see Doug Cocks, *People policy: Population Choices* (Sydney: University of New South Wales Press, 1996).

[6] For instance in the context of issues related to criminal justice, see Chris Cunneen, *Conflict, Politics and Crime: Aboriginal Communities and the Police* (Crow's Nest, NSW: Allen and Unwin, 2001) and Nicholas Cowdery, *Getting Justice Wrong: Myths, Media and Crime* (St Leonard's, NSW: Allen and Unwin, 2001).

[7] The cultural landscape of Aboriginal Australian nations is partly discussed by Peter Sutton, 'Archaeology and Linguistics: Aboriginal Australia in Global Perspective' (2001) 72 *Oceania*.

[8] See Greg Marks, 'Avoiding the International Spotlight: Australia, Indigenous Rights and the United Nations Treaty Bodies' (2002) 2(1) *HRLR* 19–57.

responsibilities over intakes of refugees, establishing a 'clearing house' on Nauru to keep refugees away from the Australian mainland.[9]

The peopling of Australia was arguably one of the world's more sophisticated projects of social engineering of recent centuries.[10] While the early documented history of Australia is no different from that governing other territories under colonization, its development raised fundamentally different problems. At its heart is the question of the status of territory in international law and the basis on which it was effectively occupied.[11] This will be tackled in some detail in this chapter. Until 1992, the 'legal fiction' of Australia being *terra nullius* dominated legal reasoning and justified policies of repression against the indigenous population.[12] Over two centuries the very fabric of Australian society, including the establishment of the state itself, took place on the basis that the territory, prior to the arrival of the colonizers, was empty and therefore justifiably open to occupation.[13] That this occupation consisted of waves of individuals expelled from their home state under harsh penal systems added to the complexity of the emerging state. One history of Australia reads as the gradual dismantling and de-recognition of the region's indigenous population,[14] while a more mainstream historical reading emphasizes the extent to which diverse communities, initially European, subsequently Asian, and with a steady trickle from the Pacific Islands, peopled the continent and came to shape its current society.[15]

This chapter will emphasize the causes of violations against minorities and indigenous peoples within the state. It seeks to explain the extent to which law has sought to address the position of the more vulnerable groups in Australian society. There are a host of caveats that need to be identified to ensure a thorough analysis of the situation.

[9] For an overview of the factors that led to this direction in Australian foreign policy, see Stewart Firth, *Australia in International Politics: An Introduction to Australian Foreign Policy* (Crow's Nest, NSW: Allen and Unwin, 2005) esp 254–8.

[10] This is especially important in light of the subsequent motivation for the British to hold Australia: in establishing a penal colony for the excess 'criminal classes' of Georgian England. See Robert Poirier and David Ostergren, 'Evicting People from Nature: Indigenous Land Rights and National Parks in Australia, Russia and the United States' (2002) 42 *National Resources J* 331–52, at 335. More generally, see Maria Nugent, *Botany Bay: Where Histories Meet* (Crow's Nest, NSW: Allen and Unwin, 2005) and Rosemary Neill, *White out: How Politics Is Killing Black Australia* (St Leonard's, NSW: Allen and Unwin, 2002).

[11] For general reading on this issue, see Anthony Barker, *What Happened When: A Chronology of Australia from 1788* (St Leonard's, NSW: Allen and Unwin, 2000).

[12] Diane Otto, 'A Question of Law or Politics? Indigenous Claims to Sovereignty in Australia' (1995) 21 *SJILC* 65–103.

[13] For general reading on the position in international law *vis-à-vis* territory, see Joshua Castellino, 'Territorial Integrity and the "Right" To Self-determination: An Examination of the Conceptual Tools' (2008) 33 (2) *BJIL* 503–68.

[14] For general reading on the history of the decimation of indigenous Australian society Philip Clarke, *Where the Ancestors Walked: Australia as an Aboriginal Landscape* (Crow's Nest, NSW: Allen and Unwin, 2003).

[15] For a general reading of the celebration of the creation of Australia, see Anthony Moran, *Australia: Nation, Belonging, and Globalization* (New York: Routledge, 2004).

First, there is the status of the territory itself and the extent to which any discussion of 'Australia' in its current form already pre-judges and excludes aboriginal communities that have existed on the territory since time immemorial. It needs to be highlighted that while this is a study primarily focused on vulnerable groups and indigenous peoples, it nonetheless remains part of a broader analysis of the extent to which states reflect on the need to include all, in their historical, sociological, political, and, most importantly, legal regimes. The exclusion of Aboriginals and Torres Strait Islanders from the state-building process will be emphasized as a violation of the rights of these groups.

Secondly, any emphasis on the legal regime in Australia has the handicap that it fails to reflect indigenous values, and was allied to political interests to subjugate the region's native populations. A focus on law could be seen to represent an unquestioning acceptance of this unequal regime, and an argument may be made that a better, more useful frame of reference could be the study of a *sui generis* system of aboriginal law.[16] This is addressed in section 2.3, and emphasis will be laid on the extent to which the exclusion of native thought and culture from the framing of mainstream legal rules has limited the extent to which indigenous Australians can enjoy the fruits of human rights.

Thirdly, this chapter addresses the important question of what contemporary visions of a multicultural state mean in the Australian context. There will be a brief focus on asylum seekers, refugees, and others defined differently from the mainstream population based on their personal or collective identities. These groups are traditionally outside the realm of minority rights literature (even though the groups fit within the wider notion of 'vulnerable groups'),[17] but to present an accurate picture of contemporary Australia it is important not to exclude them. While emphasis throughout the chapter will be on indigenous Australians, it will include commentary on the experiences of other minority groups and the tensions that they face in contemporary society.

The key theoretical issues relevant to this study have been briefly introduced in the previous chapter, but the following remain particularly pertinent to Australia:

(a) title to Australian territory;
(b) 'people hood' of Australian Aboriginals and Torres Strait Islanders;
(c) nature of occupation and colonization;
(d) the prohibition of racial discrimination;
(e) the importance of self-determination and identifying the 'consent of the natives';

[16] For a general theoretical discussion of the notion of a *sui generis* system of protection for indigenous rights, see Benedict Kingsbury, 'Reconciling Five Competing Conceptual Structures of indigenous Claims in International & Comparative Law' (2001) 34 *NYUJILP* 189–250.

[17] For a discussion on the difference between the notion of 'minorities' and that of 'vulnerable groups', see Elvira Domínguez Redondo, 'Vulnerability and the Principle of Non-Discrimination' presented at the *EU-China Experts Network Meeting*, Beijing, 9 November 2003. Hard copy available with the author.

(f) the human rights mechanisms and their implementation;

(g) the territorial dimensions of the state in terms of accepting claims for asylum; and

(h) the obligations of the state party with regard to international wrongs.

This chapter is divided into four main sections. Section 2.1 identifies the key historical moments that are important in understanding the backdrop to the plight of minorities and vulnerable peoples in Australia. The objective is to provide the necessary historical background to arrive at a nuanced understanding of contemporary problems within Australian society. Section 2.2 focuses on an identification of 'Minorities', 'Indigenous Peoples', and others that are covered by this chapter. While it is possible to be general about the various vulnerable groups in any given society, their differing cultural beliefs, locations, and values must be examined to understand the barriers to their empowerment. Section 2.3 provides an analysis of the legal framework that regulates indigenous peoples' and minorities' entitlements in Australia. The sources are the Constitution and attendant statutes that concern minority and indigenous peoples' rights. The possibility of a *sui generis* system through customary law is an equally compelling, if not equally real, basis for the rights of indigenous peoples that is also explored. The second part of this section addresses six specific issues in a bid to document the experience of minorities and indigenous peoples in Australia. Section 2.4 reflects on the existing remedies available in Australian law, testing their efficacy. Other remedies that have been articulated by jurists, indigenous peoples' spokespersons, and other commentators are given, in order to understand whether they can provide a basis for future reconciliation. The chapter ends with a short conclusion that seeks to address the question of what 'Australian-ness' means and how its construction impacts the experience of vulnerable groups within society.

2.1 History

William Jansz, generally attributed as the first European to see Australia in 1606, claimed that the territory was inhabited by 'savage, cruel, black barbarians', a crucial assessment that was probably responsible for influencing the subsequent view of aboriginal peoples.[18] The peopling of Australia is relatively well-documented.[19]

---

[18] See William Jansz, 'Uncultivated, Savage, Cruel, 1606' in Tim Flannery (ed), *The Explorers* (New York: Grove Press, 1999) 17, as quoted in fn 9, p 334.

[19] For a general reading of the history of Australia, see Marjorie Barnard, *A History of Australia* (New York: Frederick A. Praeger, 1963). Also see C.M.H. Clark, *A History of Australia: From the Earliest Times to the Age of Macquarie* (Melbourne: Melbourne University Press, 1962) which portraits a very specifically racist perspective of Australian history prior to the arrival of the European colonists. For a more nuanced reading, see Frank G. Clarke, *The History of Australia* (Westport, CT: Greenwood Press, 2002). Clarke devotes a chapter to aboriginal history, though it is worth

The purpose of this section is not to reduce the complex analyses of Australian history. Rather, it describes how native Australian populations were undermined and provides an insight into the extent to which the history of the state informs contemporary efforts to forge a strong national identity.

Before any historical analysis can proceed it is vital to state emphatically that genocide, the 'crime of crimes',[20] took place in the context of the peopling of the region, as reflected in official reports such as that by the Australia Law Reform Commission entitled *Recognition of Aboriginal Customary Laws (1986).*[21] This report underlines the fact that the aboriginal population fell from 300,000 to a mere 60,000 in the first 100 years of British occupation.[22] While there has been a recovery in population numbers,[23] there has never at any point since the colonization of Australia been a return to the original numbers that existed on the territory at the arrival of the occupying powers. In addition the 'Stolen Generations', discussed in the following section, also raise the spectre of genocide.

In dispatching Lieutenant James Cook in 1768 to Australia, the British Admiralty acted within a national strategy to acquire new territories to develop trade. The instructions given to the Lieutenant were clear:

You are...to observe the genius, temper, disposition and number of the natives, if there be any, and endeavour by all proper means to cultivate a friendship and alliance with them, making them presents of such trifles as they may value, inviting them to traffick, and shewing them every kind of civility and regard; taking care however not to suffer yourself to be surprised by them, but to be always on your guard against any accident.

You are also with the consent of the natives to take possession of convenient situations in the country in the name of the King of Great Britain, or if you find the country uninhabited take possession for His Majesty by setting up proper marks and inscriptions as first discoverers and possessors.[24]

---

noting that this is then mainly a history of the development of the Australian state, which by its nature tends to marginalize the accounts of indigenous history. Other accounts that focus more on indigenous Australian readings are: Bain Attwood and Andrew Markus, *The Struggle for Aboriginal Rights: A Documentary History* (St Leonard's, NSW: Allen and Unwin, 1999); Richard Broome, *Aboriginal Australians: Black Responses to White Dominance, 1788–2001* (Crow's Nest, NSW: Allen and Unwin, 2002) and Nonie Sharp, *Saltwater People: The Waves of Memory* (Crow's Nest, NSW: Allen and Unwin, 2002).

[20] For a general reading on genocide, see William A. Schabas, *Genocide: The Crime of* Crimes (Cambridge: Cambridge University Press, 2002). For the Australian context, see Michael Legg, 'Indigenous Australians and International Law: Racial Discrimination, Genocide and Reparations' (2002) 20 *BKJIL* 387, 408–10 (capturing a discussion that began when the UN Committee for the Elimination of Racial Discrimination took objection to Australia's Native Title Act). A similar discussion from the perspective of Australian foreign policy is offered by Firth (n 9).

[21] Australian Law Reform Commission, *Recognition of Aboriginal Customary Laws* (Report No 31, 1986) 18, available at <http://www.austlii.edu.au/au/other/IndigLRes/1986/1/index.html> [last accessed 25 March 2009].

[22] ibid 18.

[23] The current estimate based on 1991 figures puts the native Australian population at 265,459 which would account for a mere 1.6% of the total population of the state.

[24] H. McRae, G. Nettheim, and L. Beacroft, *Aboriginal Legal Issues: Commentary and Materials* (Sydney: Law Book Company of Australasia, 1991).

The arriving fleet was required to take possession of convenient trading locations, but it was made explicit that such possession needed to be gained through the 'consent of the natives'.[25] It was only if the country was found uninhabited that the instructions urged the taking of possession through discovery. Another quotation, this time from a court of law 200 years later, shows the extent to which legal justification was consistently provided for the violation of Captain Cook's orders. In *Coe v Commonwealth* [1979], Gibbs J refuted any argument for the 'sovereignty' of the natives, stating:

The annexation of the east coast of Australia by Captain Cook in 1770, and the subsequent acts by which the whole of the Australian continent became part of the dominions of the Crown, were acts of state whose validity cannot be challenged: see *New South Wales v Commonwealth* (1975) 135 CLR 337 at 388, and cases there cited. If the amended statement of claim intends to suggest either that the legal foundation of the Commonwealth is insecure, or that the powers of the Parliament are more limited than is provided in the Constitution, or that there is an Aboriginal nation which has sovereignty over Australia, it cannot be supported.[26]

These contrasting statements 200 years apart contextualize the Australian discussion over its treatment of indigenous peoples, against trends such as the recognition of 'domestic dependent nations' as articulated in other jurisdictions, notably the United States of America.[27] While there were periods of limited acceptance in Australian jurisprudence of this concept,[28] it was categorically rejected by Burton J in *R v Murrell* [1836] because aboriginal culture had not achieved the level of institutional and political sophistication that would merit the recognition given to Native American tribes in the United States of America. He went on to rule:

[A]lthough it be granted that the aboriginal natives of New Holland are entitled to be regarded as Civilised nations as a free and independent people, and are entitled to the possession of those rights which as such are valuable to them, yet the various tribes had not attained at the first settlement of the English people among them to such a position in point of numbers and civilization, and to such a form of Government and laws, as to be entitled to be recognised as so many sovereign states governed by laws of their own.[29]

While this line of thinking is perhaps indicative of the tone and superiority of law in the context of 1836, more recent sentiments expressed by Gibbs J in *Coe v*

---

[25] For a discussion that draws out this aspect of 'consent' of the natives, see Garth Nettheim, ' "The Consent of the Natives": *Mabo* and Indigenous Political Rights' (1993) 15 *SYLR,* 223–46 at 223.

[26] (1979) 53 ALJR 403.

[27] See the Marshall cases in the US esp *Worcester v Georgia,* 31 US 515 (1832). For a general reflection on the extent to which courts have addressed indigenous rights of this nature, see Siegfried Wiessner, 'Rights and Status of Indigenous Peoples: a Global Comparative and International Legal Analysis' (1999) 12 *HHRJ* 57–128.

[28] *R v Bonjon* 1844 British Parliamentary Papers at 146ff.

[29] See *R v Jack Congo Murrell* (Supreme Court of New South Wales) in *Sydney Herald* (8 February 1836).

Commonwealth indicate the refusal to accept the 'domestic-dependent nation' doctrine, advanced by the Marshall law cases in the United States as early as 1832. Instead, Gibbs J ruled:

…the history of the relationship between the white settlers and the Aboriginal peoples has not been the same in Australia and in the United States, and it is not possible to say, as was said by Marshall CJ, at 16, of the Cherokee Nation, that the Aboriginal people of Australia are organized as a 'distinct political society separated from others', or that they have been uniformly treated as a state. The Aboriginal people are subject to the laws of the Commonwealth and of the States or Territories in which they respectively reside. They have no legislative, executive or judicial organs by which sovereignty might be exercised. If such organs exist, they would have no powers, except such as the laws of the Commonwealth, or of a State or Territory might confer upon them. The contention that there is in Australia an Aboriginal nation exercising sovereignty, even of a limited kind, is quite impossible in law to maintain.[30]

There were occasions for discussion of sovereignty, land rights, and the possibility of a treaty between indigenous Australians and the government,[31] but the legal fiction that Australia was *terra nullius* and therefore open to colonization was maintained until the *Mabo* decision of 1992. This attitude, whereby indigenous Australians were objects rather than subjects of law,[32] undoubtedly is the root cause of the exclusion of Aboriginal and Torres Strait Islanders from Australian society.[33] In claiming that the territory was unoccupied, the occupiers were effectively claiming title to the territory on the basis of original discovery,[34] and discounting the native populations that were clearly visible on the territory as subjects of international law.[35]

Instead, the general belief was adopted that the territory, being unoccupied, was open to colonization, with no legal effect given to the occupation and

[30] *Coe v Commonwealth (No 1)* (1979) 53 ALJR 403 at 403.

[31] This is reflected upon by Nettheim (n 25) 234–5 where the author writes of the positive response that phrases such as 'self-determination' 'self-governance' and 'self-management' received in official government circles. It is clear that political events clearly overtook this discussion in Australia and that at international level the language of self-determination has always been more problematic. For more on this at international and Australian level, see (2003) 3 *Macquarrie L J* [Special Issue on Self-Determination].

[32] This is explored in R.L. Barsh, 'Indigenous Peoples in the 1990s: From Object to Subject in International Law?' (1994) 7 *HHRJ* 33–62.

[33] The issues around the issue of *terra nullius* and particularly the impact of such a declaration in terms of international law are explored in Joshua Castellino (n 13).

[34] For a general reading of the doctrine of discovery in international law, see Robert Jennings and Arthur Watts (eds), *Oppenheim's International Law: Volume 1 Peace* (9th edn. London: Longman, 1992) at 687.

[35] This discussion of indigenous peoples as subjects and objects has been well articulated by Barsh (n 32). Essentially the differentiation means that were they considered 'subjects of international law' then their rights would include those against their dispossession. If on the other hand they could be considered 'objects of international law' then they would be treated much the same as any other inanimate substance, without the necessary attribution of rights.

existence on the territory of indigenous peoples.[36] This historical treatment of the existing population is a separate issue, although it underpins the development of policies that essentially treated the native populations as inferior, resulting in the absorption of indigenous Australians into mainstream population,[37] and the assimilation of all 'non-full blood' Australians.[38]

Early documents concerning first European contact with the populations had not envisaged any of the subsequent violations. Instructions given to Governor Philip of New South Wales towards the end of the eighteenth century stated that the colonizers were required to 'treat the natives with kindness':[39]

You are to endeavour by every possible means to open an intercourse with the natives and to conciliate their affections, enjoining all our subjects to live in amity and kindness with them. And if any of our subjects shall wantonly destroy them, or give them any unnecessary interruption in the exercise of their several occupations, it is our will and pleasure that you do cause such offenders to be brought to punishment according to the degree of offence.[40]

The actual treatment could not have been more different, and two linked policies that arose in this context can be seen as precursors to modern discrimination and stigmatization of indigenous populations in the settled Australian state. The first was the decision not to recognize the existing populations as being the legitimate owners and occupiers of the land, and the second was the decision not to treat Australia as an occupation, but as a title acquired through discovery.[41] Both of these factors combined at the outset to ensure that there was no treaty to be signed between the incoming colonizers and the native populations, unlike in New Zealand, Canada, and the United States.[42]

Dorsett suggests three reasons for this failure to agree a treaty: the lack of a serious military threat and no other European competition; a belief that the aboriginal population was not large and that there was no sustained cultivation of lands; and a perceived difficulty in the negotiation process, for example in identification and understanding of tribal hierarchy.[43] In other colonial contexts treaties were

---

[36] *Mabo v Queensland (No 2)* (1992) 175 CLR.

[37] See Alexander Reilly, 'A Constitutional Framework for Indigenous Governance' (2006) *28 Sydney L Rev* 403–35 at 416, fn 59.

[38] As discussed in *Royal Commission into Aboriginal Deaths in Custody: National Report* (1991). See HREOC Report, *Bringing Them Home* (1997).

[39] Shaunnagh Dorsett, 'Civilisation and Cultivation: Colonial Policy and Indigenous Peoples in Canada and Australia' (1995) 4 (2) *GLR* 214–38 at 223. For more on the background of the appointment of Philip as Governor, see Barnard (n 19) 31–4.

[40] Instructions to Governor Philip, *HRNSW* (23 April 1787) Vol 1 (2) 52.

[41] For more on the discussions leading to these decisions, see Clarke (n 19) 41–60.

[42] For more on a comparison between these states in terms of issues concerning indigenous peoples and especially their treatment in law, see e.g. Theresa Simpson, 'Claims of Indigenous Peoples to Cultural Property in Canada, Australia, and New Zealand' (1994–1995) 18 *HICLR* 195–221.

[43] Dorsett (n 39) 214–38.

often signed with native populations more as a guarantor of exclusivity in the colonial process than as any genuine recognition of the international personality of the incumbent sovereign.[44] In the absence of European competition, the sole interested colonial power in Australia saw no serious military threat from the scattered indigenous populations. The second reason is based on a misconception of the size of population at the time of colonization of Australia, with the prevailing suggestion being that it consisted of isolated communities rather than true 'peoples' with sovereignty.[45] This was later found to be untrue—the populations were far more numerous than previously imagined.[46] Nonetheless it is clear that the failure not to cultivate territory was read, in racialized terms, as indicating an underdeveloped population that was, for some, sub-human.[47] While there has been a material change in this relationship in the latter half of the last century, much of the progress was undermined more recently under John Howard's government.[48]

The impact of treating Australia as *terra nullius* was significant in terms of the applicable legal regime. Unlike in other British colonial projects, there was no progressive recognition of the rights of inhabitants on newly acquired territories.[49] The assertion of the legitimacy of the Crown on *terra nullius* proclaimed British sovereignty over a perceived legal and political vacuum.[50] The

---

[44] For reading on colonial experiences such as that in Africa, see C.H. Alexandrowicz, *The European-African Confrontation* (Leiden: A.W. Sijthoff, 1973).

[45] For an authoritative discussion of the term peoples and the entitlement of self-determination, see Antonio Cassese, *Self-Determination of Peoples, A Legal Reappraisal* (Cambridge: Cambridge University Press, 1995).

[46] See Clark (n 19) 4.

[47] This link between cultivation of the land and 'civilization' is an interesting one and has been explored in the literature by Jared M. Diamond, *Guns, Germs and Steel: The Fates of Human Societies* (W.W. Norton & Co, 1997). In addition, the issue also rose in the *Western Sahara* case *vis-à-vis* the extent to which the indigenous Saharawis could have been considered a people in the region. For an analysis of the ICJ's advisory opinion, see Joshua Castellino, 'National Identity & the International Law of Self-determination: The Stratification of the Western Saharan "Self"' in Stephen Tierney (ed), *Accommodating National Identity: New Approaches in International and Domestic Law* (The Hague: Kluwer Law International, 2000) 257–84.

[48] While the government of John Howard has come in for significant criticism over its policy on indigenous peoples, criticism that is well-founded in the opinion of the authors, it may also be suggested that the Howard government was at times reflecting a populist position that existed within Australian society, one that had been chastened by the progressive *Mabo* decision (see above n 36) and which had, as a consequence, become more caustic toward any potential loss of privileges in a reconciliation process. For more on the Howard government and its impact on law in general in Australia, see Marion Maddox, *God under Howard: The Rise of the Religious Right in Australian Politics* (Crow's Nest, NSW: Allen and Unwin, 2005).

[49] As Strelein suggests, in other contexts: 'The implications of colonization became primarily a matter of domestic law [once international recognition had been gained fait accompli).... British courts had always purposed to recognize the rights of inhabitants of newly "acquired" territories where their traditions and values were similar to those of the British'. [parenthesis added]. See Lisa Strelein, 'From *Mabo* to *Yorta Yorta*: Native Title Law in Australia' (2005) 19 *WUJLP* 225–72 at 228.

[50] Strelein identifies the different types of regimes that flowed from the assertion of the 'test' of civilization that would ultimately identify the applicable regime of property law, drawing on the

'usual' colonial practice was to allow local law to continue unless found contrary to British concepts of morality or justice, or until specifically altered by the Crown.[51] In Australia, the determination of a legal vacuum left the Crown:

... [free to] discover an uninhabited country and settle it with English subjects, and by which the laws of England as appropriate to the circumstances would be immediately transplanted.[52]

The result was not only the subjugation of a people and the accompanying dismissal of their laws and customs.[53] As Reynolds shows, the benefits of assuming the absence of people on the continent outweighed other factors and contributed to this 'fiction' becoming the founding myth of the Crown's claim to Australia.[54]

The manner in which Australian courts interpreted the application of law to the aboriginal personality reflected the maintenance of this fiction over 200 years.[55] Aboriginal nations were not deemed 'domestic dependent nations' and, as a consequence, were not entitled to undisturbed possession of their territories save for the Crown's right to pre-emption.[56] For example, in *MacDonald v Levy* [1833],[57] Justice Burton denied that indigenous peoples had rules, rather describing them as 'wandering tribes... living without certain habitation and without laws'.[58] Against this were isolated court judgments where evidence was admitted that the indigenous peoples had their own complete system of punishment and the introduction of common law to the colony did not by itself extinguish indigenous laws and jurisdiction.[59]

---

work of William Blackstone,*Commentaries on the Laws of England* Vol 1 (London: Legal Classics Library, 1983) 104. See Strelein (n 49) 229.

[51] The basis for this is identified by Strelein as coming from the decision in *Campbell*, 98 England Reports at 895–6, and is also reflected in *Blankard v Galdy* (1693) 90 Eng Rep 1089 and *Calvin's Case* (1608) 77 Eng Rep 377. See Strelein (n 49) 229.

[52] ibid.

[53] As Strelein puts it: The interests of the emerging colonial state were best served by the complete denial of the rights of the Indigenous inhabitants of the 'acquired territory'. The fiction of *terra nullius* fulfilled the imperial imperative for control over resources, allowing the state to govern the use of land and resources to serve its own purpose. Strelein (n 49) 235–6.

[54] Henry Reynolds, *Aboriginal Society: Reflections on Race, State and Nation* (Crow's Nest, NSW: Allen and Unwin, 1996). This view of sparse population was allowed to stand despite the contradictory evidence presented (of the area around Sydney Harbour being more populated that believed in Europe) almost immediately after the arrival of the First Fleet. This has been captured in Watkin Tench, *Sydney's First Four Years* (Botany Bay, NSW: Angus and Robertson, 1961) 51–2.

[55] This is discussed in some detail throughout the chapter but more concertedly in section 2.4.1 under remedies.

[56] See Justice Willis in *R v Bonjon* (New South Wales Supreme Court).

[57] (NSW Supreme Court) in *Sydney Herald* (11 March 1833).

[58] ibid.

[59] One such exception is articulated by Justice Willis who questions how a 'native' could be tried in 'his native land by a new race to him, and by laws of which he knows nothing'. See as quoted by Strelein (n 49) 237, fn 65.

Australian jurisprudence appears tacitly to subscribe to a 'scale of organization' test to determine the lack of legal personality of the indigenous incumbents in terms of law.[60] This is captured by Reynolds:

[T]he distinctive and unenviable contribution of Australian jurisprudence to the history of relations between Europeans and the Indigenous peoples of the non-European world...was not to provide justification for conquest of cession of land or assumption of sovereignty...but to deny the right, even the fact, of possession to people who had lived on their land for 40,000 years.[61]

Strelein highlights the impact of politics on law at the time, a *realpolitik* that continues to this date:

Regardless of any natural rights to retain even private rights or possessions, prescriptions for peaceful settlements would not be observed in practice as the battles for land were already being fought and lost at the hands of colonists. The settlers and squatters were aware of the claims of indigenous peoples to particular tracts of lands, but they had the intellectual affirmation of superiority and the sanction of the state. In effect, the absence of an Indigenous legal system became an irrebuttable presumption.[62]

In *Cooper v Stuart* [1889], the Privy Council backed the view that New South Wales, as a colony, had been practically unoccupied, and rejected any notion of the assertion of *sui generis* indigenous rights.[63] It was not until 1971, in *Milirrpum v Nabalco*, that indigenous peoples were able to present evidence of their continuing relations over traditional lands.[64] The admission in that case by Justice Blackburn of the existence of a 'subtle and elaborate system' of aboriginal laws and customs was a return to the early articulation of Willis J in the *Bonjon* case that had been lost in the annals of regressive judgments.[65] Irrespective of this, the *lex specialis* governing property was deemed not to fit within the rubric of the 'subtle and elaborate system' and the finding in *Cooper* was upheld.[66] The courts' general attitude to indigenous peoples can probably be captured in the statement of Justice Chamberlain in *R v Skinny Jack* [1964], where he suggested that assimilation was the goal of law and adjudication.[67]

The progression to the *Mabo* decision was logical and built-up over a period of time from the adverse *Milirrpum* decision in the 1970s.[68] In *Coe v Commonwealth*

---

[60] Strelein (n 49) 238.

[61] Henry Reynolds, *The Laws of the Land* (2n edn. Sydney: Penguin Australia, 1992) 3–4.

[62] Strelein (n 49) 238.   [63] *Cooper v Stuart* (1889) 14 App Cas 286.

[64] *Milirrpum v Nabalco* (1971) 17 FLR 141.

[65] ibid 237, see above in fn 59.

[66] ibid 272–3, where the notion between aboriginal 'property' and common law perceptions of property are found to be at significant odds. This leads Strelein to comment that this case remains the 'best illustration of the fracture between law and fact that has characterized much of Australia's legal history'. See Strelein (n 49) 241.

[67] In that case Justice Chamberlain is attributed as saying: '[T]heir first lesson should be to obey our laws', *R v Skinny Jack* (unreported decision, 13 July 1964) cited by Strelein (n 49) 241.

[68] For a commentary on this decision, see Kent McNeil, 'A Question of Title: Has the Common Law Been Misapplied to Dispossess the Aboriginals?' (1990) 16 *Monash U L Rev* 91.

[1979], the door towards sovereignty was opened a fraction despite the rejection of the central plea of the plaintiffs,[69] and questions were posited about the efficacy of the *Cooper* decision.[70] The reservations were more clearly expressed in *Gerhardy v Brown* where the discussion about the rights of 'original inhabitants', including their claim to retain 'occupancy of traditional lands', was addressed.[71] The *Mabo* judgment when it came was a 'substantial pebble' with a significant 'ripple effect',[72] although its result has proven to be underwhelming.[73] The immediate optimistic viewpoint, that the decision laid a 'strong foundation for the recovery of land' and a strengthening of the bargaining powers of indigenous Australians,[74] was soon undermined. Subsequent events also show that the belief that the decision would lead to a growth of settlements over control of resources, as well as general socio-economic and environmental issues, was misguided.[75]

Irrespective of the colonial policy in Australia, subsequent Australian governments were clear about their 'civilizing mission' with regard to the indigenous peoples.[76] In 1814 Governor Macquarie[77] issued two specific proposals:

a. the creation of a Native Institution, Parrammatta, for 'educating, Christianising and giving vocational training to Aboriginal children';[78] and
b. the granting of land to aboriginal peoples in order to enable them to learn to farm.[79]

As with many facets of attempts to interfere with native culture, it appeared to have 'good Christian values' at the heart of it, with 'Christian' in this sense a reference to a belief in humane values and the desire to assist those in need. The overtly Christian and therefore alien belief that underlay the projects often resulted in a failure to alleviate the situations of the populations, resulting in an imposition of alien values detrimental to local culture. In the context of Macquarie's proposal, it is interesting to see the recognition as early as 1814 of the need to grant indigenous autonomy, in whatever sense envisaged. However, the emphasis on farming and cultivation immediately restricted the potential good that would come from the scheme, drawing on an unfounded prejudice

The decision also merited criticism in *Calder v Attorney-General of British Columbia* [1973] 34 DLR 3d 145 at 218.

[69] *Coe v Commonwealth (No 1)* (n 30) at 408.   [70] ibid 411–12.
[71] *Gerhardy v Brown* (1985) 159 CLR 70.
[72] Nettheim (n 25) 223.   [73] ibid 224.   [74] ibid.
[75] ibid 236.   [76] Dorsett (n 39) 224–6.
[77] For more on Governor Macquarie, see Gordon Greenwood, *Australia; a Social and Political History* (London: Angus and Robertson, 1955) esp 1–45. Also see Clark (n 19) 261–380.
[78] As described in R. Broome, *Aboriginal Australians* (2nd edn. Sydney: Allen and Unwin, 1994) 31.
[79] The details of this are reflected upon by Dorsett (n 39) 214–38, fn 35 in a letter sent by Governor Macquarie to Earl Bathurst, marked No 15 of 1814, per ship Seringapatnam, *Historical Records of Australia* vol VII, July 1813–December 1815, Library Committee of Commonwealth Parliament 1916, 368 (copied fn 35). Also see Greenwood (n 77) 10.

on the ability to cultivate territory and the perceived ability of a society to develop.[80]

The recognized value of indigenous peoples underpinned projects such as that proposed by Governor Macquarie in 1814.[81] Following the limited success of this scheme, Archdeacon Scott suggested the establishment of a more comprehensive institution that united 'farming occupations with instruction'.[82] Like the earlier proposals, this had the approval of the Colonial Office (precursor to the Foreign and Commonwealth Office) in London, who continued to express concern for the plight of the 'natives' and remained eager for programmes that would contribute to the civilizing mission.[83] The persistence with trying to create an agrarian culture was ingrained in Australian policy through the active encouragement of missionaries and the appointment of superintendents with mandates to monitor progress.[84]

Changes in representatives elected to the British Parliament, especially the presence of a strong anti-slavery movement, led to policy development in ostensibly more progressive directions.[85] A House of Commons select committee appointed under the chairmanship of T.F. Buxton, a leading humanitarian of the time,[86] considered what measures ought to be adopted towards territories with British settlements.[87] It presented two reports that had a significant impact on colonial policy in general.[88] In Australia, the reports called for an increase in expenditure for protectors of Aborigines, and also for the reservation of lands to 'enable them to continue without molestation' until 'agriculture ceased to be distasteful to them'.[89] The decision to decentralize for reasons of political expediency, resulting in the transfer of 'aboriginal policy' from the centre to the constituent

---

[80] ibid.

[81] Of course, in a specifically Australian context the impact of the work of Charles Darwin cannot be underestimated. As seen in the opening chapter to this book, this clearly contributed to the notion that as a 'weaker' race, Aboriginals would inevitably die out...of special importance is the growing hold of theories such as polygenism (that human races were biologically separate) as articulated by Darwin. It could be argued that it was the provision of this 'scientific' basis that justified the subsequent decisions of Australian governments *vis-à-vis* its populations. See A. Markus, *Australian Race Relations* (St Leonard's, NSW: Allen and Unwin, 1994) 13. Also see Jeffrey R. Dafler, 'Social Darwinism and the Language of Racial Oppression: Australia's Stolen Generations' (2005) 62 *A Rev of General Semantics*.

[82] Quoted as Governor Darling to Right Hon W. Huskisson, 27 March 1828, Despatch No 50, per ship Eliza, Enclosure 1; Archdeacon Scott to Governor Darling, 1 August 1827, *Historical Records of Australia* at 59.

[83] Clark (n 19) 44–6.   [84] Dorsett (n 39) 225.

[85] See particularly the notes of historian Henry Reynolds entitled 'The Law of the Land' available at <http://www.austlii.edu.au/au/journals/AboriginalLB/1987/57.html> [accessed 2 April 2008].

[86] See Attwood and Markus (n 19) 227.

[87] ibid.

[88] See Douglas Pike, *Paradise of Dissent: South Australia, 1829–1857* (Melbourne: Melbourne University Press, 1957) 29–51.

[89] Dorsett (n 39) 225, also see her citation fn 40.

states in the 1840s and 1850s, was to expedite the decline of Australia's indigenous peoples.[90]

The *Stolen Generations Scheme* is a manifestation of the kinds of policies of the period. It operated in different guises from the latter part of the nineteenth century until the late 1960s, and under its terms aboriginal children were taken away from their families and given to 'good Christian families' to rear, by the national and state governments, missions, and even the *Aborigines' Protection Board*.[91] The stated reason underlying this policy was to rescue the children from a backward aboriginal life and offer them a chance to participate fully in Australian society. In terms of public international law such behaviour clearly falls within the definition of genocide as articulated by Article 2(e) of the Genocide Convention.[92] In this context Prime Minister Rudd's apology to the Aboriginal Nations of Australia is particularly welcome,[93] as is the positive reaction in the press.[94]

While a *rapprochement* with indigenous Australians remains distant it appears that the current government is motivated to pursue such a path. In order to move fully towards a society that respects indigenous and minority rights, the discussion needs to be widened to include the many communities that have migrated to Australia. While many sources claim that the immigration process in Australia has thrived,[95] it is clear that some of the wider problems that arise in the Australian context stem from the original dispossession of indigenous territory.[96]

2.2 Identification of Minorities and Indigenous Peoples

Minority rights literature is rich with analyses of the contours of the definition of who constitutes a minority within a state.[97] The discussion here does not seek to

---

[90] ibid 226.

[91] For a detailed report on these events, see *Bringing Them Hope: The Report* available at <http://www.austlii.edu.au/au/other/IndigLRes/stolen/> [accessed on 25 March 2009].

[92] art 2 of the Genocide Convention reads: 'In the present Convention, genocide means any of the following acts committed with intent to destroy, in whole or in part, a national, ethnical, racial or religious group, as such: (a) Killing members of the group; (b) Causing serious bodily or mental harm to members of the group; (c) Deliberately inflicting on the group conditions of life calculated to bring about its physical destruction in whole or in part; (d) Imposing measures intended to prevent births within the group; (e) Forcibly transferring children of the group to another group'.

[93] The full text of the speech delivered in Parliament on 13 February 2008 has been reproduced electronically and is available at the Herald Sun Newspaper website at <http://www.news.com.au/heraldsun/story/0,21985,23206474-661,00.html> [accessed 3 July 2008].

[94] See e.g. 'Thunderous applause in Sydney for Rudd's speech', *Australian Associated Press*, *Sydney Morning Herald* (13 February 2008).

[95] For a discussion of this in an Australian context, see Martin Krygier, *Between Fear and Hope: Hybrid Thoughts on Public Values* (Sydney: ABC Books, 1997).

[96] See Michael Dodson and Lisa Strelein, 'Australia's Nation-Building: Renegotiating the Relationship between Indigenous Peoples and the State' (2001) 24 *UNSWLJ*-40.

[97] The discussion of 'who' constitutes a minority is a rather turgid one, although there is some consensus for the less than successful definition proposed by UN Special Rapporteur Francesco

make any new contribution to the literature in this regard,[98] rather proceeding on the following basis:

(a) it accepts that the two key definitions in human rights literature provided by Capotorti[99] and Cobo,[100] with all their inherent flaws, are indicative of the substantive content of the communities that are covered under the title 'minorities' and 'indigenous peoples' respectively;

(b) for the purpose of Australia, the pre-eminent group that is vulnerable in terms of rights violations are the communities that fall under the banner of 'indigenous peoples' under which the Aboriginals and Torres Strait Islanders are subsumed;[101]

(c) while there are discussions about whether immigrants can justifiably claim minority status, this is often factored around the length of time of their stay within a territory and the recognition of the rights they have acquired. From a historical reading, all non-native populations would fall under the title of 'immigrants'. Evidently some immigrants in Australia have acquired fewer rights than others, and remain in a non-dominant position.[102] Thus many Pacific Islanders fall within the definition, and more recent Asian migrants, whether or not they have acquired citizenship,[103] ought to be covered on the grounds that if their basic rights are not met, the state is in violation of fundamental human rights;

(d) more controversially, refugees and asylum seekers have been included for several reasons but mainly on grounds of their vulnerability in recent years due to the harshness of Australian governmental policy.

Capotorti, see 'Study on the Rights of Persons Belonging to Ethnic, Religious and Linguistic Minorities' UN doc E/CN.4/Sub.2/384/Rev.1 (1977).

[98] While it could be argued that much of the literature is based on a European reading of what constitutes a 'minority', including the insertion of the word 'national', the authors believe an overt discussion in this context is not conducive towards an assessment of the perpetration of violations against vulnerable groups. Thus we posit acceptance of accepted definitions, though mindful of various inconsistencies.

[99] See Capotorti, (1977) (n 97).

[100] See José Martinez Cobo, Special Rapporteur, 'Study of the Problem of Discrimination Against Indigenous Populations', UN doc E/CN.4/Sub.2/1986/7/Add.4 (1986).

[101] The distinctions between the two different peoples needs to be acknowledged—as does the diversity among the indigenous nations of Australia. It could be argued that the diversity of the different nations was a contributing factor in the colonial confusion on how to deal with them. For a greater understanding of these issues especially the hypothesis of 'country' and its value to indigenous peoples' thinking in Australia, see Steve Kinnane 'Indigenous Sustainability: Rights, Obligations, and a Collective Commitment to Country' in J. Castellino and N. Walsh (eds), *International Law and Indigenous Peoples* (Leiden/Boston: Martinus Nijhoff, 2005) 159–94.

[102] i.e. the issue of 'non-dominance'. In this context a distinction needs to be made between 'vulnerable groups' and minorities and indigenous peoples. See Domínguez Redondo (n 17).

[103] For more on international human rights standards on this issue, see CERD *General Recommendation XI on Non-Citizens*, 42nd Session, 1993 and CERD *General Recommendation 30 Discrimination against Non-Citizens*, 64th session, 2004.

Thus an underlying caveat to this chapter is that while focused on a discussion of Aboriginals and Torres Strait Islanders, some comment will also be offered where minority provisions concerning Australia's diverse immigrant communities are affected.

2.2.1 Aboriginals

Aboriginals and Torres Strait Islanders are distinguished in this section to show the specific differences that exist between these two peoples, and the extent to which the portrayal of Australian indigenous populations as one was an inaccurate generalization. Nonetheless, their similarities need also to be acknowledged, particularly in terms of their joint advocacy efforts to achieve systemic change within Australia.

Anthropologists and historians studying Australian pre-history suggest that: 'Australia's aboriginal peoples are the oldest continuous culture in the world, having inhabited the continent of Australia for at least 30,000 years by conservative estimates'.[104] The aboriginal population that greeted the first colonizers from Europe was recorded as being small. In an entry in Captain James Cook's diary in 1770, he writes:

Neither are they very numerous, they live in small parties along by the Sea Coast, the banks of Lakes, Rivers creeks &c. They seem to have no fix'd habitation but move about from place to place like wild beasts, in search of food, and I believe depend wholly upon the success of the present day for their subsistence.[105]

It was in this connection that programmes described in the previous section were articulated to seek to 'civilize' the population. Many argue that Aboriginals had a sense of private property rights before the arrival of the Europeans.[106] Irrespective of the existence of private property rights, there is a deep spiritual element to how land is perceived among the different aboriginal nations that centres on the qualities that the land possesses, which are deemed sacred in most aboriginal cultures.[107]

2.2.2 Torres Strait Islanders

The application of *terra nullius* to Torres Strait Islanders was even more problematic since, unlike Aboriginals from the main Australian island, Torres Strait

[104] See John Mulvaney and Johann Kamminga, *Prehistory of Australia* 1–2 (Smithsonian, 1999).

[105] Cook's Journal, 23 August 1770, in J.C. Beaglehole (ed), *The Journals of Captain James Cook* (Cambridge: Cambridge University Press, 1974) 396.

[106] This has been studied in the context of indigenous peoples in North America, notably in the work of Kenneth H. Bobroff, 'Retelling Allotment; Indian Property Rights and the Myth of Common Ownership' (2001) 54 *VLR* (2001) 1571. An analogous argument in connection with Australia's indigenous peoples is presented by Henry Reynolds, *Aboriginal Sovereignty* (Sydney: Allen and Unwin, 1996).

[107] As discussed by Poirier and Ostergren (n 10) 335–8.

Islanders were never nomadic, having had a settled agricultural society long before European colonization of the continent.[108] There were significant links between the Torres Strait Islanders and the peoples across the Torres Strait in Papua New Guinea. Diamond engages in a detailed discussion about the potential links between the two communities while noting the extent to which they appeared to maintain their distinct traits. They are described as being Austronesian sea-farers that have shown evidence of sustained cultivation. The distinction in Australian policy between Aboriginals and Torres Strait Islanders is relatively new, with all indigenous Australians classed as a single group in the past. Despite the differences the two distinct groups are treated as one in the context of this chapter, since they face similar forms of discrimination and exclusion. A final point to bear in mind is that the central figure in the famous *Mabo* decision, discussed in further detail in the section on land rights, was Eddie Mabo, a Torres Strait Islander.

2.3 Rights of Minorities

2.3.1 Competing Bases for Legitimacy

The constitution normally provides the key elements to understanding the legal values that underpin a society.[109] In the Australian context it is equally important to identify a competing base of legitimacy through 'customary' legal systems, which, along with the constitutional provisions, are examined in the first part of this section. The second part of this section looks at the various legal regimes that have been created to address specific issues pertaining to minority and indigenous peoples' rights.

2.3.1.1 *The Australian Constitution and the 'Race Power'*

The *Commonwealth of Australia Constitution Act 1900* was passed as an Act of the Parliament of the United Kingdom at Westminster on 9 July 1900. It calls on the Queen's authority in its preamble,[110] and excludes the aboriginal populations from its outset:

... Whereas the people of New South Wales, Victoria, South Australia, Queensland, and Tasmania, humbly relying on the blessing of Almighty God, have agreed to unite in one indissoluble Federal Commonwealth under the Crown of the United Kingdom of Great Britain and Ireland...

---

[108] See Clive Turnbull, *A Concise History of Australia* (London: Thames and Hudson, 1965).

[109] Thus in the book on Asia, a constitutional analysis was the starting point for any examination of the legal regime within a state. See Joshua Castellino and Elvira Domínguez Redondo, *Minority Rights in Asia: A Comparative Legal Analysis* (Oxford: Oxford University Press, 2006).

[110] See Arthur B. Keith, *The Dominions as Sovereign States: Their Constitutions and Governments* (London: Macmillan & Co, 1938) 100–48.

The 'people' in this context consisted of the subjects of law, namely those of European descent who were in Australia, with the indigenous populations excluded from constitution-making.[111] In fact, as originally drafted, there were only exclusionary references to Aboriginals in the Constitution,[112] which were finally expunged by referendum in 1967.[113] The 1900 Act was celebrated as the 'coming of age' of the state of Australia, and, through its passage, the earlier *Federal Council of Australasia Act 1885* was repealed.[114]

As it stands, the Constitution does not contain a declaratory preamble, with the text that serves as a preamble merely explanatory. A proposed amendment, put to referendum in 1999, suggested the insertion of the following preamble:

With hope in God, the Commonwealth of Australia is constituted as a democracy with a federal system of government to serve the common good.

We the Australian people commit ourselves to this Constitution:

proud that our national unity has been forged by Australians from many ancestries;

never forgetting the sacrifices of all who defended our country and our liberty in time of war;

upholding freedom, tolerance, individual dignity and the rule of law;

honouring Aborigines and Torres Strait Islanders, the nation's first people, for their deep kinship with their lands and for their ancient and continuing cultures which enrich the life of our country;

recognising the nation-building contribution of generations of immigrants;

mindful of our responsibility to protect our unique natural environment;

supportive of achievement as well as equality of opportunity for all;

and valuing independence as dearly as the national spirit which binds us together in both adversity and success.

This insertion did not get the attention it deserved in the context of other, politically more expedient, questions asked of the population.[115] Less than 40 per cent of Australians agreed with the insertion.[116] Had the preamble been inserted, it would have acknowledged the rich ancestral heritage of Australia

[111] This is a good example of what Barsh would call the difference between subjects and objects of law. See (n 31).

[112] Specifically s 127 of the Constitution (since repealed) which excluded aboriginal natives (sic!) from the census figures. See Garth Nettheim, 'Indigenous Australian Constitutions' (2001) 24 (3) *UNSWLJ* (2001) 840–9 at 843.

[113] See generally, Jackie Huggins, 'The 1967 Referendum: Thirty Years On' (1997) 1997/1 *Australian Aboriginal Studies* 3–4; Bain Attwood and Andrew Markus *The 1967 Referendum: Race, Power and the Australian Constitution* (Canberra: Aboriginal Studies Press, 2007).

[114] Commonwealth of Australia Constitution Act 1900, preamble, para 7.

[115] The main question put to referendum concerned the de-recognition of the British monarch as head of the state, towards a more republican model.

[116] Under Australian law, rules governing referendums are contained in the *Referendum (Machinery Provisions) Act 1984*. For an amendment to carry it needs to be approved by a double majority i.e., a national majority of electors countrywide; and a majority of electors in the majority (four out of six) states. Details of the last referendum are available from the official website of the Australian Election Commission at <http://www.aec.gov.au/Elections/referendums/Referendums_Overview.htm> [accessed 17 March 2008].

and provided explicit recognition of Aborigines and Torres Strait Islanders as the first people of Australia. The assertion of the kinship of indigenous peoples with their land would also have been an important acknowledgment in the battle over land rights.[117]

The conspicuous absence of any mention of indigenous heritage in the Constitution is put into perspective by the continuing controversy over the powers of Parliament contained in section 51 (xxvi). The current Constitution still has provision for what has been labelled 'race powers' under section 51 (xxvi). This section is the primary article listing the powers of parliament, and begins:

The Parliament shall, subject to this Constitution, have power to make laws for the peace, order, and good government of the Commonwealth with respect to:

...

(xxvi.) The people of any race, for whom it is deemed necessary to make special laws...[118]

These powers, sitting amidst a host of powers for animate and inanimate things, have been extremely controversial, not least since they have been invoked to facilitate harmful policies to indigenous nations including the Stolen Generations Scheme.[119] There have been several attempts to modify these powers. However section 51 (xxvi) is a major improvement on the original wording of the Constitution. The referendum of 27 May 1967 sought a vote on the *Constitutional Alteration (Aboriginals) 1967* which remains one of only eight major successful amendments to the Constitution.[120] The referendum, passed with an overwhelming majority in all six states, removed two sections from the original text of the Constitution: the exclusion of Aboriginals from the 'race powers' section; and the

[117] Nettheim (n 112) 843.

[118] Some of the other powers listed under the preceding and subsequent sub-sections are: (i) trade and commerce; (ii) taxation; (iii) bounties on production or export of goods; (iv) public borrowing; (v) postal, telegraphic, etc; (vi) naval and military defence; (vii) lighthouses etc; (viii) astronomical and meteorological observations; (ix) quarantine (x) fisheries; (xi) census and statistics; (xii) currency, coinage, and legal tender; (xiii) banking; (xiv) Insurance; (xv) weights and measures; (xvi) bills of exchange and promissory notes; (xvii) bankruptcy and insolvency; (xviii) copyrights, patents of inventions and designs, and trade marks; (xix) naturalisation and aliens; (xx) foreign corporations; (xxi) marriage; (xxii) divorce and matrimonial causes; (xxiii) invalid and old-age pensions; (xxiiiA) provision of social payments; (xxiv) civil and criminal processes; (xxv) laws, the public Acts and records, and the judicial proceedings of the states; (xxvii) immigration and emigration; (xxviii) the influx of criminals; (xxix) external affairs; (xxx) external relations with the Pacific states; (xxxi) acquisition of property; (xxxii) railways; (xxxiii) acquisition of railways; (xxxiv) railway construction; and (xxxv) conciliation and arbitration (xxxvi).

[119] The paternalism of this provision is akin to that expressed in *ILO Convention No 107* (1957). It is instructive to note that Australia is not a party to either the *ILO Convention No 107* nor its more progressive and supervening Convention No 169 *Concerning Indigenous and Tribal Peoples in Independent Countries* (1989). However, as we shall see below, its interpretation does not necessarily have to be in keeping with any parental responsibility towards the good of the offspring.

[120] Of the forty-four attempts to modify the Constitution only eight have been successful. See generally H.K. Colebatch, *Beyond the Policy Cycle: The Policy Process in Australia* (Sydney: Allen and Unwin, 2006).

exclusion of aboriginal populations from the census numbers of Australian states. The original text of the Constitution on the two issues, prior to amendment, read as follows:

On the race powers issue:

... the people of any race, *other than the Aboriginal race in any State,* for whom it is deemed necessary to make special laws.[121]

And on the issue of non-counting of Aboriginals and Torres Strait Islanders, section 127 of the Constitution previously read:

In reckoning the numbers of the people of the Commonwealth, or of a State or other part of the Commonwealth, Aboriginal natives shall not be counted.[122]

The meaning and substantive content of the provision was adjudicated upon in the context of *Kartinyeri v Commonwealth*,[123] often referred to as the *Hindmarsh Island Bridge Case*. The court was asked to address the question of whether this specific power of enactment implied a positive obligation for the state to enact legislation beneficial to indigenous peoples. Interestingly, after thorough analysis, the ruling found against this proposition, implying that the power was granted to legislate, not to legislate necessarily for the benefit of the indigenous population.

Irrespective of the ruling in *Hindmarsh*, the 1967 referendum was widely believed as providing the federal authorities the opportunity to claw-back aboriginal policy from regional state jurisdictions. Despite this optimism the federal government took no measures to act on its new powers in the first five years, and it was only after the *Aboriginal Tent Embassy*[124] embarrassment for the federal government that some action was taken. Since then the race powers have been used on various occasions to pass statutes on a host of issues concerning aboriginal affairs (as detailed in sub-section 2.3.2 of this chapter.)

The relative success in 1967, and the failure to amend in 1999, are part of a series of proposals that have been tabled at various times to address the underlying tension around the legal status of indigenous nations of Australia, and the settlers who arrived on their land. Undoubtedly the issue of land rights has been at the forefront of these proposals, although this has taken on other guises in the context of political participation, criminal justice, and protection against hate speech. Nettheim also addresses three other notable propositions intended to

---

[121] Italicized section expunged by *Constitution Alternation (Aboriginals) Act 1967*.

[122] s 127 *Constitution of Australia 1900*, repealed by No 55, 1967, s 3.

[123] *Kartinyeri v Commonwealth* (1998) 195 CLR 337 (*Hindmarsh Islands Bridge Case*).

[124] This event, on 26 January 1972 (Australia Day), saw the erection of a tent embassy on the lawns of the federal Parliament, where indigenous peoples staged a protest over their disappointment in the lack of progress on issues such as land rights. The result is widely believed as locating aboriginal issues within the politics mainstream, leading to the election later that year of the Whitlam government that established a Royal Commission into Land Rights in the Northern Territory under the stewardship of Justice Woodward.

tackle these long-standing problems, including: *a*) a repeal of section 25 (which contemplates the possibility of states excluding certain voters, with only minor penalties);[125] *b*) complete revision of the 'race power'; and *c*) the adoption of legislation on the prohibition of racial discrimination.[126]

While each of these proposals has sought to bring indigenous rights closer to the centre of Australia's national policy questions, the most significant attempt to re-define relations between indigenous Australians and settled Australians has been the move towards the articulation, signature, and ratification of a treaty between the government and the indigenous populations. The possibility of a treaty is addressed in detail in the context of remedies in the final substantive section of this chapter. At this stage it is sufficient to identify the key moments in Australian history when this discussion has been most close to conclusion. Among these are:

(a) 1768: the Admiralty's instruction to Lieutenant James Cook (seeking consent of natives);

(b) 1979–1983: National Aboriginal Conference and Aboriginal Treaty Committee;[127]

(c) 1988: the *Barunga Statement of Northern Territory Aboriginal Peoples;*[128]

(d) 1995: ASTSIC support for a treaty as part of a 'social justice package';[129]

(e) 2000: Corroboree and the presentation of the Reconciliation Council's report entitled *Towards Reconciliation.*[130]

2.3.1.2 A Sui Generis *Claim to Rights?*

The attempt to sign a treaty between the Australian government and the indigenous people of the territory asks a more fundamental question on the relationship between existing national law and the subjecthood of indigenous peoples. Benedict Kingsbury suggests that there are at least five competing conceptual bases for addressing the claims of indigenous peoples.[131] These include the discourse of human rights and non-discrimination, claims as minorities, claims for self-determination, claims based on extinguished historical sovereignty, and finally *sui generis* claims.

---

[125] s 25 refers to the exclusion of persons of 'race' in line with the older and since repealed s 127 of the Constitution as discussed above note 122.

[126] Garth Nettheim, 'Indigenous Australians and the Constitution' (1999) in 74 *Reform* 29; also 'Reconciliation and the Constitution' (1999) 22 *UNSWLJ* 625.

[127] Stewart Harris, *Its Coming Yet…An Aboriginal Treaty Within Australia between Australians* (Canberra: Barossa Vintage Books, 1979).

[128] McRae, Nettheim, and Beacroft (n 24) 469.

[129] ibid, chs 3 and 10.

[130] Council for Aboriginal Reconciliation *Corroboree 2000: Towards Reconciliation* (2000). Also see Council for Aboriginal Reconciliation *Roadmap for Reconciliation* (2000).

[131] Kingsbury (n 16) 189–245. For a different more 'multicultural' approach, see W. Kymlicka, 'Theorizing Indigenous Rights' (1999) 49 *UTLJ* 281–92.

It is clear that indigenous claims overlap on several of the criteria. In Australia, the human rights and non-discrimination claim is contextualized by the *Racial Discrimination Act 1975*[132] that remains the bulwark of indigenous and minority rights protection within Australia. The 'minority claims' basis is underpinned in the provision of special measures, not least the 'race powers' of the federal government to legislate on aboriginal affairs. The self-determination claim forms the basis of the movement for the signing of a treaty. This leaves the historical sovereignty claim and the *sui generis* claim as indigenous peoples. The two are intrinsically linked, with the former posited as justificatory grounds for the latter. Any reconciliation with Australia's indigenous peoples needs to be mindful of these alternative legal settings and claims.

At the root of this discussion is the contested notion of 'sovereignty', and its imputed meaning and significance. One of the definitions of sovereignty advanced by the *National Aboriginal and Islander Health Organization* in 1983 is indicative:

Sovereignty can be demonstrated as Aboriginal people controlling all aspects of their lives and destiny… It is Aborigines doing things as Aboriginal people, controlling those aspects of our existence which are Aboriginal. These include our culture, our economy, our social lives and our indigenous political institutions.[133]

Yet in international terms sovereignty is defined very differently.[134] For Reilly, the notion of sovereignty is encapsulated in 'indigenous governance', a process of 'reclaiming the concept of sovereignty' even though its political force may be compromised by its formal legal limits.[135] This contrasts with the view of Alfred, who suggests that among the indigenous population of Australia, the quest for sovereignty should be abandoned as it is an 'exclusionary concept rooted in an adversarial and coercive Western notion of power'.[136] While the spirit of non-compliance with a system loaded against fundamental concepts underlying indigenous claims is understandable, opting out of the quest for sovereignty could have a significant impact. Though there are good reasons for the rejection of a *sui generis* claim,[137] the dropping of the claim to sovereignty and its associated rights and privileges may, on balance, adversely affect the future fate of indigenous communities in Australia.

Reilly's main argument towards a pragmatic reading of the notion of indigenous governance suggests the adoption of a lower, less problematic threshold

---

[132] No 52 (1975).

[133] National Aboriginal and Islander Health Organization *Sovereignty* (1983) quoted in Reilly (n 37) 410, fn 30.

[134] See e.g. J.S. Barkin & B. Cronin, 'The State & the Nation: Changing Norms and the Rules of Sovereignty in International Relations' 48(1) *Intl Organization* 107–30.

[135] See Reilly (n 37) 410.

[136] Taiaiake Alfred, *Peace, Power, Righteousness: An Indigenous Manifesto* (New York: Oxford University Press, 1999) 59.

[137] Kingsbury (n 16) 189–245.

for indigenous governance as a way through the impasse that subsumes discussions concerning 'indigenous sovereignty', 'native title', and the right to 'self-determination'.[138] It remains important that indigenous Australians maintain their position as 'persistent objectors'[139] to the construct of sovereignty and, as a corollary, to native title, in keeping with the spirit of providing subsequent generations with a legacy that may be exercised in better political climates.[140] Basing his argument on the work of John Griffiths,[141] Reilly argues that the concept of 'legal pluralism' offers a useful framework for the discussion of Indigenous governance, since '. . . it emphasises the system of laws and regulation that really governs the behaviour of groups, regardless of the formal legal position'. He holds this view despite an admission that federalism is a weak form of legal pluralism, since the federal system remains a single legal order with different components.[142]

Australian courts have, somewhat justifiably, sought to avoid making pronouncements on aboriginal sovereignty and *sui generis* status.[143] It has arisen in several cases although the *Mabo* judgments studiously avoided it, as did the previous judgment in *Wacando v Commonwealth and Queensland*,[144] where the issue turned on discrepancies in old colonial and imperial instruments believed resolved through the *Colonial Boundaries Act 1885* (UK).[145] It was raised more recently in *Coe v Commonwealth* in conjunction with land rights arguments,[146] and has also arisen on occasion in the context of criminal justice where aboriginal defendants have sought to challenge the jurisdiction of the settler court system.[147]

---

[138] Reilly (n 37) 411.

[139] See Jonathan Charney, 'The Persistent Objector Rule and the Development of Customary International Law' (1985) 56 *BYIL* 1. Also see Michael Byers, *Custom, Power and the Power of Rules: International Relations and Customary International Law* (Cambridge: Cambridge University Press, 1999).

[140] Of course, it is possible to argue that questions of legacy may be irrelevant if aboriginal communities gradually disappear as a result of a failure to compromise on questions such as these. This argument has merit, but on balance the partial implicit or explicit abandoning of such claims could be a big step towards the defeat of such claims in the future, which would act as a counterweight to the survival of indigenous communities and cultures. For more, see Noel Pearson, *Our Right to Take Responsibility* (Cairns, Queensland: Noel Pearson and Associates, 2000) 13–14.

[141] John Griffiths, 'What is Legal Pluralism?' (1986) 24 *JLP* 1, 38.

[142] ibid 412.

[143] An analogy that is worth highlighting is the extent to which the Human Rights Committee has sought to fence its way around the issue of self-determination. The notion is captured in the work of David Kretzmer when writing about the doctrine of political exception, see David Kretzmer, *The Occupation of Justice: The Supreme Court of Israel and the Occupied Territories* (Albany: State University of New York Press, 2002).

[144] (1981) 148 CLR 1.

[145] 1895 c 34 58_and_59_Vict. Available at <http://www.bailii.org/uk/legis/num_act/1895/1064725.html> [last accessed 1 August 2008].

[146] Nettheim (n 25) 223.

[147] *R v Murrelli* (1836) Legge 72; *R v Bonjon* (1844) British Parliamentary Papers at 146ff; *R v Wedge* [1976] 1 NSWLR 581.

While the question of a *sui generis* system is arguably beyond the realm of any state's legal apparatus,[148] the Australian Law Reform Commission did engage in a discussion about the validity of aboriginal customary law. This ninety-one page discussion paper, released in November 1980, was entitled *Aboriginal Customary Law—Recognition?*[149] It was the culmination of four years of research, travel, and debate by the Commission in response to a specific question raised by then Attorney-General Ellicott in 1977.[150] The Report opens with a statement about the special interest of the Commonwealth in the welfare of the Aborigines, and the need to ensure their racial identity, traditional lifestyle if they so wish, and equitable, humane, and fair treatment under the criminal justice system. The terms of reference directed the Commission to inquire only into the extent to which customary law should be recognized and applied by existing courts, whether aboriginal communities should be empowered to enforce their own laws, and 'any other related matter'.

In examining the Report, David Weisbrodt makes important criticisms that reveal the difficulty of unravelling this area of law. Among these was an over-emphasis on criminal law reform, while avoiding problems of 'personal law' such as marriage, adoption, and inheritance,[151] and a failure to address land rights issues. In addition, it treated customary law as static,[152] and failed to take into account other experiences of customary law that may have provided greater illumination.[153] Highlighting the dangers of viewing customary law as fixed, Weisbrodt warns:

> ...a major argument against codification of customary law in African and Pacific states, despite the superficial attraction of such a means of facilitating ascertainment, recognition and enforcement of customary law, is that codification would result in 'freezing' custom at a particular point in time, robbing customary law of its flexibility and dynamism

---

[148] The *Secession of Quebec Case* in Canada could be seen as one example where a court contemplated the impact of secession through the lens of domestic law. However, by and large this discussion tends to fall outside the jurisdiction of the court systems and the nature of the topic (i.e. a rival bid for legitimacy) makes governments reluctant to clarify its contours. For more on self-determination claims in national identity settings, see Stephen Tierney, *Accommodating National Identity* (Leiden/Boston: Martinus Nijhoff, 1999). For a different set of papers examining how the claim of self-determination for indigenous peoples has been articulated in different domestic and regional settings, see Castellino and Walsh (n 101).

[149] Australian Law Reform Commission, *Aboriginal Customary Law—Recognition?* Discussion Paper No 17 (Canberra 1980) 91.

[150] For more on the discussion related to this report, see Elizabeth A. Povinelli (ed), *The Cunning of Recognition* (Durham/London: Duke University Press, 2002).

[151] For more on personal laws or personal autonomy and how they can be effectively constructed, see Castellino and Domínguez Redondo (n 109) esp chs 2 and 4.

[152] This is attributed to the substantial work of Professor Sthrethlow, see Mark Harris "...Another Box of Tjuringas Under the Bed": The Appropriation of Aboriginal Cultural Property to Benefit Non-Indigenous Interests' in J. Castellino and N. Walsh (eds), *International Law and Indigenous Peoples* (n 101) 133–57.

[153] David Weisbrot, 'Comment on the ALRC Discussion Paper: Customary Law' (1981) 2 *ALB* 1(1), 3.

and will ultimately lead to a gap between custom as codified and custom as evidenced by practice.[154]

He argues that the non-existence of customary law in a pure form ought not to be construed as meaning customary law is not worthy of recognition.[155] Nonetheless, the lack of codification makes it difficult to ascertain its nuances, let alone judicially assess its application to a given set of complex circumstances. The ambivalence of lawyers and judges trained in a western legal tradition towards such forms of law and the belief in the supremacy of case law and statute and the rules governing procedure and evidence, make the task particularly difficult.[156] Weisbrodt's recommendation for achieving recognition for aboriginal custom and jurisprudence is to establish:

...a semi-autonomous Aboriginal community court system applying customary law with an emphasis on mediation and conciliation, with jurisdiction parallel (as a minimum) to Courts of Petty Sessions, and appellate review available only for allegations of denial of natural justice.[157]

The underlying basis for law in Australia *de facto* remains the Constitution. This is at odds with some articulations of indigenous rights which define 'constitution' as '... our systems of Aboriginal law and Aboriginal structures of law and governance, which have been in place since time immemorial'.[158] As articulated by one indigenous leader:

Aboriginal people have got our own constitution to run our way, not whitefella way. We were self government right from the start and we ran it pretty good. And now we're still going to run it.[159]

Support for this position is drawn from Yolgnu law which has been at the centre of some Australian nations' legal system:

White man's system may be different, but if we are going to live here the two laws need to come and meet in between. I'm talking about negotiating and having rights in law to negotiate. We need to put our law in the system of Australian law so that the two law systems balance and are dealt with equally.[160]

Processes begun in Northern Territory (with 28.5 per cent of the aboriginal population of Australia) were echoed in central Australia when indigenous peoples convened in August 1998 as the 'Constitutional Convention of the

---

[154] ibid. This issue is discussed again in ch 5 in the context of the potential codification of customary law in Papua New Guinea. See ch 5.1.2, esp above n 87.

[155] ibid.　　　[156] ibid.　　　[157] ibid.

[158] As contained in *Indigenous Constitutional Strategy: Northern Territory,* reflected in Nettheim (n 112) 846.

[159] ibid 847. A quote attributed by Nettheim to Max Stuart, Co-Chair, Northern Territory Indigenous Constitutional Convention, see fn 28.

[160] ibid, fn 29. Quote attributed to Galarrwuy Yunupingu, AM. Co-Chair, Northern Territory Indigenous Constitutional Convention, quoted by ATSIC.

Combined Aboriginal Nations of Central Australia', and passed the *Kalkaringi Statement*.[161]

2.3.2 Thematic Assessment of Rights

Having identified the general legal basis for the protection of indigenous peoples and minorities, the specific statutory provisions that exist on various themes will now be examined. It is not possible to be exhaustive on the various rights of indigenous peoples and minorities that exist within Australian statute books. This section examines land rights, rights of political participation, environmental and intellectual property rights, protection against hate speech, and involvement with the criminal justice system.

2.3.2.1 Land Rights

The most important issue that has been raised in the statutes, case-law, and in discussions within Australian civil society in the context of indigenous peoples is land rights. As stated earlier, it was not until 1992 that Australia acknowledged the legal fiction contained in the widely held belief in the continent's status as *terra nullius* at the time of the arrival of the British.[162] While the steps towards the important decision concerning the claim of Mabo have been well-documented[163] and discussed,[164] this brief sub-section examines significant aspects of the decision and its legal consequences.

Eddie Koiki Mabo and four other plaintiffs from the Murray Islands (Torres Strait) had claimed title to the territory under Meriam land law.[165] In substantiating their claim they convinced the court that traditional indigenous titles to land in the Murray Islands had survived colonization of the continent,[166] based on a finding that common law recognized and protected traditional indigenous

---

[161] The statement itself and its impact is examined in greater detail by Sarah Pritchard, 'Constitutional Developments in Northern Territory' (1998) 4(15) *Indigenous L Bulletin*.

[162] See n (11).

[163] Writing in 1994 Sarah Pritchard offers a useful analysis in understanding the key contemporary milestones in Australia *vis-à-vis* land rights. These are; a) *Mabo v State of Queensland (No 2)* (n 36); b) *Native Title Act 1993* (Cth); c) *Native Title Amendment Bill 1996* (Cth); d) *Wik Peoples v State of Queensland* (1996); e) *Native Title Amendment Bill 1997* (Cth); f) The Senate Debates, 1997; g) *Native Title Amendment Act 1998* (Cth). In such a short analysis here it will only be possible to focus on a key salient issues. See Sarah Pritchard, 'Native Title from the Perspective of International Standards' (1997) 18 *AYIL* 127–74, at 130–6. Also see Frith Way and Simeon Beckett, 'Governance Structures for Indigenous Australians On and Off Native Title Lands' Discussion Paper 4—Land-Holding and Governance Structures under Australian Land Rights Legislation (University of New South Wales and Murdoch University, unspecified date) available at Indigenous Law Resources: Reconciliation and Social Justice Library at <http://www.austlii.edu.au/au/other/IndigLRes/1998/3/4.html> [last accessed 27 January 2009].

[164] See above n (11).

[165] For a general exposé of the issues in the lead up to this case, see Nonie Sharp, *No Ordinary Judgment* (Canberra: Aboriginal Studies Press, 1996).

[166] *Mabo v Queensland (No 2)* (n 36) at 1.

title. In addition the earlier doctrine denying aboriginal rights was found to be based on a scale of organization that was discriminatory,[167] and on a false and unacceptable theory.[168] The judgment relied heavily on positive and normative international law and shared colonial jurisprudence,[169] culminating in the famous statement by Justice Brennan:

The fiction by which the rights and interests of Indigenous inhabitants in land were treated as non-existent was justified by a policy which has no place in the contemporary law of this country... Whatever the justification advanced in earlier days for refusing to recognize the rights and interests in land of the [I]ndigenous inhabitants of settled colonies, an unjust and discriminatory doctrine of that kind can no longer be accepted.[170]

There are precedents for this decision in Privy Council cases[171] and from jurisprudence in other British colonial settings.[172] It had repercussions in jurisdictions as far removed as Malaysia,[173] Nicaragua,[174] and Kenya.[175] In Australia, *Mabo* provided a vehicle for the recognition of native title based on existing rights and interests of Aboriginals singly or collectively.[176] A distinction was drawn between common law title and *sui generis* title, since the latter was an entitlement outside any potential accommodation within Australian property rights regimes.[177]

Speaking at the *UN Working Group on Indigenous Populations*, noted aboriginal leader Mick Dodson described the decision as no more that an act of 'sterile symbolism' which would neither return the ancestral heritage of indigenous Australians nor pay adequate compensation for the loss.[178] Yet at the time it was heralded as providing the much-needed impetus to bring Australia into line with other common law jurisdictions in recognizing the land rights of its indigenous populations.

In response to the decision the government passed the *Native Title Act 1993* (since amended), the purpose of which was to provide an effective starting point

---

[167] ibid at 42.   [168] ibid at 40.

[169] Strelein (n 49) 244.   [170] *Mabo v Queensland (No 2)* (n 36) at 42.

[171] Notably *Amodu Tijani v Secretary, Southern Nigeria* [1921] 2 AC 399 (PC).

[172] Notably *R v Symonds* [1847] NZPCC 387 in the context of New Zealand. Also see Strelein (n 49) 118.

[173] Castellino and Domínguez Redondo (n 109) ch 3, esp *Jau Jok Evong v Marabong Lumber Sdn Bhd* [1990] 2 CLJ 625 and *Woon Tan Kan v Asian Rare Earth Sdn Bhd* (1992) 4 CLJ 2207.

[174] Notably in the way that the Inter-American Commission decided the *Awas Tingni* case, see *The Mayagna (Sumo) Indigenous Community of Awas Tingni v The Republic of Nicaragua*, Judgment of 31 August 2001 [2001] IACHR Petition No 11 577.

[175] For a discussion of the case-law and statutory framework in Kenya on this issue, see Albert K. Barume, 'Indigenous Battling for Land Rights: The Case of the Ogiek of Kenya' in J. Castellino and N. Walsh (eds), *International Law and Indigenous Peoples* (n 101) 365–91.

[176] *Mabo v Queensland (No 2)* (n 36) at 57.

[177] This is reflected in the Native Title Act preamble.

[178] Michael Dodson, 'Statement on Behalf of the Northern Land Council' in *The Australian Contribution: UN Working Group on Indigenous Populations* (Xth session, Geneva, July 1992) 35.

for the determination of the title claims of indigenous peoples.[179] The main objects of this Act are defined in section 3 as:

(a) to provide for the recognition and protection of native title;
(b) to establish ways in which future dealings affecting native title may proceed and to set standards for those dealings;
(c) to establish a mechanism for determining claims to native title; and
(d) to provide for, or permit, the validation of past acts, and intermediate period acts, invalidated because of the existence of native title.[180]

The Act (as amended) recognizes and protects native title, ensuring that it is not extinguished in any manner contrary to the Act.[181] It covers acts affecting title,[182] and a mechanism for determining whether native title exists and providing compensation for acts affecting such title.[183] In section 4 (an overview of the Act itself), the kinds of acts affecting native title,[184] the consequences of past and future acts,[185] and the actions are all identified for events in the intermediate period (before the High Court decision in *Wik Peoples v Queensland* (1996) 187 CLR 1).[186] The *Native Title Act* also made provisions for the confirmation of extinguishment of native title[187] and identified the mechanisms (including the establishment of a *National Native Title Tribunal*) through which issues covered under the Act are to be addressed.[188]

While the passage of the *Native Title Act*[189] appeared to solidify the gains of *Mabo*, the intervening years significantly undermined this. An early important challenge arose in *Wik Peoples v Queensland* [1996],[190] where the fundamental question of conflict of laws was raised in the specific instance of the extent to which native title could co-exist with other interests, in this case, pastoral leases. The relevance of this question had enormous consequences, since much of occupied Australian territory is held on such leases. By finding that pastoral leases could co-exist, the courts failed to grant exclusive native title rights, thereby questioning the efficacy of such title.[191]

Even before this decision there had been signs that the courts would not allow the Act a smooth passage.[192] While the original *Native Title Act* sought to

---

[179] *Native Title Act 1993.* [180] s 3, ibid. [181] s 4(1), ibid.
[182] s 4(3–6), ibid. [183] s4(7), ibid. [184] s 4(3)(a)(b), ibid.
[185] s 4(4), ibid. [186] s 4(5), ibid. [187] s 4(6), ibid.
[188] s 4(7), ibid.
[189] *Native Title Act 1994* No 71 notified 1 November 1994 (Gaz 1994 No S229).
[190] (1996) 187 CLR 1.
[191] For a general discussion on the acquisition of territory in international law, see Castellino (n 13). It could be argued that 'title' in customary international law has usually been considered exclusive. The notion of a co-existing system of title seems absurd, though this needs to be distinguished from the concept of *usus fructus* which, while signifying usage of land in custom, is now akin to 'title' per se.
[192] For instance, see *Fejo v Northern Territory of Australia* (1998) 156 ALR 721. Under the *Commonwealth Aboriginal Land Rights (Northern Territory) Act 1976* aborigines had the inalienable, statutory title to land that they could prove they traditionally owned through claims

provide a process for the recognition and protection of native title, certainty for land management and a framework for dealing with native title in the future,[193] this was gradually undermined by subsequent legal developments. The ridicule expressed in sections of the media exaggerating the nature of indigenous claims to territory succeeded in creating a tense environment.[194] Another key decision that contributed to the need for a re-examination of the statute was *Brandy v HREOC* where it was found that the statutory body created to oversee the grant of native title, the *National Native Title Tribunal* (NNTT), did not have constitutional power to make such determinations.[195] In *Northern Territory v Lane* (1995)[196] it was decided that native title claims needed to be registered as soon as they were lodged, giving claimants automatic access to the right to negotiate, whether or not the applicant would satisfy the acceptance test established in the *Native Title Act*. Finally, in *Wik* the assumption that native title had been extinguished by a grant of lease was deemed wrong since native title was determined as being able to continue to exist on land subject to a pastoral lease.[197]

The range of uncertainties surrounding the grant of native title provided justification for the John Howard government to amend the statute. The state argued that the *Native Title Act* had become obsolete and inadequate on the following grounds:

a) it failed to determine the competing rights between Native Title Act holders and pastoralists on pastoral lease land;

b) the fact that the right to negotiate could be gained directly on registration of claim with NNTT with negotiating rights, without proper determination of its validity;

c) it failed to design a mechanism to address co-existing interests in land, since the 'freehold test'[198] was no longer adequate;

d) decisions had been taken by the government after 1 January 1994 on pastoral lease land on the basis that no native title existed, which had since been proved invalid;

---

filed by 5 June 1997. Critics of the Act point to the disadvantages of proving such ownership in urbanized and pastoral communities (due to the exceptions in the law). The *Miscellaneous Acts Amendment (Aboriginal Community Living Areas Act 1989* (NT) has attempted to respond to some of these concerns for large pastoral holdings to the further detriment of aboriginal claims. Also see *Commonwealth v Yarmirr* (2001) 208 CLR1.

[193] CERD *Findings on the NTAA 1998 (Cth)*, UN Doc CERD/C/54/Misc.40/ Rev. 2 (18 March 1996) at 6.

[194] The general human rights context for the regulation of hate speech is discussed in some detail by Luke McNamara, *Regulating Racism: Racial Vilification Laws in Australia* (Sydney: Sydney Institute of Criminology Monograph Series No 16, 2002).

[195] (1995) 183 CLR 245.

[196] (1995) 50 FCR 332.

[197] *Wik Peoples v Queensland* (1996) 187 CLR 1, 133 (Toohey J with the concurrence of Gaudron, Gummow, and Kirby JJ).

[198] Whereby governments cannot generally undertake acts on land where native title exists if those acts could not be done over freehold land.

e) problems in the administration and final determination of claims—in this context, by December 1998, only one offshore and four mainland decisions regarding NTAS had been made out of over 700 existing applications before the NNTT;[199]

f) the imposition of 'unintended restrictions and cumbersome procedures' on claimants and defendants;

g) agreements between native title holders and governments were deemed unsatisfactory, yielding no definitive legal determination of native title;

h) provisions intended to permit low impact mining and petroleum exploration in the absence of usual right to negotiate had proved ineffective; and

i) the established need for greater recognition of Aboriginal and Torres Strait Islander representative bodies.[200]

The modifications made to the *Native Title Act* were passed by Parliament as the *Native Title (Amendment) Act 1998*.[201] It made crucial changes to the NTA, including:

1. the requirement that all claims to native title were made directly to the Federal Court;[202]

2. validation of acts in the intermediate period (1 January 1994 and 23 December 1996), as long as this was done on current or former leasehold or freehold land;[203]

3. pastoralists, governments, and land and environmental regulatory regimes were permitted to continue activities under pastoral leases, even though there may be competing co-existing native title claims;[204]

4. governments could continue to grant off-farm grazing and irrigation rights, and remove resources from pastoral leases, though native title holders were given procedural and compensation rights;[205]

5. new registration test (for claimants to have right to negotiate) based on new criteria;[206]

6. the right to negotiate was streamlined, reworked, and replaced;[207]

7. past extinguishment by grant of exclusive possession tenures were made confirmable by states and territories;[208]

---

[199] Commonwealth of Australia, 'Australian Government Response to the UNCERD Request for Information under art 9(1) of the ICERD' (9 July 1999) 5. Other determinations of title through the native Title Act included consent orders in favour of the Dunghutti people at Crescent Head, NSW north coast; Hopevale in North Queensland; and Western Yalanje people (North Queensland).

[200] See Gillian Triggs, 'Australia's Indigenous Peoples and International Law: Validity of the Native Title Amendment Act 1998 (Cth)' (1999) 23 *MULR* 400–2.

[201] For a general discussion of this issue, see Gillian Triggs, ibid 372–415.

[202] s 61.   [203] s 22F and s 22A.   [204] ss 24 GA-24GC.

[205] ss 24GD-24GE.   [206] ss 190A-190D.

[207] ss 26A-26C, 43A.   [208] s 23 in general.

8. registered native title claimants were assured existing access to pastoral land while the claim is processed;[209] and

9. new systems of registration were created over indigenous land-use agreements.[210]

Commentators such as Triggs,[211] Strelein, Dodson, and others registered concern about the diminution or extinguishment of Native Title Rights,[212] and the erosion of the right of indigenous peoples to negotiate.[213] Triggs concludes:

These provisions, individually and cumulatively, diminish the right to consultation and negotiation in relation to native title land. While it is thought likely that the High Court will uphold the constitutional validity of the NTAA, the restrictions on the RTN [right to negotiate] fail to meet international legal standards.[214]

The *Ward* decision subsequently clarified the status of the *Native Title Act 1993*, establishing it as the more logical starting point for the investigation of native title, rather than the *Mabo* decision.[215] In *Yorta Yorta* the High Court further identified this as the applicable regime for the regulation of the determination, protection, and extinguishment of native title, where applications under this mechanism are instigated.[216] This is governed by section 223 of the *Native Title Act*, which states:

(1) [T]he expression *native title* or *native title rights and interests* means the communal, group or individual rights and interests of Aboriginal peoples or Torres Strait Islanders in relation to land or waters, where:
    a. The rights and interests are possessed under the traditional laws acknowledged, and the traditional customs observed, by the Aboriginal peoples or Torres Strait Islanders; and

---

[209] s 47.

[210] Div 3(b)–(e).

[211] Commenting on the NTAA Triggs argues that it violated basic principles of the Racial Discrimination Convention, particularly where the amendments extinguish native title or reduce opportunities to make a claim in the future. She felt the sanction by CERD did not go far enough since The Native Title Amendment Act had wide, long-term, and discriminatory effects upon Australia's indigenous people which violated the *jus cogens* norm against racial discrimination. See Triggs (n 201) 377.

[212] This is characterized by the confirmation of past extinguishments; the validation of intermediate period titles; an expansion of rights of pastoralists and corresponding diminution of other existing indigenous rights. See ibid 405.

[213] With a significant reduction in areas to which the right to negotiate (RTN) would apply; a reduction of the range of future acts to which RTN would apply; and the exclusion of RTN in the context of inter-tidal zones and in relation to mining. In the context of mining exploration future acts relating solely to land and waters was excluded, as also in the context of approved gold and tin mining acts. For more, see ibid 406–8.

[214] ibid 408. In a section entitled 'Does the NTAA comply with international Law' the author highlights specific international standards that have been breached, including ILO 107 art 11; ILO 160 art 4, 13,14, 16; CERD 1, 2, 5(v), (vi); CCPR 2(1), 27; CBD 10.

[215] *Western Australia v Ward* (2002) 191 ALR at 16.

[216] *Members of the Yorta Yorta Aboriginal Community v Victoria* (2002) 194 ALR 538 at 549.

b. The Aboriginal peoples or Torres Strait Islanders, by those laws and customs, have a connection with the land and waters; and

c. The rights and interests are recognized by the common law of Australia.[217]

According to the High Court in *Ward*, this requires two forms of action:

a. an identification of the applicable traditional laws and customs; and

b. evidence against that regime, demonstrating native title.[218]

This two-part test was enhanced by the High Court in *Yorta Yorta* where Justice Olney had rejected the native title claim of the community in 1998, on the grounds that any such claim had been washed away by 'the tide of history'.[219] This was on the grounds of the forced settlement of missions within the territory,[220] the suppression of older forms of cultural expressions,[221] and the taking-up by the local population of employment on offer.[222] This led him to conclude that, by 1881, the *Yorta Yorta* had lost their culture and status as a 'traditional society' and thereby their claim to any native title was effectively nullified by the flow of history.[223]

On appeal, in validating indigenous laws and customs as the source for such rights, the claimants suggested that such determinations ought to be gleaned from rules with normative content rather than merely 'observable patterns of behaviour'.[224] The court made it clear that the continuation of the system depended on its maintenance and observance by the group who consider themselves bound by it, and that, conversely, the society was probably defined by adherence to these laws. This creates difficulty of proof, as Strelein points out:

> The Court introduced a logical disjunction into the doctrine of native title that creates a schism between the existence of Indigenous law and the legal consequences thereof... Thus by requiring proof of continued acknowledgement of a system of laws as a precondition for the recognition of native title, the Court has disavowed any continuing authority within Indigenous societies capable of recognition by the courts. The Court relied on the act of state doctrine to reassert that the acquisition of sovereignty cannot be challenged by a municipal court. This abdication of judicial responsibility was exacerbated by the Court's adherence to the suggestion that it is the NTA which limits the ability to recognize indigenous peoples' rights to their lands, and that there is no continuing role for the common law in determining the underlying concepts of proper interpretation of the NTA.[225]

Similar conclusions were reached in *De Rose v South Australia*,[226] which addressed the claim of an aboriginal group to a pastoral property in the

---

[217] Native Title Act 1993 s223.

[218] *Western Australia v Ward* (2002) 191 ALR at 17.

[219] *Members of the Yorta Yorta Aboriginal Community v Victoria* [1998] FCA 1606 (18 December 1998).

[220] ibid at 36–49. [221] ibid at para 118. [222] ibid paras 119–20.

[223] ibid at para 129. [224] ibid at paras 42 at 551.

[225] Strelein (n 49) 255–6. [226] [2002] FCA 1342 para 106 (1 November 2002).

north-west of South Australia. At trial the physical and spiritual connection between the communities claiming the title was determined to have been lost.[227] The decision was overturned on appeal, with a critical finding over the judgment that Justice O'Loughlin had appended in deciding compliance with traditional law.[228]

Cases such as these and others like *Neowarra v Western Australia*[229] have led Strelein to conclude:

The proof of a coherent and continuous society defined by a pre-sovereignty normative system creates an enormous grey area in the requirement of proof. The nature of the group has emerged as a fundamental threshold question for native title claimants. The High Court's defence of the views of the trial judge in *Yorta Yorta* demonstrates the vagaries of an assessment based to a significant degree on the judge's perceptions of the group. The High Court has done little to guide trial judges away from their pre-existing biases and prejudices in making such an assessment. Native title claimants must rely on the ability of a non-indigenous judiciary to conceive the contemporary expressions of Indigenous identity, culture and law. What native title is able to recognize in terms of rights and interests derived from indigenous society is affected by judicial understandings of the relationship between traditional and pre-colonial society.[230]

As a result:

The final determination of native title and its pendant rights and interests requires more than just the translation of a normative system that regulates behaviour among a group into a proprietary title understandable in the Australian property system. This may, in itself, seem a difficult task, but the process is further complicated by the associated task of determining the impact of extinguishment. The conflation of these two processes in devising a final determination has created significant obstacles for the proof of native title and has undermined titles in many instances.[231]

It is clear that the *Native Title Act* and the *Native Title Amendment Act 1998* have played a key role in shaping the extinguishment of native title.[232] The possibility opened by *Mabo* in 1992 for the recognition of native title has come full circle, and raises the question as to whether the formulation of a statutory regime is in any way superior to the courts' reliance on common law to establish native title. The advantage of the NTA and NTAA regime is that it established a procedure for the recognition of native title and created a detailed technical regime of statutory extinguishment.[233] Against this it failed to clarify:

---

[227] ibid at 911.
[228] *De Rose v South Australia* (2003) 133 FCR 286 and a final decision in *De Rose v South. Australia II* [2005] FCA 110 (8 June 2005).
[229] [2003] FCA 1402 at 395 (8 December 2003).
[230] Strelein (n 49) 259–60.
[231] ibid 260.   [232] ibid 263.
[233] *Western Australia v Ward* (2002) 191 ALR 1. Also see *Erebum Le (Darnley Islanders) v Queensland* [2003] FCA 227 (14 October 2003).

a. the extent to which *sui generis* sovereignty and associated rights exist for native Australians;[234]
b. how the cycle of hierarchy that inevitably places indigenous interests at a lower level than that of others in society could be challenged;[235]
c. the value to be attributed to different kinds of evidence and testimony;[236]
d. the extent to which competing interests, such as long term pastoral leases, are to be adjudicated upon; and, most importantly,
e. a formula that adequately compensates indigenous Australians for the long term and continuing damage done to the community through the instrument of law itself.

Strelein comments:

The Australian courts and the legislature have been compliant in the subjugation of native title to the interests of the Crown and to private interests. Nevertheless, the *Mabo* decision set a benchmark for recognition, even though it may not have met its potential or the expectations of Indigenous peoples. However, the *Mabo* decision still provides an unprecedented level of protection over indigenous land rights that is binding on the state—the courts, the legislature and the executive—as well as on its guarantees... However, the inconsistent treatment of the theory of Indigenous rights has meant that indigenous sovereignty is excluded from the scope of rights that can be claimed before the courts. While the tenor of recent judgments appears respectful of Indigenous peoples, the law they set down still contains vestiges of the assumptions of superiority. The requirements of proof of social organization and traditional connection since the assertion of sovereignty, as well as the emphasis on tenure history and extinguishment, are all examples of the way in which the law has subordinated Indigenous society. An approach that begins from the premise that all peoples are equal, and that their rights are worthy of protection against the excesses of the state, would produce a different result.[237]

In other words, the 'machinery of the Australian legal system has acted as the legitimising arm of colonialism'.[238]

2.3.2.2 *Political Participation*

The erosion of the right to negotiate in the context of the amended *Native Title Act* is arguably one of many manifestations of the general erosion of the

---

[234] As several authors have pointed out Australian courts have avoided this issue. For a commentary on this in the context of a generally positive commentary on the impact of the *Mabo* decision, see Nettheim (n 25) 228–32 and 234–5.

[235] Strelein (n 49) 265, 267.

[236] See *Western Australia v Ward* (2002) 191 ALR 1 where the court discussed the notion of indigenous peoples' land laws and customs. While highlighting that indigenous peoples could and did make laws to regulate their relationship with the land, they undermined this authority by imputing extinguishment of native title on the basis of decisions taken in regard to access and use, at 627.

[237] Strelein (n 49) 268–9.

[238] Michael Dodson, 'From Lore to Law: Indigenous Rights and Australian Legal Systems' (February 1995) *ALB* 2.

right to political participation of indigenous peoples in Australia.[239] While
some argue that the right of political participation ought to take the form
of indigenous self-governance,[240] other arrangements for the realization of
this right have been proposed. Recently indigenous governance was premised on the *Aboriginal and Torres Strait Islander Commission Act 1989*.[241] This
Act laid the foundation for the creation of the *Aboriginal and Torres Strait
Islander Commission* (ATSIC) with a mandate for representing Aboriginal and
Torres Strait Islanders, and working towards the efficient delivery of services
to members of the community.[242] The Act also provided for the establishment of a network of elected indigenous representatives who were to play a
key role in Commonwealth government decisions, not only in relation to
service delivery, but with regard to questions of resource-allocation to indigenous communities.[243]The governmental decision to create this structure was
an acknowledgment of the need for indigenous involvement at the higher
echelons of governance, especially in the context of decisions affecting the
community.[244] The creation of a network of elected aboriginal representatives
nationwide owes its existence to the progress made in the 1970s where significant national indigenous representative bodies were created.[245] The policy
was controversially reversed in 2005,[246] on the grounds of its inefficiency,[247]

[239] In the context of environmental rights (discussed below). See T. Keyes, 'Indigenous Rights
Sidelined Again: The Federal Environment Protection and Biodiversity Conservation Bill (1999)
4 *ILB* 22, 14–15.

[240] e.g. Reilly (n 37) 405. The author distinguishes 'governance' from 'government', suggesting that the latter refers to official institutions organized by the constitution of a state, while the
former, as a concept has much broader connotations.

[241] No 150 of 1989.

[242] The objects of the Act are described in s 3, with the functions of the Commission outlined
in s 10 of the Act.

[243] See Commonwealth of Australia, Department of Immigration and Multicultural and
Indigenous Affairs, 'In the Hands of the Regions: A New ATSIC: A Report of the Aboriginal and
Torres Strait Islander Commission' (Canberra: 2003).

[244] Reilly (n 37) 404.

[245] This includes the *Department of Aboriginal Affairs and the National Aboriginal Consultative
Committee* [Whitlam Labour Government] and the *National Aboriginal Conference* [Fraser
Coalition Government].

[246] There was a significant uproar about this reversal with many reports submitted to the
UN Commission on Human Rights, see, among others, *Report of the Special Representative of
the Secretary-General*, Hina Jilani UN doc E/CN.4/2006/95/Add.1 (22 March 2006) para 20;
*Report submitted by the Special Representative of the Secretary-General on human rights defend-
ers*, Hina Jilani UN doc E/CN.4/2006/95/Add.5 (6 March 2006) at para 123–4 and *Report
of the Special Rapporteur on the situation of human rights and fundamental freedoms of indigenous people*, Rodolfo Stavenhagen UN doc E/CN.4/2006/78/Add.1 (18 January 2006) para 11.
Also see written statement submitted by Society for Threatened Peoples International, a non-
governmental organization in special consultative status UN doc E/CN.4/2005/NGO/239
(9 March 2005).

[247] See Second Reading of the Attorney-General and Minister for Justice, the Hon Daryl
Williams, 4 September 1997, in *Native Title* (2nd edn—Native Title Act 1993 and Regulations)
[Australian Government Solicitor, 1998] 7886–93.

with the Commission abolished and many of its activities transferred to mainstream government departments.[248] Instead the policy was premised on the need for 'practical reconciliation' which advocated a 'focus on practical measures to alleviate Indigenous disadvantage'.[249] The abolition of ATSIC took place despite positive reviews of the system commissioned by the Department of Immigration, Multiculturalism, and Indigenous Affairs (DIMIA).[250] It was justified by the government as follows:

The vision is of a whole-of-government approach which can inspire innovative national approaches to the delivery of services to Indigenous Australians, but which are responsive to the distinctive needs of particular communities. It requires committed implementation. The approach will not overcome the legacy of disadvantage overnight. Indigenous issues are far too complex for that. But it does have the potential to bring about generational change.[251]

The emphasis of the new arrangements was on 'direct dealing with local communities through Shared Responsibility Agreements,[252] cutting the red tape and making mainstream agencies accountable'.[253] There has been a shift towards a focus on allocation of resources, with the new bodies (National Indigenous Council and various Indigenous Coordination Centres) expected to act as links between the communities and the governments,[254] and mindful of the need to form regional partnerships.[255]

Yet indigenous governance, as Reilly argues, is inevitable, and while it may be distasteful politically, it nevertheless takes place on a regular basis within Australian society. The challenge is how the government chooses to recognize these processes.[256] While Reilly does not advocate formal recognition of Indigenous governance models, he argues that a lack of such

---

[248] See Senate Select Committee on the Administration of Indigenous Affairs, 'After ATSIC: Life in the Mainstream?' [2005] AILR 33; 9(2) 89 which remains extremely critical about the decision to abolish the commission.

[249] Reilly (n 37) 404.

[250] ibid 418.

[251] See Speech to the Australian Public Service Commission Leadership Development Network, 20 July 2005 entitled 'Leadership in a Changing Environment'. The full text of the speech is available at <http://www.apsc.gov.au/media/tim200705.pdf> [last consulted 25 March 2009]. For more on the content of the new arrangements please see <https://www.indigenous.gov. au/NewArrangementsBrochure.pdf>.

[252] For detailed views of these arrangements, see <www.oipc.gov.au/About_oipc/new_ arrangements.asp> [last accessed 1 April 2008].

[253] As contained in the text of Senator Amanda Vanstone's Press Release (11 July 2005), quoted in Reilly (n 37) 418.

[254] Senator Amanda Vanstone, 'Minister Announces New Indigenous Representation Arrangements' Press Release (20 June 2005) as quoted in Reilly, ibid 419.

[255] For more on regional partnership agreements, see <http://www.indigenous.gov.au> [last accessed 1 August 2008].

[256] Reilly (n 37) 404.

recognition at a practical level undermines governmental policy.[257] He makes the case for:

> ...law makers to recognise that Indigenous governance is already a constitutional reality in Australia and, as such, that it must be accounted for in developing laws to protect and maintain Indigenous social, cultural and political rights.[258]

The argument for this position is based on three central tenets: the need to adopt a legally pluralist position for a society that is as pluralist as Australia;[259] the notion that the political legitimacy of a society is only enhanced '...when the political integrity of different social groups within society is recognised';[260] and the belief that such a policy is the only one likely to achieve improvement in the social and economic conditions facing the group.[261] Reilly distinguishes his three categories of governance on the basis that self-governance is the 'capacity of social entities to govern themselves autonomously';[262] co-governance utilizes 'organised forms of interactions [collaboration/co-ordination] for governing purposes';[263] while hierarchical governance consists of 'bureaucratic government, with control coming from the top'.[264]

In terms of strategy, Reilly distinguishes the call for a constitutional framework recognizing indigenous governance from other calls for recognition of sovereignty, self-government, or self-determination.[265] Recent Australian history supports the argument that self-determination and sovereignty can prove a red-herring, stalling progressive discussions on other aspects of indigenous peoples'

---

[257] Reilly does not appear to consider self-determination and sovereignty as crucial. The argument he is offering is based on a nuanced reading of the Australian constitution, the Australian federal system, and the evidence of indigenous self-governance. The author problematically suggests that indigenous rights were established in international human rights law in the 1970s and 1980s whereas indigenous communities assert that this was when states began to awaken to the existence of these communities who had continued to exist alongside other communities, though maintaining their own systems of governance.

[258] Reilly (n 37) 404.

[259] For this the author draws on the work of Griffiths (n 142); and William Connolly, *The Ethos of Pluralization* (Minneapolis: University of Minnesota Press, 1995).

[260] Reilly (n 37) 404.

[261] This sentiment is extrapolated from the findings of the Harvard Project on American Indian Development which stressed the importance of the quality of governance structures to the economic well-being of the American Indian communities. See Stephen Cornell, Catherine Curtis, and Miriam Jorgensen, 'The Concept of Governance and its Implications for First Nations' *Joint Occasional Papers on Native Affairs*, No 2004–02 available at <http://www.jopna.net/pubs/JOPNA05_Governance.pdf> [last accessed 1 August 2008].

[262] Reilly (n 37) 406 drawing on a definition provided by Jan Kooiman, *Governing as Governance* (London: Sage, 2003) at 78.

[263] ibid.   [264] ibid.

[265] As contained in joint art1(2) of the *International Covenant on Civil and Political Rights* and the *International Covenant on Economic, Social, and Cultural Rights* (both 1966). For more on this distinction, see Joshua Castellino and Jeremie Gilbert, 'Self-determination, Indigenous Peoples and Minorities' (2003) 3 *MQLJ* [Special Issue: Self-determination] 155–78.

rights.[266] For Reilly it would be more productive to view indigenous governance as a potential remedy under the existing provisions for federalism contained in the Australian constitution.[267] Instead he argues that focusing on 'governance' rather than 'government' may be advantageous.[268] The concept of indigenous governance would allow for a more unified strategy through which the aboriginal community would be able to self-govern or co-govern rather than engage the issue of hierarchical governance.[269]

While this position ought to be appreciated for the extent to which stalled discussions can be revived, from a strategic perspective, foregoing the right to self-determination and the claim to sovereignty appears to erode the basis for the claim in the first place. It could be argued that unlike minorities who do not have a claim to self-determination,[270] indigenous claims to *lex specialis* are based first on the historical basis of their rights prior to the limited European contact and conquest, and second as a remedy for the denial and violation of these rights through legal subterfuge. In reality this means locating a space in society for its indigenous people, as socio-economic improvements without redress of historical grievances would fail to uphold principles of sovereignty and self-determination.

Under international human rights law, a focus on political participation (under Article 25 of the *International Covenant on Civil and Political Rights* (ICCPR)) is more feasible and enforceable than self-determination (Article 1 of the ICCPR and the *International Covenant on Economic, Social, and Cultural Rights* (ICESCR)). Yet in terms of the intent of the drafters of the Covenants, it would be clear that the situation of indigenous peoples comes more within the discussion of Article 1 than Article 25. It seems that a focus on political participation may be the only way of addressing the issues enshrined under Article 1 of the Covenant,[271] even though it may fail to realize a central premise on which the community is staking a claim to governance. For many Australian nations, the subjugation of indigenous sovereignty lies at the heart of the destruction of indigenous governance structures, and a return to such systems requires that this fundamental violation be recognized. While a focus on self-governance and co-governance may be a practical solution out of a current impasse, it is unlikely

---

[266] This is very much the perspective taken by leading indigenous commentator Patrick Thornberry. See *Indigenous Peoples and Human Rights* (Manchester: Manchester University Press, 2002) 4–6.

[267] As discussed in pt 3, below.

[268] Reilly (n 37) 406. For more on the notion of governance and 'self-governance', see Kooiman (n 264) 177–232.

[269] Reilly, ibid.

[270] See Human Rights Committee *General Comment No 23: The rights of minorities* (art 27) (08/04/94) UN doc CCPR/C/21/Rev.1/Add.5, paras 3.1 and 3.2.

[271] There is little theoretical work done on the overlap between arts 1 and 25 of the Covenant's rights. Though there is much in political science on the right to democratic governance. One legal jurist who seeks to explore these links is Stephen Wheatley, *Democracy, Minorities and International Law* (Cambridge: Cambridge University Press, 2005).

to satisfy the grounds on which claims for indigenous governance are being advanced in the first place.[272]

The Australian government response to this has not changed and has been re-articulated in several forums since:

> ...advocates for ethnic, indigenous or linguistic minorities sometimes rely upon the principle of self-determination in international law as a basis for claims to political or legal regulation. So far, however, the principle has been confined in international practice to situations involving separate ('colonial') territories politically and legally subordinate to an administering power.[273]

From an indigenous perspective it is difficult to imagine what 'colonial' refers to if their situation is excluded. While this restrictive view is not shared in the literature,[274] it is clear that since aboriginal peoples have been found to have been 'subjugated and oppressed', as *Mabo* confirms,[275] some of the conditions raised in the above quote have been satisfied. Nonetheless the discourse on self-determination remains highly sensitized,[276] and while the adoption of a position of self-determination may be instinctively appropriate, many groups are forced to resist the temptation to articulate claims under this heading.

2.3.2.3 Environmental and Ecological Rights and Intellectual Property Regimes

This section is a blend of several issues that underpin the battle for recognition of indigenous rights in Australia. It focuses on intellectual property regimes and their impact on indigenous communities, and environmental and ecological rights, especially the protection of sacred places and objects.[277]

---

[272] esp in the context of claims for 'country' among aboriginal nations. For more, see Steve Kinnane in Castellino and Walsh (n 101).

[273] Australian Law Reform Commission, *Recognition of Aboriginal Customary Law* (Report No 31, 1986) p 128.

[274] For a general reading on self-determination, see Lee C. Buchheit, *Secession: The Legitimacy of Self-Determination* (Yale University Press: New Haven, 1978); Antonio Cassese, *Self-Determination of Peoples, A Legal Reappraisal* (Cambridge: Cambridge University Press 1995); Hurst Hannum, *Autonomy, Sovereignty and Self-determination: The Accommodation of Conflicting Rights* (Philadelphia: University of Pennsylvania Press, 1990); Anthony Whelan, 'Wilsonian Self-Determination and the Versailles Settlement' (1994) 43 *ICLQ* 99–115, and esp Ivor Jennings, *The Approach to Self-Governance* (Cambridge: Cambridge University Press, 1956).

[275] *Mabo (No 2)* (n 36) 451.

[276] For a discussion of the controversy over the term in the then 'Draft Declaration', see Patrick Thornberry (n 267) 382–5.

[277] For general reading on this issue, see Steve Kinnane in Castellino and Walsh (n 101); also see D. Smyth, 'Understanding Country: The Importance of Land and Sea in Aboriginal and Torres Strait Islander Societies' Council for Aboriginal Reconciliation, Key Issues Paper No 1 [where the author examines and explains the importance of land and the links that aboriginal and TS people have with it].

2.3.2.3.1 Traditional Knowledge and Intellectual Property Rights

In commenting on the extent to which indigenous environmental knowledge has been appropriated, O'Bryan highlights the need for an emphasis on the protection of aboriginal intellectual property rights.[278] There are difficulties associated with recognition and definition of 'traditional knowledge' in order to protect it as crucial to the propagation of indigenous identity. The parameters must not be too rigid and so fail to recognize traditional knowledge when it falls outside these narrow lines. Traditional knowledge has been defined as:

> ... practical (instrumental) and normative (enabling) knowledge about the ecological, socio-economic and cultural environment. Traditional knowledge is people centred (generated and transmitted by people as knowledgeable, component and entitled actors), systematic (inter-sectional and holistic), experimental (empirical and practical), transmitted from one generation to the next and culturally valorised. This type of knowledge promotes diversity; it valorises and reproduces the local (internal) resources.[279]

The protection of traditional knowledge is justified as it is part of the fundamental protection that ought to be afforded under indigenous cultural rights.[280] Globally, the need to protect traditional knowledge is often explained in terms of the potential that such knowledge may have in addressing solutions to contemporary problems such as HIV/AIDS, ecology, or climate change.[281] Given that the resource held by indigenous peoples is valuable, several questions arise that ought to be of significant concern to national legislators, indigenous leaders and communities, commercial enterprises that seek to exploit or harness the given resource, and wider society that could potentially benefit. Among these questions are: Who owns traditional knowledge? How can it be transferred from the 'traditional' to the 'formal/commercial' realm? And what are the rewards/dangers inherent in the process?

---

[278] Katie O'Bryan, 'The Appropriation of Indigenous Ecological Knowledge: Recent Australian Developments' (2004) 1 *MQJICEL* 29–48.

[279] Ad Hoc Open-Ended Inter-sessional Working Group on Article 8j and related provisions of the Convention on Biological Diversity entitled 'Assessment of the effectiveness of existing sub national, national and international instruments, particularly intellectual property rights instruments, that may have implications on the protection of the knowledge, innovations and practices of indigenous local communities' See UNEP/CBD/WG8j/2/7, 27 November 2001, 9–10.

[280] In *Wongatha People v State of Western Australia and ors (No 5)* [2003] FCA 218 the plaintiffs raised an interesting argument about the notion of 'cultural knowledge' and the manner in which it can be transmitted.

[281] This is based on the argument that western science may be limited and that traditional sources may have the answers currently evading science, see O'Bryan (n 278) 31. The author warns; '...the race to discover new products and processes, the use of traditional ecological knowledge can shorten the odds tremendously'. Also see UN Special Rapporteur Daes' finding that the use of traditional knowledge had increased the efficiency of screening plans for medicinal purposes by 400 per cent, see E. Irene Daes, *Protection of the Heritage of Indigenous Peoples* (1997) presented by Special Rapporteur of the Sub-Commission on Prevention of Discrimination and Protection of Minorities and President of the Working Group on Indigenous Populations, Geneva, 49th Session, E/CN.4/Sub.2/1997/28.

The first question has generated much case-law in Australia. It has been resolved in other areas (notably in the law of the sea) through the adoption of the 'global commons' norm.[282] The difficulty with blanket acceptances of this norm is that it opens up a range of exclusive indigenous ownership to general owner-ship, without the active consent of the indigenous population who risk being marginalized. If the 'global commons' approach is unsatisfactory, the other end of the ownership spectrum, the notion of individual ownership, would also be inappropriate. Michael Davis puts the debate in context:

Biological knowledge in Indigenous communities is generally regarded as being a community resource, and is shared and transmitted 'freely' within communities according to customary rights, rules and obligations. The private ownership rights which patent laws confer for inventions are thus antithetical to indigenous peoples' world views.[283]

While international patent regimes may be developed with western scientific researchers and commercial firms in mind,[284] they are inappropriate when applied to traditional knowledge and indigenous peoples.[285] Contemporary developments,[286] such as the 1994 General Agreement on Tariffs and Trade (GATT)[287] and the World Trade Organization's Agreement on Trade-Related Intellectual Property Rights (TRIPs),[288] are of particular concern to

[282] This term has also been explored in greater depth in the context of indigenous peoples' rights by Michael Davis, 'Law, Anthropology, and the Recognition of Indigenous Cultural Systems' (2001) *Law and Anthropology* 11, 306.

[283] Michael Davis, 'Indigenous Peoples and Intellectual Property Rights' (Research Paper No 20, Australian Parliamentary Library) at 6.

[284] See 'Patents, Indigenous Peoples, and Human Genetic Diversity', *RAFI Communique* (Ottawa, Canada: Rural Advancement Foundation International, May 1993).

[285] In general, see Darrell A. Posey and Graham Dutfield, *Beyond Intellectual Property: Toward Traditional Resource Rights for Indigenous Peoples and Local Communities* (Ottawa: International Development Research Centre, 1996).

[286] The following constitutes a range of international instruments that address this issue in international society: The *Rio Earth Summit* esp *Agenda 21* (see ch 26); the *Statement of Forest Principles*. The *Rio Declaration* (esp Principles 9 and 10); the *Convention on Biodiversity* esp arts 8j, 10c, 17(2), and 18(4). For an indigenous peoples response to the latter, see 'The Biodiversity Convention: The Concerns of Indigenous Peoples' (1996) AILR 84. Among the chief criticisms is the constant affirmation in the CBD that the states rather than indigenous or 'peoples' have the right to biological resources—for a closer reading, see O'Bryan (n 279) 37. Also to be included in this list now is art 29 of the *Declaration on the Rights of Indigenous Peoples*, 2007. Other soft law standards that exists in this area include: *Declaration of Belm* (1992), the *Kunming Action Plan* (1992), the *Manila Declaration Concerning the Ethical Utilization of Biological Resources* (1992), the *Kari-Oca Declaration* (1992), the *Mataatua Declaration on Cultural and Intellectual Property Rights* (1993), the *Julayinbul Statement on Indigenous Intellectual Property Rights* (1993), and the *Declaration Reaffirming the Self Determination and Intellectual Property Rights of Indigenous Nations and Peoples of the Wet Tropics Rainforest Area* (1993).

[287] For general reading an analytical index on GATT, see the WTO website summary available at <http://www.wto.org/english/res_e/booksp_e/analytic_index_e/gatt1994_01_e.htm> [last accessed 1 August 2008].

[288] For an updated reading on TRIPS, see the WTO website available at <http://www.wto.org/english/tratop_e/TRIPS_e/TRIPS_e.htm> [last accessed 1 August 2008].

indigenous peoples.[289] Many believe that these agreements will raise the risk of 'bio-piracy'[290] by recognizing only private rights and making no provision for intellectual property that may be collectively held within a community. Most problematically, the agreement provides that the 'products of scientific research become the private property of the product's corporate sponsors'.[291]

Australia has discharged its obligations under the *Convention on Biodiversity* through a national strategy as well as through legislation.[292] The *National Strategy for Ecologically Sustainable Development* (1992) recognized the value of indigenous knowledge in objective 22.1 which states the principle that:

> To ensure effective mechanisms are put in place to represent Aboriginal and Torres Strait Islander peoples' land, heritage, economic and cultural development concerns in resource allocation processes...Governments will encourage greater recognition of Aboriginal Peoples and Torres Strait Islanders' values, traditional knowledge and resource management practices relevant to ESD.[293]

In 1996, the Commonwealth, along with state and territory governments, endorsed the National Strategy for the Conservation of Australia's Biological Diversity with a specific mention of indigenous peoples in Objective 1.8, with a call to implementation framed in Action 1.8.2:

> ...that the use of traditional biological knowledge in the scientific, commercial and public domains proceeds with the co-operation and control of the traditional owners of that knowledge and ensure that the use and collection of such knowledge results in social and economics benefits to traditional owners.

Passed in 1999, the *Environment Protection and Biodiversity Conservation Act*[294] purports to implement Australia's obligation arising out of Article 8 of the *Convention on Biodiversity*, and has been called 'the most significant change to Commonwealth environmental laws since they were first introduced'.[295] Despite the obvious relevance of this statute to indigenous peoples, they were sidelined[296] in what became a highly politicized debate in Australian society.[297] Instead the Act seeks to promote the use of indigenous peoples' knowledge of biodiversity

---

[289] See Richard Howitt, *Rethinking Resource Management: Justice, Sustainability and Indigenous Peoples* (London/New York: Routledge, 2001).

[290] O'Bryan (n 278) 34. [291] ibid 34, see ff 21/22.

[292] It is important to note that Australia Ratified the Convention on Biodiversity on 18th June 1993 and implemented it in domestic law through the *Environment Protection and Biodiversity Conservation Act 1999* (Cth) and *Native Title Act 1993* (Cth), thus showing the close links between this issue and that of land rights discussed in section 2.3.2.1 above.

[293] Commonwealth of Australia, 'National Strategy for Ecologically Sustainable Development' (1992) 82, (objective 22.1) with ESD standing for 'ecologically sustainable development'.

[294] *Environment Protection and Biodiversity Conservation Act 1999* (Cth).

[295] L. Ogle, 'The Environment Protection and Biodiversity Conservation Act 1999 (Cth): How Workable is it?' (2000) 17 EPLJ 468.

[296] See Keyes (n 239) 14–15.

[297] 800 amendments were put to the bill before it was finally passed in its final format—O'Bryan (n 278) 39.

with the use of the phrase 'involvement of and in co-operation with the owners of the knowledge',[298] in order to 'promote a partnership approach'.[299] However 'partnership' is explicitly declared not to affect the operation of the *Native Title Act*,[300] placing several stipulations over bilateral agreements in this realm, with a special section, 305, that provides indigenous peoples with 'usage rights'.[301]

The question of access to resources is governed by section 301, which contains the major flaw in the legislation, since it can only be invoked in Commonwealth lands or lands under section 26(2). In addition the legislation contains further limitations as it only applies in the context of a potential negative impact of 'national environmental significance', a standard left undefined, and as a result it is not clear when the mechanism is triggered.[302]

The discretionary powers given to ministers under sections 201, 216, and 158 are also problematic. A person could be issued a permit by a minister to undertake activities in relation to particular endangered, migratory, or marine species or communities on Commonwealth land, where the minister is satisfied that the action is of particular significance to indigenous communities and would not affect the survival or recovery in nature of a particular species. Once again the failure to consult indigenous peoples over the general framing of the law is compounded by the fact that the minister need not seek the prior informed consent of the indigenous peoples' concerned. This suggests a paternalistic approach not in line with contemporary standards of indigenous peoples' rights protection.[303]

The Act also defines indigenous traditions in section 201(4) as:

... the body of traditions, observances, customs and beliefs of indigenous persons generally, or of a particular group of indigenous persons'. ...

Thus indigenous peoples are allowed to maintain access to certain scarce ecological or biological sources for traditional purposes if they have obtained permission through the relevant permit and their action does not impact on the survival of a particular species. In addition these conditions only apply to Commonwealth lands, with state lands exempt.[304] The participation envisaged under the Act is articulated as including indigenous representation on the *Biological Diversity Advisory Committee*[305] and in the creation of a separate *Indigenous Advisory*

---

[298] EPBC Act s 3(1)(g).   [299] EPBC Act s 3(2)(g)(iii).
[300] EPBC Act s 8.   [301] EPBC s 305.
[302] O'Bryan (n 278) 34.
[303] This discussion is captured in the contrast between ILO Convention No 107 (1959) and ILO Convention No 169 (1989). While the former had a paternalistic approach, this is substituted in the later document for one that gives indigenous peoples a central role in decisions affecting them. For a similar discussion in the context of Brazil and Indians in the Amazon, see M.G.M. Rodrigues, 'Indigenous Rights in Democratic Brazil' (2002) 24(2) *HRQ* 487–512. Also see Moore and Lemos, 'Indigenous Policy in Brazil: The Development of Decree 1775 & the Proposed Raposa/Serra do Sol Reserve, Roraima, Brazil' (1999) 21(2) *HRQ* 444–63.
[304] O'Bryan (n 278) 42.   [305] EPBC Act 504(4)(ea).

Committee,[306] although neither body's recommendations are binding on the minister.

2.3.2.3.2 Aboriginal Art

According to Bulun:

> The unauthorised reproduction of art works is a very sensitive issue in all Aboriginal communities...[The] creation of works remains very important in ceremonys and the creation of art works is an important step in the preservation of important traditional custom...[It] represents an important part of the cultural continuity of the tribe.[307]

Providing protection for aboriginal art raises problems as legal protection is afforded to the individual. Many aboriginal cultures commonly hold the belief that the protection of the collective is more important, as it can allow the due enrichment of the community that would in turn provide for the right of the individual.[308] *Yumbulul v Aboriginal Artists Agency Ltd and anor* [1991][309] illustrates the difficulty. An argument was put forward suggesting that a painting was owned collectively by the Yolngu clan, where 'paintings are part of the corpus of ritual knowledge, which includes the paintings, songs, dances, power names and sacred objects, that can be referred to as *madayin* ("sacred law")'.[310] The Walpiri Aborigines of the central western part of Northern Territory made similar claims:

> In producing paintings, individuals lay claim to aspects of the ancestral realm...Painting tends to be a social activity, directly involving several individuals and catching the interests of many others...Designs are discussed, and the layout of the painting is determined through consultation and negotiation...A proper painting is one that well reflects the collective Walpiri vision of reality.[311]

This raises the difficulty, common to discussions on the nature of collective rights, of protecting collective rights while allowing individuals to opt out. A corollary question is whether the collective right could still remain undisturbed

---

[306] EPBC S505A.

[307] Affidavit of John Bulun Bulun in proceedings issues in 1989 cited by Fleur Johns (n 308 below) and attributed to C. Golvan, 'Aboriginal Art and the Protection of Indigenous Cultural Rights' (1992) 7 *EIPR* 227 at 228. For a more detailed commentary of the issues raised, see C. Golvan 'Aboriginal Art and the Copyright: The Case for Johnny Bulun Bulun' (1989) *10 EIPR* 346.

[308] Fleur Johns, 'Portrait of the Artist as a White Man: The International Law of Human Rights and Aboriginal Culture' (1995) 16 *AYIL* 173–97, at 173.

[309] Unreported decision of French Justice, sitting in the Federal Court at Darwin, 23–5 July, 1991 as cited in n 26 ibid 178.

[310] H. Morphy, 'Now you Understand: An Analysis of the Way Yolngu Have Used Sacred Knowledge to Retain their Autonomy' in M. Langton and N. Peterson (eds), *Aborigines, Land and Land Rights* (Canberra: Australian Institute of Aboriginal Studies, 1983) 110 at 117.

[311] P. Faulstich, '"You Read 'im This Country": Landscape, Self and Art in an Aboriginal Community' in P. Dark and R. Rose (eds), *Artistic Heritage in a Changing Pacific* (Bathurst: Crawford House Press, 1993) 140 at 156.

by opt-out processes seeking to invalidate them. In other words, is it necessary to insist that no aboriginal artist could create a painting in her or his name and the community always needs to be given the benefit? Would such a law discriminate against an aboriginal artist in comparison with her or his non-aboriginal counterparts? While it can be suggested that protecting the collective interests of the cultural heritage of the aboriginal community imposes 'special duties and responsibilities',[312] determining where the boundary lies between the collective and the individual is a question that the courts have had to determine. In *Commonwealth v Tasmania* [1983], Justice Murphy opined that law in Australia had failed to prevent the destruction of aboriginal culture.[313]

This gap was highlighted by a federal government working party on the *Protection of Aboriginal Folklore*, which concluded that the *Copyright Act 1968* (Cth) provided inappropriate and inadequate legal protection for aboriginal 'folklore', since its precondition for protection was 'originality'.[314] Other problems with protection include the prohibition upon breach of confidence which provides little protection, since material is unlikely to be regarded as legally confidential after disclosure of publication has taken place.[315] The principle of equitable ownership is not useful to communities owning traditional designs or 'cultural heritage' in its broadest sense, since 'ownership' in the legal sense is difficult to prove under the *Copyright Act 1968*.[316] Fleur argues that one of the ways in which aboriginal cultural rights could be protected would be to view them through the lens of the protection of minority cultural rights, rather than through freedom of expression.

As Johns concludes:

In Australia, notwithstanding State and Federal Governments' adoption of 'positive measures' (such as establishment of an Aboriginal Arts Board within the Australia Council) and despite action taken by Aboriginal people themselves (such as the establishment of the Aboriginal Artists Agency Ltd), the fact remains that the system of production and circulation of images and artefacts is not in Aboriginal hands.[317]

He suggests that the patchwork of legislation, unequally applied in various states, 'fails to guarantee Aboriginal peoples access to, or control over, Aboriginal cultural property that is already in non-Aboriginal hands'.[318] Without a positive right protecting this realm, aboriginal peoples have been unable to access the right to culture that may exist at the international level. As a result they have been unable to guard against the 'opposing incremental processes of cultural homogenisation

---

[312] As indicated in art 19 of the ICCPR, 1966.

[313] *Commonwealth v Tasmania* (1983) 158 CLR 1 at 180.

[314] Commonwealth Department of Home Affairs and the Environment, 'Report of the Working Party on the Protection of Aboriginal Folklore' (1981) 13. Also see S. Gray, 'Wheeling, Dealing and Destruction; Aboriginal Art and the Land Post-Mabo' (1993) 63 *ALB* 10.

[315] See S. Gray, 'Aboriginal Designs and Copyright' (1992) 66 *LIJ* 46 at 49.

[316] Johns (n 308) 180.   [317] ibid 187.   [318] ibid.

and cultural expropriation'.[319] As in the pursuit of land rights, the difficulty of using 'self-determination' to guard against cultural encroachment has met with little success. The controversial nature of the term in general application to indigenous issues has made it a less than useful negotiating ploy, even though it may capture the central claim of aboriginal and other indigenous peoples.

Another effort to enshrine protection for aboriginal heritage in Australian law was the *Aboriginal and Torres Strait Islander Heritage Protection Act* (ATSIHPA) 1984,[320] ostensibly passed to protect places deemed sacred to indigenous Australians. However, by 1997, of the ninety-nine areas submitted for protection, the Act had only provided protection to one aboriginal site near Alice Springs (Niltye/Tnyere-Akerte).[321] Writing in the aftermath of the Hindmarsh Island affair,[322] Russell Goldflam stated:

The *ATSIHPA* has foundered on the rocks of Federalism, political partisanship, judicial review and, perhaps most importantly, the underlying, unresolved and generally unacknowledged conflict between Australia's Indigenous and colonial legal systems.[323]

The Act was reviewed by noted jurist Elizabeth Evatt,[324] who criticized the lack of consultation and negotiation between the drafters and the indigenous communities of Australia. Some of Evatt's findings were:[325]

a. aboriginal customary law should be recognized and respected, and its rules regarding the disclosure of restricted information be observed, with

[319] ibid 188. The author uses the example of the boomerang that has been transformed into a commodity that has managed to separate itself from aboriginal culture to become an Australian symbol.

[320] *Aboriginal and Torres Strait Islander Heritage Protection Act 1984* (Cth).

[321] Russell Goldflam, 'Noble Salvage: Aboriginal Heritage Protection and the Evatt Review' (1997) *ALB* 2; 3(88) at 2.

[322] The Hindmarsh Island affair is prominent in writings about indigenous peoples in Australia. It refers to the discussion of a plan in 1988 for the construction of a bridge in South Australia between Goolwa and Hindmarsh Island in the Murray River estuary. The planning application met with an objection by a group of women from the Ngarrindjeri aboriginal nation, who refused to specify the grounds for their objection, claiming that the island was sacred for reasons that their beliefs would not allow them to articulate in public. They initiated action to prohibit construction, with the evidence contained in two sealed envelopes marked 'Confidential; To be Read by Women Only'. This led to the then Minister of Aboriginal Affairs, Robert Tickner (a man) to place a 25-year construction ban on bridge construction in the area. The controversy resurfaced in 1995 when other Aborigines were quoted in the press as suggesting that the secrecy issue was a hoax, and escalated when Shadow Minster Ian McLachlan tabled some of the documents in Parliament, and was forced to resign over how he obtained them. This led to the establishment by the South Australian government of the Hindmarsh Island Royal Commission—who suggested in December that the claim was a fabrication. John Howard's government subsequently passed the *Hindmarsh Island Bridge Act 1997* overturning the previous ban. A claim was also raised by the developers, which however failed. See *Chapman v Luminis Pty Ltd (No 5)* [2001] FCA 1106 (21 August 2001).

[323] Goldflam (n 321) 4.

[324] This attempt to redeem the Act by Evatt was deemed by Goldflam a 'noble salvage attempt', see ibid.

[325] Commonwealth of Australia, Elizabeth Evatt AC, 'Review of the Aboriginal and Torres Strait Islander Heritage Protection Act 1984' (Canberra: 1996).

traditional laws only overridden in cases of a demonstrated compelling public interest;

b. questions of the significance and threatened desecration of asserted heritage property should be conclusively determined by appropriately constituted state/territory or Commonwealth aboriginal heritage bodies, based on a subjective test. Applicants would not be expected to breach customary law regarding the disclosure of information, and third party involvement in the assessment should be minimal;

c. procedures under the Act should encourage developers to address possible indigenous heritage protection issues at an early stage of the planning process to ensure fairness;

d. existing mediation procedures should be strengthened and made legally enforceable through a registration procedure;

e. understanding that the decision of whether or not to protect an item of property is a matter of political discretion, it should be determined by the government, but with a duty to provide reasons and effectively consult aboriginal communities;

f. the creation of an independent, expert-led, gender-balanced Commonwealth Aboriginal Heritage Protection Agency with a majority of Aboriginal people and supported by an Aboriginal Cultural Heritage Advisory Council; and

g. the Act should remain a measure of last resort with minimal standards for regional regimes under which complying states and territories could accredit their processes and agencies.

A national policy would cover both the provision of legal protection, and the establishment of a range of aboriginal-controlled programmes for the active and appropriate management of aboriginal cultural heritage property.[326]

2.3.2.4 *Stigmatization and Hate Speech*

The discussion in Australia on racism has echoed through the media and has yielded a complaint to the Committee on the Elimination of Racial Discrimination (CERD) over pejorative language.[327] Whilst racist sentiment has continuously been expressed against the Aborigines, the inflow of immigrants and asylum seekers has widened this particular debate. Legislation concerning racial vilification is widespread at national and provincial level. At national level the applicable regime combating racial hatred in society is the *Racial Hatred Act 1995*, which introduced section 18C(1) into the existing *Racial Discrimination Act 1975* which:

Makes unlawful, public acts which are reasonably likely in all the circumstances to offend, insult, humiliate or intimidate another person or a group of people where the act

---

[326] Summary of key findings as identified by Goldflam (n 321) 4.
[327] This case arose in the context of art 4 of the International Convention for the Elimination of All Forms of Racial Discrimination.

is done because of race, colour, or national or ethnic origin of the other person or group members.[328]

Within this section, incitement is defined as '… a conscious and motivated act', requiring subjective judgment by the court.[329] Inevitably there have been few prosecutions under the Act, owing to the limitations in place provided by section 60 (see below), but also owing to the high threshold for proving beyond a reasonable doubt that a given offence falls foul of the Act.[330] In view of discussions that have taken place elsewhere on the appropriate exceptions to hate speech,[331] Article 60 of the Act holds that nothing said or done:

…in reasonably good faith in the course of any statement, publication, discussion or debate made or held for an academic, artistic or scientific purpose, or any other purpose in the public interest' will be prohibited.[332]

The Act establishes the right to complain to the Human Rights and Equal Opportunities Commission (HREOC), which can be individually activated.[333]

It is at the provincial level in Australia that the regimes are more nuanced. In New South Wales the applicable regime, the *Anti-Discrimination Act 1977*, has been utilized in the battle to combat hate speech,[334] and in this context the particularly relevant sections of the Act are sections 20C(1) and 20D. The former makes the phenomenon of hate speech or 'racial vilification' unlawful though not criminal, while the latter defines a criminal offence as including physical threat or an incitement to physical threat.[335] In keeping with the importance of ensuring that the legislation does not unduly impinge on freedom of expression, the Act delineates that certain actions could be exempt.[336] Among these are 'fair' reporting, absolute privilege, good faith, and public interest. The Act also sets up an *Anti-Discrimination Board* whose mandate is to regulate its implementation.

---

[328] Unlawful behaviour includes: writing racist graffiti in public places; wearing Nazi insignia in a public place; making racist speeches at a rally; placing racist posters or stickers in a public place; racist abuse in public places such as shops, workplaces, parks, public transport; offensive racist comment in a publication.

[329] s 18C(1).

[330] This is discussed in detail in the context of the different 'racial vilification' laws in Australia. See McNamara (n 194).

[331] See esp A. Harel and G. Parchomovsky, 'On Hate & Equality' (1999) 109(3) *YLJ* 507–39.

[332] s 60.

[333] As given by pt III of the Act. To date evidence suggests that there have been few complaints with no success.

[334] See e.g. *Wagga Wagga Aboriginal Action Group v Eldridge* (1995) (EOC 92–701); *Patten v State of NSW* (1995) (EOT 91/92) (21 January 1997).

[335] Fine Australian Dollars 10,000/six months' imprisonment—individual; 100,000—corporation. Attorney-General must consent—four cases—prosecution never recommended.

[336] s 18D lists the exemptions as follows; (a) in the performance, exhibition or distribution of an artistic work; or (b) in the course of any statement, publication, discussion or debate made or held for any genuine academic, artistic or scientific purpose or any other genuine purpose in the public interest; or (c) in making or publishing: (i) a fair and accurate report of any event or matter of public interest; or (ii) a fair comment on any event or matter of public interest if the comment is an expression of a genuine belief held by the person making the comment.

Western Australia does not have a specific regime of protection against hate speech, instead arguing that this falls within the remit of the *Criminal Code 1913* as amended in 1989, which regulates acts of racial hatred, a response to poster campaigns.[337] The extent of the crime consists of the possession of material that is threatening or abusive with intent to publish, distribute, or display such material in order that racial hatred can be instigated, promoted, or increased.[338]

In Queensland the hate speech provision is contained in section 124A of the *Anti-Discrimination Act 1991*.[339] This section states that 'persons must not, by advocating racial or religions hatred or hostility, incite unlawful discrimination of another contravention of the act'.[340] The penalties for such action are fines, though corporations violating the section face higher sanction than individuals.[341] In South Australia the offence of racial hatred and stigmatization is included in the *Racial Vilification Act 1996*.[342] While this Act gives hate speech a higher profile and contains higher penalties than other provincial legislation,[343] the requirement of the Attorney-General's consent has restricted the extent to which the Act has been used. Finally, among the states and territories that have any provision for hate speech, the Australian Capital Territories has three sections in its *Discrimination Act 1991* that closely mirror the New South Wales Act.[344]

In a thorough though now dated commentary on Australian regimes for protection against racial vilification, McNamara makes some important points on the need to seek an appropriate balance in regulating hate speech. This will require: posing the question as to the advantages and disadvantages of engaging criminal law as opposed to civil law models; identifying the difficulty in ascertaining the threshold that ought to be put in place for prosecutions; and accepting the importance of creating a transparent process that is not inundated with complaints, while at the same time ensuring that genuine complaints are processed adequately.[345]

The collective experience from Australia would seem to indicate that it remains difficult to gain criminal prosecutions for hate speech or racial vilification. This could be attributed to a number of factors, including the current design of the legislation with its high thresholds, the inevitable bias in society that prevents serious consideration of such types of activities as crimes, and the general malaise

[337] See McNamara (n194) 222–58.

[338] McNamara ibid 227. Also the penalty deemed payable by the Act is as follows: for summary offence $2,000 and/or six months' imprisonment; for an indictable offence—two years' imprisonment. To date there have been no prosecutions under this provision.

[339] Sub-section (1) of this art states: (1) A person must not, by a public act, incite hatred towards, serious contempt for, or severe ridicule of, a person or group of persons on the ground of the race, religion, sexuality, or gender identity of the person or members of the group.

[340] s 126, *Racial Discrimination Act 1991*.

[341] The penalty is as follows: $3,500 (individual) 17,000 (corporation).

[342] (No 92) 1996.

[343] Once again the penalties are distinguished between individuals: Aus $5,000 and corporations Aus $25,000.

[344] ss 65–76 *Discrimination Act 1991*.   [345] McNamara (n 194) 304–13.

and lack of confidence on the part of litigants over the probability of receiving a fair hearing. In addition, the onerous requirements of the legislation (for example, the requirement of the Attorney-General's consent), the technical difficulty of being able to prove a case of incitement in a court of law,[346] and the general fear of political or social repercussions, render the avenue less than useful.[347] There is also the fear among applicants that such actions could provide persons with a platform from which to advocate racially discriminatory views to the wider community.[348]

2.3.2.5 *Criminal Justice*

There are two specific elements to an examination of the effect of criminal justice on indigenous Australians: the high proportion of those from outside the majority within the criminal justice system and the existence of a *sui generis* system that makes a case for *lex specialis* over criminal justice.

In the 1970s Senator Neville Bonner, concerned with the extent to which aboriginal peoples and other islanders were receiving a fair trial, sought to introduce a private member's bill into the Senate entitled *Aborigines and Islanders (Admissibility of Confessions) Bill*.[349] The Bill sought to regulate the manner in which police were allowed to question Aborigines, Torres Strait Islanders, and Pacific Islanders.[350] Its main thrust was that confessional evidence obtained through questioning ought to be excluded unless in accordance with clearly enumerated procedures. Envisaged as applying to the Commonwealth and the states, the Bill was designed as an extension of the statutory and common law rules

---

[346] For general reading on this issue and especially for an interesting echo of how the issue has historically been tackled in the United States of America, see M.T. Gibson, 'The Supreme Court & Freedom of Expression From 1791 to 1917' (1986) 55 *FOLR* 263.

[347] This is particularly true under the Howard government: there is documented evidence of a belief among leading NGOs that criticism of the government would lead to indirect sanctions. See Sarah Maddison, Richard Denniss, and Clive Hamilton, 'Silencing Dissent: NGOs and Australian Democracy' Canberra: The Australian Institute, Discussion Paper No 65, June 2004, available at: <http://www.tai.org.au> [last accessed 1 August 2008]. This issue is also reflected in the *Report of the Special Rapporteur on Adequate Housing as a Component of the Right to an Adequate Standard of Living*, Miloon Kothari, Mission to Australia 31 July to 15 August 2006 UN doc A/HRC/4/18/Add.2 (11 May 2007) at p 30 paras 114–19.

[348] Notwithstanding this several cases have been raised which include: *Australian Capital Television v Commonwealth* (1992) 177 CLR 106; *Nationwide News v Wills* (1992) 177 CLR 1; *Stephens v West Australian Newspapers* (1994) 182 CLR 211; *Theophanous v Herald and Weekly Times* (1994) 182 CLR 104; *Langer v Commonwealth* (1996) 186 CLR 302; *Muldowney v South Australia* (1996) 186 CLR 352; *McGinty v Western Australia* (1996) 186 CLR 140; *Levy v Victoria* (1997) 189 CLR 579; *Lange v ABC* (1997) 189 CLR 520 and *Kruger v Commonwealth* (1997) 146 ALR 126. For more reading on the issue, see the host of Australian Human Rights Law journal articles—as well as N. Aroney, *Freedom of Speech in the Constitution* (Australia: The Centre for Independence Studies, Policy Monograph 40, 1998).

[349] For more on this issue, see Greg Lyons, 'The Portland Case: Onus and another v Alcoa of Australia Ltd' (1981) *ALB* 14, 1(1) at 9.

[350] For a general discussion of the Bill and its effect, see Neil Rees, 'Police Questioning of Aborigines and Islanders: The Bonner Bill' (1981) *ALB* 1 available at <http://www.austlii.edu.au/au/journals/AboriginalLB/1981/5.html> [last accessed 31 March 2008].

governing police interrogation. When the Bill was first introduced in 1976 (it was subsequently reintroduced on two further occasions), Senator Bonner stated that:

... the special need experienced by Aboriginals and Islanders in respect of oral and written confessions springs out of a real difficulty they experience when conversing in English; a real ignorance as to their civil rights; a real ignorance of the law; and a different set of social values.[351]

The Bill provided that a confession would not be admissible if it was not obtained voluntarily, if there were doubts over whether the confessor fully understood the effect of the confession at the time it was made, and if procedural safeguards were not followed. The safeguards envisaged were nuanced, and depended on the nature of the offence. The general rule was articulated as follows:

When an Aborigine is under restraint in respect of 'an offence', there is to be no interrogation unless s/he has been:

(i)   informed that s/he is under 'restraint' and told the nature of the offence;
(ii) given the standard caution; and
(iii) informed that communication may be made with a friend or relative.[352]

It is clear that despite the over-representation of indigenous Australians and minorities in the criminal justice system, criminologists have not devoted adequate attention towards understanding the problem and appropriate steps have not been taken to ensure its rectification.[353] A study by Smandych, Lincoln, and Wilson is a notable exception, and the authors highlight:

... in Australia, the treatment of aboriginal people in the criminal justice system at both the state and the federal level has long been investigated. The Australian Law Reform Commission (1986) examined the possible use of customary law methods as a measure of reducing overrepresentation of Aboriginal people in arrest and imprisonment statistics. More recently, public concern about the number of deaths of Aborigines held in police and prison custody culminated in the *National Report of the Royal Commission into Aboriginal Deaths in Custody* (1991).[354]

The greater politicization of aboriginal issues means that there is more attention on such problems than in the past.[355] The authors point to some factors that may contribute towards the over-representation of Aboriginals and other vulnerable groups in the criminal justice system of Australia, including: racist bias; visibility; cultural factors that sit uneasily within the Anglo-Celtic criminal justice

---

[351]   Senate, Debates, 15 September 1976 699.
[352]   Rees (n 350).
[353]   Russel Smandych, Robyn Lincoln, and Paul Wilson, 'Towards a Cross-Cultural Theory of Aboriginal Culture: A Comparative Study of the Problem of Aboriginal Overrepresentation in the Criminal Justice Systems of Canada and Australia' (1993) 3 *ICJR* 1–24 at 2.
[354]   ibid.
[355]   Through politically active groups calling for greater accountability, see ibid 4.

system such as linguistic challenges and different interpretations of right to silence; legal factors, including the significant incursion of laws into aboriginal lifestyles; extralegal factors, such as value judgments of police; and overpolicing of the communities.[356]

The more recent trend towards seeking to correct the treatment of indigenous Australians started with the work of *The Royal Commission into Aboriginal Deaths in Custody* (RCIADIC), established in 1987. This Commission produced its report in 1991, which was met with widespread criticisms.[357] One of the major findings that emerged in the report was that the proportion of Aborigines in police and prison custody was of a similar proportion to the aboriginal deaths in each case.[358] Smandych *et al* highlight the raw figures in the report,[359] computing them to show that aboriginal adults were twenty-three times more likely to die in police custody than their non-aboriginal counterparts. This led another author to emphasize that were the same rate to have been maintained for non-aboriginal adults, it would have seen 8,500 custody deaths in the period under study, and would no doubt have been the cause for a significant outcry.[360]

The inter-sectionality of ethnicity and gender in the criminal justice system is another major concern in Australia. Stubbs and Tolmis examine battered woman syndrome (BWS) and argue that in looking at the intersection between race, culture, and BWS, it is important to take into account the extent to which the cultural context informs the positions of both the protagonist and the victim.[361] They cite a number of cases that arise in this context,[362] though few appear to cite ethnic or racial background as a factor. *R v Kina* [1993][363] is something of an exception in this regard,[364] where the authors highlight:

...the incidence of homicide and patterns of homicide vary substantially by race/ ethnicity and gender. This issue is particularly important in Australia where empirical evidence indicates that Aboriginal people are significantly over-represented as victims

---

[356] ibid 9.   [357] ibid 3–5.   [358] ibid 5.

[359] 75 aboriginal deaths per 100,000 of the adult aboriginal population as compared to 3.3 non-aboriginal deaths per 100,000 non-aboriginal adult population.

[360] Robert Tickner, 'Government response to the final report of the RCIADIC' (1992) *Aboriginal and Islander Health Worker J* 16–19.

[361] Julie Stubbs and Julia Tolmie, 'Falling Short of the Challenge? A Comparative Assessment of the Australian Use of Expert Evidence on the Battered Woman Syndrome' (1999) *23 MULR* 709–48 at 745.

[362] *R v Hickey* (Unreported, Supreme Court of New South Wales, Slattery AJ, 14 April 1992); *R v Secretary* (1996) 5 NTLR 96; *R v Muy Ky Chhay* (1994) 72 A Crim R 1; *R v Gadd* (Unreported, Supreme Court of Queensland, Maynihan J, 27 March 1995); *R v Terare* (Unreported, Supreme Court of New South Wales, Levine J, 20 April 1995); *R v Simon* (Unreported, Supreme Court of New South Wales, Bruce J, 21 July 1995); *R v Varagnolo* (Unreported, Supreme Court of New South Wales, McInerney J, 21 March 1996); *R v Buzzacott* (Unreported, Supreme Court of South Australia, Bollen J, 21 July 1993) and *R v Gilbert* (Unreported, Supreme Court of Western Australia, Scott J, 4 November 1993).

[363] (Unreported, Supreme Court of Queensland, Court of Appeal, Fitzgerald, P, Davies and McPherson JJA, 29 November 1993).

[364] Also see *Runjanjic v Kontinnen* (1991) 56 SASR 114 and *R v Osland* (1998) 150 ALR 170.

and offenders in homicide generally and in intimate homicides... [a cited Report][365] found that Aboriginal victimisation rates were 10 times higher for women and 8 times higher for men, and that Aboriginal homicide offence rates were 14 times higher for men and 13 times higher for women. In most homicides, victims and offenders shared the same racial backgrounds... [and] 51 percent of all Aboriginal homicide victims were killed by a spouse as compared with only 21 percent for 'white' Australians.[366]

In addition, aboriginal women were found to be particularly vulnerable owing to their isolation, the violence directed against them and their children,[367] and their lack of resources in seeking remedies. The authors report that their experience in conducting field research inevitably brought out a disproportionate number of cases involving aboriginal women, most of who continued to live in difficult and isolated circumstances.[368] It led them to conclude:

Race and ethnicity may mark out different life circumstances, experiences and options for women. Race and ethnicity may also be associated with particular stereotyped understandings of women.[369]

While crediting Kirby J as being the first Australian judge to acknowledge the relevance of race and ethnicity in the context of defending battered women who kill their abusers,[370] the authors suggest that his perspective was nonetheless limited by a stereotyped understanding of battered women as passive.[371] Instead, they believe that while it is true that women from different cultural backgrounds react differently to violence, it is necessary to understand:

...how the intersection of their gender and their identity might impact on the range of social options available to them in coping with the violence, and might also affect the way in which they are constructed and their behaviour is understood by the legal system.[372]

2.4 Remedies

2.4.1 The Courts

The role of Australian courts in overturning the legal fiction of *terra nullius* has been noted. However, in doing so, the courts merely arrived at a position that other jurisdictions had reached a long time ago. Furthermore, even in *Mabo*,

---

[365] Heather Strang, *Homicides in Australia 1990–1991* (Canberra: Australian Institute of Criminology, 1992) —data for the work was collected on the basis of 'racial appearance' and thus could be inaccurate to an extent.

[366] Stubbs and Tolmie (n 361) 746.

[367] Pam Greer, 'Aboriginal Women and Domestic Violence in New South Wales' in Julie Stubbs (ed), *Women, Male Violence and the Law* (Sydney: Institute of Criminology, 1994) 64.

[368] Stubbs and Tolmie (n 361) 746–7.   [369] ibid 747.

[370] *Osland* (1998) 150 ALR 170, 213–14.

[371] Stubbs and Tolmie (n 361) 747.

[372] ibid 748.

some prejudices show through clearly. Dorsett finds that one of these is the pre-ponderant importance of agriculture, recognized by Brennan J in *Mabo*:

> [The European powers] recognized the sovereignty of the respective European Nations over the territory of 'backward peoples' and, by such State practice, permitted the acquisition of sovereignty over such territory by occupation rather than by conquest. Various justifications for the acquisition of sovereignty over territory of 'backward peoples' were advanced. The benefits of Christianity and European civilization had been seen as a sufficient justification from medieval times. Another justification for the application of the theory of *terra nullius* to inhabited territory...was that new territories could be claimed by occupation if the land were uncultivated, for the Europeans have a right to bring land into production if they were left uncultivated by the indigenous inhabitants.[373]

Dorsett suggests that the intrusion of agriculture into law in the colonizing period was due to influential writers of the time, who, while theorizing on the basis of their particular experiences, remained determined to generate theories with general application.[374] Although Australian courts in *Mabo* abandoned the 'fiction' of *terra nullius*,[375] the doctrine of 'occupation' per se remained part of their interpretation.[376]

Despite the court's positive view of native title,[377] it nonetheless asserted that indigenous sovereignty was non-justiciable in domestic law and more a question of politics than of law.[378] This was echoed immediately after in *Isabel Coe (on behalf of the Wirajduri Tribe) v Commonwealth*.[379] The Wiradjuri Tribe's assertion of exclusive sovereignty since time immemorial over contested lands was rejected by Chief Justice Mason on the grounds that the sovereignty argument 'tainted proceedings' due to an improper political purpose. This argument is premised on the difficulty of adjudicating on the acquisition of Australia by the British, which, as an act of state, could be construed to be immune from legal challenge.[380]

---

[373] *Mabo (No 2)* (n 36) at 32–3. It needs to be asserted that this merely echoed the famous judgment of Marshall CJ in *Johnson v Macintosh* where he described Indians as '... ... fierce savages, whose occupation was war, and whose subsistence was drawn chiefly from the forest. To leave them in possession of their country, was to leave the country a wilderness; to govern them as a distinct peoples was impossible. *Johnson and Graham's Lessee v M'Intosh* 21 UK (8 Wheat) 543 (1823) at 590.

[374] Thus Dorsett shows how the relevance of Locke's view could be traced to a utilitarian argument over the economics emphasizing the importance of agriculture, and how Vattel's de-coded these values into *jus gentium*. See Dorsett (n 39).

[375] Otto (n 12).

[376] In *Coe v Commonwealth (No 1)* (n 30) 118, 137, Murphy J stated the legal doctrine of occupation: Occupation was originally a legal means of peaceably acquiring sovereignty over territory otherwise than by secession or conquest. It was a cardinal condition of valid occupation that the territory should be *terra nullius*—a territory belonging to no-one—at the time of the act alleged to constitute occupation.

[377] And effectively 'rewriting Australian history' in the words of Otto (n 12) 66.

[378] See *Mabo (No 2)* (n 36) 50–11.   [379] (1993) 68 ALJR 110.

[380] Otto (n 12) in fn 66.

As Otto points out, the notion of sovereignty itself is contested, with Australia's indigenous peoples having a unique perspective on what this constitutes.[381] Thus *Mabo* created 'an overdue impetus for a post-colonial reconceptualization of the Australian nation'.[382] In the decade and a half since *Mabo*, recognition of indigenous peoples' right to traditional land has undergone significant change, as discussed above in the decisions of *Ward*[383] and *Yorta Yorta*.[384] The fundamental question that the courts appear to have wrestled with, post-*Mabo*, is how native title fits into the regime of Australian property law.[385]

A further important point is the role the courts have played in the recognition or denial of the existence of indigenous law. An analysis of the courts' track record shows four clear epochs:

a) Early Phase (1820–1841): a number of decisions addressed aboriginal law and determined that disputes between aboriginal peoples would be governed under customary law;[386]

b) Sovereignty and Laws of Crown deemed to apply (1847–1979): two cases in particular held that Australia was to be considered a settled colony of the British Crown and thereby the only law that could be applicable to disputes upon the territory of Australia were those made by, or in the name of, the British Crown;[387]

c) Re-opening of the question of sovereignty (1979–1992): this phase was instigated by Paul Coe's failed challenge on behalf of the aboriginal community and nation of Australia. The case questioned the sovereignty of the Crown as being 'contrary to the existing rights, privileges, interests and entitlements of the aboriginal peoples'.[388] The acknowledgment of uncertainty by virtue of how sovereignty entered Australia began the claw-back process of the

[381] ibid 68–79. The author discusses the various guises of sovereignty in this section of the article.

[382] ibid 70.

[383] *Western Australia v Ward* (2002) 191 ALR 1. In fact it could be argued that the doctrine of extinguishment as developed in *Ward*, 'has played a significant role in the case law by limiting the recognitions and protections of indigenous peoples' interests'. See Strelein (n 49) 226.

[384] *Yorta Yorta* (n 217).

[385] Strelein examines these issues in some detail while also commenting on the history of the doctrine of discovery in Australia with a particular focus on the doctrine of extinguishment and its impact on the level of evidence required to prove native title. See Strelein (n 49) 225–72.

[386] *R v Ballard or Barrett*, Supreme Court of New South Wales, Forces CJ, 21 April 1829, published in the Sydney Gazette 23 April 1829; *R v Murrell and Bummaree* (Supreme Court of New South Wales, Forbes CJ, 5 February 1836, published in *Sydney Herald*, 8 February 1836); *R v Bonjon*, Supreme Court of New South Wales, Willis J, 16 September 1841, published in Port Phillip Patriot, 20 September 1841 and *R v Ballard, R v Murrell and R v Bonjon* [1998] ALR 27.

[387] The notable cases in this context are *Attorney-General (NSW) v Brown* (1847) 1 Legge 312; *Cooper v Stuart* (1899) 14 App Cas 286. This sentiment was echoed more contemporaneously in *Milirpum v Nabalco Pty Ltd (1971)* 17 FLR 141—where Blackburn J held that the laws of the Yolgnu that suggested land rights for the community were not in fact recognized in law, on the basis that such a relationship between the community and the land were not recognized by the Crown or in common law as being based upon the notion of 'property' as existed under this regime.

[388] *Coe v Commonwealth (No 1)* (n 30) and *Coe v Commonwealth (No 2)* (1993) 118 ALR 193.

previous era. The material finding was that neither the High Court nor the Privy Council had ever determined whether or how sovereignty had entered Australia, and that this would be a relevant question, especially in the context of a determination as to whether title was acquired under the Doctrine of Settlement or one of conquest;[389]

d) Overturning the legal fiction of *terra nullius* (1992): *Mabo* was the culmination of this discussion since it established that British sovereignty had entered Australia as a result of occupation or settlement,[390] but in a reversal of *Milipuram*, it held that common law in a settled colony was capable of recognizing property laws that were based on a different system of laws.[391]

While *Mabo* may have been instrumental in opening up the discussion of land rights for aboriginal communities, and indicating a shift in the constitutional framework of Australia,[392] its importance lay in the assertion of the existence of aboriginal law that had been submerged through forces of colonization. In raising this, it hinted at the complexity of such a legal regime, based on the different rules of diverse communities rather than a centrally organized, recognizable system of law across the indigenous nations.[393]

Despite developments in common law in relation to indigenous rights, including the 'sovereign obligation of nations towards indigenous persons' and a corresponding 'judicial duty to embrace ... tribal perspectives on land and national resources', this has not been effectively translated to indigenous peoples' environmental rights. This is mainly due to the fact that the courts rely heavily on 'non-indigenous forms of evidence and other proof requirements'.[394] For instance, as Manus claims, environmental rights of indigenous peoples remain unsettled despite contemporary attention, leading him to conclude that:

... the foremost factor in the survival of tribal cultures in nations with common law court systems may be the courts' willingness to accept as part of its judicial role a responsibility to both recognize and impose the sovereign obligation to understand, value and preserve the environmental interests of native populations.[395]

In *Mabo*, the court relied on common law power to define native rights,[396] where competing property interests in the Murray Islands were examined. In an antecedent to the case, the Meriam peoples' prayer in 1982 seeking a declaration that they were: (*a*) owners by custom of the territory; (*b*) holders of traditional native

---

[389] *Coe v Commonwealth (No 1)* (n 30) at 136.   [390] At 32–42.

[391] At 86–95 (Deane and Gaudron JJ).

[392] As stated by Justice Gummow in *Wik Peoples v Queensland* (1996) 187 CLR 1.

[393] As Reilly puts it: '*Mabo* is significant not only for the extent of the legal rights it recognised, but also for its acceptance of a system of Aboriginal governance that must be acknowledged and taken seriously by law' (n 37) 421.

[394] Peter Manus, 'Indigenous Peoples' Environmental Rights: Evolving Common Law Perspectives in Canada, Australia and the United States' (2008) 33 *BCEALR* 1–86 at 1.

[395] ibid 3.   [396] *Mabo v Queensland (No 2)* (n 36) 58–63.

title; and (c) holders of usufructuary rights on their territory, was rejected.[397] In 1992, faced with a similar claim, the court agreed with the tribe and determined that Australian common law recognized 'native title' which preserves the 'entitlement of the indigenous inhabitants, in accordance with their laws or customs, to their traditional lands'.[398] Howitt is critical of *Mabo* because, despite its celebration as a validation of indigenous rights, it paradoxically also defines native title as fragile and incomplete. Thus:

> Rather than recognising and creating a robust legal version of the interests and responsibilities between people and their country (native title), the High Court constructed native title as a highly circumscribed recognition space—a limited set of artefacts of customary law and aboriginal title that the British (and subsequently Australian) common law was able and obliged to recognise as 'property'.[399]

Thus for Howitt, *Mabo* reduced robust and ancient jurisdictions of the 'dreaming' in aboriginal customary law to the fragility of native title by a 'sleight-of-hand'.[400] The result was to introduce the amorphous concept of 'co-existence' and to create an abstract conceptualization of legal interests that allowed what was ostensibly a *sui generis* category to exist within the confines of established Australian property law. On this basis it could be argued that the courts have played a mixed role in the furtherance of indigenous rights in Australia, though this role has been significantly more positive in recent decades.

2.4.2 Development of Statutory Standards or a Unifying Treaty

The means of implementing human rights law in dualist states such as Australia is the passage of domestic legislation that upholds international standards that the state has agreed to, in signing and ratifying international human rights law instruments. Ever since the attempt to frame the first Australian constitution, indigenous peoples have, more often than not, been excluded from consultations that have led to policy and statute. It is also arguable that the passage of statutes has, to a certain extent, done little for indigenous peoples who continue to live under their customary law in many instances.[401] The lack of legal status has been a constant barrier restricting indigenous participation, and as a result the international legal system has not been able to grasp the nuance of the destruction to indigenous people that is wreaked by a system that treats its members more as individuals and less as members of a collective group.[402] In

---

[397] *Mabo v Queensland* (1988) 166 CLR 186.

[398] *Mabo (No 2)* (n 36) 15.

[399] Richie Howitt, 'Scales of Coexistence: Tackling the Tension Between Legal and Cultural Landscapes in Post-Mabo Australia' (2006) 6 *MQLJ* 49–64 at 51.

[400] ibid.

[401] e.g. see Paul Bann, 'Customary Adoption in Torres Strait Islands; Towards Legal Recognition' (1994) 3(66) *ALB* 8.

[402] Otto (n 12) 75–6.

recent years the attempt to unravel this problem has seen an increasing focus on land rights:

Something more than property rights is involved in the settlement of the violation of indigenous territorial integrity and in acknowledgement of land use, occupation, management and spiritual association since time immemorial. For many indigenous peoples, the notion of sovereignty comes closest to the expression of a satisfactory resolution.[403]

Towards this end the real difficulty seems to lie in reframing the 'colonial creation story' that is 'grounded in racism and elitism'.[404] Fundamental to the discussion is the re-articulation of the notion of sovereignty and its composite meanings. To view sovereignty in the guise of the attribute to statehood is likely to return the discussion to a position from where no negotiation or understanding is possible.[405] A re-interpretation of sovereignty does not appear to be pressing enough for it to result in concerted action that will enhance solutions to the problems. In describing the problem in greater detail, Otto identifies the 'legal construction' of indigenous personality and that of sovereignty,[406] and suggests four means of reconciling these aims: decolonization, secession, human rights, and indigenous peoples' rights.[407] On the potential scope of legal remedies, Reilly cautions:

The law's capacity to recognise another sovereign entity is limited by the origin and extent of the law's own authority. In the concept of native title, the law managed a limited recognition of the rights derived from Indigenous law without acknowledging Indigenous sovereignty. However, native title created a different barrier to legal recognition of Indigenous governance. Native title is derived only from laws of pre-sovereignty Indigenous communities.[408]

It remains difficult to envisage how, in practical terms,[409] the unravelling of the notion of sovereignty could resolve the inevitable conflict of rights likely to arise between the indigenous and settled populations of Australia.[410] Many in the 'Reconciliation' movement within Australia have argued for the adoption of a treaty.[411] While a treaty would maintain the 'construction of indigenous

---

[403] ibid 77.   [404] ibid.   [405] ibid 79.

[406] ibid 80–4.   [407] ibid 84–92.

[408] This was established in *Yorta Yorta* (n 217) 445–7 (Gleeson CJ, Gummor, and Hayne JJ).

[409] Otto (n 12) 94, posits faith in the international system suggesting '. . . international law is also a site for contesting the social realities that it produces. . . . the international legal system is a forum for challenging dominant constructions of reality'. However, international fatigue in these types of issues is well demonstrated. In the Australian context what could have been achieved through the 'international' has already been maximized in the context of the engagement with the human rights machinery. Further change could arguably only come through domestic reconciliation.

[410] For Otto's three suggestions on this score, see ibid.

[411] On an issue of appropriate terminology the term preferred to treaty among some indigenous nations was the Yolgnu term 'makarrata'—this issue was important and was taken up by the Senate Standing Committee on Constitutional and Legal Affairs, who submitted its report 'Two Hundred Years later: A Report on the Feasibility of a Compact or "Makarrata" between the Commonwealth and Aboriginal People' (1983). Treaty is used here in line with the comparative nature of this work.

peoples as Other', it could nonetheless, if framed right, have a salutary effect on re-interpreting the notion of sovereignty and finding a common ground between politics and law. The closest point in recent history where such a treaty was possible was the commitment made (but not honoured) in a speech by then Prime Minister Hawke in 1988 at the Barunga Festival in Northern Territory.[412]

ATSIC's own paper on the treaty issue, entitled *Treaty: Let's Get it Right!*, is important in identifying what the substance of such a document could entail. Its proposed strategy is a variety of activities such as information and aware-ness campaigns, the adoption of policy framework strategies, and the creation of a treaty framework development team, with a view towards seeking con-firmation of the wishes of the aboriginal nations through a plebiscite in the first half of 2002. Rather than negotiating directly with the Commonwealth, ATSIC sought to create the framework through which discussion and debate over the treaty could be stimulated.[413] In this process, seventeen substan-tive headings were identified for action: equality, distinct characteristics and identities, self-determination, law, culture, spiritual and religious traditions, language, participation and partnerships, economics and social development, special measures, education and training, land and resources, resource devel-opment, self-government, constitutional recognition, treaties, and agreements and legislation.[414]

The arrival at a point where a treaty of co-existence and mutual respect could be signed would itself be an indicator that Australian society was at a viable pos-ition in search of a new basis of interaction between the indigenous and non-indigenous communities.

2.4.3 Protection of Sacred Places

Land is central to indigenous ideology, especially in the context of the notion of the sacred. One area where significant progress is visible is the protection of sacred places. While this is nowhere near as extensive as advocates desire, in places where there is a genuine attempt to create a regime of protection, it has worked relatively well. It could be argued that extension of this model could provide a basis through which indigenous nations could regenerate themselves unmolested, while nonetheless having the interaction necessary for the survival and flourishing of the communities themselves.[415] Poirier and Ostergren articu-late the substantive content of such a model in a comparative analysis of how states such as Australia, Russia, and the United States of America treat heritage sites, especially national parks, which tend to be located within territories where indigenous peoples live. While recognizing the host of factors that explain the

---

[412] Reilly (n 37) 418.   [413] Nettheim (2001) (n 112) 845.
[414] ibid 845–6.   [415] Poirier and Ostergren (n 10) 331.

general treatment of colonized indigenous populations,[416] the general thrust of their study suggests that the impact of policy towards the overlap between indigenous peoples' rights and protected natural areas is moving towards 'a recognition of the role that humans have played in the natural landscape'.[417] For the purpose of their analysis, they adopt the definition of a national park provided by the International Union for the Conservation of Nature, as a place where:

> The highest competent authority of the nation, having jurisdiction over it, is vested with the responsibility to protect that area and allow visitors to enter for inspirational, educational, cultural and recreational purposes at a level which will maintain the area in a natural or near natural state.[418]

The rules of protection for these kinds of environments have traditionally treated resident indigenous populations as an 'unfortunate blight', and an 'affront to the sensibilities of tourists'.[419] In Australia national parks were created for the preservation of natural beauty rather than the protection of the heritage and territories of indigenous peoples. The earliest park in Australia is the Royal Park (now a Sydney suburb), established in 1879.[420]

The applicable rules for the protection of open spaces and traditional ways of life at the international level (seeking to guarantee autonomy of a different kind), consists of the *Zaire Resolution on the Protection of Traditional Ways of Life 1975*,[421] and the *World Heritage Conservation Act 1983* which Australia was one of the first to sign and one of the only states to have put in place specific legislation to protect World Heritage Areas.[422] Poirer and Ostergreen argue that World Heritage status has clear advantages for indigenous peoples, since, besides protection against encroachment, it guards against actions that may be contrary to the management plans of the applicable areas.[423] Australia has fourteen World Heritage sites with

---

[416] ibid. These interacting factors and attitudes are identified as spanning 'politics, sociocultural norms and economics'.

[417] ibid 332. The authors point to the tense relation between indigenous peoples and the articulation of environmental issues. There is often an assumption that indigenous peoples live in harmony with the environment. While it is true they have not contributed to the onset of climate change and global warming, the assumption that their lifestyles are in harmony with nature is simplistic. For more on this interesting issue, see Jared Diamond, *Guns, Germs and Steel* (New York: W.W. Norton, 1997).

[418] Poirier and Ostergren (n 10) 333.

[419] ibid. The authors highlight the role played by the famous essay by George Perkins Marsh entitled 'Man and Nature'. See George P. Marsh, 'The Earth as modified by Human Action; A Last Revision of man and nature' (1885) cited at p 333 fn 5.

[420] ibid 334. This was done soon after the declaration of Yellowstone National Park in the USA as a park (the oldest such park in the world).

[421] Resolutions of the 12th General Assembly of the IUCN (18 September 1975), International Union for the Conservation of Nature and Natural Resources, 6 IUCN Bulletin, Special Supplement 1 (November 1975).

[422] For a clear indication of the importance of the issue of National Parks in Australian law and politics, see David Lawrence, *Kakadu: The making of a National Park* (Carlton South, Victoria: Miegunyah Press, 2000) esp 216.

[423] Poirier and Ostergren (n 10) 342.

the most prominent being *Uluru-Kata Tjuta* (Ayers Rock and the Olgas) and
Kakadu National Park (both Northern Territory) and the Great Barrier Reef.[424]
Levels of protection have risen owing to the legal expertise among indigenous
populations and the emerging activism of non-governmental organizations advocating for indigenous and environmental rights.[425]

The issue of native title in natural parks has yet to be raised before the courts;[426]
as it currently stands, there appears to be nothing in Australian law specifically
enhancing or diminishing claims to native title within national parks. Thus the
applicable regime remains the controversial *Racial Discrimination Act 1975*, which
could be read alongside the *Australian National Parks and Wildlife Conservation
Act 1975*.[427]

A brief exposé of three key National Parks illustrates the existing model:

1. *Uluru-Kata Tjuta*, (meaning 'gathering place' in the local Anangu language)
   close to the geographic centre of Australia, consists of approximately 800
   square miles and attracts over 250,000 visitors a year. It is considered to
   represent the essence of what is referred to as 'Dreamtime creation myth-
   ology' in local aboriginal culture. The land was returned to the Anangu
   people in 1985, and leased back to the *Australian Nature Conservation
   Agency* with conditions in keeping with the *World Heritage Convention* and
   the *Zaire Resolution* guidelines.[428] The management board of the Park consists of six Anandu members selected by the local leadership, the Director
   of Parks Australia, a nominated member appointed by the *Federal Minister
   of Tourism*, and a scientist appointed by the Australian National Parks and
   Wildlife Service;[429]

2. *Witjara National Park* covers more than 4,000 square miles of territory associated with the lower Southern Arrernte and Wangkangurru people, who
   formed the Irrwanyere Aboriginal Corporation in 1989. It has a similar management structure to *Uluru-Kata Tjuta* and seeks to uphold the principle that
   aboriginal customs must be part of the management plan protected through
   some form of tenure over the park;[430]

---

[424] Such heritage sites are protected by the regime entitled *Indigenous and Traditional Peoples
and Protected Areas* which consists of a set of guidelines that are indicative of best practice in the
enhancement of protected areas as compiled by the IUCN-World Conservation Union. See World
Conservation Union, Javier Beltran (ed), *Indigenous & Traditional Peoples and protected Areas:
Guidelines and Case Studies* (Gland, Switzerland: IUCN Gland, Switzerland and Cambridge, UK
and WWF International, 2000).
[425] See Poirier and Ostergren (n 10) 343.
[426] For more on this see Beth Ganz, 'Indigenous peoples and Land Tenure: An Issue of Human
Rights and Environmental Protection' (1996) 9 *GIELR* 173.
[427] Poirier and Ostergren (n 10) 345.
[428] For an elaboration of the mythological connections of this particular area, see Anna Voigt
and Neville Drury, *Wisdom from the Earth* (Boston: Shambhala Publishers, 1997). For information
pertaining to contemporary issues surrounding the park, see Uluru-Kata Tjuta National Park,
'*Informational Handout*'.
[429] See Poirier and Ostergren (n 10) 346.   [430] ibid.

3. *Kakadu National Park* is the largest of Australia's national parks consisting of over 12,000 square miles and attracting over 200,000 visitors. It is described as an important example of the complex nature of joint management policies with parts of the park aboriginal owned, and others held under lease. It has a similar management board structure to the other parks, though there is also additional remuneration through the payment of an annual rent and 25 per cent of various fees collected (gate receipts, fees, penalties, etc.).[431]

Poirier and Ostergeen make it clear that the literature and evidence throughout the world suggests that native access to resources is generally prohibited.[432] It could be argued that Australian indigenes have had considerably greater success than their counterparts elsewhere in the world.

2.4.4 Autonomy (Indigenous Governance/ Federalism)

While highlighting the importance of ensuring that indigenous governance remains in the forefront of the discussion towards the amelioration of indigenous peoples' rights in Australia, the difficulty of the plurality of traditions among the various aboriginal nations makes any unified approach impossible.[433] There is also no clear determination of what the indigenous nations of Australia collectively want.[434] It has been argued that the focus on formal recognition of indigenous rights through the court system with an overt focus on concepts such as sovereignty and self-determination have done much to raise legal and political aspirations within the community.[435] Conversely, few of these aspirations have been met through the formalistic processes engaged. As a result, while indigenous aspirations for recognition involve a formal challenge to the legal basis for the British assertion of sovereignty over Australia tracing back to 1788,[436] there has been little gain in this direction, even though the allegiance to 'alternative sources of law'[437] has been acknowledged in Australian jurisprudence.[438] The federal nature of Australia ought to have made it easier to engage indigenous autonomy claims. Federalism in this context needs to be defined as a philosophy '... according to which relations between two or more groups are organised on the basis of a combination of the principles of centralisation,

---

[431] ibid 347.
[432] ibid 350. Also see Patrick West and Stevin Brechin (eds), *Resident Peoples and National Parks* (Arizona: University of Arizona Press, 1991).
[433] Reilly (n 37) 407.
[434] ibid. Reilly also points to an ambitious project being undertaken by the Centre for Aboriginal Economic Policy Research (CAEPR).
[435] ibid 408.
[436] As discussed in *Coe v Commonwealth (No 1)* (1979) 24 ALR and *Coe v Commonwealth (No 2)* (1993) 118 ALR 193.
[437] Reilly (2006) 408.
[438] *NSW v The Commonwealth* (1975) 133 CLR 337 (esp at 338, Gibbs J) and the more famous *Mabo (No 2) v Queensland* (1992) 175 CLR (esp 31–2, Brennan J).

non-centralisation and power sharing'.[439] Tully refines this further in the context of indigenous peoples:

Free and equal peoples can mutually recognise the autonomy and sovereignty of each other in certain spheres and share jurisdiction in others without incorporation or subordination. This is a form of treaty federalism.[440]

The crux of the debate over land rights that has formed such a major part of this chapter is that Australian indigenous identity, like its settled counterpart, is territorially based, and as a result, co-habitation is reduced to a competition over land.[441] Another viewpoint is that some form of autonomy, or, 'indigenous governance', has existed in Australia since time immemorial, but more pertinently that such governance has been recognized by the government, although not posited in such terms.[442] Reilly believes that there are advantages in negotiating self-government arrangements directly with state governments rather than relying on the centre and suggests that existing legal regimes at Commonwealth and state government level show evidence of recognition, both formally and informally, of indigenous governance.[443] He argues that official recognition of indigenous governance remains central to addressing the plight of indigenous Australians, eliminating 'distracting politics' and creating space through which institutional arrangements can be made for effective co-existence.[444]

The question of reparations, especially where an 'international wrong' has occurred, needs to be addressed.[445] There are important arguments against any engagement with reparation for historical violations.[446] The scale and systematic

---

[439] Eghosa Osaghae, 'Federalism in Comparative Perspective' (1997) 16 *Politeia* 1.

[440] James Tully, 'The Struggles of Indigenous Peoples for and of Freedom' in Duncan Ivison, Paul Patton, and Will Sanders (eds), *Political Theory and the Rights of Indigenous Peoples* (Cambridge: Cambridge University Press, 2002).

[441] Reilly (n 37) 413.

[442] ibid 413–15. Also see <http://www.nit.com.au/Opinion/story.aspx?id=7223> also 'CoAG: A Black Hole of Government Approach' *National Indigenous Times* (10 November 2005) [last accessed 25 March 2009].

[443] ibid 415–22. This recognition of indigenous governance in legislation and policy can be gleaned in several different events and mechanisms; The attempt to fight for equality: Freedom Ride 1965 in Western NSW; Pastoral Workers' Strike, Newcastle Waters; Wave Hill Cattle Stations Strike Northern Territory; some attempts to isolate and identify Indigenous specific rights: claim for land, 1927; representation of Aboriginal on land claim board; creation of advisory board consisting of aboriginals—and settled; and also the specific recognition through legislative mechanisms that created Indigenous corporations and land councils. For more on these issues also see Ann Curthoys, *Freedom Ride: A Freedom Rider Remembers* (Sydney: Allen and Unwin, 2002); see generally Attwood and Markus (n 19); *Aboriginal Councils and Associations Act 1976* (Cth) since repealed through the Corporations (Aboriginal and Torres Strait Islander) Bill 2005 (Cth).

[444] ibid 423.

[445] See André Nollkaemper's analysis of the impact of an 'international wrong' in 'Internationally Wrongful Acts in Domestic Courts' (2007) 101 *AJIL* 760–99.

[446] Jeremy Waldron, 'Superseding historic Injustice' (1992) 103 *Ethics* 4. Waldron's central argument is that reparation in the present for past violations fail to take into account the necessary disjuncture between the past and the present. He suggests that reparation based on past conditions will simply result in harm to people with competing interests in the present.

nature of the violation of Australian indigenous rights, and the extent to which they have been reduced to an existence close to subsistence as a direct consequence of actions undertaken by the state through the guise of law, suggests that some reparatory mechanisms are needed. At the very least there should be a *lex specialis* seeking to enshrine specific protection and promotion of indigenous rights. Another possible remedy would be to guarantee indigenous governance, though this meets with difficult, though arguably not insurmountable, hurdles on such issues as the degree of independence of interlocutors and the determination of indigenous communities.[447]

2.4.5 Human Rights Law as a basis for Equality and Non-Discrimination

Since Australia does not have a Bill of Rights some have advocated the passage of something akin to a 'Commonwealth Charter of Espoused Rights and Freedoms', passed as an ordinary statute in Canberra.[448] This is perceived as applying primarily to Commonwealth actions and legislation and would not be able to address the significant rights violations that take place at state level. In addition, such legislation could be overturned by the passage of subsequent legislation, thus robbing it of stability.[449] Examples of such regimes from elsewhere suggest they may be of limited effectiveness, especially where political stakes, in the context of indigenous land rights for instance, are so high.[450]

One partial success story in terms of the upholding of cultural rights was the appeal lodged against a decision handed down by Brooking J, before the Supreme Court of Victoria, by the *Victorian Aboriginal Legal Service* on behalf of Sandra Onus and Christina Frankland, two Gunditj-Mara people. The plaintiffs sought to restrain the construction company, Alcoa from damaging or interfering with aboriginal relics on the site of a proposed aluminium smelter at Point Danger, near Portland in south-western Victoria. Their argument relied on section 21 of the *Archaeological and Aboriginal Relics Preservation Act 1972* (Vic.), which makes it a criminal offence to wilfully or negligently deface, damage, or interfere with a relic. Fearing Alcoa's construction works would contravene this section, the

---

[447] For a general explanation and understanding of the Australian federal system especially the relationship between the centre and the states, and also for commentary on the seminal case in the area, the *Tasmania Dam Case, Commonwealth v Tasmania* (1983) 158 CLR 1, see Brian R. Opeskin and Donald R. Rothwell (eds), *International Law & Australian Federalism* (Melbourne: Melbourne University Press, 1997).

[448] 'Reconstituting Australia without a Bill of Rights'.

[449] For a general discussion of these issues see the various contributions contained in 'The 1998 Constitutional Convention: an Experiment in Popular Reform' *UNSWLJ* Vol 4, No 2. The precedent cited for such action is the manner in which the Racial Discrimination Act 1975 was overturned by subsequent Hindmarsh Bridge legislation, see above section 2.3.

[450] See Castellino and Domínguez Redondo (n 109) for the extent to which a similar body (albeit more focused on minorities) set up in Singapore to scrutinize legislation had a limited effect and was in effect only a rubber-stamping process for legislation.

Australia

plaintiffs sought an interlocutory injunction. Their principal concern was to ensure continued access for Gunditj-Mara people to land which belonged to their ancestors by tradition, and to preserve the relics and sacred sites on the land. Brooking J ruled against the plaintiffs' standing,[451] refusing the plaintiffs' right to private action, and dismissing the claim that the plaintiffs would suffer special damage if Alcoa contravened section 21 in relation to a relic on the proposed development site. The aboriginal appellants argued non-economic interest standing, suggesting that this was sufficient 'special interest' to generate *locus standi*.[452] The potential engagement of public interest litigation of this kind may become an option for rights-based claims of indigenous Australians in the future.

There has been considerable engagement with the United Nations system in the protection of human rights in Australia.[453] This engagement has focused in recent years on the rights of indigenous Australians, but has also seen significant commentary on the rights of migrants, immigrants, refugees, and asylum seekers.[454] The state has at times been robust in defending itself against criticism

---

[451] Citing as authority the High Court's decision in *Australian Conservation Foundation Inc v Commonwealth of Australia and ors* (1980) 28 ALR 257.

[452] Lyons (n 349).

[453] See particularly the UNCERD finding concluding observation 18 March 1999...NTA— 'discriminates against indigenous title holders by validating past acts, extinguishing native title, upgrading primacy production and restricting the right to negotiate'... 'wind back protections of indigenous title offered in *Mabo*'...also particularly highlights lack of participation.

[454] Australia has had more than its share of scrutiny by the special procedures of the United Nations. Of particular note are the following reports, which all point to a critical approach to the Howard government's various actions: Report of the Special Rapporteur on Adequate Housing as a Component of the Right to an Adequate Standard of Living, Miloon Kothari, Mission to Australia 31 July to 15 August 2006 UN doc A/HRC/4/18/Add.2 (11 May 2007); Report of the Working Group on Arbitrary Detention Visit to Australia 24 May to 6 June 2002, UN doc E/CN.4/2003/8/ Add.2 of 24 October 2002, 1; Report of the Special Rapporteur on the independence of judges and lawyers, Leandro Despouy UN doc A/HRC/4/25/Add.1 (5 April 2007); The right to freedom of opinion and expression Report of the Special Rapporteur, Amebyi Ligabo UN doc A/HRC/4/27/ Add.1 (26 March 2007); Report of the Special Rapporteur on the Situation of Human Rights and Fundamental Freedoms of Indigenous People, Rodolfo Stavenhagen UN doc A/HRC/4/32/Add.1 (19 March 2007); Report of the Special Rapporteur on the Promotion and Protection of Human Rights and Fundamental Freedoms while countering Terrorism UN doc A/HRC/4/26/Add.1 (15 March 2007); Report submitted by Jorge G. Bustamante, Special Rapporteur on the Human Rights of Migrants UN doc A/HRC/4/24/Add.1 (15 March 2007); Report of the Special Rapporteur on Extrajudicial, Summary or Arbitrary Executions, Philip Alston UN doc A/HRC/4/20/Add.1 (12 March 2007); Report of the Special Rapporteur on Freedom of Religion or Belief, Asma Jahangir UN doc A/HRC/4/21/Add.1 (8 March 2007); Report of the Special Rapporteur on the Right of Everyone to the Enjoyment of the Highest Attainable Standard of Physical and Mental Health, Paul Hunt UN doc A/HRC/4/28/Add.1 (23 February 2007); Report of the Special Rapporteur on the Promotion and Protection of Human Rights and Fundamental Freedoms while countering Terrorism, Martin Scheinin UN doc A/HRC/4/26/Add.3 (14 December 2006); Extrajudicial, Summary or Arbitrary Executions: Report of the Special Rapporteur, Philip Alston UN doc E/CN.4/2006/53/Add.1 (27 March 2006); Report of the Special Representative of the Secretary-General, Hina Jilani UN doc E/CN.4/2006/95/Add.1 (22 March 2006); Torture and Other Cruel, Inhuman or Degrading Treatment or Punishment Report of the Special Rapporteur, Manfred Nowak UN doc E/CN.4/2006/6/Add.1 (21 March 2006); Report of the Special Rapporteur on the Situation of Human Rights and Fundamental Freedoms of Indigenous People, Rodolfo Stavenhagen UN doc E/CN.4/2006/78/Add.1 (18 January 2006); Report of the

by UN treaty-based and charter-based monitoring bodies, creating some difficulties at the international level.[455]

Conclusion

Australia has had a long and troubled history with regard to minorities and indigenous peoples. Successful accommodation of the new populations taking up residence in Australia will determine the extent to which the state continues to flourish at the international level. In the context of this transformation it is crucial that questions over the accommodation of difference are at the forefront in Australian society. It could be argued that a significant component of its difficulties have stemmed from the myth of the creation of the Australian state in *terra nullius*. The Rudd government's apology to the indigenous nations indicates a willingness to acknowledge past violations against indigenous Australians. Greater legal entitlements from a range of available remedies must be explored.

A worrying trend from a historical perspective is that on each occasion in Australian history where the state has recognized a component of indigenous rights, the backlash from society has been significant enough to sweep away some of the gains from that recognition. More than anything else, this indicates that a true reconciliation in Australia is only possible after a society-wide discussion about the nature of the future of Australia, rather than through the imposition of laws and statutes. This is a debate that needs to be engaged by all components of Australian society.

Special Rapporteur on Adequate Housing as a component of the Right to an Adequate Standard of Living, Miloon Kothari UN doc E/CN.4/2006/41/Add.1 (23 December 2005); Opinions adopted by the Working Group on Arbitrary Detention, UN doc E/CN.4/2006/7/Add.1 (19 October 2005); Report of the Special Rapporteur on the Situation of Human Rights and Fundamental Freedoms of Indigenous People, Rodolfo Stavenhagen UN doc E/CN.4/2005/88/Add.1 (16 February 2005); Report submitted by Ms. Gabriela Rodríquez Pizarro, Special Rapporteur on the Human Rights of Migrants UN doc E/CN.4/2005/85/Add.1 (4 February 2005); Report by Mr. Maurice Glèlè-Ahanhanzo, Special Rapporteur on Contemporary Forms of Racism, Racial Discrimination, Xenophobia and Related Intolerance, submitted pursuant to Commission on Human Rights resolution 2001/5 UN doc E/CN.4/2002/24/Add.1 (26 February 2002); Report of the Special Rapporteur on Violence against Women, its Causes and Consequences, Ms Radhika Coomaraswamy UN doc E/CN.4/2002/83/Add.1 (28 January 2002).

[455] For more on this issue, see Triggs (n 201) 372–415.

3

New Zealand

Introduction

Although similar in terms of a shared history and direct link with Australia, the manner of engagement with indigenous and minority rights in New Zealand is strikingly different.[1] New Zealand is held up globally as one of the standard-bearers for indigenous rights, with the Maori entrenched at the heart of the state structure. As we shall see in this chapter, the historic *Treaty of Waitangi*, signed in 1840, is a crucial component of New Zealand's legal system which has had the effect of enshrining the protection of Maori at the heart of the colonial state project.[2] The deliberations of the *Waitangi Tribunal*, seeking to arrive at reconciliation with the Maori, means that the status of Maori rights are constantly changing, mostly in a positive direction.[3] Though there are positive signs in

[1] For a general comparison between Australia and New Zealand on a host of issues, see: Allan Hawke, 'New Zealand and Australia: Three Years Later' (2006) 31 *NZIR* (a reflection by the outgoing Australian High Commissioner in New Zealand); also see Emmet McElhatton, 'Australia and New Zealand: Like minded Defense Partner?' (2006) 31 *NZIR*; Greg Unwin, 'Australia, New Zealand and the South Pacific' (2006) 31 *NZIR*; Bruce Billson, 'Australia and New Zealand: A Shared Purpose in the Pacific' (2006) 31 *NZIR* and Howard Barnsey, 'Protecting the Environment; A Trans-Tasman Synergy' (2003) 28 *NZIR*. Also see Gary Hawke, 'New Zealand and Australia: Moving Together or Drifting Apart?' (2002) 27 *NZIR*; Denis McLean, 'Australia and New Zealand: Two Hearts Not Beating as One' (2001) 26 *NZIR*.

[2] There has been a rich vein of writing on the Treaty of Waitangi from various perspectives. A selection of these sources, chosen for the different perspectives they offer are: Andrée Lawrey, 'Contemporary Efforts to Guarantee Indigenous Rights under International Law' (1990) 23 *VJTL* 703; Paul McHugh, *The Maori Magna Carta: New Zealand Law and the Treaty of Waitangi* (Auckland: Oxford University Press, 1991); Geoff McLay (ed), *Treaty Settlements; The Unfinished Business* (Wellington: NZ Institute of Advanced Legal Studies, 1995); Claudia Orange, *The Treaty of Waitangii* (Wellington: Allen and Unwin, 1987); K. Upson-Hooper, 'Slaying the Leviathan: Critical Jurisprudence and the Treaty of Waitangi' (1998) 28 *VUWLR* 683; Jennifer S. McGinty, 'New Zealand's Forgotten Promises: The Treaty of Waitangi' (1992) *VJTL* 681; J.G.A. Pocock, 'Law, Sovereignty and History in a Divided Culture: The Case of New Zealand and the Treaty of Waitangi' (1998) 43 *MGLJ* 481; Mason H. Durie, *Te Mana Kawanatanga: The Politics of Maori Self-Determination* (Auckland: Oxford University Press, 1998).

[3] As recently as 25 June 2008, the New Zealand government handed back nearly half a million acres of Crown forestry land in a settlement estimated to be worth NZ$ 418 million (approximately £160 million). See Kathy Marks, 'A £160m apology to the Maoris for shameful history of injustice' *The Independent Newspaper* (26 July 2008) 19; the statement of Michael Cullen, Treaty Minister is instructive: 'We are a lesser nation for failing to uphold our obligations to generations of Maori'.

relation to New Zealand's protection and promotion of the Maori, there remain controversial questions concerning minority and indigenous rights, notably for Pacific islanders and recent immigrants from different parts of Asia.[4]

As in the case of Australia, this chapter will concentrate on indigenous peoples, but will also seek to address the other significant minorities in contemporary New Zealand. In contrast to Australia, a theme that has been constantly emphasized in New Zealand is the notion of biculturalism.[5] This posits the notion of parity and partnership between the indigenous New Zealanders and the *Parekha* (New Zealanders of European origin).[6] The principle derives from the *Treaty of Waitangi*, but was inconsistently and at times maliciously misapplied.[7] In more recent years, there has been a genuine move towards rectifying some of the misapplications. The overt stress on biculturalism in a society that is increasingly multicultural has created barriers of exclusion for many of the newer groups.[8] While the most disenfranchised by this process are migrants of Asian origin, the impact on Pacific Islanders cannot be understated.[9] Docker has described the quest as 'layers of a discourse which is at one and the same time a quest for identity and a struggle for recognition',[10] which is:

... first of all, the basic question of how to negotiate the universalist, egalitarian demand of the liberal-democratic state and its foremost principle, based on the rule of law, of equal treatment of all citizens (regardless of colour, creed, sex, ethnic or geographic origin) on the one hand, and the call for recognition of cultural specificity on the other...

secondly, the realisation of competing and sometimes contradictory claims and demands for recognition put forward by different groups, presented simultaneously in the same public arena. The interests of indigenous people and of groups of immigrant minority settlers need to be acknowledged both in relation to each other as much as in relation to the majority group of settlers and their descendants. The 'post-colonial project' in countries like Australia and New Zealand implies the development of the whole

---

[4] For an examination of the contemporary sociology of New Zealand, esp on in-groups interactions, see John Docker and Gerhard Fischer, *Race, Colour and Identity in Australia and New Zealand* (NSW: University of New South Wales Press, 2000).

[5] For more on a New Zealand application of this term, see Vince Marotta, 'The Ambivalence Of Borders: The Bicultural And The Multicultural' in John Docker and Gerhard Fischer, *Race, Colour and Identity in Australia and New Zealand* (NSW: University of New South Wales Press, 2000) 177–90 esp 181.

[6] The literature on New Zealand uses a liberal sprinkling of terms drawn from the Maori language. The main purpose of this is to reflect the fact that English terms have not been adequately translated, and to avoid the possibility of misinterpretation which, as we shall see in the context of the discussion below on the Treaty of Waitangi was malicious. In keeping with the comparative nature of this book an emphasis will be placed on reliable English translations of words with Maori words where appropriate.

[7] For a detailed discussion about the treaty, its legal value, and controversies, see Ian Brownlie, *Treaties and Indigenous Peoples* (Oxford: Clarendon Press, 1992).

[8] This is discussed in detail by Marotta (n 5).

[9] *Concluding Observations of CERD*, New Zealand, UN doc CERD/C/NZL/CO/17 (15 August 2007) para 21. In this context the Committee calls on New Zealand to address this issue with some urgency.

[10] Docker and Fischer (n 5) 6.

of society as independent and free, unencumbered by the limiting influences of cultural and social hegemony exerted by the ex-colonial master society, regardless of whether these influences are the result of still-existing direct links to the former home country or whether they are the product of neocolonial conditions manufactured by the descendants of the original settlers, who are clinging to familiar colonial notions of 'home'.[11]

Docker also highlights the perceived need that these essentially post-colonial questions include a strong push for reconciliation, which for him is a '... coming to terms with a history and the continuing legacy of oppression, dispossession, discrimination, forced assimilation, of attempted genocide'.[12] The result is a series of overlapping and competing contradictions, as a 'nation' comes to terms with its identity in the modern world, and tries to understand how this reconciles with its older identities. Some contest the value of this soul-searching and reconciliation in New Zealand, based as it is on the notion of the principle of first occupancy.[13] This view is encapsulated in Waldron's analysis of what he labels 'indigeniety', suggesting that while this principle may be used to condemn colonial invasion, it could not be used to justify any reversion to the *status quo ante*.[14] In addition he suggests this focus:

... legitimises occupancy which is not disruptive of anyone else's occupancy, but it puts too much weight on history and is insufficiently sensitive to subsequent changes in circumstance and to the conditions that face us today.[15]

New Zealand is perceived as a 'staunch supporter of human rights' globally,[16] and has undertaken a committed programme seeking to understand how these values can be applied domestically.[17] At the international level, this commitment to human rights values is reflected in its signature and ratification of the principal human rights instruments,[18] and at home, to a committed policy of

---

[11] ibid.   [12] ibid.

[13] See Jeremy Waldron, 'Indigeneity? First Peoples and Last Occupancy' (2003) 1 *NZJPIL* 56–82.

[14] ibid 56.   [15] ibid.

[16] New Zealand was described as such by its Permanent Representative in Geneva in the context of a defence to the criticism of the Foreshore and Seabed Act, discussed below. See Claire Charters and Andrew Erueti, 'Report from the Inside: The CERD Committee's review of the Foreshore and Seabed Act 2004' (2005) 36 *VUWLR* 284–8.

[17] See Paul Gordon Lauren, 'A Very Special Moment in History: New Zealand's Role in the Evolution of International Human Rights' (1998) *NZIR*. Lauren narrates how by 1933 states in favour of human rights regarded New Zealand as an adversary. The dramatic about-turn in New Zealand's support for international human rights is attributed to: (*a*) the experience of World War II; and (*b*) the leadership of Peter Fraser and his colleagues Walter Nash and Carl Berendsen. For the changing nature of New Zealand, see Alan H. Grey, *Aotearoa & New Zealand: A Historical Geography* (Canterbury: Canterbury University Press, 1994), esp Vol X.

[18] New Zealand ratified CERD on 22 November 1972, the CCPR on 28 December 1978; Optional Protocol to the CCPR on 26 May 1989; the Second Optional Protocol to CCPR on 22 February 1990; the CESCR on 28 December 1978; CEDAW on 10 January 1985; Optional Protocol to CEDAW on 7 September 2000; CAT on 10 December 1989; Optional Protocol to CAT on 14 March 2007; CRC on 6 April 1993; and the Optional Protocol to CRC on Child

reconciliation with its indigenous peoples that would bring 'envious tears' to the eyes of others in a similar situation.[19]

The structure of this chapter follows the model used through this volume. Section 3.1 articulates the relevant history in order to understand the contemporary issues facing protection of indigenous and minority rights in the state. Section 3.2 identifies the groups that come within the purview of the definition of 'minority and indigenous peoples' and the range of needs these communities face. As stated, the emphasis is on the 'dominant' minority, the Maori, but to exclude other groups would be to fall foul of the same principles this book seeks to challenge. Section 3.3 portrays the range of 'rights' that currently exist in New Zealand law, drawing from the Constitution, special regimes as created through statutes, interpretation of case-law, and crucially the *Treaty of Waitangi* and its interpretation by the statutory body, the Waitangi Tribunal. This is a particularly challenging section of the chapter since it draws together varying strands of development in many different areas, including the political and the legal.[20] Section 3.4 concentrates on the remedies available in New Zealand to tackle violations of the rights of indigenous peoples and minorities. It assesses the institutional framework for rights, and reassesses the remedies needed to arrive at a regime respectful of the rights of minorities and indigenous peoples. The concluding section will offer a brief comment on the future protection of indigenous peoples and minorities in New Zealand.

3.1 History

It is usual to focus on the arrival of the colonizer to territories. While this is abhorrent owing to the credence it gives to this single event in the context of ancient communities that pre-dated colonization, it is nonetheless a necessary focal point in any examination of minority and indigenous peoples' rights.[21] The justification is simple: it is the arrival of 'settlers' and the creation of a legal regime that began the process of disempowerment. A modern analysis of human rights

Soldiers on 12 November 2001. It signed but has not ratified the Optional Protocol to CRC on the Sale of Children (7 September 2000) and the Disability Convention (30 March 2007).

[19] Waldron (n 13) 58. Waldron says this in the context of bringing tears to the eyes of even the most liberal Supreme Court judge—though the point is somewhat overstretched.

[20] One author argues that there has been a gradual shift towards bringing Maori issues back into the political realm and away from the legal realm where they can be less well controlled by the government of the day. See Kerry David, 'Self-Determination and Constitutional Change' (2000–2003) 9 *AULR* 235–47 esp 237–40.

[21] For an understanding of the calibration of the term 'native' and the expectations raised at the time of the arrival of the settlers in New Zealand, see John Miller, *Early Victorian New Zealand: a Study of Racial Tension and Social Attitudes, 1839–1852* (Oxford: Oxford University Press, 1958).

within any given state needs to focus on the actions of the government whose obligation it is to ensure access to human rights.[22]

The relevant backdrop to this discussion in New Zealand contains several key eras: i) pre-invasion society; ii) the settlement process; iii) the Treaty of Waitangi; iv) the politics of retraction of parity; v) the modern quest for social equality; and vi) the issue of immigration—which has contributed large numbers of populations and continues to change the demographics of the state. In seeking to provide an adequate yet succinct historical narrative, this section will focus on pre-invasion history, the settlement process, and the contemporary context in which the discussion of 'national' identity is framed.

3.1.1 Pre-invasion History

Much of New Zealand's history is 'shrouded in preliterate times' with many legends to explain aspects of culture.[23] According to one of these legends the islands were discovered by the Maori explorer Kupe around 925 AD (according to the European calendar), who after having returned to Hawaiki (Tahiti), widely accepted as the Maori ancestral home, instructed others on its location.[24] Legend has it that a group of Maori may have subsequently been blown off-course in a storm, and arrived and settled on what was identified as *Tiritiri o te Moana*, followed by numerous delegations.[25] This would be in line with the fact that many modern Maori trace their descent to fleets of canoes such as *Tainui, Te Arawa, Aotea, Takitimu, Tokomaru*, and others, from around the middle of the fourteenth century. The history of these Polynesian groups has been traced by some anthropologists to Austronesians who arrived at the islands from Asia,[26] and by others to groups having sailed across on rafts from South America.[27]

The dispersal of the Maori across the two islands took a few centuries, with group cohesiveness maintained through the association of descent from the original canoeists. The *Ngapuhi* occupied the far north; the *Atiawa, Taranaki*, and *Ngatiruanui* settled in the northern part of North Island; the *Ngatihua*, the *Ngatimaniapoto*, and the *Waikato* tribes settled to the south of modern day Auckland; and the east coast was occupied by the *Ngatiporou*, the *Arawa* confederation, and others. Few Maori sought to occupy the significantly colder climes of the South Island, even though anthropologists and historians have found traces of Maori there through the presence of hunting artefacts.[28] The Maori societies

---

[22] This approach has also been adopted in the chapter on Fiji; see ch 4, section 4.1.1.

[23] One founding myth is the story of the hero Maui. For more, see Keith Sinclair, *A History of New Zealand* (Harmondsworth: Penguin Books, 1959) 13–14.

[24] ibid 15.   [25] ibid.   [26] ibid.

[27] This argument is bolstered by the prevalence of South American plants and vegetation among the species cultivated by the early settlers. For more on this, see Jared M. Diamond, *Guns, Germs and Steel: The Fates of Human Societies* (New York: W.W. Norton, 1997).

[28] Sinclair (n 23) 20.

were well-organized internally, with a clear hierarchy under often despotic rulers,[29] and a strong element of the 'sacred' in their spiritual beliefs. Sinclair highlights the prevalence of demarcated roles within society and the designation of public places for robust intra-tribe debate.[30]

Unlike Australia, there is evidence of well-established pre-colonial communities in New Zealand,[31] making the declaration of *terra nullius* less plausible.[32] The point made on the relationship between 'cultivation' and legal personality in Australia is also borne out by the treatment of the Maori in New Zealand, which contrasts sharply to their indigenous cousins in Australia.[33] By the time of the arrival of European settlers:

> ... there was, in the North Island no waste land which was not used for hunting birds, or for cultivating or gathering food. Tribal boundaries were precisely defined. Warfare was endemic. The fortified hill-top village, the *pa*, was capable of offering effective resistance to weapons much more formidable than those of the Maori. The intricate combinations of buildings, terraces, trenches and scarps, the stockades of tree trunks, lashed together with creepers and crowning either a terrace or the parapet of a ditch, made the *pa* extremely difficult to storm. Even when the outer wall was breached, the enemy found each inner terrace or house a fortress still to be taken. Many of the hills of northern New Zealand, carved with the great encircling terraces of ancient pa, remain as a memorial to forgotten enmities.[34]

Arguably herein lies the crux of the difference of the colonial experience of Australia and New Zealand—the level of sophistication of indigenous political organization and evidence of the use of land suggests that the dynamic that had worked so well in declaring Australia *terra nullius* could not function in New Zealand. In addition, being warriors experienced in strategic warfare, subjugating the Maori in open warfare would have proved difficult for the limited numbers of settlers. While the numbers of Maori in New Zealand were not significantly high at the time of the arrival of the colonizers, their greater organization meant that the experience of Australia (often erroneously justified on the basis of the existence of low numbers) could not apply in New Zealand.[35]

---

[29] ibid 20–1. Sinclair provides insight into internal tribal structures with an emphasis on *whanau* (sub-tribes), and the notion of collective rights, deemed crucial by the Waitangi Tribunal articulating collective claims to territory.

[30] ibid 22–4.

[31] For an insight into the vibrant Maori economy prior to the arrival of the Europeans, see Paul Monin, 'The Maori Economy of Hauraki 1840–1880' (1995) 29 *NZJH* 197–210.

[32] One gauge of the difference would be the extent of the work of rationalization of title being engaged upon during the settlement process in New Zealand, as epitomized by the functioning of Land Courts, with no similar process available in Australia. For more, see Cathy Marr, *Public Works Takings of Maori Land, 1840–1981* (1997) [Report for the Treaty of Waitangi Policy Unit] (Rangahaua Whanui National Theme G) (Wellington: Waitangi Tribunal).

[33] For an analysis of 'push factors' in New Zealand's colonization, including the role played by Dutch seaman Abel Janszoon Tasman, see Sinclair (n 23) 29.

[34] ibid 24–5.

[35] See ch 2.1. For an explanation of the prevalence of cannibalism and the extent to which it played a role in shaping the discourse around the Maori in New Zealand, see Miller (n 21) 35–69.

As a result New Zealand was colonized differently from Australia, and, arguably, differently from other avenues of British colonization since. Banner explains:

New Zealand was the colony in which the greatest proportion of the land was acquired by purchase rather than conquest. After some uncertainty in the earliest years, the British government recognized the indigenous people, the Maori, as possessing full property rights in all of the colony's land. Over the course of the 19th century, the British bought the vast majority of New Zealand. In 1800, the Maori had owned over 60 million acres of land; by 1911, they owned only 7 million, much of which was not well suited for farming. A few million acres had been confiscated by the colonial government after the midcentury wars, but the rest was purchased in transactions with all the formalities of real estate sales back in England.[36]

These facts, alongside the signing of the *Treaty of Waitangi*, give the impression of a different kind of colonialism, driven less by the imposition of the classical agenda of the 3Cs (civilization, Christianity, and commerce),[37] than one where 'natives' were treated with respect, with their consent sought before the engagement of colonial activities. This positive impression needs to be tempered against two crucial factors. First the *Treaty of Waitangi* was a problematic document as a contract owing to its varied interpretations. Second, the result of colonization was the same: at its least problematic, involving a siphoning away of community resources; at its worst, bearing similar machinations of subjugation foisted upon colonial peoples elsewhere. As Banner admits:

...at the end of this process the Maori were nearly as poor, and formed as much of an underclass, as Aboriginal Australians or North American Indians. Property ownership—the opportunity to sell land at negotiated prices, to hold out for a better price, or to refuse to sell land at all—had done them very little good. Had the British simply conquered New Zealand by force and herded the Maori onto reservations, the result from the Maori perspective would scarcely have been worse.[38]

3.1.2 Settlement and the Treaty of Waitangi

It was clear at the outset that New Zealand was envisaged as a vital component in the Australian empire.[39] Yet it was the Dutch who displayed initial interest in New Zealand, with seaman Abel Janszoon Tasman given a mandate by the

[36] Stuart Banner, 'Conquest by *LSR* 47–8. For a discussion on the identity of the purchasers of Maori land and the impact of the market upon them, see further 54–71.

[37] A general source examining British colonial rule, especially in the African context is L.H. Gann and P. Duignan (eds), *The Rulers of British Africa 1879–1914* (London: Croom Helm, 1978) and *Colonialism in Africa 1870–1960* (Cambridge University Press: Cambridge, 1969–75).

[38] Banner (n 36) 48.

[39] The *Sydney Gazette* of 1831 made clear the general political and 'logical' direction of the future of New Zealand when it opined 'Nothing is more evident than that New Zealand must, at no distant period, form an integral and productive part of the immense Australian empire'. As cited by Sinclair (n 23) 29.

Governor General of the Dutch East Indies that, should he encounter 'any civilization', he was to:

>...find out what commodities their country yields, likewise inquiring after gold and silver, whether the latter are by them held in high esteem; making them believe that you are by no means eager for precious metals, so as to leave them ignorant of the value of the same.[40]

As Sinclair documents:

>Tasman charted part of the west coast of the country, which he called Staten Landt, hoping that the Staten Landt which had been discovered by one of his countrymen off Tierra del Fuego might stretch so far; but he did not linger long on this inhospitable shore. The Governor-General and Councillors were disappointed. True, Tasman had discovered Van Diemen's Land (now Tasmania) and Staten Landt (which was soon renamed Nieuw Zeeland, after the Dutch province, when the original Staten Landt was found to be an island); but 'in point of fact no treasures or matters of great profit' had been found. Nieuw Zeeland was left to its savage inhabitants for another century, though its existence was recorded in a few charts and books.[41]

It was not until Captain James Cook came across the islands in 1769, drawing up the first maps of the state, that settlement became a possibility. Cook was impressed by his interaction with the Maori, describing them as 'a brave, warlike people, with sentiments void of treachery'.[42] As the number of whaling and trading expeditions mounted from Sydney Harbour grew, settlement became ever more probable. However this settlement was never going to be easy against the warlike Maori with numbers of 'wars of races' breaking out.[43] While curiosity and respect for the Maori made the colonization different,[44] for the Maori there remained extraneous factors for this war, mainly instigated by the influence that the new cultures were bringing upon ancient traditions. As Sinclair narrates:

>Their community began to pass through a moral and technological revolution more comprehensive and more painful than contemporary industrialization in Europe. Old beliefs, customs, everyday habits of eating or dress, were abandoned or altered, not always for the better. In some places the tribal structure itself was tottering.[45]

---

[40] ibid 30.   [41] ibid.

[42] ibid 32. Sinclair narrates the impression that foreigners made on one Maori chieftain, who years later described how the Maori thought of the strangers as goblins and how they were impressed by the rifle that was used to bring down a bird, believing it to be a magic walking stick.

[43] This phrase is attributed to New Zealand's first historian Dr A.S. Thompson who published *The Story of New Zealand* (London: John Murray, 1859).

[44] Early historical accounts of New Zealand portray the Maori in more positive terms than corresponding histories of Australia. Missionary Samuel Marsden claimed to understand Maori culture to be able to preach, and became immersed in it. He subsequently engaged with two Maori chiefs (Hongi and Waikato), brought them to England in 1820, and introduced them to Cambridge linguist Professor Lee, beginning the first transliteration of the Maori script. See Sinclair (n 23) 35–8. It is also clear that the missionaries commanded respect but had little impact in converting the Maori to Christianity.

[45] Sinclair (n 23) 40.

In addition, health problems never encountered before began to affect the Maori,[46] whose social fabric was being eroded through the introduction of alcohol, prostitution, and venereal diseases.[47] This led to a demand for *utu* (revenge) within the Maori population, which was to change the relations between the Europeans and the indigenous peoples. In addition, the easy purchase of weapons from traders meant that society was increasingly armed and engaged in internecine inter-tribal warfare, which, while not new, wreaked higher levels of devastation.[48]

In seeking to determine what kind of intervention was required, an initial plan to empower the traders and residents[49] was rejected as being useless against an indigenous population that could rise up easily in defiance.[50] Instead, opinion mobilized behind the proposal of William Hobson, a sea captain, who recommended the signing of treaties with the Maori for the acquisition of certain pockets of territory, very similar to the 'factories' set up by the East India Company in India.[51] While this may have led to the *de facto* annexation of New Zealand, the British Crown did not exercise effective control outside the areas of the settlements, or 'factories'.[52] Between the 1840s and 1860s there were significant discussions and philosophical arguments between 'organized colonizers' and 'humanitarianists' over the direction of British policy in New Zealand.[53] The debate culminated in a decision that while parts of New Zealand annexed by Hobson would become dependencies of New South Wales, the indigenous populations would be dealt with fairly, and all land was to be acquired on the basis of a Crown grant.[54] Sinclair concludes:

These instructions marked a new and a noble beginning in British colonial policy. The history of New Zealand was to be distinguished from that of earlier settlement colonies; the fate of the Maoris was to differ from that of the American Indian, the Bantu, the Australian or Tasmanian aborigine; for the new colony was being launched in an evangelical age. Imperialism and humanitarianism would henceforth march together. Even the Colonial Office, without much conviction, hoped that New Zealand would be the scene of a Utopian experiment.[55]

A meeting took place on 5 February 1840, at Waitangi, where a group of Maori chiefs met to deliberate over whether or not to negotiate with Hobson, weighing up potential benefits against the experiences they had heard of in the ill-treatment of

---

[46] Including typhoid, tuberculosis, pneumonia, epidemic influenza, and measles.

[47] This is in line with the thesis of Diamond (n 27) who attributes particular 'germs' and bacteria as one of the factors that explains the dominance of Europeans over others.

[48] The rivalry between various missions and the racism inherent in Charles Darwin's portrayal of New Zealand shows that the spirit of domination and superiority, so closely aligned with the colonial experiences everywhere was very much still in evidence. See Sinclair (n 23) 38–44.

[49] Estimated at the time to be a few thousands, living along the coast near what was to become Auckland.

[50] Sinclair (n 23) 54.   [51] ibid.   [52] ibid 55.

[53] For more, see ibid 55–66.   [54] ibid 66.   [55] ibid 67.

the Aborigines in Tasmania.[56] A reluctant consensus emerged to accept relations with the British in the hope that 'Christianity, trade and tribal peace' would replace the pagan past and the 'anarchic present'. Hobson was called upon to:

... remain for us a father, a judge, a peacemaker. You must not allow us to become slaves. You must preserve our customs, and never permit our lands to be wrested from us.... Stay then, our friend, our father, our Governor.[57]

The *Treaty of Waitangi* was signed on 6th February 1840 by fifty chiefs, followed by five hundred others. Several influential chiefs refused to sign, including those of *Arawa*, the *Ngatihaua*, the *Ngatimaniapoto*, and the *Waikato*.[58] By Article 1 of the Treaty, the chiefs ceded sovereignty to the Queen for the guarantee of their continued possession of the territories on which they lived and possessed individually or collectively. The sole right of purchase of land was granted to the Queen, and the chiefs were given the same rights and privileges as British subjects.[59]

By 21 May, in the shadow of competition from others,[60] Hobson proclaimed British sovereignty over both islands through discovery, occupation, and cession.[61] Crucially,

... the acquisition of sovereignty ... proceeded from an assumption which was unquestionably as just as it was unusual. The Government accepted that the country, or at least the populous North Island, belonged to its native inhabitants, and neither ignored their rights nor attempted to qualify their dominion out of existence by appealing to international law.[62]

The *Treaty of Waitangi* was envisaged as laying the ground through which indigenous peoples and settlers could live in harmony on the basis of equality, despite the fact that it was a compromise not fully in accord with any of the interested parties in New Zealand.[63] The early years under the new arrangement have been described as consisting of growing European settlements on

---

[56] According to Alves information about the activities of the Crown in Tasmania in particular and in Australia flowed to New Zealand through the activities of the whalers and sealers, see Dora Alves, *The Maori and the Crown: An Indigenous People's Struggle for Self-Determination* (Westport, Connecticut/London: Greenwood Press, 1999) 11–13.

[57] Sinclair (n 23) 69.

[58] For the extent to which these events escalated to full-fledged war, see Keith Sinclair, *The Origins of the Maori Wars* (Wellington: New Zealand University Press, 1957).

[59] One leader used the analogy of the Queen owning the shadow of the land while the Maori owned its substance—a sentiment that led an under-secretary in the Colonial Office to wonder how the chiefs would react when they discovered that the 'shadow' was not as insubstantial as presumed. See Sinclair (n 23) 69.

[60] ibid 69–70.

[61] For more on these concepts in a historical and contemporary context of public international law, see Joshua Castellino, 'Territorial Integrity and the "Right" to Self-determination: An Examination of the Conceptual Tools' (2008) 33(2) *BJIL* 503–68.

[62] Sinclair (n 23) 70.

[63] The British government was forced to accept more responsibility than bargained for; the New Zealand Settlement Company saw its access to land restricted; the missionaries had lost their

the fringe of Polynesia, though increasing land speculation was threatening this equilibrium.[64] Unlike in Australia, Maori land ownership meant that land could not be acquired as easily by the settlers, leading to significant tensions among European populations, notably those who viewed New Zealand as a home for British immigrants as well as humanitarians who insisted on the maintenance of indigenous rights.[65]

The new regime also depended heavily on the Maori economy for its survival.[66] During the early years of settlement the Maori economy thrived, mainly through control over coastal regions and the lucrative shipping lanes of North Island. Increased cultivation among the Maori led to food surpluses that were sold and exported for profit. Meanwhile land acquired by speculators was left idle awaiting projected masses of settlers that never materialized.[67] The Maori also acquired sophisticated agricultural tools, received English education through missionaries,[68] and found gainful employment in the colonial regime. This led Grey, Governor General in the 1850s,[69] to the conclusion that he had established a basis for 'peaceful co-existence', with '... the two races ... well on their way to the humanitarian goal of "amalgamation"'. In his report to the Secretary of State as narrated by Sinclair, he claimed that:

...both races already form one harmonious community, connected together by commercial and agricultural pursuits, professing the same faith, resorting to the same Courts of Justice, joining in the same public sports, standing mutually and indifferently to each other in the relation of landlord and tenant, and thus insensibly forming one people'.[70]

This optimistic gloss obscured disparities in entitlements that had begun to appear.[71] It would probably be more accurate to record that the Maori lived segregated within their communities under their laws, deriving marginal benefit from the schools. This contradicts the notion of a move towards a unified state, though there was apparently some truth in this statement in and around

special status; and the Maori tribal chiefs would naturally have preferred not to cede sovereignty. ibid 70–2.

[64] For the motivations of settlers and especially for more detail on the intricate political manoeuvrings among them to gain ascendancy in New Zealand, see J.S. Marais, *The Colonization of New Zealand* (Oxford: Oxford University Press, 1927).

[65] Sinclair (n 23) 72–4.

[66] ibid 84. For an impression of the Maori economy during the arrival and consolidation of settlement, see Monin (n 31).

[67] Sinclair (n 23) 84.

[68] For an interesting discussion on the substantive content of this education and how it was received, see Harry C. Evison, *The Long Dispute: Maori Land Rights and European Colonisation in Southern New Zealand* (Christchurch: Canterbury University Press, 1997) 115–25.

[69] For more on Governor Grey, his biography, motivations and impact, see ibid 158–76.

[70] As quoted by Sinclair (n 23) 85.

[71] The early denial of franchise and representation to the Maori and the lack of recognition for the Maori language blatantly belies this process. See Phil Parkinson, 'Strangers in the House: The Maori Language in Government and the Maori Language in Parliament 1865–1900' (2001) 32 *VUWLR*, Monograph 1–60.

the European settlements.[72] Despite this, Grey successfully negotiated the Constitution of 1852, which, though 'democratic' in setting up six provinces with elected representatives, inevitably excluded Maoris on the basis that franchise was given to individual land owners.[73]

While the European state was being consolidated, Maoris were getting organized on the basis of nationalism (*kotahitanga*) with the goal of eliminating colonization.[74] This led to the election of a Maori King in 1858, the Waikato chief, Te Wherowhero, under the title of Potatau 1.[75] He adopted the trappings of sovereignty through a flag, Council of State, code of laws, magistrate and police force. The royal entourage included a land surveyor, a reflection of the competition for land that was unfolding. The rise in tensions resulted in an intensive war from 1854–1864, though historians argue that in some parts the conflict continued until the late 1880s.[76]

With pressure on the British exchequer, colonies were asked to become self-reliant, a promise that brought Frederick Weld to power in New Zealand in 1864.[77] The resultant policy saw blatant violation of the *Treaty of Waitangi* in a series of land confiscations, with nearly three million acres of Maori land requisitioned in Waikato, the East Coast, and Taranaki.[78] The war also changed the dimension of Maori land possession.[79]

In addition, the passage of the *Maori Land Court Act 1865*[80] saw a justified attempt to redress the legal balance, which resulted in a legal subterfuge, separating the Maori from their lands. The ostensible function of the court was to convert customary Maori title to freehold title, but in its first decade of operation, the court was required to name a restricted number of holders in the title deeds in contravention of conventional Maori custom of collective ownership, rendering significant numbers of Maori landless. In the meantime, Parliament passed

---

[72] Sinclair (n 23) 85.   [73] ibid 85–6.

[74] ibid 109.

[75] For an analysis of the issues leading to the 'King Movement', see Thomas Buddle, *The Maori King Movement in New Zealand* (Auckland: New Zealander Office, 1860) (reprinted by AMS Press, New York, 1979).

[76] Sinclair (n 23) 138.

[77] The House of Commons decided this in 1862; see ibid (n 23) 140.

[78] These have subsequently become the key milestones in the growing influence of the Waitangi Tribunal in later years, as it seeks to undo the damage of these illegal acquisitions. See Waitangi Tribunal *Taranaki Report; Kaupapa Tuatahi*,(Wai 143)(1996). Also see (all Waitangi Tribunal) The *Hauraki Report*, (Wai 686) (2006); *Ngati Awa Raupatu Report*, (Wai 46)(1999); *Turanga Tangata Turanga Whenua: Report on the Turanganui Kiwa Claims*, (Wai 814)(2004).

[79] By the end of the war there were eleven million acres left (of twenty-one million before the war) of which two and a half million was leased to settlers. See Sinclair (n 23) 140–1. For more on confiscations also see Miller (n 21) 70–96.

[80] For commentary on the early functioning of this court, see Judith Binney, 'The Native Land Court and the Maori Communities, 1865–1890' in Judith Binney, Judith Bassett, and Erik Olssen (eds), *The People and the Land* (Wellington: Allen and Unwin, 1990) 143–64. Also see F.D. Fenton, *Important Judgements Delivered in the Compensation Court and the Native Land Court 1866–1879* (Auckland: Native Land Court, 1879).

a number of pieces of legislation,[81] and as a result, Maori were easily duped by opportunists who dispossessed them in return for pitiful consideration.[82] Many of these issues will be discussed in detail in subsequent sections, suffice to stress at this point that despite the vaunted ambitions of partnership between the Maori and Parekha, the experience at the start of the twentieth century was clearly tilted towards domination of the Maori by the settlers, with law serving as a hand-maiden of dispossession.

3.1.3 The Changing Identity of New Zealand: New Arrivals and the Quest for Equality

It is easy to describe Asian migration to New Zealand as a twentieth century phenomenon. This is inaccurate since Polynesians, the first occupants of New Zealand, are believed to have migrated from Asia themselves. There has also been a regular trickle of more contemporary Asians to New Zealand alongside European settlement.[83] Nevertheless at the start of the twentieth century:

…Maori were in a distinct minority. The 1901 census reported 42,900 Maori, 2,200 half-castes living as Europeans, and 772,700 Pakeha. Maori owned very little land on the South Island and only 11 million acres, or 39 percent, of the North Island.[84]

The first wave of 'non-indigenous' migration to New Zealand took place mainly from the British Isles between 1850 and 1870.[85] The migrants were mostly labourers who were finding it increasingly difficult to find work at home.[86] Around this time support existed for New Zealand to be a 'white' state,[87] with xenophobic tendencies towards Asians and Pacific islanders seeking work in the whaling and trading industries.[88] One manifestation of this tone is captured in the *Otago Witness* newspaper in 1919:

If there is one subject on which there is acute feeling… it is the recognition of the coloured races. And although the American Declaration of Independence begins by asserting all men are born equal in the sight of God it makes no mention of niggers and Japanese.[89]

---

[81] Many of which were not translated into Maori, despite their obvious impact on their community. See n 71.

[82] Sinclair (n 23) 143.

[83] For a reading on theories of the peopling of the Pacific States, see Diamond (n 27).

[84] See Steven C. Bourassa and Ann Louise Strong, 'Restitution of Land to New Zealand Maori: The Role of Social Structure' (2002) 75 (2) *PA* 227–60.

[85] Marotta (n 5) 178.

[86] Marotta (n 5) 178.

[87] At the Paris Peace Conference in 1919, (then) prime ministerial candidate Massey famously pledged to keep New Zealand 'clear of coloured and undesirable immigrants', see P.S. O'Connor, 'Keeping New Zealand White, 1908–1920' (1986) 2 *NZJH* 41–65.

[88] Marotta (n 5) 179.

[89] *Otago Witness*, 23 April 1919.

The underlying tensions that drive this ideology are still manifest in certain seg-
ments of society[90] who feel marginalized by the contemporary inflow of migrants
from China, India, and parts of South-east Asia.[91]

The issue of equality is a persistent theme in contemporary New Zealand
politics, based on the question of how entitlements accrue. As experienced by
other states, this pits the notion that meritocracy remains the only justifiable
way to determine success in society, to a more nuanced approach that suggests
that in the pursuit of individual or collective goals, it is important to be mindful of the different and unequal starting points of different individuals, usually
determinable on personal identifiers such as race, gender, ethnicity or religion.[92]
The latter view, central to the pursuit of 'minority rights law', requires the state
to actively pursue avenues designed to narrow socio-economic gaps in society.
In contemporary New Zealand politics, discussion of this in the run-up to the
last general election in 2005 focused around issues such as 'tax cuts, the role and
function of the *Treaty of Waitangi*, and affirmative action policy'.[93] This led one
author to conclude that:

> ... ideologies of equality and issues of who gets what were central to the NZ 2005 elec-
> tion campaign in much the same way that ideologies of national security and the war on
> terrorism were central to election campaigns in the United States that occurred at around
> the same time.[94]

Commenting on 'meritocracy', Sibley suggests:

> The culture-specific positioning of equality-as-meritocracy may have allowed political
> elites and their constituents to express opposition to resource allocations favoring minor-
> ity groups in the NZ context while still maintaining discourses of plausible deniability
> in much the same way as symbolic racism is thought to operate within the United States.
> In this way, the NZ-specific re-formulation of equality positioning assessed ... may have
> provided an axis of meaning that aided in the creation and mobilization of public opin-
> ion regarding resource-allocations, land claims, affirmative action programs, and a host
> of other material issues leading up to the 2005 NZ general election ... the mobilization
> of public opinion in this way exerted unique effects on political party preference that
> were not reducible to universal and broad-bandwidth measures of personality, ideo-
> logical attitudes, or attitudes toward biculturalism and ethnic group relations in the NZ
> context.[95]

---

[90] See Keith Tuffin, 'Racist Discourses in New Zealand and Australia: Reviewing the Last
20 Years' (2008) 2(2) *SPPC* 591–607.

[91] For a governmental source that explains the rationale and processes of migration to New
Zealand, see <http://www.immigration.govt.nz/> [last accessed 21 January 2009].

[92] For a discussion of this in an Asian context, see Joshua Castellino and Elvira Domínguez
Redondo, *Minority Rights in Asia: A Comparative Legal Analysis* (Oxford: Oxford University Press,
2006) esp ch 4.

[93] Chris G. Sibley, 'Political Attitudes and the Ideology of Equality: Differentiating Support for
Liberal and Conservative Political Parties in New Zealand' (2007) 36 *NZJP*.

[94] ibid.   [95] ibid.

3.2 Identification of Minorities and Indigenous Peoples

It is worth remembering that '...between 1945 and 1971 there were 90,082 assisted migrants entering New Zealand and 76,673 were from Great Britain and Ireland'.[96] Census figures, available from 2006, still show an overwhelming majority of Parekha in New Zealand.[97] Of the total population of over 4.2 million, over two and a half million (67 per cent of the total population) are classified 'European'. The Maori are the most significant minority, numbering over half a million, close to 15 per cent of the population, while the next biggest group is the fast growing category counted under 'Asian', accounting for close to 10 per cent. Pacific Islanders account for nearly 7 per cent of the population. The other category included in the census was the curious amalgam of 'Middle Eastern/Latin American/African' which accounted for close to 1 per cent of the population.[98] The figures include an 'ethnic' category entitled 'New Zealander' with just over 11 per cent reporting under this title. Another anomaly about the census was that individuals could represent themselves as belonging to several categories; as a result the figures are merely rough indicators of true populations.[99] In order to be able to understand minority rights protection in New Zealand, this section will portray the three main groups that fall within this category: the Maori, the 'Asians', and the Pacific Islanders.[100]

3.2.1 The Maori

The Maori are acknowledged as the 'indigenous people' of New Zealand on the basis of first occupancy. It has been proven that the ancestry of the Maori is distinctly Polynesian rather than Melanesian.[101] As highlighted above, they arrived at New Zealand in canoes and still maintain group cohesions reflecting descent from ancestors sharing the same canoe. Their intra-tribe organization, culture, and warrior nature were key factors in the difference in treatment they

[96] Marotta (n 5) 180. For a detailed history of immigration to New Zealand with a particular emphasis on Asian immigration, see Malcolm McKinnon, *Immigrants and Citizens: New Zealanders and Asian Immigration in Historical Context* (Wellington: The Printing Press, 1996).

[97] For a full list of the 2006 figures, see <http://www.stats.govt.nz/census/census-outputs/quickstats/snapshotplace2.htm?id=9999999&tab=CulturalDiversity&type=region&ParentID> [accessed 23 May 2008].

[98] These figures are available from the New Zealand Census Office online at <http://www.newzealandcensus.nz> [last accessed 7 August 2008].

[99] For further explanations about the census figures including a reflection of the discussions of multiple response classification and an explanation of the 'New Zealander' category, see <http://www.stats.govt.nz/census/default.htm> [Last accessed 23 May 2008].

[100] For general reading on the process of the peopling of New Zealand, see James Belich, *Making Peoples: A History of the New Zealanders from Polynesian Settlement to the End of the Nineteenth Century* (Auckland: Penguin Books, 1996).

[101] Sinclair (n 23) 15.

received from settlers in comparison to their aboriginal cousins in Australia. With the arrival of the Parekha in their lands, Maori culture began to come under significant pressure, even though the Maori economy continued to thrive. Early fears that the Maori would be wiped out in New Zealand through disease and exposure to Europeans dissipated by the dawn of the twentieth century, when Maori population figures began to recover after touching a nadir of 42,000 in 1896.[102] This represented a significant drop from the estimated 250,000 Maori on the two islands in the mid-1700s, and had already dropped dramatically to 60,000 by 1854.[103] It still took close to three-quarters of a century (until 1921) before the population returned to the numbers recorded at the first census in 1858.[104] The significant dip in numbers during that period is attributed to exposure to diseases that came with the Europeans, against which the Maori had no immunity.[105] Concerned at the state of health and diminishing population, Maoris united to form the Young Maori Party in the last decade of the nineteenth century, in a bid to focus on measures to improve the living conditions of their communities. In 1900, Mauri Pomare, a Maori, was appointed Medical Officer of Health to the Maoris and, together with others, began the job of providing medical assistance and education about preventative measures against ill-health and disease.[106]

While these measures are credited with the rise in health, and the concurrent recovery in numbers, the loss of land through the sixty years tracing back to the *Treaty of Waitangi* was considerably more difficult to overcome. Writing in the 1950s, Sinclair's image of the Maori shows the extent of this decimation:

The Maori...have lost the land. They have only four million acres, of which two-and-a-half are thought capable of being farmed successfully. The one hundred and thirty thousand Maoris, in other words, own about twenty acres of good land each, which is probably less than the European's holdings (per capita) of good land.[107]

An aggravating factor in the plight of the Maori then, which remains today, was the urban-rural divide, with significant numbers living in rural communities while most Europeans lived in cities and towns. As a result, the Maori found it difficult to access services that were readily available in large population densities. A manifestation of this divide in the 1950s was the difference in child mortality rates,[108] and the difficulties that Maori encountered in seeking access to business

---

[102] ibid 190.   [103] Bourassa and Strong (n 84) 234.

[104] The first census taken in 1858, before the Maori wars, recorded Maori numbers at 56,000. See Sinclair (n 23) 90.

[105] One of the central arguments made by Diamond in assessing any scientific basis to Europeans colonization is that germs, brought by Europeans to other parts of the world, had the impact of instigating disease in local populations, which assisted the subjugation of locals. See Diamond (n 27).

[106] Sinclair (n 23)190–1.   [107] ibid 289.

[108] Sinclair documents the difference as 74 child deaths in every 1,000 Maori births, as opposed to 23 in every 1,000 European births.

and professions.[109] Criticizing the claim that New Zealand had found a system of harmonious co-existence, Sinclair argues:

Although only about half the present Maori population (135,000 in 1955) are full-blooded, 'amalgamation', the humanitarian ideal of a century ago, has occurred neither physically nor socially. To a large degree the two races retain different social patterns and values. The Maoris, though Christian, have not generally adopted puritanical attitudes towards work or pleasure; though engaged in money-making, they have not abandoned their traditional community life in favour of economic individualism. Thus, though they share the same opportunities, rights, and duties as the Europeans, the Maoris are not 'equal' in the sense of being the same.[110]

Optimism over the future came mainly in the maintenance of a healthy birth-rate among the Maori,[111] and this could be considered as much a factor as any other in making the Maori, and the state of New Zealand, a beacon for indigenous peoples elsewhere. Despite this progress it is clear that 'equality' remains far away—the deliberations of the *Waitangi Tribunal* have done much to address the historical imbalance, but difficult questions over future inclusion still remain. A significant factor that has become increasingly relevant to New Zealand society, and one not foreseen by Sinclair in the 1950s, was the increasing nature of Asian migration. While he did suggest that lower birth rates among Europeans was off-set by the increase in white immigration,[112] the strong rise in contemporary Asian migration has played a more significant role in changing the social fabric of New Zealand.

3.2.2 'Asians'

The 'Whites Only' policy of the newly formed government of New Zealand (consisting entirely of Parekha) meant that foreigners (i.e. Asians and Pacific Islanders) were actively discouraged from seeking work in New Zealand. Despite this policy, numerous Asians and Pacific islanders managed to find work in the whaling and trading industries, though their situation would often become precarious in times of economic downturn, only to recover when the work returned and prosperity was on the rise. To regulate the flow of Asian populations the New Zealand government proposed legal bars on such immigration, including the *Asiatic Restriction Bill (1879)*[113] and the *Chinese Immigrants Act (1881)*.[114]

Despite these barriers to the inflow of Chinese and other Asian workers, some did find manage to find employment in goldfields[115] and other labour

---

[109] ibid 289–90.

[110] ibid 290. However, the relatively high-rate of inter-marriage between Maori and Parekha (nearly 19 per cent able to claim mixed heritage) suggests that the communities are not that separate.

[111] ibid 289–90.   [112] ibid 290.

[113] As discussed by Docker and Fischer (n 5) 179.   [114] ibid.

[115] For a discussion about the Gold Rush and its impact on the population dynamics, see Evison (n 68) 287. Evison provides some precise figures of Europeans and Maori in the South

intensive economic pursuits.[116] Drawing on the work of Borrie, Marotta provides an interesting insight into the population of New Zealand in 1871:

By 1871, 3000 Chinese still remained, and between 1870 and 1880, there were 3000
Germans, 4600 Scandinavians, and a small inflow of immigrants from Italy and France,
who settled in both the South Island and the North Island. There was a bias towards the
Scandinavians and Germans because, according to government officials, they seemed to
assimilate more quickly to the 'British way of life'.[117]

The significant change in population dynamics came around 1890, due to a
downturn in the economy and flow of settlers to Australia, resulting in a changed
emphasis in immigration policy towards the encouragement of settler immigrants rather than landless labourers.[118] This was accompanied by xenophobic
attitudes towards Asians as a whole, who were accused of stealing scarce jobs
and so threatening the 'racial purity' of New Zealand.[119] While encouraging
resettlement of Britons, Asians were actively discouraged from entry through
the passage of the *Immigration Amendment Bill 1920*.[120]

The ambivalent attitude towards Asian migration finally changed in 1987
when the government passed the *Immigration Act*.[121] The policy of opening its
doors to skilled immigrants was driven by the economic need for New Zealand to
become less isolationist and seek a bigger role in the global economy. This turn of
events is probably responsible for the distinct change in focus of New Zealand's
immigration policy, and the corresponding move towards a pluralistic society.
By the end of the 1980s, European immigration had fallen, replaced by growing numbers from the Pacific Islands and various parts of Asia. By 1991, there
was a large presence of several Asian populations, among them Chinese (45,000)
Indians (30,000), Cambodians (5,000), Filipinos (4,000), Sri Lankans (3,000)
and Vietnamese (2,000).[122]

This relatively sudden inflow of Asian migration caused tensions in a state
that had hitherto seen itself as 'bicultural'. The interpretation of this biculturalism had been narrow enough to exclude Pacific Islanders from the general category of Maori in the mid-1970s, and this was compounded by the fact
that the Asian immigrants had little in common with white settlers, the Maori,
or even the Pacific Islanders. In addition the strong connections between the

---

Island: The European population of the South Island was 138,540 in December 1867, with nearly
50,000 in Otago... In 1868, the European population of Canterbury passed 40,000, while the
total Maori population of southern New Zealand was recorded as 1,626: Kaikoura 77, Buller
48, Westland 68, Tuahiwi 176, Rapaki 76, Port Levy 52, Akaroa 29, Wairewa 87, Taumutu 25,
Arowhenua 86, Waimate 76, Moeraki 97, Waikouaiti 106, Purakaunui 19, Otakou 98, Taieri
58, Molyneux 22, Tuturau 11, Aparima 64, Kawakaputaputa and Oraka 68, Oue 22, Omaui 23,
Ruapuke 102, Stewart Island 88, Bluff 48. He does not record any numbers for Pacific Islanders
and Asians.

[116] Marotta (n 5) 180.   [117] ibid.   [118] ibid.
[119] ibid.   [120] ibid.
[121] Public Act 1987 No 74, date of assent 21 April 1987.
[122] McKinnon (n 96) 51.

communities and their countries of origin, their mercantile sense, and their intra-community support system saw Asians rise up the socio-economic, if not the political, hierarchy.

3.2.3 Pacific Islanders

Unlike Asian migrants to New Zealand, who managed to ascend the socio-economic ladder, Pacific Islanders have continued to languish near the bottom on all indicators. Pacific Islanders are disproportionately represented among the urban poor and unemployed in New Zealand.[123] Although they were the first real group to make an impact in terms of numbers on the New Zealand population, they have remained marginalized.[124] More recently, Pacific Islanders (many of whom are New Zealand citizens) have gravitated to New Zealand in search of employment from New Zealand-controlled Pacific territories. As Mackinnon demonstrates, this distinct group had risen in numbers to 61,000 by 1976.[125] The oil crises led to a freezing of immigration as unemployment rose, and with economic conditions worsening, Pacific Islanders came under scrutiny as scapegoats for the economic downturn.[126]

The overtly bicultural nature of the rights discussion has had a particularly negative impact on these communities who have been excluded from policy discussions. This raises questions of the nature of 'indigenous identity' and the importance and basis of the Maori claim to redistributive justice.[127] The concept of 'indigenous identity' within New Zealand continues to merit some debate,[128] as reflected upon by Marotta:

The role of indigenous groups, in particular, has become central to the debate over the cultural composition of New Zealand. New Zealand has been described as both multi-cultural and bicultural. To describe New Zealand as multicultural is to argue that it is made up of many ethnic groups besides Maori and Pakeha...and thus deny the unique importance of Maori people. Those on the left have argued that multiculturalism is a smokescreen which allows the Pakeha dominant group to hold onto their power and wealth and avoid dealing with Maori Pakeha relationships. On the other hand, to describe New Zealand society as bicultural, according to liberals and conservatives, is

---

[123] See Emma Eastwood and Farah Miller, 'Asia' in *State of the World's Minorities 2008* (London: Minority Rights Group International, 2008) 127.

[124] For a particular insight into immigration of Fijians to New Zealand, see Azmat Gani, 'Some Empirical Evidence on the Determinants of immigration from Fiji to New Zealand' (1998) 32 *NZEP*.

[125] McKinnon (n 96) 40.

[126] This phenomenon impacted Australia-New Zealand relations as Pacific Islanders accessed the open immigration policy between the two states to move to Australia in search of work. See McLean (n 1).

[127] e.g. Waldron asks whether the Maori claim is based on the principle of first occupancy or the principle of prior occupancy (n13) 56.

[128] Marotta (n 5) 181.

unfair and hence undemocratic because it singles out Maoris, who are simply one of many minority groups.[129]

The discussion of biculturalism or multiculturalism is seen in many societies.[130] Its particular manifestation in New Zealand lies in the fact that the state was mindful of the need, early on, to promote the equal rights of the Maori. This became the bed-rock on which policy was pursued, even though many argue that this pursuit was superficial and resulted more in assimilation of the Maori than a unique version of two cultures living alongside each other as equals.

Marotta concludes:

The hybrid experience [of New Zealand] has destabilised the boundaries between the Anglo self and the non-Anglo other, and it has allowed particular individuals to reconstruct their identities. At this level the problematicisation or removal of boundaries is said to have some positive outcomes—for example, greater tolerance of difference. However…the removal of cultural boundaries may suppress the identity of the other, while trying to foster and celebrate this very same identity. One has to be careful not to treat borders as if they are inherently oppressive. One needs to give special recognition to those boundaries which are the products of human action. Boundaries which the Anglo self and the non-Anglo other construct around themselves may be seen as exclusionary, but they should be respected if they are socially constructed and not imposed upon individuals.[131]

The notion that 'shared' does not need to mean uncontested is supported by Bottomley who acknowledges that shared forms of culture may be highly contested sites through which the protagonists seek to maintain their uniqueness *vis-à-vis* the 'Other'.[132]

---

[129] ibid. This debate is reflected upon by a number of different authors, most compellingly by Richard Mulgan, *Maori, Pakeha and Democracy* (Auckland: Oxford University Press, 1989). Mulgan's other work entitled *Democracy and Power in New Zealand: A Study of New Zealand Politics* (Auckland: Oxford University Press, 1989) provides further insights into how the issue of democracy and inclusion has played out within domestic politics.

[130] Canadian philosopher Will Kymlicka's work discusses the parameters of this issue in detail, and from many perspectives. See e.g. *Multicultural Citizenship: A Liberal Theory of Minority Rights* (Oxford: Oxford University Press, 1995) and Multicultural Odysseys: Navigating the New International Politics of Diversity (Oxford: Oxford University Press, 2007). Also see Bhikhu Parekh, *Rethinking Multiculturalism: Cultural Diversity and Political Theory* (Basingstoke: Palgrave Macmillan, 2006). Also see Alexandra Xanthaki, 'Multiculturalism and Extremism: International Law Perspectives' in Javaid Rehman and Susan Breau (eds), *Religion, Human Rights Law and International Law* (The Hague: Martinus Nijhoff Publishers, 2007) 443–64.

[131] Marotta (n 5) 181.

[132] For discussions about the majority identity, see Sarah Dugdale, 'Chronicles of Evasion: Negotiating Pakeha New Zealand Identity' in Docker and Fischer (n 5) 190–202. For visions of 'Otherness' especially as viewed through a literary lens, see Nina Lola, 'Exploring Disallowed Territory: Introducing The Multicultural Subject into New Zealand Literature' ibid 203–17.

3.3 Rights of Minorities

Having identified the key minorities in New Zealand, it is time to turn to the rights provided for them in New Zealand law. It is important to state at the very outset that the focus on a reconciliation process with the Maori has meant that significant measures are in place to tackle the manner in which this group was disenfranchised in the process of settlement. A significant proportion of this section will focus on the extent to which the government has attempted to accommodate Maori rights. It could be argued that this section best reflects the overtly bicultural nature of the discussion over inclusion in New Zealand society. To meet the objective of being able to provide an accurate picture of the rights available to identified minorities, this section will be divided into two sub-sections. The first seeks to offer a commentary on the *Treaty of Waitangi 1840*, the Waitangi Tribunal set up by the *Treaty of Waitangi Act 1975*, as well as the *Bill of Rights Act* and the *Human Rights Act*, to show the provisions that exist for minorities and indigenous peoples. The second sub-section focuses on thematic issues that remain fundamental to minority rights in New Zealand. Amongst these are: *a*) land rights (including the foreshore and seabed); *b*) education and linguistic rights; *c*) fishing rights; *d*) resource management; and *e*) issues related to immigration.

3.3.1 The Treaty and Statutory Framework for Indigenous and Minority Rights in New Zealand

There are a number of different interlocking statutes that bear some relevance to indigenous and minority rights.[133] The first part of this sub-section will provide an insight into the *Treaty of Waitangi* and attendant processes that remain at the core of the identifiable regime of indigenous rights; the second addresses two key statutes that frame human rights in New Zealand, namely the *New Zealand Bill of Rights Act 1990*[134] and the *Human Rights Act 1993*.[135]

3.3.1.1 The Treaty of Waitangi

The *Treaty of Waitangi* is one of the most significant pieces of law in New Zealand with significant impact on indigenous peoples globally. It represents a definitive

---

[133] The following would be particularly important: *New Zealand Bill of Rights 1990* (Public Act 1990 No 109, date of assent 28 August 1990); *Human Rights Act 1993* (Public Act 1993 No 82, date of assent 10 August 1993); *Te Ture Whenua Maori Act 1993* (Public Act 1993 No 4, date of assent 21 March 1993); *Protection of Personal Property Rights Act 1988* (Public Act 1988 No 4, date of assent 12 March 1988); *Maori Language Act 1987* (Public Act No 176, 20 July 1987); *Ministry of Maori Development Act 1991* (1991 No 145); *Immigration Act 1987* (Public Act 1987 No 74, date of assent 21 April 1987).

[134] Public Act 1990 No 109, date of assent 28 August 1990.

[135] Public Act 1993 No 82, date of assent 10 August 1993.

moment of New Zealand history, and is at once a key explanation of the way in which the Maoris were perceived at the time of settlement, and a source of rights in the context of the subsequent disregard for Maori heritage. As indicated in the historical section, the Treaty itself was signed by William Hobson, Consul and Lieutenant-Governor, on behalf of the Crown, and a number of Maori chiefs. Further signatures were received as the document made its way around the territory of New Zealand. In the words of Brownlie:

It is by any standards an instrument from which heavy duty performance is expected. At one and the same time it is a part of the mana of Maori, the source of a political agenda, and a means of achieving particular ends... The importance of the Treaty cannot be doubted...[136]

The document itself is short, consisting of a preamble and three short articles. Any discussion of the content of the Treaty runs into difficulties owing to the significant distortions between the English and the Maori language versions of the Treaty. The main difficulties are over the narrow interpretation in the English text of words such as *'tino rangatiratanga'* and *'taonga'* which many suggest need to be interpreted more as 'self-determination' and 'treasure' rather than the interpretation they merited in the English text.

The preamble to the Treaty expresses the wish by the Queen of England to 'protect the chiefs and sub-tribes of New Zealand', to 'preserve their chieftainship and their lands', and to 'maintain peace and good order'. To achieve this the Queen suggests that it is 'just' to appoint an administrator (Hobson), to negotiate with the people of New Zealand, '... to the end that their chiefs will agree to the Queen's Government being established over all parts of this land and adjoining islands'. The preamble indicates that one of the reasons why this would be 'just' would be the presence of many of the Queen's subjects already living on the islands, and '... others yet to come'.[137] In addition the rationale identified by the Queen for this extension of sovereignty is suggested as being '... so that no evil will come to Maori and European living in a state of lawlessness'.[138] The three 'laws' identified in the Treaty are as follows:

The first

The Chiefs of the Confederation and all the chiefs who have not joined that Confederation give absolutely to the Queen of England for ever the complete government over their land.

The second

The Queen of England agrees to protect the chiefs, the sub-tribes and all the people of New Zealand in the unqualified exercise of their chieftainship over their lands, villages and all their treasures. But on the other hand the Chiefs of the Confederation and all the

---

[136] Brownlie (n 7) 77.   [137] preamble *Treaty of Waitangi 1840*.
[138] ibid.

Chiefs will sell land to the Queen at a price agreed to by the person owning it and by the person buying it (the latter being) appointed by the Queen as her purchase agent.

The third

For this agreed arrangement therefore concerning the Government of the Queen, the Queen of England will protect all the ordinary people of New Zealand and will give them the same rights and duties of citizenship as the people of England.[139]

At face value the Treaty signifies a transaction between the Queen and the Maori chiefs whereby the Queen gains overall sovereignty over New Zealand and the exclusive right to purchase lands from the Maori.[140] In return, the Maori leadership appears to have gained an administrative head who would govern the territories; protection and 'unqualified' exercise of their chieftain-ship over the territory and all its treasures; and equal rights and duties in line with the 'people of England'.

The real issue with the Treaty was not so much what was gained by the parties, but what was lost.[141] From this perspective it would appear that the Crown lost nothing while the Maori chiefdom lost significantly. In addition, when the mis-interpretation of the Treaty and its subsequent violations are taken into account, it is clear that the Treaty did little in terms of the promises made.[142]

Even though the Treaty has been the subject of significant debate over its legal significance,[143] its political manifestations,[144] and even its philosophical leanings,[145] it is only in the last few decades that there has been a concerted effort at undoing some of the dramatic violations of the Treaty, through a range of remedies discussed in the subsequent sub-section of this chapter. Much of the historical writings on the Treaty concern the severe imperfections around the process and the validity and content of the text. More recently, discussions have been instigated over the relevance of the Treaty to questions facing the communi-ties today. It is clear that the Treaty is an 'eccentric document',[146] but with a clear

---

[139] *The Treaty of Waitangi* (Modern English translation) as contained in app 1, Evison (n 68) 356–7.

[140] For a criticism of Captain Hobson by the Colonial Office, see Orange (n 2) 98–100.

[141] As Bourassa and Strong put it, irrespective of the significance of the laws, it is clear that all exchanges were skewed to be beneficial to the European settlers (n 84) 251.

[142] See Douglas Graham, *Trick or Treaty?* (Victoria University of Wellington, Wellington: Institute of Policy Studies, 1997).

[143] See, generally, Brownlie (n 7) and Archie, Carol, *Maori Sovereignty: The Pakeha Perspective* (Aukland: Hodder Moa Beckett, Auckland, 1995) Ken S. Coates and P.G. McHugh (eds), *Living Relationships Kokiri Ngatahi: The Treaty of Waitangi in the New Millennium* (Wellington: Victoria University Press, 1998).

[144] F.M. Brookfield, 'The Treaty of Waitangi, the Constitution and the Future' (1995) 8 *BRNZS* 4–20 and F.M. Brookfield, 'Sovereignty: The Treaty, the Courts and the Tribunal' [1989] *NZ Rec L Rev* 292–8.

[145] Waldron (n 13) 58.

[146] Brownlie uses this phrase, identifying, among its 'eccentricities' issues over its objectives; the fact that it was not negotiated through any form of representative democracy and the fact that it has been rescinded in 1865 and also supplanted more recently through the *Native Lands Act*. Brownlie

impact on the framing of law between Maori and settlers, differentiating the settlement of New Zealand from the Australian experience.

In hindsight, the redressals of *Treaty of Waitangi* violations monitored by the
Waitangi Tribunal since its inception in 1975 have, in many cases, successfully
addressed issues that would have continued to be a barrier to genuine reconciliation between the Maori and the state of New Zealand. Recent governments
have been keen to enshrine the Treaty at the heart of New Zealand law, whether
as a 'vehicle for legal developments' or as an 'assemblage of vehicles relevant to
inter-communal relations'.[147] Thus the Treaty finds expression in the *Constitution
Act 1852*[148] (discussed briefly below), the *Treaty of Waitangi Act 1975*[149] and the
Treaty of Waitangi (State Enterprises) Act 1988.[150]

Legal writings have debated whether reconciliation is necessary[151] and whether
the concept of 'indigeneity' adds specific value.[152] Several scholars have examined
the provisions of the Treaty as well as its intrinsic legal value.[153] Questions of interpretation have centred around the meaning of the phrase *te tino rangatiratanga*
and the extent to which it respects the notion of self-determination (as discussed
below).[154] While protocol-related difficulties have been discussed elsewhere,[155]
what is more interesting from the perspective of this book is the question of interpretation of the Treaty, and the meanings ascribed to it by the signatories.

The discrepancies are visible in the original translation of the *Treaty of
Waitangi*—among the copies distributed to English missionaries to obtain
signatures was one version in English, which raised important questions over
the difference in meanings. Principally, this involved the interpretation of the
original term *kawanatanga*, which was broadly translated as 'sovereignty', while
the relatively wide meaning of the term *tino rangatiratanga* was diminished to
meaning possession.[156] A widening of *kawanatanga* (attributed in the Treaty

---

also goes on to show several contradictions that exist in the process and substance of the Treaty. See
Brownlie (n 7) 79.

[147] ibid 77.
[148] Newcastle-Grey (2 February 1853) and Ms Grey Letters 54.
[149] No 114 of 1975 (commenced 10 October 1975); *Treaty of Waitangi Amendment Act 1977* (23
December 1977). As amended by various schedules leading up to the *Treaty of Waitangi Amendment
Act 2006* No 077 (commenced 13 December 2006).
[150] No 105 (commenced 9 December 1987). As amended by *Treaty of Waitangi (State Enterprises)
Acts 1988–1991* No 006.
[151] Waldron (n 13) 56–82.   [152] Waldron (n 13) 60.
[153] See n 144 above.
[154] See Section 3.4.1. For more detail on the early days of the Waitangi Tribunal, see Michael
Belgrave (ed), *The Recognition of Aboriginal Tenure in New Zealand, 1840–1860* (WAI 45/G4)
(Wellington: Waitangi Tribunal). For early sources that reflect on the debate over land rights, see
James Busby, *The Pre-emption Land Question* (Auckland: Richardson and Sansom Publishers,
1859). Also see Louis Alexis Chamerovzow, *The New Zealand Question and the Rights of Aborigines*
(London: T.C. Newby, 1848). Also see Bryan D. Gilling, 'Engine of Destruction? An Introduction
to the History of the Maori Land Court' (1994) 24 *VUWLR* 115–39.
[155] The *Treaty of Waitangi* (Modern English translation) as contained in app 1, Evison (n 68) 96.
[156] ibid.

to the Queen and the Crown) and narrowing of *tino ranatiratanga* (addressing the rights of the chiefs) significantly changed the dimension of the Treaty. In addition, under Article 2, the original Maori language version called for the selling of Maori land to the Queen at mutually agreed prices, but this element was lost in the English version, where this was translated as giving the Queen the exclusive 'right of pre-emption' over Maori lands[157] What exacerbated these difficulties was that the English version of the Treaty was official, even though it only received thirty-nine of the five hundred-plus signatures.[158] It is clear that the meaning attributed to 'pre-emption' in English law was the right of the monarch to commandeer necessities exclusively, at especially favourable terms, a right usually exercised only in times of emergencies such as wars.[159] As Evison states:

The Treaty of Waitangi's guarantee of '*tino rangatiratanga*' was not what it had seemed. Chiefs had signed the Treaty equally with the Crown's representatives. But this equality vanished with the proclamation of British sovereignty, for the sovereignty of the British Crown is absolute and unconditional. British subjects are subject to parliamentary statutes. These, and not the Treaty, would determine Maori rights, and what land Maoris could have. Whether ministers would regard the Treaty of Waitangi as morally binding remained to be seen: it was certainly not going to be legally binding. This useful distinction was a refinement unknown to the Maori.[160]

As Brownlie highlights, the assumption of *te tino rangatiratanga* did not signify that tribal lands could be attributed to traditional forms of government to the exclusion of the rest of the system of law in New Zealand. This would contradict the notion of common citizenship as granted in Article 3, and legal principles that lean towards equality and representative government.[161] This is also borne out by the fact that the later *Treaty of Waitangi Act 1975*, does not address this claim. Rather Brownlie favours an approach that treats the Treaty as a living document:

The words of a statute or a treaty have a life of their own and, except in certain extreme cases, the positive elements can be developed. After all is said and done, the hypocrisy of power gives hostages to fortune. For the determinist all is lost from the start, and the concept of law is essentially denied.[162]

Irrespective of its original value, the phrase 'in accordance with the Treaty of Waitangi principles' has entered New Zealand's legal lexicon.[163] With

---

[157] ibid.   [158] ibid 96–101.

[159] For more on the concept of pre-emption and its comparative application, see, Brendon Edgeworth, 'Tenure, Allodialism, and Indigenous Rights at Common Law: English, United States, and Australian Law Compared After Mabo v Queensland' in 23 *AALR* (1994) 397. Also see the Waitangi Tribunal findings in the *Ngai Tahu Report*, (Wai 27) (1991), where the Crown's acquisition through pre-emption of large tracts of the South Island came in for serious criticism.

[160] Evison (n 68) 115.   [161] Brownlie (n 7) 38.

[162] ibid.

[163] ibid. Also see the *Huakina Development Trust v Waikato Valley Authority* [1987] 2 NZLR 188 where the court refers to the Treaty. Numerous statutes also refer to this phrase.

questions over its 'international status', its modern content with regard to pre-emption would fall foul of the peremptory norm of international law— the principle of non-discrimination on the basis of race.[164] Fundamental to the discussion of the Treaty and its validity is the notion of what constitutes 'traditional law', 'common law', and 'indigenous titles' to territory. This has been the source of significant questions posed to the Waitangi Tribunal, which have been resolved, mostly in favour of the applicants.[165] The onus of treaty interpretation and guardianship has fallen to the Waitangi Tribunal which has exercised its jurisdiction mindful of the need to foster reconciliation, placing overt emphasis on direct negotiations between the claimants and the Crown through a process of genuine dialogue.[166] The impact of the Tribunal has also been significant through the take-up of its recommendations by the Crown and the extent to which the courts have drawn on its reports, as well as the quality of its mandate in terms of binding decisions (in the specific context of the State Enterprises Act).

There are three key procedural issues: (*a*) only Maori can bring a claim before the Tribunal;[167] (*b*) claims over land can only relate to Crown land and not private ownership;[168] and (*c*) the procedure, being non-contentious, has been suggested as being open to legal uncertainties.[169]

---

[164] See generally, Michael Banton, *International Action Against Racial Discrimination* (Oxford: Oxford University Press, 1996).

[165] See e.g. Waitangi Tribunal [all] *Manukau Claim*, (Wai 8) (1985); *Orakei Claim*, (Wai 9) (1985); *Waiheke Claim*, (Wai 10)(1987); *Te Roroa Report*, (Wai 38)(1992); *Muriwhenua Land Report*, (Wai 45) (1997); *Hauraki Report*, (Wai 686)(2006); *Ngati Rangiteaorere Claim*, (Wai 32) (1990) ; *Poukani Report*, (Wai 33)(1993); *Te Ika Whenua Energy Assets Report*, (Wai 212)(1998); *Te Whanganui-a-Orotu Report*, (Wai 55)(1995); *Mohaka Ki Ahuriri Report*, (Wai 119)(2004); *Te Whanganui a Tara me ona Takiwa: Report on the Wellington District*, (Wai 145)(2003); *Treaty of Waitangi Act and Whanganui River*, (Wai 167)(1999); *Rekohu: A report on the Moriori and Ngati Mutunga Claims in the Chatham islands*, (Wai 64)(2001) and *Te Runanga o Wharekauri Rekohu Incorporated v Attorney-General* [1993] 2 NZLR 301; *Te tau Ihu o te Waka a Maui: Preliminary Report on Te tau Ihu Customary Rights in the Statutory Ngai Tahu Takiwa*, (Wai 785)(2007) and *Waimumu Trust (SILNA) Report*, (Wai 1090)(2005).

[166] The mandate of this Tribunal and its functioning are discussed below under 'remedies'.

[167] See Waitangi Tribunal, *Claim Relating to Maori Privilege*, (Wai 19)(1985) where a non-Maori's claim of discriminatory privileges accruing to Maori was dismissed as outside the scope of the Tribunal's jurisdiction, since only Maori could bring claims before it.

[168] This is a similar issue to that in Australia raised by pastoral leases. However, any entertainment of private claims in New Zealand would fall foul of the existing Torrens system of registration of land title established by *Land Transfer Act 1952* [Public Act No 52 1952]. Also see Law Commission 'Issues paper: Review of the Land Transfer Act (October 2008, available at <http://www.lawcom.govt.nz> [last accessed 23 January]). For more, see G.W. Hinde, D.W. McMorland and P.B.A. Sim, *Land Law* (Wellington: Lexis Nexis, 1978). The discussion in *Te Weehi v Regional Fisheries Officer* [1987] NZLR 63 at 67 focused on whether non-territorial Maori rights in common law may have survived over private claims despite the existence of firm registered titles. This argument remains relatively unproven and would not impact territorial rights. For more, see P.G. McHugh, 'Aboriginal Servitudes and the Land Transfer Act' (1986) 16 *VUWLR* 313.

[169] Brownlie (n 7) 85.

3.3.1.2 *The Contemporary Human Rights Framework:* New Zealand Bill of Rights Act 1990[170] *and the* Human Rights Act 1993[171]

If the *Treaty of Waitangi* provides the rights framework for the claim of indigenous rights, the *New Zealand Bill of Rights Act* (BORA) and the *Human Rights Act 1993* provide the contemporary human rights framework. BORA enshrines human rights values into New Zealand law but addresses specific rights that could be considered particularly relevant to minorities. Administered by the Ministry of Justice, the Act seeks

(a) to affirm, protect, and promote human rights and fundamental freedoms in New Zealand; and

(b) to affirm New Zealand's commitment to the International Covenant on Civil and Political Rights.[172]

Among the substantive rights contained in the Bill are the following that are of special interest to indigenous and minority rights protection:

(a) Freedom of thought, conscience, and religion;[173]
(b) Freedom of expression;[174]
(c) Manifestation of religion and belief;[175]
(d) Freedom of peaceful assembly;[176]
(e) Freedom of association;[177] and
(f) Freedom of movement.[178]

In addition, BORA also has provisions for the protection of human rights in the context of search, arrest, and detention.[179] The Bill has a specific section entitled 'Non-Discrimination and Minority Rights', in Articles 19 and 20. Article 19 focuses on freedom from discrimination and is framed in the following terms:

(1) Everyone has the right to freedom from discrimination on the grounds of discrimination in the Human Rights Act 1993;

(2) Measures taken in good faith for the purpose of assisting or advancing persons or groups of persons disadvantaged because of discrimination that is unlawful by virtue of Part 2 of the Human Rights Act 1993 do not constitute discrimination.[180]

---

[170] Public Act 1990 No 109, date of assent 28 August 1990.
[171] Public Act 1993 No 82, date of assent 10 August 1993.
[172] preamble, New Zealand Bill of Rights 1990.
[173] art 13, ibid.   [174] art 14, ibid.   [175] art 15, ibid.
[176] art 16, ibid.   [177] art 17, ibid.   [178] art 18, ibid.
[179] This includes protection against unreasonable search and seizure (art 21); liberty of persons (art 22); an articulation of the rights of persons arrested or detained (art 23); the rights of persons charged (art 24); minimal standards of criminal procedure (art 25); guarantees against retroactive penalties and double jeopardy (art 26); and a particularly interesting 'right to justice' (art 27). This is further supplemented by the *Victims' Rights Act 2002* Public Act No 39 (as at 29 November 2007) which aims to improve provisions for the treatment and rights of victims of offences.
[180] This section was substituted, as from 1 February 1994, by s 145 *Human Rights Act 1993* (Public Act No 82, 1993).

Article 20 of the New Zealand Bill of Rights specifically reflects on the rights of minorities, stating:

A person who belongs to an ethnic, religious, or linguistic minority in New Zealand shall not be denied the right, in community with other members of that minority, to enjoy the culture, to profess and practise the religion, or to use the language, of that minority.[181]

This wording is based on Article 27 of the *International Covenant on Civil and Political Rights*, recognizing the need specifically to protect minorities, highlighting the same traditional grounds for identification of minorities, framing the right as individually based but collectively enjoyed, and outlining similar substantive content.[182]

While BORA focuses on traditional civil and political rights, provisions for social security are addressed through the *Social Security Act 1964*,[183] the purpose of which is identified[184] as enabling provision of financial and other support,[185] including the alleviation of hardship.[186]

The *Human Rights Act 1993* was passed in New Zealand with a view to consolidating and amending the *Race Relations Act 1971*[187] and the *Human Rights Commission Act 1977*,[188] and providing overall protection for human rights in New Zealand.[189] The Act continues the Commission on Human Rights created by the *Human Rights Commission Act 1977*, with one of its primary functions identified as encouraging '... the maintenance and development of harmonious relations between individuals and among the diverse groups in New Zealand society'.[190] Among other relevant functions for minorities and indigenous peoples are: the power to advocate for human rights;[191] make public statements;[192]

---

[181] art 20, New Zealand Bill of Rights 1990.

[182] In its last report to the UN Human Rights Committee, New Zealand reported on measures taken for the promotion of the Maori and the Pacific Islanders. No mention was made of measures to address the rights of new immigrants, though this would be in keeping within the parameters of what are universally agreed as 'minorities'. See *New Zealand State Report* (fourth period report) UN doc CCPR/C/NZL/2001/4 (14 May 2001) 63–71.

[183] Public Act 1964 No 136, date of assent 1964.

[184] This provision was inserted into the Act on 24 September through s 23 of the *Social Security Amendment Act 2007* (Public Act 2007, No 20).

[185] As articulated in art 1A(a)(i), (ii), and (iii).

[186] art 1A(b).

[187] No 150 (commenced 1 April 1972); as amended by *Race Relations Amendment Act 1989* (No 127) (commenced 12 December 1989).

[188] No 049 (commenced 1 September 1978); (23 October 1981) *Human Rights Commission Amendment Act 1981*; (23 November 1982) *Human Rights Commission Amendment Act 1982*; (1 February 1984) *Human Rights Commission Amendment Act 1983*; (8 March 1985) *Human Rights Commission Amendment Act 1985*.

[189] A short description of the Act is as available at <http://www.legislation.govt.nz/act/public/1993/0082/latest/DLM304212.html?search=qs_all%40act_Human+Rights&sr=1> [last accessed 14 April 2008].

[190] art 5(1)(b), *Human Rights Act 1993*.   [191] art 5(2)(a), ibid.

[192] art 5(2)(b), ibid.

receive representations from the public;[193] undertake inquiries;[194] bring and appear in proceedings;[195] and intervene in issues concerning human rights.[196] One important feature is the role envisaged for the Commission in understanding the human rights dimensions of the *Treaty of Waitangi*.[197]

The Commission is required to report to the prime minister over issues such as the desirability of action to better promote human rights;[198] the desirability of joining new international instruments;[199] and the implications of any proposed policy that may affect human rights;[200] as well as to develop national action plans around human rights.[201] Unlike human rights bodies in other jurisdictions, New Zealand's Commission has a particular role in relation to aliens, expressed as follows:

The Commission has, in order to carry out its primary functions under subsection (1), the following functions:

(l) to make public statements in relation to any group of persons in, or who may be coming to, New Zealand who are or may be subject to hostility, or who have been or may be brought into contempt, on the basis that that group consists of persons against whom discrimination is unlawful under this Act.[202]

The Act does not create special provisions for members of minorities or indigenous groups to be represented in the Commission of Human Rights, although the possession of knowledge and/or experience of the *Treaty of Waitangi* and the rights of indigenous people is one of the criteria for appointment.[203]

The Act identifies thirteen grounds on which discrimination is prohibited. This includes sex,[204] marital status,[205] religious belief,[206] ethical belief,[207] colour,[208] race,[209] ethnic or national origin (including nationality or citizenship),[210] disability,[211] age,[212] political opinion,[213] employment status,[214] family status,[215] or sexual orientation.[216] The Act also identifies and seeks to prohibit other kinds of discrimination, including racial disharmony,[217]

---

[193] art 5(2)(f), ibid.　　　　[194] art 5(2)(h), ibid.
[195] art 5(2)(i), ibid.　　　　[196] art 5(2)(j), ibid.
[197] The text of art 5(2)(d) states the function as being: 'to promote by research, education, and discussion a better understanding of the human rights dimensions of the Treaty of Waitangi and their relationship with domestic and international human rights law' ibid.
[198] art 5(2)(k)(i), ibid.　　　　[199] art 5(2)(k)(ii), ibid.
[200] art 5(2)(k)(iii), ibid.　　　[201] art 5(2)(m), ibid.
[202] art 5(2)(l), ibid.　　　[203] art 11(1)(a)(iii), ibid.
[204] art 21(1)(a), ibid.　　　[205] art 21(1)(b), ibid.
[206] art 21(1)(c), ibid.
[207] Envisaged as being the lack of a religious belief and covered under art 21(1)(d), ibid.
[208] Which is not defined but is covered under art 21(1)(e), ibid.
[209] art 21(1)(f), ibid.　　　[210] art 21(1)(g), ibid.　　　[211] art 21(1)(h), ibid.
[212] art 21(1)(i), ibid.　　　[213] art 21(1)(j), ibid.　　　[214] art 21(1)(k), ibid.
[215] art 21(1)(l), ibid.　　　[216] art 21(1)(m), ibid.　　　[217] art 61, ibid.

sexual harassment,[218] racial harassment,[219] indirect discrimination,[220] victimization[221] and advertisements.[222] The provisions on racial disharmony and racial harassment are particularly important to this study.

3.3.2 The Rights Package: Thematic Analysis

The Treaty and statutes discussed above, along with the modern *Constitution of New Zealand*,[223] provide the framework for indigenous and minority rights in New Zealand. To be able to obtain a nuanced understanding of the range of rights that merit attention, it is necessary to focus on key thematic areas. The rest of this section will focus on *a*) Land Rights; *b*) Public Participation, Education and Linguistic Rights; *c*) Fishing and Resource Management; *d*) the Foreshore and Seabed Act; and *e*) Immigration and its impact on rights.

3.3.2.1 Land Rights

The notion of the pre-emption of the Crown's rights to acquire property was not a new phenomenon since it had already been crucial to the acquisition of territory in North America.[224] The first real challenge to this notion arose in 1847, where the relatively newly-formed New Zealand Supreme Court, echoing precedent from North America, found that since the Crown was the source of all land titles, no title obtained from any other source could be sustained against this type of title.[225] This interpretation, while drawing on the spirit intended by the drafters of the English version of the *Treaty of Waitangi*, was in line with one of the first statutes in New Zealand on this issue which stated that '. . . the sole and absolute right of pre-emption from the said aboriginal inhabitants vests in and can only be exercised by Her said Majesty'. Consequently other purchases that may have occurred without the consent of the Government 'would simply be null and void.'[226]

The creation of a special court to address questions of native title may have been the way to avoid further conflict, though for a variety of reasons articulated by Banner, this failed to address Maori dispossession or their distaste for the manner in which it was achieved.[227] Banner identifies reasons why the legal

---

[218] art 62, ibid.   [219] art 63, ibid.   [220] art 65, ibid.
[221] art 66, ibid.   [222] art 67, ibid.
[223] *Constitution Act 1986* No 114 (commenced 1 January 1987).
[224] McHugh (n 2) 102–3.   [225] *R v Symonds* (1847) at 388–9.
[226] See *An Ordinance to Repeal* (1841) NZ Stat, No 2, para 2. For other pieces of early legislation concerning land rights, see *Native Land Purchase Act* (1846), NZ Stat, No 19; *Native Lands Act* (1867) NZ Stat, No 43; *Native Lands Act* (1869) NZ Stat, No 26; *Immigration and Public Works Act (Amendment) I* (1871) NZ Stat, No 75; *Native Land Act* (1873) NZ Stat No 56; *Native Land Act 1873* (Amendment Act 1878) NZ Stat, No 1; *Native Land Administration Act* (1886) NZ Stat, No 23; *Native Land Act* (1888) NZ Stat, No 36; *Native Land Court Act* (1894) NZ Stat, No 43 and *Native Land Act* (1909) NZ Stat, No 15.
[227] Banner (n 36) 71.

regime set up to adjudicate the transfer of property from Maori to settlers was less than successful in guaranteeing Maori rights.[228] Among these were the imperfections in the process and interpretation (whether deliberate or unwitting);[229] the distance and time involved in accessing the Court;[230] and the direct and indirect costs associated with the application process.[231] Summing up the extent to which market ideology rather than the actions of individuals dictated the flow of land resources away from the Maori, Banner states:

> Some Maori losses over the course of the 19th century were caused by outright fraud by the English. Some were caused by an inability to bargain as well as the English. Some sellers frittered away the proceeds. But much of what the Maori lost in the 19th century cannot be attributed to the actions of individuals, whether sharp practice by buyers or imprudence by sellers. Those losses were due instead to the structure of the market in which buyers and sellers operated. There is no way to calculate the relative magnitude of each cause of loss, because that would require a case-by-case accounting of each transaction, and in each case one would have the theoretically impossible task of constructing the non-existent baseline of a 'neutral', or 'free', market and then estimating what the land's value would have been in the market so constructed. But even if we cannot apportion relative causal weight between the market and its occupants, we can at least recognize that the occupants do not bear all the blame; some belongs to the market itself.[232]

Some may argue that this analysis is misleading. While it is true that individuals may not bear direct responsibility for engaging in activities calculated to raise the level of their financial gain, the state, by failing to control such individuals, could not deny culpability. Banner's argument, in conjunction with Waldron's scepticism about measures of restorative justice,[233] could effectively invalidate any attempt to do so.[234] In the literature to date[235] the notion of state responsibility for past violations is generally accepted,[236] even though it inevitably breaks down in the face of understanding the practical implications of how

[228] In addition for an insight into the deviousness with which some land deals were concluded, see Miller (n 21) 108–14.

[229] Banner (n 36) 73–82.   [230] ibid 82–9.

[231] ibid 86–8.   [232] ibid 90.

[233] See Jeremy Waldron 'Redressing Historical Injustice' in Lukas H. Meyer (ed), *Justice in Time: Responding to Historical Injustice* (Baden-Baden: Nomos Verlagsgesellschaft, 2004) 55–77. In addition, any attempt at restorative justice in this realm would naturally need to be mindful of the current regime protecting property as enshrined in the *Protection of Personal Property Rights Act 1988* [Public Act 1988, No 4, date of assent 12 March]. See esp arts 31A-B, inserted on 1 July 1993 via s 362(1) *Te Ture Whenua Maori Act 1993* [Public Act 1993, No 4].

[234] For more on this kind of argument, see Peter Karsten, *Between Law and Custom: 'High' and 'Low' Legal Cultures in the Lands of the British Diaspora: The United States, Canada, Australia and New Zealand, 1600–1900* (Cambridge: Cambridge University Press, 2002).

[235] For a recent welcome addition to the literature on this topic, see Federico Lenzerini (ed), *Reparations for Indigenous Peoples: International & Comparative Perspectives* (Oxford: Oxford University Press, 2008).

[236] The general difficulties of addressing historic wrong has been addressed by M. Chowdry and C. Mitchell, 'Responding to Historic Wrongs: Practical and Theoretical Problems' in 27(2) *OJLS* (2007) 339–54.

reparations could be made, their magnitude, and who the bearers of the repara-
tive costs should be.[237]

Bourassa and Strong show the extent to which the New Zealand government
has sought to accommodate the issue of restitution of land to the Maori, while at
the same time showing the extent to which the Maori social structure has been
a factor in the process.[238] Using the example of the successful Waikato-Tainui
claim,[239] Bourassa and Strong show how:

...the decentralized power structure of Maori society makes it difficult to resolve land
issues, but that tribes with unusually strong leadership will tend to fare relatively well.[240]

Also:

...the greater visibility and involvement of Maori in mainstream New Zealand
society works to their advantage when compared with indigenous groups in other
countries.[241]

The recent attempt to adjudicate on Maori territory can be traced back to the
restitution law underlying the establishment of the Waitangi Tribunal in 1975.
The scope of the Act was restricted to grievances post-1975, and could not be
considered a general provision addressing the dispossession of the Maori.[242] The
Act was amended in 1985 to extend coverage back to 1840, deemed as the first
point at which land acquisitions began.[243] The 1985 Act provided for the creation
of a special court, the Waitangi Tribunal, which was mandated to hear claims
and make recommendations to the government on indigenous land settlement
disputes.[244] Of the high proportion of claims that have been filed by numerous tribes, priority is given to historical claims of tribes concerning alienation of
property (mainly land) and fishing rights.[245]

Summarizing the history of Maori dispossession, Bourassa and Strong state:

...the tribes were dispossessed of all or almost all of their lands: some losses occurred
through transactions viewed by Maori as leases and by settlers as sales; some through
sales to private purchasers in violation of tribal and Crown law; some through sales to

---

[237] See Dinah Shelton, 'Reparations for Indigenous Peoples: The Present Value of Past Wrongs'
in Federico Lenzerini (ed), *Reparations for Indigenous Peoples: International & Comparative
Perspectives* (Oxford: Oxford University Press, 2008).

[238] See Steven C. Bourassa and Ann Louise Strong (n 84) 227–60.

[239] See *He Whakatakotoranga Kaupapa; Submission to the Treaty of Waitangi Tribunal, Makaurau
Marae, Ihumatao,* Centre for Maori Studies and Research, University of Waikato, Occasional Paper
No 25, 1984. Also see *Bed of the Wanganui River* [1962] NZLR 600; *Tai Whati: Judicial Decisions
Affecting Maori Land* (Maori Affairs Department, 1981) 96–8.

[240] See Bourassa and Strong (n 84) 228.   [241] ibid.

[242] ibid.

[243] *Treaty of Waitangi Amendment Act 1985* (Public Act No 148, commenced 9 January 1986).

[244] art 3, ibid.

[245] Bourassa and Strong (n 84) 228. The authors offer a comprehensive if dated view on the
settlement of such claims, highlighting the complex discussions that have emerged, some of which
will be the focus of this sub-section.

the Crown where there was no mutual understanding of the terms of the contract and/or violation of the sales contract by the Crown; some through confiscation by the Crown; and some through the enforcement of laws designed to terminate tribal communal ownership.[246]

As in any other jurisdiction where there are competing legal regimes, the difficulty in New Zealand law has been the extent to which ordinary courts have a role to play in Waitangi deliberations over land and other rights. The best proponent of the role the courts have had to play is captured in the *Maori Council case*,[247] where the court acted beyond the normal bounds of justiciability and played a 'rescue act' in maintaining coherence and balancing interests.[248]

3.3.2.2 Public Participation, Education, and Language

Several authors have argued that while there are some discussions over the manner in which levels of educational attainment are measured, the difference in the quality of education inevitably created inequalities in the job market, proving disadvantageous to non-European New Zealanders (as opposed to immigrants who come in on the basis of their qualifications).[249] It can also be stated with some certainty that language and education is an important axis through which the distinct Maori identity has been maintained from its earliest manifestation after the arrival of the settlers,[250] to more contemporary discussions. Even though in theory the Maori were promised the rights and privileges of British subjects by the *Treaty of Waitangi*, in practice Maori voting rights were not taken seriously until 1858, with formal representation only achieved in 1868.[251]

Parkinson traces the manner and extent to which the use of the Maori language in the official public realm grew by studying documents and events between 1865–1900 in government and in Parliament.[252] The process of official bilingualism begun by the two versions of the *Treaty of Waitangi* was interrupted almost immediately by the threat of war during the 1840s. In fact, Maori was rarely used in government between 1840 and 1865, and even after the election of representatives in 1868, the four token Maori in Parliament were 'encouraged' to speak English.[253] Thus, even though eighty-five Acts were passed by Parliament in 1866, none were translated into Maori, not even the ones directly affecting the

---

[246] For instance during discussions occurring in the context of the *Native Reserves Act 1856* the *Ngai Tahu* were urged to privatize their land holdings, ostensibly to promote 'moral and religious progress'. Yet, as Evison documents, the real motive behind this was to weaken tribal influences and encourage competitiveness among the Maori. See Evison (n 68) 271.

[247] [1987] 1 NZLR 641.   [248] Brownlie (n 7) 87.

[249] For analysis and explanation of the problem of gathering such evidence in New Zealand, see John Gibson, 'Sheepskin Effects and the Returns to Education in New Zealand; Do They Differ by Ethnic Groups?' (2000) 34 *NZEP*.

[250] Miller (n 21) 178–91.

[251] See General Assembly, *Maori Representation Act 1867* as discussed by Parkinson (n 71) 1.

[252] ibid.   [253] ibid 3.

'natives'.[254] In more contemporary times under the *Maori Language Act 1987*[255] the New Zealand government and administration has two official languages. Maori (referred to as the New Zealand language) is recognized as a *taonga* (cultural property or treasure) that merits direct protection in the *Treaty of Waitangi*. The earliest attempt to engage Maori participation in government can be traced back to the *Kohimarama Conference* in July and August of 1860.[256] The token four seats granted to Maori were authorized under the *Maori Representation Act 1867*.[257]

The issue of representation, language, and education has also come up before the Waitangi Tribunal. An interesting case arose over exactly who had the mandate to represent the Maori. In the *Te Whanau o Waipareira* claim[258] a Maori urban group, not linked through tribal kinship, constituted themselves into an association and sought to negotiate with the Crown over claims for social welfare. While it was clear that Maori had exclusive *locus standi* before the Tribunal, it had been assumed that collective claims would need to be made on the basis of existing tribal and kin-based structures. However, the Tribunal found in favour of the group, arguing that as long as it was advocating Maori claims against the Crown it merited standing before the Tribunal.[259]

The closure of the Mokai School by the government was the cause of complaint in one claim before the Tribunal. The claimants argued that:

This isn't really just about education. This is about who we are. Our identity. This is about our whole being, our wairua, our tinana, our tikanga, our kawa...And it is time for us to stand up, as we are doing, and reclaim that...It comes from an inbuiltness to strive and to fight for who we are. You take away a man's identity, he has no face. You move these Tamariki out of Mokai, they have no face. They are faceless out in the world. You keep them here, you give them solid roots and solid foundations, and they go out to the world and they can face them with a face. So that when people ask them, 'Ko wai koe?' 'Ae ko au', and [they] say who they are with pride and with dignity.[260]

The Tribunal called upon the government to re-open the school which the Department of Education duly did. The positive obligation regarding education

---

[254] ibid 37.

[255] No 176 (commenced 1 August 1987); as amended by the *Maori Language Amendment Act 1991* (Public Act No 040, commenced 20 June 1991).

[256] Parkinson (n 71). For more on the early parliamentary debates concerning Maori participation, see 7–11.

[257] Available in app B in Dora Alves, *The Maori and the Crown: An Indigenous People's Struggle for Self-Determination* (Connecticut: Greenwood Press, 1999) 153.

[258] Waitangi Tribunal, (Wai 414)(1998).

[259] The Tribunal has also addressed claims for better representation of Maori on various bodies, see e.g. Waitangi Tribunal [all] *Claim relating to Maori Representation on the Auckland Regional Authority*, (Wai 25)(1986); *Te Arawa Mandate Report: Te Wahanga Tuarua*, (Wai 1150)(2005); *Rekohu: A Report on the Moriori and Ngati Mutunga Claims in the Chatham Islands*, (Wai 64)(2001); *Appointment to Treaty of Waitangi Fisheries Commission Report* (Wai 321)(1992), and the *Maori Electoral Option Report*, (Wai 413)(1993).

[260] See Waitangi Tribunal, *Mokai School Report*, (Wai 789)(2000).

was also addressed by the Tribunal in its *Report on the Aoteraoa Institute Claim concerning Te Wananga o Aotearoa*.[261] A definitive claim addressed by the Tribunal was *Te Reo Maori Claim* which arose in the context of the official recognition of the Maori language. The claimants argued that a failure to protect the language constituted a violation of Article 2 of the *Treaty of Waitangi* and called for official recognition of the language as part of national heritage. Having analysed the arguments put forward by the claimants, the Tribunal made specific recommendations. It called on the Crown:

a) to pass legislation enabling any person who wishes to do so to use the Maori language in all courts of law and in any dealings with government departments, local authorities, and other public bodies;
b) to create (by statute) a supervisory body to foster use of the Maori language;
c) to institute an inquiry into the education of Maori children ensuring that those wishing to learn Maori be able to do so from an early age through state aid;
d) to formulate a broadcasting policy in line with the Crown obligation of recognizing and protecting the Maori language; and
e) to make the necessary amendments to move towards bilingualism in Maori and in English as a prerequisite for appropriate positions of public employment.

The Tribunal did not advocate the establishment of *Te Reo Maori* as a compulsory subject in school, nor (as is usual in policies of official bilingualism) did it request the transmission of all documents in both languages. The justification used was an interesting one—the tribunal stressed that it would be more profitable to promote the language as a valuable national possession rather than imposing it on those who may be unwilling to grasp its importance.[262] The impact of the discussion was visible the following year, when *Te Reo Maori* was made an official language of New Zealand.[263] The recommendation of a supervisory body saw the creation of *Te Taura Whiri i te Reo Maori* (the Maori Language Commission) with the mandate of promoting the language. This Maori Language Act is administered in *Te Puni Kokiri* (Ministry of Maori Development).[264]

---

[261] Waitangi Tribunal, (22 December 2005) available at <http://www.waitangi-tribunal.govt.nz/reports/view.asp?reportID=9982ADF5-40C6-420E-8899-A86640DA6D0C> [last accessed 4 August 2008].
[262] This is in sharp contrast to the policy around national language in Ireland. See Joshua Castellino, 'Affirmative Action for the Protection of Linguistic Rights: An Analysis of International Human Rights Legal Standards in the Context of the Irish Language' (2004) 25 *DULJ* 1–43.
[263] Act No 176 (20 July 1987).
[264] The words *Te Puni Kokiri* (Ministry of Maori Development) were substituted, as from 1 January 1992, for the words Iwi Transition Agency pursuant to s 9(3)(a) *Ministry of Maori Development Act 1991* (1991 Public Act No 145).

3.3.2.3 Fishing[265] and Resource Management[266]

As Boast writes, one of the most valuable features of the work of the Waitangi Trubunal was its analysis of customary environmental and conservation law in the context of the management of fishing.[267] It did this through a consideration of numerous claims early in the life of the Tribunal,[268] but more importantly, in identifying the applicable law as '...the collective wisdom of generations of peoples whose existence depended upon their perception and observation of nature'.[269]

In the specific context of fishing and management of fisheries, the Waitangi Tribunal established a set of 10 tribal rules in *Muriwhenua*:

(i)   Fisheries were tribally owned in 1840. Individual use rights were subject to and flowed from the tribal overright.

(ii) The Maori text guarantees a tribal control of Maori matters. That includes the right to regulate the access of tribal members to tribal resources.

(iii) The tribal overright was customarily unstructured. Long held family rights were recognized. Rules were simply known. Individual use rights were based on kinship and marriage and not merely on boundaries.

(iv) The past Maori failure to make by-laws for fishing grounds, under enabling laws from 1900, was not due to tribal disinterest, for the Governor reserved no fishing grounds.

(v)   The right of regulation has become a duty in our time, to protect the resource and to bring a certainty to the law. This is now required through population and other changes. It is also contrary to the public interest when Maori purporting to exercise customary fishing rights cannot be made bound by their own tribal rules.

---

[265] For more on the controversy concerning fishing rights and the Maori, see R.P. Boast, 'The Treaty of Waitangi; A Framework for Resource Management Law' (1989) 19 *VUWLR* 1–68 Also see Richard A. Finnigan, 'Indian treaty Analysis and Off-reservation Fishing Rights: A Case Study (1975) *51 WLR* 61 and John R. Schmidhauser, 'The Struggle for Cultural Survival: The Fishing Rights of the Treaty Tribes of the Pacific Northwest' (1976) *52 NDL* 30, for the extent to which the situation in New Zealand merits comparison with the experiences in Washington and Oregon in the United States of America.

[266] For an overview of New Zealand's performance against USA benchmarks on resource management and environmental legislation issues, see Tim Kelley and David Slaney, 'A Comparison of Environmental Legislation and Regulation in New Zealand and the United States' (2006) 69 *JEH* 20–2.

[267] Boast (n 265) 10.

[268] See e.g. *Kaituna* (Sir Charles Bennet and ors, Te Arawa) Re Kaituna River, (Wai 4) (1984); *Mangonui Sewerage Report* (Mangonui Sewerage, Ngati Kahu), (Wai 17) (1988); *Manukau Report*, Nganeko Minhinnick and ors (Ngati Te Ata and Tainui, re Manukau), (Wai 8) (1985); and *Report of the Waitangi Tribunal on the Muriwhenua Fishing Claim*, Interim Report re Maori Fishing Rights (Wai 262) May 1988, Hon Matiu Rata and ors (Ngati Kuri and ors, Re Muriwhenua lands and Fisheries).

[269] *Motonui Report*, (Te Atiawa, re Motonui), (Wai 6)(1983) 34.

(vi)   It is the right of tribes to determine their own membership, to license their own members and to deny tribal fishing rights to those of its members who do not observe its rules.

(vii)   It is the right of tribes to permit persons outside the tribal group to enjoy any part of the tribal fishing resource, whether generally or for any particular purpose of occasion.

(viii)   As a matter of custom, Maori individuals have no greater fishing rights than members of the general public when fishing outside their tribal areas, except to the extent that they have an authority from the local tribe and abide by its rules.

(ix)   Neither custom nor the Treaty confers on any Maori the right to destroy the resource.

(x)   It is consistent with the Treaty that the Crown and the tribes should consult and assist one another in devising arrangements for a tribal control of its treaty fishing interests, that they should aid one another in enforcing them, and that the tribes should furnish the Crown with all proper returns.[270]

This shows the push in the Tribunal for greater participatory rights in the management of fisheries resources, mindful of the needs of general public interest. The emphasis in each of the rules, and in all of them collectively, is on use and management rather than ownership. In terms of fishing rights, a study of the relevant case law[271] and Waitangi Tribunal pronouncements[272] strongly suggests that Maori fishing rights cannot be denied unless voluntarily extinguished by the Maori or expressly abrogated by Crown legislation.[273] The *Conservation Act 1987*[274] also enshrines statute-based protection for Maori fishing rights, through a direct reference to Waitangi treaty rights,[275] and through an explicit caveat of non-molestation of Maori fishing rights.[276] In the context of the discussion on introduced species, the Court's ruling in the *McRitchie* case was explicit, finding:

[No] justification for treating Maori fishing rights reserved by Article II of the Treaty more narrowly than has been said by the Waitangi Tribunal to be the proper approach in

---

[270] Muriwhenua, (Wai 22)(1998) 230.

[271] esp *Te Runanga o Muriwhenua Inc v Attorney-General* [1990] 2NZLR 641; and more recently in the context of introduced species, see *Taranaki Fish and Game Council v McRitchie* (High Court, Wellington) AP No 19/97 (14 May 1998). Also see *Te Weehi v Regional Fisheries Officer* [1986] NZLR 680 (which examined the difference between general aboriginal rights and specific treaty-based rights in the context of non-exclusive subsistence rights *vis-à-vis* rights to subsequent commercial development).

[272] esp see Waitangi Tribunal, *Muriwhenua Fishing Report*, (Wai 22) (1998).

[273] This is reiterated by Kiri Chanwai and Benjamin Richardson, 'Re-working Indigenous Customary Rights? The Case of Introduced Species' (1998) 2 *NZJEL*157–86 at 167. Support for this statement is found in the (now dated but nonetheless relevant) work of McHugh (n 168) 57.

[274] *Conservation Act 1987* (reprint as at 30 June 2005) No 035.

[275] s 4, *Conservation Act 1987*.

[276] See s 26Z, *Conservation Act 1987*.

respect of sea-fisheries; that what is protected by Article II are the available fish, the places where fish are caught and the methods and practice of fishing.[277]

And crucially, the further pronouncement that:

... as a general proposition it would follow that a Maori fishing right in respect of a particular place would extent to all fish found in that place whether indigenous or not.[278]

It could be argued that one key component of the right of self-determination would be access for Maori to self-manage natural resources in a manner that is in harmony with indigenous culture, and probably more in keeping with contemporary environmental standards. The regime that currently governs this area is enshrined in the *Resource Management Act 1991*[279] and, to a lesser extent, the *Conservation Act 1987*,[280] the *Reserves Act 1977*,[281] and the *Wildlife Act 1953*.[282] A related question is the extent to which the regimes allow Maori to manage introduced species, an issue that has generated considerable controversy over the years.[283] The dispossession of traditional lands and erosion of lifestyles and means of subsistence has, frequently, led Maori to look for non-traditional resources. This raises fundamental questions over the extent to which customary legal regimes for traditional resources can be applied to non-traditional resources.[284] According to Chanwai and Richardson, resolution of this issue lies in being able to frame the problem more coherently, and then searching for suitable processes. Thus:

... these issues may be best resolved by broadening the terms of the problem from one of rights of *access* to the resources to rights of *management*. The notion of access to a resource without management responsibilities is anathema to notions of environmental stewardship ... in indigenous culture. Enduring solutions are unlikely to be found when the problem is framed solely in terms of 'do Maori have recognisable customary *rights?*'... Rather, the focus must be broadened to the establishment of institutional processes that allow Maori to critically develop and articulate their values in response to new circumstances or threats, and for these values to operate at the formative stage of government policy development.[285]

This raises fundamental questions over the relationship between Maori and the state, and whether the relationship is to be governed by the *Treaty of Waitangi* and

---

[277] *Taranaki Fish and Game Council v McRitchie* (High Court, Wellington) AP No 19/97, 14 May 1998, at 25.

[278] ibid.

[279] *Resource Management Act 1991* (Reprint as at 28 March 2007) No 013.

[280] *Conservation Act 1987* (Reprint as at 30 June 2005) No 035.

[281] No 066 (commenced 1 April 1978); as amended by subsequent Acts until the *Reserves Amendment Act 2005* No 068 (commenced 17 May 2005).

[282] *Wildlife Acts (1953 to 1996) by Parliamentary Counsel* No 006.

[283] For a greater exploration of this issue, see Chanwai and Richardson (n 273).

[284] This is controversial in the context of trout fishing and kiore rat eradication programmes. ibid 158.

[285] ibid.

the notion of lost rights that need recovering or a notion of partnership seeking solutions to future challenges. It could be argued that the ethos of the regime leans towards a partnership,[286] while its practical experience has focused on a recovery of lost rights. The need for future partnership has been emphasized by the World Conservation Union in its study entitled *Indigenous Peoples and Sustainability*[287] which supports the views of indigenous peoples as guardians of the environment and as ideal conservationists.[288] There are a number of studies that show that this general view is in line with Maori customary values,[289] suggesting that they would make ideal partners in the conservation battle. Against this, the society-wide discussion of the issue has raised questions about the Maori attitude to conservation, as expressed in:

> ... their historical record, especially in relation to forest management, and the hunting of moa and other birds, and the suggestion that the traditional tribal nature of Maori society denied the possibility of universal conservation rules as these varied in relation to the group in question.[290]

The thrust of these arguments, as pointed out by Chanwai and Richardson, appears to be that while it is uncontested that Maori are conservationists on issues that are treasured in their customary value system, this does not necessarily extend to a wider principle outside that remit.[291]

The *Waitakere Ranges Heritage Area Act 2008*[292] governs the heritage area of Waitakere which consists of the foothills and coast of the region, a total of 27,720 hectares of land between Auckland and the west coast of Waitakere City and Rodney District.[293] Its preamble explains the significance of the legislation and its rationale,[294] identifying the area of great national significance owing to its 'terrestrial and aquatic ecosystems, which include large continuous areas of primary and regenerating lowland and coastal rainforest, wetland, and dune systems with intact ecological sequences'.[295] The area is particularly important from the perspective of its human history since it is described as the 'distinctive cultural domain for Maori' lying with the 'rohe of both Te Kawerau A Maki and Ngati

---

[286] See Department of Conservation, *Kaupapa Atawhai Strategy* (1997) which argues for this approach.

[287] IUCN Inter-Commission Task Force on Indigenous Peoples, *Indigenous Peoples and Sustainability: cases and Actions (1997)*.

[288] See D.L. Crengle within *Indigenous Peoples and Sustainability: cases and Actions* (1997) 339–52.

[289] Notably J. Patterson, 'Maori Environmental Values' in 16 *Environmental Ethics* (1994) 397 ff.

[290] Chanwai and Richardson (n 273) esp 162.

[291] ibid esp 163.   [292] Local Act 2008, No 1, date of assent 8 April 2008.

[293] See (2) preamble, *Waitakere Ranges Heritage Act 2008*.

[294] The first line of the preamble contains a statement from Waitakere Chief Te Waatarauihi who spoke of his relationship to the area in his opening speech at the *Kohimarama Conference* in 1860. The Chief makes reference to the land being a fish, which had been fished up by Maui, and his intent to remain upon it until death.

[295] See (3), ibid.

Whatua'.[296] It is instructive to note that European settlement began in this area in 1841, with significant negative impact.[297] The Act provides a window to study the manner in which the land rights question was engaged in New Zealand, suggesting that the park was established over a period of 110 years through various modes of the transmission of land rights.[298] The resource issue also makes this an important zone, with the Waitakere Ranges including significant water catchment and storage and supply areas for the metropolitan Auckland area since 1902.[299] The rationale for the current legislation is the intense pressure caused by the urbanization and extension of metropolitan Auckland. This affects 21,000 people that live in the area, but presents a risk to the 'unique natural, landscape, cultural, historic, and community features of the area, including its farming and rural character'.[300] In this context the scheme envisaged by the Act provides for local statutory guidance in terms of:

(a) managing the cumulative and precedent effects of development on the landscape, the desired future character and amenity of the area, and the ecological and biological environment;
(b) maintaining a rural character for the communities in the foothills;
(c) maintaining low-density urban areas and coastal villages in which the built environment is subservient to the natural landscape;[301]
(d) managing activities adjacent to the boundary between urban and rural areas (particularly in relation to the metropolitan urban limit boundary); and
(e) protecting heritage features.[302]

It is instructive to note that the protection of residents does not feature explicitly. Rather in identifying twelve objectives, the Act tends towards the protection of ecological and heritage values of the site, without making any admission as to the importance of preserving an epitome of Maori culture.[303]

Boast offers insights into the extent to which the *Treaty of Waitangi* has contemporary relevance for resource management, especially in light of the resource management law review project that was undertaken by the government of New Zealand in 1988.[304] This resulted in two specific policy documents, *Directions*

---

[296] See (5), ibid.

[297] This admission is implied in the text of contained (5), ibid.

[298] s 6, ibid, identified this as consisting of 'gifts, grants, purchases, and vestings (including legislation promoted by Auckland City Council in 1941 to create the Auckland Centennial Memorial Park, commemorating the centenary of the Metropolitan District of Auckland)'.

[299] s 7, ibid.   [300] s 9, ibid.

[301] In terms of the protection of existing rights the Act makes clear provision in art 35 which restricts the Act to the Preservation of existing rights including title or ownership; and does not prejudice any potential land claim that may arise in the context of the Treaty of Waitangi, an Act, the common law, or in any other manner; or in relation to heritage area land or its natural resources.

[302] s 10, ibid.   [303] See art 8, ibid.   [304] Boast (n 265) 16.

for Change: A Discussion Paper[305] and *People, Environment and Decision Making: the Government's Proposal for Resource Management Law Reform.*[306]

3.3.2.4 Foreshore and Seabed Act

One of the rare occasions when New Zealand's contemporary record on human rights has been criticized was in the context of the passage of the *Foreshore and Seabed Act* (2004) (henceforth FSA).[307] The issue arose out of a decision in the New Zealand Court of Appeal in *Ngati Apa v Attorney-General (Ngati Apa)*[308] concerning the jurisdiction of the *Maori Land Court*.[309]This court has been examining the conversion of customary title to dry land into freehold title. The challenge arose as to whether the court had the mandate to exercise that same jurisdiction in relation to questions concerning the foreshore and seabed. The key issue arising was whether, under Maori customary law, there was any distinction between dry land and the foreshore and seabed. The mandate of the *Maori Land Court* is made explicit in *Te Ture Whenua Maori Act 1993*.[310] The controversy merited detailed comment in an urgent hearing held under the auspices of the Waitangi Tribunal. In its summary report of the proceedings, the Tribunal stressed, under the heading 'terminology':

From the outset, it is essential to be clear what we are talking about when we refer to the foreshore and seabed. First, what is the foreshore? It is the intertidal zone, the land between the high- and low-water-mark that is daily wet by the sea when the tide comes in. It does not refer to the beach above the high-water mark. The seabed is the land that extends from the low-water mark, and out to sea. The need to distinguish the foreshore from the adjacent dry land and seabed arises from the English common law, which developed distinct rules for that zone. In Maori customary terms, no such distinction exists.[311]

---

[305] *Directions for Change: A Discussion Paper* (Auckland: New Zealand Ministry for the Environment, 1988).

[306] *People, Environment and Decision Making: the Government's Proposal for Resource Management Law Reform* (Auckland: New Zealand Ministry for the Environment, 1988). Also see *Protected Areas Legislation Review: Issues for Public Comment* (Auckland: New Zealand Department of Conservation, 1988) and *Historic Places Legislation Review: Issues for Public Comment* (Auckland: New Zealand Department of Conservation, 1988).

[307] No 093 (2004). For an inside view of the issues, processes and results of the urgent appeal made by the Maori to the UNCERD, see Claire Charters and Andrew Erueti, 'Report from the Inside: The CERD Committee's review of the Foreshore and Seabed Act 2004' (2005) 36 *VUWLR* 257–90. This was the second instance of censure for New Zealand, the first on indigenous rights that is acknowledged as progressive. The first censure was by the Human Rights Committee in *Rameka v New Zealand* (15 December 2003) CCPR/C/79/D/1090/2003. As discussed elsewhere in this chapter the claim of a violation of indigenous rights made before the Human Rights Committee in *Apirana Mahuika v New Zealand* (27 October 2000) a/56/40 was not upheld by a majority of the Committee.

[308] [2003] 3 NZLR 143 (CA).

[309] This court was created in 1865 with the mandate of investigating ownership of tribal areas in accordance with Maori customary law, with the mandate to award freehold titles to those determined as owners. Its mandate is made explicit in the *Native Lands Act 1865*.

[310] *Te Ture Whenua Maori Act 1993* (Reprint as at 10 February 2005) No 003, s 1, arts 6–49.

[311] Waitangi Tribunal, *Report on the Crown's Foreshore and Seabed Policy*, (Wai 1071) (2004).

In many ways what was at stake in legal terms was a clash over the extent that customary law and formal common law could co-exist.[312] This question arises often where any system recognizes more than one system of law,[313] though in this case the concern appeared to be more a fear on the part of the government that access to the beach could be cut off for non-Maori New Zealanders.[314] In *Ngati Apa* the Court of Appeal overturned its previous decision in 1963 in *Ninety Mile Beach*[315] to state that, according to well-established principles of native law (as opposed to common law), customary title had survived the Crown's assertion of sovereignty in 1840, and that such title had not since been extinguished through general legislation.[316] Thus the belief that title to the foreshore and seabed in common law had been extinguished in favour of a public commons theory, was rejected. Instead the pronouncement was that title could be determined for these areas through customary native law.

While not granting title to any specific claimant, the decision opened the door for Maori claims of this nature before the *Maori Land Court*. The Court of Appeal decision extended the notion of what constituted 'Maori customary land' to include the foreshore and seabed, a reading bolstered by the lack of distinction in Maori customary law between the areas. As envisaged by the Court of Appeal decision, claimants would need to be able to appeal to the *Maori Land Court* to see whether they could change the status of any given segment of the foreshore and seabed from 'Maori customary land' into 'Maori freehold land' under the terms of the *Te Ture Whenua Maori Act 1993*.[317] This meant that Maori could claim customary title via the *Maori Land Court*, through its statutory function, and through the *High Court*, exercising inherent common law native title jurisdiction.[318]

With the possibility of the global commons argument being diluted, the Government acted swiftly to design legislation intended to overturn the decision. It released a report in August 2003 proposing legislation that would:

a) declare the entire foreshore and seabed common public domain;
b) guarantee right of public access along the foreshore;
c) remove the Maori Land Court's jurisdiction to grant freehold title in the context of the foreshore and seabed; and

---

[312] This point was also made by Professor Patrick Thornberry, Member of CERD, in closing comments at the hearing of the urgent appeal on this matter. See Charters and Erueti (n 307) 281.

[313] This arose in a similar context to *Mabo*, however with a different kind of conflict of law, between religious and constitution laws. For more, see Castellino and Domínguez Redondo (n 92) 36–44, 182–99.

[314] This fear is acknowledged by the authors of the claim at CERD level—see Charters and Erueti (n 307) 257–90. They counter that such issues could have been resolved by the courts, as in Australia, and through other processes short of exclusive Maori ownership. See ibid 266–7.

[315] *See In Re Ninety Mile Beach* [1963] NZLR 261 (CA).

[316] [2003] 3 NZLR 143 (CA).

[317] Charters and Erueti (n 307) 261.   [318] ibid.

d) establish a new Maori Land Court jurisdiction recognizing only 'customary rights' *vis-à-vis* the foreshore and seabed.[319]

The consultation took place under the shadow of hysteria and indignation among the non-Maori public, with the Maori universally rejecting the proposals.[320] In an urgent hearing the Waitangi Tribunal outlined concerns that the policy would violate due process, deny access to justice, endanger the rule of law, and result in unfair discrimination against the Maori, undermining the continuing proced-ure and spirit of reconciliation.[321] The select committee charged with managing the consultation and bringing the Bill to life received a number of submissions, the vast majority opposing the Bill.[322] Remarkably, the report of the Attorney-General, while admitting that the Bill may *prima facie* breach the freedom from discrimination requirement, justified the action in light of legal uncertainties generated by *Ngati Apa*.[323] With party politics dominating the discussion and no amendments possible, the Bill returned to Parliament in November 2004 with a *supplementary order paper* detailing a tighter sets of tests through which the High Court could determine 'territorial customary rights orders' (rather than inherent native title jurisdiction), and added mechanisms to be included under the *Resource Management Act 1991*[324] seeking to protect and enhance customary rights.[325]

An appeal was instigated to the Committee on the Elimination of Racial Discrimination (CERD) under its urgent appeal and early warn-ing mechanisms,[326] condensed by Charters and Erueti[327] as consisting of the following:

a) the notion that the action was discriminatory and fell under the jurisdiction of CERD;
b) the uncertainty generated by the *Ngati Apa* decision and the aftermath which made the issue urgent;
c) the FSA's statutory replacement regime for the recognition of Maori rights to the foreshore and seabed;
d) the need for the provision of redress;
e) the impact on the effective participation of Maori in public processes; and
f) international legal precedents from elsewhere.[328]

---

[319] See Government of New Zealand, *The Foreshore and Seabed of New Zealand: Protecting Public Access and Customary Rights* (Wellington: Government of New Zealand, 2003).
[320] Charters and Erueti (n 307) 262.
[321] *Report on the Crown's Foreshore and Seabed Policy* (n 311).
[322] Charters and Erueti (n 307) 263.
[323] See Attorney-General, 'Report on the Consistency of the Foreshore and Seabed Bill with the New Zealand Bill of Rights Act 1990' (Wellington, 6 May 2004).
[324] *Resource Management Act 1991* (Reprint as at 28 March 2007) No 013.
[325] See *Foreshore and Seabed Bill 2004*, supplementary order paper 2004 No 302.
[326] See Joshua Castellino 'A Re-Examination of the International Convention for the Elimination of All Forms of Racial Discrimination' (2006) 2 *RIDH* 1–29.
[327] Charters and Erueti (n 307) 264–73.   [328] ibid.

In setting out the complaint, the claimants' advocates articulated the concern that once legislation was enacted in New Zealand it could not be overturned on grounds of human rights (hence the process by which the Attorney-General is required to test the legislation for compliance with the Bill of Rights Act). In addition they submitted evidence of high profile speeches made by the prime minister and others that they claimed appealed to racial intolerance.[329] The CERD response, led by Thornberry, focused on the speed of the government's response, raised issues concerning procedural uncertainties that affected Maori disproportionately, and stressed that the replacement regime only provided for the possibility of a reserve or redress for the extinguishment of Maori territorial interests.[330] In addition, Thornberry concluded that the tests for establishing customary rights identified in the FSA were stringent and seemed to 'freeze' these rights in time.[331] The 'decision' handed down by the Committee, labelled 'succinct' by the claimants' advocates,[332] highlighted the haste through which legislation was undertaken, suggesting that other avenues that may have been available were not explored owing to the fear of racial tension. It concluded that:

Bearing in mind the complexity of the issues involved, the legislation appears to the Committee, on balance, to contain discriminatory aspects against the Maori, in par-ticular in its extinguishment of the possibility of establishing Maori customary title over the foreshore and seabed and its failure to provide a guaranteed right of redress, notwith-standing the State Party's obligation under articles 5 and 6 of the Convention.[333]

However, by the time of the hearing the *Foreshore and Seabed Act* had already been enacted by Parliament and the government appeared unwilling to engage in any discussion about withdrawal or modification based on the Committee's findings.[334]

3.3.2.5 *Immigration and Related Rights Issues*

Stephen Hoadley suggests there has been a steady convergence in the immigra-tion policies of Australia and New Zealand.[335] These similarities derive from a shared political view in New Zealand and Australia of immigration as a response to economic needs. Both governments recognize immigration as a necessary instrument to maintain economic growth, and so seek economically productive

---

[329] The reference here is to a speech made by Don Brash titled 'Nationhood' but labelled the 'Orewa Speech', delivered to an audience at Orewa Rotary Club on 27 January 2004.

[330] These concerns articulated by Thornberry are described in detail by Charters and Erueti (n 307) 279–80.

[331] ibid 280.   [332] ibid 284.

[333] UN CERD 'Decision 1(66): New Zealand Foreshore and Seabed Act 2004' (11 March 2005) CERD/C/66/NZL/Dec 1 at para 6.

[334] See John Dunne, Interview with Rt Hon Helen Clark, prime minister (Breakfast Show, TRN 3ZB) (14 March 2005) as portrayed by Charters and Erueti (n 307) 286–7.

[335] Stephen Hoadley, 'Immigration Policy: A Steady Convergence' (2003) 28 *NZIR*.

immigrants.[336] The heritage of the British Commonwealth means that English languages skills are emphasized and that the refugee and immigration regimes in the two countries are relatively similar. Historically, this has also been characterized by a range of subsidies to encourage European immigration, with a concomitant range of barriers such as poll taxes to discourage Asian immigrants and an ambivalent policy towards Pacific Islanders, who are tolerated in times of good growth and repelled in times of depression.[337] More recently, the arrival of large numbers of Asians and Pacific Islanders to Australia and New Zealand has triggered different types of debates over family reunion rights; rates of migration among different communities; politicized reactions to immigration; controversies over the acceptance of refugees; and processes attendant to the determination of asylum applications.[338]

The central problem in the asylum process is the question of being able to identify effectively claimants for asylum in order to determine the merits of their claim. Both countries are reported as deporting four out of five arrivals under this procedure as 'economic migrants'.[339] The Australian strategies have been touched upon in the previous chapter under the rubric of the so-called 'Pacific Solution'.[340] By contrast New Zealand had followed a policy of releasing non-lawful arrivals into the community through community groups often mobilized by religious groups.[341] This policy has been tightened owing to allegations that applicants with links to terror networks could be slipping into the country, though the notion of automatic detention has been found contrary to international refugee law by the courts.[342] New Zealand has also been shown to have been more progressive over arrivals on the ship Tampa who were deflected to Nauru.[343] The *New Zealand Immigration Service* worked efficiently to interview the asylum applicants, granting status to 134 of them, and placing them on citizenship tracks.

There has been disquiet over the immigration flows from New Zealand to Australia. New Zealand immigrants have been characterized as benefit seekers rather than genuine contributors. While immigration between the states in the past was relatively balanced, the flow of New Zealanders into Australia has begun to outflank those going in the opposite direction. A significant proportion of the incoming New Zealanders have been Pacific Islanders or Asian in origin, fuelling rising tensions in Australia. These factors have resulted in a call from Australia for a re-negotiation of the Trans-Tasman Agreement on unrestricted migration between the two countries[344] and the adoption of a 'fresh approach'

---

[336] ibid.   [337] ibid.   [338] ibid.
[339] ibid.   [340] See Unwin (n 1); Billson (n 1); and G. Hawke (n 1).
[341] Hoadley (n 335).   [342] ibid.
[343] For more, see 'Australia Ships out Afghan Refugees' *BBC Asia Pacific Desk* (3 September 2001) <http://news.bbc.co.uk/1/hi/world/asia-pacific/1522723.stm> [last accessed 4 July 2008].
[344] See Australian Department of Immigration and Citizenship, *Fact Sheet No 17* (produced by the National Communications Branch, Canberra, revised on 27 July 2007).

in New Zealand in seeking to attract Australians with improved social secur-ity packages.[345] As in Australia, there remain general concerns over rising racial tensions towards all immigrants, with attempts to tackle this through law cap-tured in Article 61 (on racial disharmony), Article 63 (on racial harassment), and Article 73 (equality provision) of the *Human Rights Act 1993*, with remedies set out under Article 92 of the same legislation.

3.4 Remedies

3.4.1 Self-determination (*tino rangatiratanga*)[346]

The 'right' or 'remedy' of self-determination has merited significant vol-umes of writing throughout the history of public international law, as authors seek to rationalize how the legal principle performs against commonly held aspirations.[347] While the 'right' at international level could be described as only applicable to 'colonial peoples',[348] in New Zealand, the norm was held to be cul-turally important and included in the *Treaty of Waitangi* in 1840. Unlike in other areas where indigenous rights to self-determination are contested,[349] in New Zealand, this notion is inscribed in the foundations of the state in the *Treaty of Waitangi* through the concept of *te tino rangatiranga*—a concept that, as one author puts it, 'existed for over one thousand years prior to colonization [and did not require] the recognition and endorsement of English law in order to exist after 1840'.[350] The substantive aspect of this principle, effectively formulated in various claims addressed by the Waitangi Tribunal, has provided an understand-ing by which the courts have interpreted Maori rights. The Court of Appeal's rul-ing in *Ngati Apa* was an inevitable effect of the growing realization of the concept of self-determination and its validity in customary law. This conclusion needs to be balanced against the inevitable caveat that while there may be a heightened

[345] Hoadley (n 335).

[346] For a Maori perspective of self-determination, see Durie (n 3).

[347] See generally, Antonio Cassese, *Self-Determination of Peoples, A Legal Reappraisal* (Cambridge: Cambridge University Press, 1995) and Martti Koskenniemi, 'National Self-Determination Today: Problems of Legal Theory and Practice' (1994) 43 *ICLQ* 857.

[348] See generally, Morton H. Halperin and David J. Scheffer with Patricia L. Small, *Self-Determination in the New World Order* (Washington DC: Brookings Institute Press, 1992); Alexis Heraclides, *The Self-Determination of Minorities in International Politics* (Cass: London, 1991). See also Meic Stephens (trs), *Luis Núñez Astrain: The Basques: Their Struggle for Independence* (Cardiff: Welsh Academic Press, 1997) discussing the Basque claim to self-determination; Denisa Kostovicova, *Kosovo: The Politics of Identity and Space* (London/New York: Routledge, 2005) dis-cussing the claim to statehood in Kosovo; Kerim Yildiz, *The Kurds in Iraq: The Past, Present and Future* (London: Pluto Press, 2004) discussing the claim of the Kurds in the context of Iraq.

[349] See Joshua Castellino, 'Conceptual Difficulties and the Right to Indigenous Self-Determination' in Nazila Ghanea, and Alexandra Xanthaki (eds), *Minorities, Peoples and Self-Determination: Essays in Honour of Patrick Thornberry* (London/Boston: Martinus Nijhoff, 2005) 55–74.

[350] David (n 20) 236.

awareness of these concepts as legal tools, this does not guarantee indigenous rights per se. The controversy over the *Foreshore and Seabed Act* demonstrates this point cogently.

One of the best explanations of the norm derives from commentary on the Treaty itself.[351] The concept of '*kawanatanga*' is equally important, as discussed by Orange in providing commentary on Article 1 of the Treaty:

> The emphasis given to an absolute and lasting yielding up seems to be conveyed clearly, but the choice of 'kawanatanga' for 'sovereignty' is not such a happy one. Williams had already used it to render 'sovereign authority' and 'civil government' in the preamble. The concept of sovereignty is sophisticated, involving the right to exercise a jurisdiction at international level as well as within national boundaries. The single word 'kawanatanga' covered significant differences of meaning, and was not likely to convey to Maori a precise definition of sovereignty.[352]

In commenting on Article 2, Orange suggested that '*rangatiratanga*' was more likely to convey sovereignty, with 'kawanatanga' implying authority in an abstract rather than concrete sense.[353] The Waitangi Tribunal, in *Motonui*, defined kawanatanga as '. . . the authority to make laws for the good order and security of the country, but subject to an undertaking to protect particular Maori interests'.[354] This interpretation is significant for two main reasons. First, it suggests that the promises exchanged at Waitangi were 'an exchange of gifts . . . the gift of the right to make laws, and the promise to do so as to accord the Maori interest an appropriate priority';[355] and second, that correctly interpreted, the *Treaty of Waitangi* acts as a constitutional fetter to legislating in New Zealand, introducing need for prioritization of Maori interest. In a subsequent report the Waitangi Tribunal clarified that the notion of complete Crown control was not in accordance with kawanatanga, suggesting that the interpretation required a restricted version of law-making rights.[356] In the context of contested claims over fishing rights, the Waitangi Tribunal found that not taking account of due Maori interests was in violation of the treaty principles.[357]

The notion of a constitutional fetter is not a widely accepted view. However, courts have determined that, in some circumstances, parliamentary sovereignty is not as absolute as envisaged.[358] It is also clear that the Waitangi Tribunal does not have the mandate to determine the existence of a constitutional fetter.[359]

---

[351] See Evison (n 68) 356–7.   [352] Orange (n 2) 40.
[353] ibid 41.
[354] *Motonui Report*, Aila Taylor (Te Atiawa, re Motonui), (Wai 6) (1983).
[355] ibid 95.
[356] See *Report of the Waitangi Tribunal on the Muriwhenua Fishing Claim*, Interim Report (re Maori Fishing Rights) (Wai 262) May 1988, Hon Matiu Rata and ors (Ngati Kuri and ors) 27–8.
[357] ibid.
[358] See esp *L v M* [1979] 2 NZLR 519, 527; *Brader v Ministry of Transport* [1981] 1 NZLR 73, 78; *New Zealand Drivers' Association v New Zealand Road Carriers* [1982] 1 NZLR 374, 390; *Taylor v New Zealand Poultry Board* [1984] 1 NZLR 394, 398.
[359] For more on the controversy concerning fishing rights and the Maori, see Boast (n 265) 6.

While the courts have been positive in interpreting obligations, they do not seem well-placed to articulate such a concept either.[360]

Boast also highlights Article II of the English language version, and the misinterpretation of the word 'guarantees':

Her Majesty the Queen of England confirms and *guarantees* to the Chiefs and Tribes of New Zealand and to the respective families and individuals thereof the full and exclusive and undisturbed possession of their Lands and Estates, Forests, Fisheries and other properties which they may collectively or individually possess.[361]

The use of the word 'guarantee' has been interpreted as construing a positive obligation by the Waitangi Tribunal[362] as well as the Court of Appeal.[363] This can be contrasted with the so-called 'race powers' in Australia which have not met with as positive an interpretation.[364] A number of claims before the Waitangi Tribunal concern issues of resource management and rights of tribal input into decisions affecting environment and resources, rather than outright ownership.[365] Ownership is often interpreted as being able to manage resources and decisions concerning resource management, as demonstrated in the *Waiheke*[366] and *Orakei*[367] claims. As Boast argues:

Tribal participation in reserve management—either in isolation or in association with other authorities—is one method of giving effect to the obligations to protect ranagatiranga which falls short of a transfer of ownership.[368]

This finds an echo in the Maori term '*kaitiaki*' (guardianship) which is reflected in the *Environmental Management and the Principles of the Treaty of Waitangi*, but which is recognized as not having the same meaning as 'ownership'.[369]

[360] Though dated the article by J.L. Caldwell 'Judicial Sovereignty' (1984) *NZLJ* 11: 357–9 does provide a good insight into the judiciary in New Zealand.

[361] art II, Treaty of Waitangi official English translation as reproduced in Boast (n 265) 7.

[362] See *Manukau* at p 94 which discusses the notion of a positive obligation on the Crown; also see *Te Reo Maori* (Huirangi Waikerepuru and ors) (Wai 11) (1986) 29; also see *Orakei* (Joseph P. Hawke and ors, Ngati Whatua) (Wai 9) (1987); and *Muriwhenua* (Wai 22) (1998) 194.

[363] See *Maori Council v Attorney-General* [1987] 1 NZLR 641.   [364] See c 2, s 2.3.1.

[365] e.g. Waitangi Tribunal [all] *Mangonui Sewerage Claim*, (Wai 17) (2000); *Ngawha Geothermal Resource Report*, (Wai 304) (1991); *Report of the Waitangi Tribunal on the Waiau Power Station Claim*, (Wai 2) (1978); *Proposed Discharge of Sewage at Welcome Bay*, (Wai 3) (1990); *Kaituna River Claim*, (Wai 4) (1984); *Turangi Township Remedies*, (Wai 84) (1995); *Te Arawa Representative Geothermal Resource Claim*, (Wai 153) (1994); *Te Maunga Railways Land Report*, (Wai 315) (1994); *Motonui-Waitara Claim*, (Wai 6) (1995); *Taranaki Maori, Dairy Industry Changes and Crown Report*, (Wai 790) (2001); *Maori Development Corporation Report*, (Wai 350) (1993); *Kiwifruit Marketing Report*, (Wai 449) (1995) and *Petroleum Report*, (Wai 796) (2003).

[366] See *Waihekei* (Hariata Gordon and ors, Ngati Paoa) *re Waiheke Island*, (Wai 10) (1987) esp 77–8.

[367] See *Orakei* (Joseph P. Hawke and ors, Ngati Whatua), (Wai 9) (1987) esp 147, 186.

[368] Boast (n 265) 9. As Boast also shows this can be interpreted as the duty of consultation—using the example of the *Manukau* claim for the transfer of ownership of Manukau Habour (which the Tribunal rejected—see 103), focusing instead on 'use' and not 'ownership'. ibid.

[369] See [Government of New Zealand] *Environmental Management and the Principles of the Treaty of Waitangi: Report on Crown response to the Recommendations of the Waitangi Tribunal 1983–1988* (Wellington: Parliamentary Commissioner for the Environment, 1988) 72.

As seen with Australia and Fiji, the difficulty with formally adopting tribal customary rules lies in their diversity, in the lack of certainty they provide, and in the potential conflicts that arise from these rules in terms of the constitution and civil laws of the land. While there have been calls in New Zealand for greater use and reliance on Maori customary law,[370] obvious difficulties lie in promulgation and enforcement, with the added problem of the translation of the 'concepts and requirements of customary codes into comprehensive regulations'.[371]

Another important Maori term mis-translated into English is *'taonga'* which could be translated as 'things treasured' and may relate to tangible as well as non-tangible objects. It is a highly elastic term and could apply at macro-level to the environment and people, or more narrowly interpreted, to a particular item. The question of how tribal and spiritual values and resources should be interpreted in law was raised by Chilwell J in the context of the *Huakina Development Trust* case.[372] The judge acknowledged the importance of Maori spiritual and cultural values in determining issues concerning water rights (in this case, in the context of a water right granted by the *Waikato Valley Authority* to a local dairy farmer for the discharge of dairy-waste into a stream). The judgment framed a three-point guideline for establishing whether and how such values could be accommodated within the law: i) that a specific custom existed and was probable; ii) that it must be lawful; and iii) that it must be reasonable, taking the whole context of the question into account.[373] Summarizing the operations of the Waitangi Tribunal in 1989, Boast suggests that its contribution could be framed as: i) making the distinction between rights and privileges; ii) identifying the key difference between balancing interests and prioritization of these; and iii) the development of the notion of partnership.[374]

3.4.2 Impact of *Treaty of Waitangi* on New Zealand Law

Judging by the impact of the *Treaty of Waitangi* on New Zealand law, it is tempting to conceive it as an articulation of indigenous customary law. However, it is precisely the opposite of this in that it sets down the terms through which the Maori ceded sovereignty to the Crown. The range of legislation that makes reference to the Treaty is significant.[375] There has also been related case-law on diverse subjects such as in *Application by City Resources (NZ) Ltd,*[376] over a planning application. The Treaty was also used as setting the 'context' in *Huakina*

---

[370] See Moana Jackson, *The Maori and the Criminal Justice System: He Whaipaanga Hou—A New Perspective* (Study Series 18, Policy and Research Division) (Auckland: Department of Justice, 1988).

[371] Boast (n 265) 14.

[372] *Huakina Development Trust v Waikato Valley Authority* [1987] 2 NZLR 188.

[373] ibid at 277.   [374] Boast (n 265) 16.

[375] See n 133.

[376] Unreported, Planning Tribunal, Wellington, 6 May 1988 (MIN 24/87).

Development Trust v Waikato Valley Authority[377] with the decision respecting Maori spiritual values in determining water rights. These also arose in *McKenzie v Taupo County Council* though the Maori objections on spiritual values, while heard, were not heeded in the decision by the Planning Council in dealing with a proposal to build a marina on Lake Taupo.[378] The Treaty has influenced law in the following areas:

(a) Freshwater resources: The Waitangi Tribunal has held deliberations on the ownership of rivers and lakes in the context of claims over the Waikato and Wanagui Rivers.[379]

(b) Freshwater fisheries: One of the early cases before the Waitangi Tribunal, the *Karaitiana Claim*,[380] highlighted the mean-spiritedness of the manner of the interpretation of the term 'indigenous fish'.[381]

(c) Geothermal Resources: Among the Maori's most valued treasures (*taonga*), these exist in places such as Ohinemutu, Whakarewarewa, Ohaki, and Orakeikorako.[382]

(d) Mining: Under New Zealand law, mineral ownership and surface ownership are severable, resulting in a complex system of laws with the potential of two separate title-holders to the surface and the mineral ownership. Mining is governed by the *Mining Act 1971*[383] and the *Coal Mines Act 1979*.[384] Maori landowners can veto mining,[385] though this right is not absolute.[386] Maori hold the right, along with others, to object to the granting of mining licences on general environmental grounds; or exclusively on the grounds of 'the relationship of Maori people and their culture and traditions with their ancestral lands'.[387]

---

[377] [1987] 2 NZLR 188.   [378] (1987) 12 NZTPA 83.

[379] For more on these issues, see Centre for Maori Studies and Research, *He Whakatakotoranga Kaupapa: Submission to the Treaty of Waitangi Tribunal, Makaurau Marae, Ihumatao* (Occasional Paper No 25) (University of Waikato, Waikato 1984). Also see *Bed of the Wanganui River* [1962] NZLR 600; *Tai Whati: Judicial Decisions Affecting Maori Land* (Maori Affairs Department, 1981) 96–8.

[380] *Report on a Claim by H T Karaitiana Relating to Lake Taupo Fishing Rights*, (Wai 18) (1986).

[381] Boast (n 265) 36.

[382] The importance is articulated as: 'An extensive body of customary rules, and an elaborate framework of myth, historical associations and memories has grown up relating to the thermal areas, and there could scarcely be a clearer example of a tribal taonga than a place such as Ohinemutu or Ohaki'. ibid 37.

[383] No 025 (commenced 1 January 1973); 1 January 1973, *Mining Amendment Act 1972*; 21 November 1973, *Mining Amendment Act 1973*; 9 October 1975, *Mining Amendment Act 1975*; 1 May 1977, *Mining Amendment Act 1975*, s 3, Schedule; 16 October 1978, *Mining Amendment Act 1978* (1 January 1978).

[384] No 021 (commenced 1 October 1979); 1 April 1980; 1 October 1979, ss 2, pt VIII, 268(1).

[385] ss 30, 35, 36 *Mining Act 1971*.

[386] In certain circumstances (s 37) of the *Mining Act 1971* such land may be declared open for mining.

[387] s 3(1)(g) *Town and Country Planning Act Commencement Order* (SR 1978/29) (as of 3 September 2007). Also see *Application by Winstone Concrete Ltd* (1987) 12 NZTPA 257 (where the argument of spiritual links was unsuccessfully raised); *Application by City Resources (NZ) Ltd*

(e) Archaeological site management: There are estimated to be 200,000 heritage sites in New Zealand,[388] with tens of thousands listed in the *New Zealand Register of Archaeological Sites* and administered by the *Historic Places Trust* and the *New Zealand Archaeological Association*. There was little Maori input into a realm of paramount significance to Maori tribes. To address this issue, the Trust engaged with the community and passed the *Historic Places Act 1993*,[389] which lists 'traditional sites',[390] delineating a separate procedure for their management, governed under section 439A of the *Maori Affairs Act 1953* (as amended in 1985).[391] Under this provision the *Maori Land Court* is given the mandate to consider proposals for any piece of land if, 'by reason of its historical significance or spiritual or emotional association with the Maori people or any group or section thereof',[392] there is a request to get it set aside as Maori reservation. Should the recommendation of the *Maori Land Court* be accepted by the government it could lead to compulsory acquisition of such land under the *Maori Affairs Act*.[393]

(f) The *Town and Country Planning Act 1977*[394] is the centrepiece of New Zealand's resource management laws.[395] While it makes no reference to *Waitangi* it does make reference to matters of 'national importance' in section 3(1)(g), listing the relationship of the Maori and their culture and traditions within their ancestral land.[396] However, as noted by the Waitangi Tribunal,

Planning Tribunal, 6 May 1988 24/87, A 26/88 (Shepherd) [where an exploration licence was denied on the duties imposed on the Crown through the Waitangi Tribunal]; *Applications by Freeport Australasian Minerals* Planning Tribunal (29 March 1989) MIN 84/87, W 25/89 [a similar case with an opposite result, though it did result in some concessions, see esp at 17–18]. The Waitangi also addressed this issue in Waitangi Tribunal, 'Manukau Report', (Wai 8) (1985). Issues concerning ownership of mineral wealth arose in *Te K Mahuta and Tainui Maori Trust Board v Attorney-General* CA 126/89. The mining complexities in New Zealand have merited special attention from a Review Team focused on such legislation. Its findings are included in Ministry of Energy, 'Report of the Review Team on Mining legislation' (Wellington, 1986).

[388] A.D. Challis, *Motueka: An Archaeological Survey* (Auckland: Longman Paul, 1978).

[389] *Historic Places Act 1993* (Reprint as at 1 August 2006) 019.

[390] A traditional site is '. . . a place or site that is important by reason of its historical significance or spiritual or emotional association with the Maori people or to any group or section thereof'. s 2, *Historic Places Act 1980*.

[391] No 94 (commenced 1 April 1954); 1 April 1968, s 235; 28 April 1931, *Finance Act 1931 (No 2)*; 28 October 1955, *Maori Purposes Act 1955*; 1 January 1956, *Maori Purposes Act 1955*, s 3; 25 October 1956, *Maori Purposes Act 1956*; 24 October 1957, *Maori Purposes Act 1957*; and *Maori Affairs Amendment Act (No 2) 1985* No 139.

[392] s 439A, *Maori Affairs Act 1953* (as amended in 1974).

[393] s 439A(2) *Maori Affairs Act 1953* (as amended in 1974).

[394] No 121 (commenced 1 June 1978); 23 December 1980, *Town and Country Planning Amendment Act 1980*; 1 June 1978, *Town and Country Planning Amendment Act 1980*, s 6; 16 December 1983, *Town and Country Planning Amendment Act 1983*; 1 February 1984, *Town and Country Planning Amendment Act 1988* No 044 (commenced 1 April 1988).

[395] Boast (n 265) 50.

[396] s 3(1)(g) *Town and Country Planning Act 1977*. Also see G. Asher, 'Planning for Maori Land and Traditional Maori Uses' (1982) 65 *TPQ*; J. Tamihere, 'Te Take Maori: Maori Perspectives of Legislation and its interpretation with an Emphasis on Planning Law' (1985) 5 *AULR* 137; S. Kenderdine, 'Statutory separateness; Maori Issues in the Planning process and the Social

listing Maori concerns alongside six other issues of national importance provides for balancing but not prioritization of indigenous rights.[397] The challenge, it seems, is to get the balance right between *kawanatanga* and *rangatiranga*, with the possibility that all Maori *taonga* be excluded from planning systems if that be the wish of the community.[398]

(g) Sea fisheries: This is an issue where the Waitangi Tribunal has contributed significantly, commencing with the *Muriwhenua* report.[399] It is established that tribal authorities are required to administer their share of resources within the tribe in accordance with tribal rules.[400] There was also consideration for the role of the *Maori Land Court* in ensuring that fisheries allocations are made following careful investigation.[401]

It is arguably through such issues that the Waitangi Tribunal has been able to substantiate customary law, effectively contributing to the codification of the principle of self-determination or *te tino rangatiranga*.[402]

3.4.3 Restitution, Reparation, and Reconciliation[403]

The initial attempts at reconciliation and restitution of Maori land were largely unsuccessful until the first breakthrough in 1975.[404] The more significant development in 1985, the extension of the Waitangi Tribunal's mandate, was accompanied by an official apology and a concrete plan towards reconciliation and settlement of all major tribal claims by the year 2000. The failure to meet

---

Responsibility of Industry' (1985) *New Zealand LJ* 249, which could be seen of the first pieces of writing to tackle the issue of corporate social responsibility and indigenous customary regimes. Also see K.A. Palmer, *The Planning System and the Recognition of Maori Tribal Plans* (Ministry of the Environment: RMLR Working Paper No 28, 1988).

[397] See 'Mangonui Sewerage Report' (Mangonui Sewerage, Ngati Kahu) (Wai 17) (1988) 7.

[398] Boast (n 265) 51.

[399] See *Report of the Waitangi Tribunal on the Muriwhenua Fishing Claim*, Interim Report (re Maori Fishing Rights) (Wai 262) May, 1988, Hon Matiu Rata and ors (Ngati Kuri and ors).

[400] These include rules over partnership between Maori and non-Maori; reciprocity, flexibility, and others that are analysed in some detail by David (n 20) 237–40.

[401] The following rulings have been singled out by David as contributing to a growing awareness of self-determination: the *Muriwhenua Fishing Report*, (Wai 22)(1988); *Ngai Tahu Sea Fisheries Report*, (Wai 27) (1992); The *Taranaki Report: Kaupapa Tuatahi*, (Wai 143) (1996); *Te Whanganui-a-Orutu Report*, (Wai 55) (1995) and *Kiwifruit Marketing Report*, (Wai 449)(1995). The full reports and summaries are available at <http://www.waitangi-tribunal.govt.nz/> [last accessed 25 March 2009].

[402] David (n 20) 237–40.

[403] For more on restitution, see Steven C. Bourassa and Ann Louise Strong, 'Restitution of Property to Indigenous People: The New Zealand Experience', (Working Paper No 7, Auckland: Real Estate Research Unit, University of Auckland, 1998). The issues of political representation of the Maori are explored by the same authors in 'Restitution of Fishing Rights to Maori: Representation, Social Justice and Community Development', (August 2000) 41(2) *APV* 155–75.

[404] This breakthrough is heralded by the passage of the *Waitangi Tribunal Act 1975*.

that deadline has seen an extension of the mandate until 2010, with all claims expected to be resolved by 2020.[405]

In discussing the manner in which Maori land claims have been articulated, Bourassa and Strong highlight particular difficulties that have been faced by the decentralized social structures of the indigenous communities in articulating a unified view and accompanying this with unified leadership.[406] The authors show that while the notion of restitution is better developed in New Zealand than elsewhere, the greater visibility of the Maori has enabled them to be successful in advancing particular claims, and even then, more centralized tribes have been significantly more successful than others. Much of this relates to the organization of Maori Society at the time of the arrival of the settlers, when:

The hapu was the main functioning unit of Maori society, comprised of several extended families, or whanau, headed by a chief (rangatira). Each hapu held its land and its fishing sites communally. Hapu came together for war or fishing in a body called the iwi.[407] Today, many Maori employ the term iwi to mean a tribe or a tribal federation. It is important to stress that Maori society is a decentralized one and that the current emphasis on iwi in the settlement process is largely Crown initiated. Dealing with a limited number of iwi rather than hundreds of hapu is simpler, whether the matter is determining responsibility or disbursing funds.[408]

The lack of a pre-agreed system for land survey in the aftermath of the Treaty, and a failure at recording meant that land was often re-sold, and in addition, the contested terminology of the Treaty meant that this land was 'sold' for misunderstood consideration, leading to significant doubt over the validity of the contract of acquisition.[409] While the Treaty corrected some deficiencies by ensuring that land title could only be valid if purchased through the Crown, and through the creation of a *Land Commission* to examine pre-Waitangi claims, the fundamental misinterpretation of the terms of the Treaty in the English and Maori versions was not addressed.[410]

The first legal challenge arose in 1847 in *R v Symonds*, where it was held that the Crown's right of pre-emption in New Zealand was held as the custodianship

---

[405] For an update on the process, see <http://www.waitangi-tribunal.govt.nz> [last accessed 5 August 2008].

[406] This is compounded by other issues viz sub-division of tribes and the rural-urban divide.

[407] For a general explanation of the settlement of the Maori in New Zealand from their original homeland of Hawaiki, see Angela Ballara, *Iwi: The Dynamics of Maori Tribal Organisation from c. 1769 to c. 1945* (Wellington: Victoria University Press, 1998).

[408] Bourassa and Strong (n 84) 256.

[409] For a general view of the progression of property regimes in international law, see Joshua Castellino and Steve Allen, *Title to Territory in International Law: An Inter-temporal Analysis* (Dartmouth: Ashgate, 2003).

[410] The *New Zealand Land Claims Ordinance* of 1841 sought to untangle the issue of pre-1840 land sales, though it met with resistance from settlers and Maori. See Bourassa and Strong (n 84) 260. For a full account of the various pieces of legislation enacted in and around this time, see Alan Ward, *National Overview*, Vol. II 255–78.

of Maori interests.[411] However, the Maori had not sold their land under the terms interpreted by the English version of the Act. The Crown acquired 91 per cent of the 37 million acres of the South Island between 1844 and 1864 under these conditions, re-selling 30,000 acres near Canterbury for £15,000 more than the original sum paid to the Maori (*Ngai Tahu*) for 34.5 million acres.[412] This issue was finally settled by the Waitangi Tribunal in 1998.[413] The arrival of British-style governance to New Zealand saw the passage of the *New Zealand Constitution Act 1852*, which, while granting suffrage to settlers to determine the political future of the state, excluded the Maori since it was based exclusively on ownership or the holding of leasehold title under single rather than collective ownership.[414]

The war with the Maori over the various discontents of the relationship between settlers and indigenous population provided cause for the passage of the *Suppression of Rebellion Act 1863*, under which further parcels of land were con-fiscated by the Crown.[415] As the Waitangi Tribunal stated in 1996:

The wars...were not of Maori making. The Governor was the aggressor, not Maori....In terms of strict law, the initial military action against Maori was an unlawful attack by armed forces of the government on Maori subjects who were not in rebellion and for which, at the time, the Governor and certain Crown officers were subject to criminal and civil liability.[416]

Thus land was taken on punitive grounds in contravention of norms of exist-ing international law, as well as against norms of collective punishment in international humanitarian law.[417] *Native Lands Acts* were passed in 1862 and 1865,[418] intended to 'encourage the extinction of native proprietary customs' and to convert modes of ownership into those derived from the Crown. The Acts established the *Native Land Court* to oversee this conversion,[419] though in the

---

[411] *R v Symonds* (1847) NZPCC 390–1.

[412] Bourassa and Strong (n 84) 260.

[413] For a discussion of the issues in *Ngai Tahu*, see Alves (n 56) 133–40.

[414] Suffrage was restricted to males. For a thorough analysis of this and other related tensions at the time of the passage of the act, see John Miller, *Early Victorian New Zealand; A Study of Racial Tension and Social Attitudes 1839–1852* (Oxford/London/New York/Wellington: Oxford University Press, 1958).

[415] This Act, similar to legislation in Ireland in 1799 and 1833 saw the confiscation of 3.5 mil-lion acres with customary title extinguished, and Crown title established. This land was given to soldiers, sold to settlers, or bequeathed to loyal Maori. Though a proportion was returned under the Confiscation Court, this was under Crown title, with the original customary title effectively permanently extinguished. ibid esp 129–47.

[416] See [Waitangi Tribunal] *Taranaki Report* (Wai 143) (1996) 8–10.

[417] For an analysis into the history of collective punishment, including around the time of these events in New Zealand, see Shane Darcy, *Collective Responsibility and Accountability under International Law* (Leiden: Brill NV, 2007).

[418] For a discussion of these, see Miller (n 45) 108–14.

[419] This was criticized by the Waitangi Tribunal as effectively eliminating collective ownership and reifying of the notion of individual held title. See Waitangi Tribunal, *Orakei Report* (Wai 9) (1987) 30–1.

process individualized land holdings excluded non-land owners from voting rights.[420] In addition, land was lost to the Crown through compulsory acquisition for public works[421] and the imposition of property taxes.[422]

The *Symonds* decision was reviewed by the Supreme Court in 1877, suggesting that the *Treaty of Waitangi* was null and void because it had not been incorporated into statutory law, rendering native title ineffective.[423] While this decision was overturned by the Privy Council in *Nireha Tamaki v Baker*,[424] reinstating the Treaty as foundational to the creation of the New Zealand state, the fragility of the question of native title was clearly visible.[425]

In the early part of the twentieth century the uncertainty over the meaning and value of native title prompted the creation of a *Commission on Native Lands* and *Native Land Tenure* in 1907,[426] with the ostensible purpose of seeking to ameliorate obvious defects of land acquisition. The progressive recommendations of the Commission were ignored by the government,[427] and it was not until the 1920s that the first steps were taken to engage in real redress of native title. A series of events[428] led to the appointment of the *Sim Commission* in 1926 to investigate the persistent Maori claims of illegal acquisition of territory. The Commission's report found unjustified confiscations and recommended payment of compensation in perpetuity.[429] Had it been implemented, this restitution would have been the most progressive in the history of indigenous rights. However, the Depression at the end of the 1920s delayed adoption of the recommendations and Maori interests were made hostage to the politics of convenience. In the meantime, Maori holdings by the 1930s had already shrunk to a mere 3.6 million acres.[430]

In the aftermath of World War II these discussions returned centre-stage in local politics with the government seeking 'final' settlements with the Taranaki, the Ngai Tahu, the Tainui, and the Whakatohea. These took the form of payments in perpetuity or payments of fixed sums over a number of years. The payments remained nominal, however, and the acts authorizing them were repealed in 1955. The discussion then lay relatively dormant until the passage of the 1975 *Treaty of Waitangi Act*. By 1975 Maori holdings accounted for only 3.1. million acres (about 5 per cent of the available land), almost all individually owned.[431] In addition there were a further 67,000 acres in native reserves, subject to the

---

[420] Bourassa and Strong (n 84) 258.   [421] Via the *Public Works Act 1864*, ibid.

[422] See *Native Lands Act 1865* which allowed the state to take as much as 5 per cent.

[423] *Wi Parata v Bishop of Wellington* (1877) 3 NZ Jur NS SC 72.

[424] *Nireha Tamaki v Baker* (1901) NZPCC 371.

[425] On this issue also see *Hoani Te Heuheu Tukino v Aolea District Maori Land Board* (1941) NZLR 590, AC 308.

[426] Often referred to as the 'Stout-Ngata Commission'.

[427] Bourasssa and Strong (n 84) 258.

[428] For more details, see ibid. Also see Alves (n 56) 38, 124.

[429] See 'Report of the Royal Commission to Inquire into Confiscation of Native Lands' (1928) 29 AJHR 11.

[430] Bourassa and Strong (n 84) 254.   [431] ibid 255.

control of government-appointed trustees, usually non-Maori. At the same time there were forces in society pushing for greater recognition of New Zealand's heritage—in 1973, 6 February was celebrated as 'Waitangi Day', even though there was little to celebrate. By 1975, the Maori mobilized under the banner of 'Not One Acre More of Maori Land' and the leadership of Dame Whina Cooper, a Maori, and marched on Wellington. This finally instigated the *Treaty of Waitangi Act*. The relative paucity of claims filed before the Tribunal between 1975 and 1985 can be attributed to: *a*) its narrow mandate; *b*) the overtly legalistic proceedings, alien to the Maori; and *c*) the fact that the Tribunal could only make non-binding recommendations to the government.[432] The appointment of Maori Edward Taihakurei Durie to chair the Tribunal is a key turning point in Waitangi history. This resulted in major changes to Tribunal operations, greater confidence in the institution, and contributed to the extension of its mandate to cover violations post-1840.[433] The work of the Tribunal on the *Motunui-Waitara* claim was significant in establishing the credentials of the institution.[434] Under the amended *Treaty of Waitangi Act 1985* claims were invited challenging historic acquisitions of property through confiscations, expropriations, title grants, and Crown and private purchases, intertwining contemporary claims with conceptual claims to rivers, lakes, minerals, and geothermal resources.[435] In keeping with the extended mandate of the Tribunal, more staff were made available and the bench increased to seven, four of whom were required to be Maori.[436] This requirement was rescinded in 1988 when the Act underwent further modification,[437] and the panel was increased to sixteen without ethnic quotas.[438]

The question of compensation has remained open in terms of how it was measured and dispensed. There is no binding precedent for proceedings before the Tribunal with settlements negotiated directly between the tribes and the

[432] ibid.   [433] See Alves (n 56) 59–66.

[434] This claim concerned the discharge of chemical effluents on fishing reefs resulting in physical and spiritual contamination, and was adjudicated upon through a combination of Maori traditional *marae* hearings as well as through reliance on western protocols. The Tribunal's findings were well received by the Government who changed the public works regime through legislation. A similar success was visible over the question of fishing rights as addressed in 1992 by the Tribunal. See Steven C. Bourassa and Ann Louise Strong, 'Restitution of Fishing Rights to Maori: Representation, Social Justice and Community Development' (August 2000) 41 (2) *APV*, 155–75.

[435] See art 3, *Treaty of Waitangi Amendment Act 1985* (Public Act No 148 of 1985, commenced 9 January 1986).

[436] This evinced strong response from right-wing nationalist parties who suggested that allowing Maori majority on the panel would be 'racist' and that re-opening issues of title back to 1840 could rend the fabric of New Zealand society by opening up long settled claims.

[437] See The *Treaty of Waitangi (State Enterprises) Act 1988*. The Act was developed in the aftermath of *New Zealand Maori Council v Attorney-General* [1987] 1 NZLR 641 and the amendment was subsequently challenged and was the focus of a Court of Appeal decision in 1989. See *Tainui Maori Trust Board v Attorney-General* (1989) 2 NZLR 513.

[438] Envisaged as being achievable in a 'spirit of partnership between the communities'.

government. Controversy also flared when the government announced its intention to set aside a fiscal cap of NZ$ 1 billion for restitution.[439]

Efforts to generate principles through which the government could respond to
Waitangi Tribunal recommendations, failed.[440] In discussions over the financial
compensation package, a strict rule was adopted placating private landowners
and excluding private property, thereby sheltering such claims from the Tribunal
and significantly reducing the volume of claims that could be adjudicated.[441]
Since 1985 the Tribunal has nonetheless made significant progress through
embedding various legislation at the heart of the claims process. Among such
laws are the *Crown Forests Assets Act*[442] (with the creation of the statutory body
the *Crown Forestry Rental*),[443] the *Environment Act 1986*,[444] the *Conservation Act
1987*,[445] the *Crown Minerals Act 1991*,[446] and the *Resource Management Act* also
of 1991.[447] The most important piece of supporting legislation remains the *Te
Tura Whenua Maori Act (Maori Land Act 1993)*.[448]

The alienability of reserve land was the subject of a Court of Appeal decision in 1994 in the context of the transfer of substantial mining rights to
Coalcorp New Zealand. The court held, on appeal from the Tainul Maori Trust
Board, that land was subject to the 1988 Amendment to the *Treaty of Waitangi*
and determined that the Crown was required to protect the plaintiffs' rights
by acknowledging that such a transfer was susceptible to a Waitangi claims
determination.[449]

*Te Runanganui o Te Ika Whenua Inc Society and anor v Attorney-General and
ors* in 1994 was also a significant decision, where the Court of Appeal ruled
on the nature and applicability of customary native title in New Zealand.[450]
According to the court:

---

[439] See Wira Gardiner, *Return to Sender: What Really Happened at the Fiscal Envelope Hui*
(Auckland: Reed Consumer Books, 1996). The cap was rescinded by the Labour-Alliance coalition
government in 2000.

[440] The most controversial of these was the condition that settlements would be subject to fiscal restraints. See *Crown Proposals for the Settlement of Treaty of Waitangi Claims*, 1994 (Office
of Treaty Settlements, 1995) available in html format on *Australian Indigenous Law Reporter* at
<http://www.austlii.edu.au/au/journals/AILR/1996/91.html> [last accessed 6 August 2008]. For
more on the Maori protests and their impact, see Sue Abel, *Shaping the News: Waitangi Day on
Television* (Auckland: Auckland University Press, 1997) 152.

[441] A similar process in Australia would make little impact on recognition of native title since a
significant proportion of Australian land is held on pastoral leases, outside the scope of a Waitangi
type tribunal. This point is addressed in the conclusion in terms of lessons learned.

[442] Public Act 1989 No 99, date of assent 25 October 1989.

[443] Under the auspices of the *Crown Forests Assets Act 1989*, since amended by the *Crown Forests
Assets Amendment Act 1995* (Public Act No 94 1995, 19 December 1995).

[444] (Public Act No 127, 19 December 1986).

[445] Public Act No 65, 31 March 1987.   [446] Public Act No 70, 22 July 1991.

[447] Public Act No 69, 22 July 1991.   [448] Reprint as at 10 February 2005, No 003.

[449] While the court did not determine that coal was covered by the Waitangi claims, it nonetheless acknowledged that there had been knowledge of the resource since 1840 with some evidence of
some modest *usus*. See *Tainui Maori Trust Board v Attorney-General* (1989) 2 NZLR 513.

[450] 2 NZLR 20, 24.

Aboriginal title is a compendious expression to cover the rights over land and water enjoyed by the indigenous or established inhabitants of a country up to the time of its colonization. On the acquisition of the territory, whether by settlement, cession or annexation, the colonising power acquires a radical or underlying title which goes with sovereignty.... But, at least in the absence of special circumstances displacing the principle, the radical title is subject to the existing native rights.[451]

A three-pronged approach is now in place. The court system is accessible to adjudicate claims and interpret the *Treaty of Waitangi*. However, the Waitangi Tribunal is the body charged with hearing claims and is the initial entry point for claimants into the legal arena, while the Office for Treaty Settlements[452] is charged with negotiating actual settlements.[453] While there is no full appeal to the decisions of the Waitangi Tribunals, the proceedings are subject to judicial review.[454]

Much needs to be highlighted in the relative success of claims for restitution, reparation, and reconciliation, not least: *a*) the significant presence of the Maori in New Zealand's demographics; *b*) the relatively high percentage of urbanized Maori with access to law and other regimes; *c*) the prevalence of high rates of inter-marriage between the dominant communities; *d*) the relatively low rate of competition from other minorities within the country which has allowed the development of a bicultural society.[455] One way of gauging the relative success of the Maori in terms of New Zealand public life is in the representation of Maori in the national Parliament. By mid-2001 there were 14 Maori-descended members of parliament out of 120. While this is not near the 15–20 per cent representation in terms of their prevalence in society, it is well beyond comparison in relation to other countries such as Canada and Australia. Of the fourteen

---

[451] (1994) 2 NZLR 20 (24).

[452] This office operates under the guidance of the Minister for Treaty Negotiations, advising the minister, and has the mandate to recommend a time period in designating negotiators. Its primary concern is the achievement of stable resolutions. The office works to acquire surplus land from government agencies to place into the Settlement Land Banks with significant annual outlays to ensure such purchases. These land banks contain: Crown Settlement portfolio (for land confiscated under the New Zealand Settlements Act 1863); fifteen regional land banks (non-confiscated non-allocated land which claimants will need to show historical significance, cultural significance, or proposed future use to be able to acquire); and claim specific land banks, such as the four established between 1944–1946 viz Muriwhenua, Whakatohea, Whandanui, and Ngai Taju.

[453] For more on the procedure and its impact, see Tom Booking, 'The Waitangi Tribunal and New Zealand History' (2006) 68 *The Historian*. Also see the official website of the Waitangi tribunal available at <http://www.waitangi-tribunal.govt.nz/> [last accessed 6 August 2008].

[454] For reading on unheard claims as of 1997, see 'Rangahaua Whanui National Overview' [Research report published in three volumes in 1997]. This brings together articles on national themes, including pre-emption, Crown purchases, and confiscation, and research articles by district. It offers suggestions to the Tribunal for addressing the historic claims, and marshals background information appropriate to historic claims. The Tribunal is aware that a critical function of its process is to address tribal grievances and is therefore reluctant to unduly shorten the claims process.

[455] Bourassa and Strong (n 84) esp Table One which provides empirical evidence of these indicators.

members elected to the 2001 Parliament, six represented specific Maori electorates, with the remaining elected from 'open' seats, suggesting a level of maturity in the politics of New Zealand that places it significantly further ahead than comparable counterparts.

In adjudicating on the *Waiheke Island* claim, Chief Judge Durie made some telling points about the goal of reconciliation:

> It ought to be recalled that the Treaty was not just with Maoris. It was a treaty with tribes and was taken about the country to be separately considered by them. Government ought therefore to be concerned not only with the development of Maori land but with an equitable development that has regard to the differences in tribal land holdings ....To compensate a tort is only one way of dealing with a current problem. Another is to move beyond guilt and ask what can be done now and in the future to rebuild the tribes and furnish those needing it with the land endowments necessary for their own tribal programmes. That approach seems more in keeping with the spirit of the Treaty and with those founding tenets that did not see the loss of tribal identity as a necessary consequence of European settlement. [T]he deployment of available lands to assist the tribes to an economic base freed from State dependence would appear to meet best a cultural need....[456]

Conclusion

The Waitangi Tribunal was created out of a genuine will to repair the relationship between the two dominant communities on the islands. It has significant Maori involvement, and claims are addressed through a combination of the legal and customary traditions of the two communities. The Maori engaged with the Tribunal once the crucial teething issues were resolved. The decisions of the Tribunal have generally been met with an appropriate response from the government of the day.

Against this there remain significant challenges that are unresolved. There is no general agreement on the scale of compensation nor the financial cap, and as a result payments depend on the exchequer, which in times of financial uncertainties can be difficult to guarantee. The process is skewed towards those tribes with responsibility for advocating the Maori cause. This is of benefit to the stronger, more organized urban tribes, undermining their rural counterparts. Furthermore the process has made a small dent in the large number of claims submitted before it. Despite working to expedite proceedings and prioritize key claims, the backlog casts serious doubt on whether the aim of achieving final settlement by 2010 can be reached. There remain key outstanding technical issues, including the question of who may instigate a claim—thus the class includes an *iwi* but not a *hapu*,

---

[456] See Waitangi Tribunal, 'Waiheke Island Report', (Wai 10) (1987) 40–1.

but in reality, these lines are often blurred in many tribes. Additionally, claimants have to bring claims only on the basis of occupation of land as of 1840, with subsequent dispossession. Thus, urban Maori can often only participate in terms of proof of ancestry, and even then the entitlement is restricted to rural rather than urban land, which tends to be privately owned and is therefore exempt. By and large however, it is clear that the New Zealand experience with the Maori, if not with its other indigenous and minority populations, offers a useful model for other parts of the world.

4

Fiji

Introduction*

It can be argued that Fiji turns the minority rights and indigenous peoples discourse on itself. The protection and promotion of the rights and cultures of minority and indigenous groups is often accused of exacerbating inequality. In this sense, conflict in Fiji has highlighted how a dominant indigenous majority can exploit the discourse of indigenous rights at the expense of other minority groups. Whether indigenous groups in Fiji would have survived at all without aggressive exploitation of indigenous rights underlies indigenous claims to enhanced legal protection. The task of the present chapter is to distil the history, identity, and participation of all groups in Fiji, with a view to supporting the role minority and indigenous rights discourse can play in resolving conflict and finding a common ground for development.

The Fiji islands consist of a group of 503 islands, of which 106 are inhabited, in the southwest Pacific between latitudes 53° and 22° south of the equator. The 180th meridian of longitude passes through the group. The islands are scattered over about 90,000 square miles of sea.[1] Two islands, Viti Levu and Vanua Levu, account for 87 per cent of the total land area.[2] The population of Fiji is approximately 775,000 with 51 per cent indigenous Fijians and the rest composed of Indo-Fijians, Chinese, European, Pacific Islanders, and 'others'.[3] There is a contradiction between the state-imposed political label of 'others' which refers collectively to those who are neither Fijians nor Indo-Fijians, and the distinctive identity of the various minority ethnic groups concerned.[4] The Indo-Fijians are the next largest ethnic group constituting nearly 45 per cent of the population.[5]

---

* See caveat in Introduction 3.
[1] John Coulter, *The Drama of Fiji: A Contemporary History* (Tokyo: Charles Tuttle, 1967) 27.
[2] Ralph Premdas, *Ethnic Conflict and Development: The Case of Fiji* (United Nations Research in Ethnic Relations Series) (Aldershot: Ashgate, 1995) 10.
[3] Fiji Census 1996, cited in Shaista Shameem, 'New Impulses in the Interaction of Law and Religion' (2003) *BYULR* 661 at 661.
[4] Paulo Baleinakorodawa, 'Minority Rights in Fiji' (Citizens' Constitutional Forum, 2007) 4–5 <http://www.ccf.org.fj/confrence/GROUP%20AND%20MINORITY%20RIGHTS.pdf> [last accessed 6 August 2008].
[5] Fiji Census 1996, cited in Shameem (n 3) 661.

Most of them are the descendants of indentured labourers brought from India in the late nineteenth and early twentieth century to work on sugar-cane fields.[6]

Fiji is the only country in the world that does not have a name for all its citizens.[7] A 1970 British Foreign and Commonwealth Office circular explains:

The term 'Fijian' is invariably used in Fiji to refer to the indigenous inhabitants of the country and institutions...specifically associated with them. It is not an appropriate term...to refer to all inhabitants of Fiji.[8]

The circular notes that 'there is unfortunately no suitable single word to describe all the inhabitants of Fiji'.[9] Baleinakorodawa recommends calling all citizens 'Fiji Islanders'.[10] The *Committee on the Elimination of Racial Discrimination*, in its 2008 Concluding Observations to Fiji's state report, also asked the state:

...to reflect further on how the concept of "indigenous Fijians" relates to the under-standing of indigenous peoples in international law, in particular as reflected in ILO Convention 169 on indigenous and tribal peoples' rights and the 2007 United Nations Declaration on the Rights of Indigenous Peoples. Furthermore, the State party is invited to explain how the concept of indigenous Fijians is applied in law and practice and its impact on the enjoyment of human rights by everyone in Fiji.[11]

A popular perception and stereotype of Fijian culture permeated early travel writings on the islands. Images of 'easy-going Melanesians and happy-go-lucky Polynesians'[12] was a myth cultivated in the interests of tourism. Norton quotes a travel feature in the *Sydney Morning Herald* from 1968:

There is no hunger, no loneliness, and no ambition...They live in the warmth of commu-nal love...free from the cult of the individual, unconcerned with egos, clapping hands around the kava bowl...banana leaf hats on their heads and flowers behind their ears.[13]

Allied to the imagery of paradisiacal village life is a political philosophy termed the 'Pacific Way', which emphasizes stability and tradition via adher-ence to chiefly rule.[14] Kamasese Mara, who became prime minister of Fiji after

---

[6] Michael Howard, *Fiji: Race and Politics in an Island State* (Vancouver: University of British Columbia Press, 1991) 4. See generally Kenneth Gillion, 'Fiji's Indian Migrants: A History to the End of Indenture in 1920' (Melbourne: Oxford University Press, 1962).

[7] Baleinakorodawa (n 4) 19. For the purposes of the chapter, the following distinguishing terms will be used: indigenous Fijians, Indo-Fijians, Fijian-Chinese (...).

[8] Foreign and Commonwealth Office South West Pacific Department, FCO 24/790 (22 December 1970) 2. It continues: 'The incorrect use of the term "Fijian" can give offence in Fiji and care should accordingly be taken to use the term only when it is specifically intended to refer to indigenous inhabitants of Fiji' 4.

[9] Foreign and Commonwealth Office (n 8) para 4.

[10] Baleinakorodawa (n 4) 19.

[11] Committee on the Elimination of Racial Discrimination, Concluding Observations—Fiji (2008) CERD/C/FJI/CO/17 [13].

[12] Coulter (n 1) 18.

[13] Robert Norton, *Race and Politics in Fiji* (St Lucia: University of Queensland Press, 1977) 15.

[14] Howard (n 6) 7.

independence in 1970, first articulated the ideology of the 'Pacific Way' to the General Assembly of the United Nations.[15] The failure and collapse of the contemporary Fijian polity has done much to dispel this image. The political climate has 'surfaced the well-founded fears and anxieties entrenched in the lives of indigenous and minority groups about their rights and interests'.[16] Shaista Shameem, director of the *Fiji Human Rights Commission*, notes that 'while the majority of Fiji's people would like Fiji to be known and admired for its beautiful beaches, stunning mountain ranges, pristine reefs and tropical forests, in reality, we are better known for the coups that took place in 1987 and 2000'.[17] Fiji has experienced four coups since independence, the most recent being 5 December 2006 when military commander Frank Bainimarama assumed the powers of the president and dismissed the prime minster, Laisenia Qarase.[18] Political developments in Fiji have placed considerable strain on democratic institutions throughout the Pacific Island Countries. Responding to the first coup in May 1987, Howard asked:

... the South Pacific has seen continuing challenges to democratic principles in country after country until many observers have come to wonder whether the entire region may soon go the way of Fiji.[19]

Therefore the major powers in the region, Australia and New Zealand, have adopted increasingly interventionist stances, in particular in the wake of the 2000 coup.

The greatest threat to stability in Fiji is the land tenure system. The British High Commissioner in 1971, J.R. Williams, warned that 'the land question is a potentially explosive issue which ticks away like a time bomb'.[20] The expiration and non-renewal of thirty-year tenancy agreements for Indo-Fijian farmers means that 'half the Indian rural population stands to lose its livelihood within a generation'.[21] As a result, 'the land tenure system in Fiji ... contains all the ingredients of serious political conflict between the Indian and Fijian communities'.[22] Those ingredients are still present and land tenure remains the greatest barrier to effective fulfilment of minority rights. The British aimed to 'leave the Fijians in ultimate control, but with full and adequate safeguards for all other communities'.[23] As a result, minorities, including the largest Indo-Fijian group, will never achieve political or territorial control in Fiji and do not seek to do so. Minority rights in this regard are a contested ground in which all groups point to deficiencies by contrast with others.

---

[15] ibid 54.   [16] Baleinakorodawa (n 4) 4.
[17] Shameem (n 3) 661.
[18] 'Fiji's History of Coups', *The Guardian* (5 December 2006).
[19] Howard (n 6) 12.
[20] J.R. Williams, 'The Land Question in Fiji', FCO 24/1143, 5 October 1971.
[21] ibid.   [22] ibid.
[23] D.P. Aiers, Foreign and Commonwealth Office South West Pacific Department, 'Discussions on Fiji at the United Nations' FCO 58/493 (5 January 1970) 13.

This chapter will commence by tracing the historical background to ethnic division in Fiji. Section 4.2 will then identify the groups that fall within the category of 'minorities' and 'indigenous peoples'. The rights of minorities are examined in section 4.3, with particular emphasis on the themes of land, religion, education, language, membership of the military/police, and hate speech. The final section will seek remedies to the continued violations of the rights of minority groups in Fiji, focusing on affirmative action.

4.1 Historical Background

4.1.1 Pre-Independence

It is generally accepted that Fiji was settled some three to four thousand years ago.[24] Derrick argues that the history of Fiji 'must be written largely from the viewpoint of the European, for the period preceding European discovery is entirely undocumented'.[25] Sutherland is less dismissive, but nevertheless highlights the relative lack of materials from the pre-colonial period:

Considerable gaps exist in our knowledge about conditions in Fiji prior to contact with Europeans. Most written materials are concerned either with the remote past, particularly the original peopling of the islands, or the post-contact era. Little is known of the intervening period which Thomson, displaying the ethnocentrism and paternalism typical of Fiji's early historians, described as 'the centuries which lie between the age of myth and the age of history'.[26]

Europeans knew nothing of Fiji until the middle of the seventeenth century, when its existence was first reported by Dutch sailors from the East Indies.[27] Tasman sighted and reported the islands in 1643, but did not land. Cook was the next navigator known to have observed Fiji, when he sighted Vatoa, which he named Turtle Island, in 1774. Bligh, expelled from the *Bounty* by mutineers, charted thirty-nine islands from the ship's launch in 1789, but like Tasman and Cook, did not land on these. For nearly 200 years navigators added new features to a growing map, without leaving their vessels to explore the islands. These captains' '... chief business was anything but discovery'.[28]

---

[24] Howard (n 5) 16.

[25] R. Derrick, *A History of Fiji* (Suava, Fiji: Printing and Stationery Department, 1946) v.

[26] William Sutherland, *Beyond the Politics of Race: An Alternative History of Fiji to 1992* (Canberra: Australian National University, 1992) 7. The reference is to B. Thomson, *The Fijians: A Study in the Decay of Custom* (London: Dawsons, 1908, reprinted *Fiji Times*, Suva, Fiji, 1981). Tribal histories based on oral sources which pre-date European contact have been preserved by the Fijian National Commission. They are generally 'full of accounts of turmoil', although extensive genealogies tell also of times when 'fighting was unknown and a profound peace prevailed'.

[27] Derrick (n 25) 30.   [28] ibid 31.

The precise date of the first landing is unknown. It took place sometime in the opening years of the nineteenth century when the schooner the *Argo*, on a voyage from China with a cargo for the penal settlements at Norfolk Island and Port Jackson, was blown off course and struck the Bukatatanoa Reefs. A number of the crew were taken off by canoes drawn from Oneata Island and a few of these survivors reached Lakeba, and from there, the larger islands of western Fiji. Derrick remarks: 'The changes that were to sweep over Fiji, and the disasters that were to result from contact with the outside world, were heralded by a wreck'.[29]

In the pre-colonial period, eastern Fijians were more highly stratified than their western (and interior) counterparts. Eastern Fiji had a Polynesian character influenced by Tonga, resulting in a rigid hierarchy; while western Fiji was characterized by a Melanesian, more egalitarian society.[30] From the mid-nineteenth century a handful of relatively powerful eastern chiefs emerged with close ties to Christianity and European traders and settlers, who were attracted in growing numbers by the availability of sandalwood.[31] In 1865, a number of eastern Fijian chiefs agreed to form a government under the leadership of Cakobau at the suggestion of British consul. The government collapsed within a year, but Howard identifies this agreement as the formation of:

...an enduring alliance between foreign business and political interests and Fiji's ranking eastern chiefs, an alliance that was to coalesce into a ruling oligarchy in colonial and postcolonial Fiji.[32]

Fiji was formally and unconditionally taken over by Britain in 1874, ostensibly at the request of the Fijian chief, Cakobau. The *Deed of Cession* of 10 October 1874 bound Britain to protect the Fijians from European commercial interests and to preserve the Fijian way of life,[33] although the text itself states only that '...the rights and interests of the said Tui Viti [Cakobau] and other high chiefs the ceding parties hereto shall be recognised (...)',[34] and in relation to land, 'that all claims to title to land by whomsoever preferred... shall in due course be fully investigated and equitably adjusted'.[35]

According to Howard, 'the colonial state transformed much of what had existed before, creating a neotraditional order among the indigenous Fijians which it sought to rule indirectly through a chiefly elite'.[36] That order, in place from 1874 until independence in 1970, is described as an oligarchy, composed of three ruling elements: first, the colonial administration; second, a largely expatriate business elite; and third, a native Fijian elite.[37] It was structured along ethnic and regional lines. The eastern social structure with its emphasis on hierarchy provided the model for rule through its chiefs, resulting in major changes to western Fijian societies, and ensuring the eastern chiefs '...a position at the

---

[29] ibid 37.   [30] Howard (n 6) 17.   [31] ibid 20.
[32] ibid 22.   [33] Premdas (n 2) 10.
[34] Deed of Cession of 10 October 1874, art 7(1) in Derrick (n 25) app 251.
[35] ibid.   [36] Howard (n 6) 14.   [37] ibid 6.

top of the native administration'.[38] The British governed the Fijians indirectly through a 'state within a state' that allowed Fijian chiefs to continue to govern their own people. The institutional basis was the *Fijian Administration* and the *Great Council of Chiefs*, both colonial constructs.[39] The administration was supposed to act in the interests of the Fijian people, but the reality was that such communalism was essentially envisaged for the smooth operation of a trade that was to prove exploitative, helping the chiefdoms at the inevitable expense of commoners.[40] The administration thus assisted in the transformation of hereditary chiefs into colonial bureaucrats.[41]

From 1879 to 1916 indentured labour programmes brought in workers from India to work on the plantations. The drive for indentured labour was fuelled by '... racist conceptions of inherent Fijian capabilities'.[42] Carens describes the indenture system as 'hard and degrading'.[43] In the period of indenture some 60,000 labourers arrived, with about half returning to India and the rest remaining as legal residents.[44] Gujaratis began arriving from India around 1904 as goldsmiths and tailors, and established themselves as leaders of the Indo-Fijian business community.[45] By this process, a new population was grafted onto the extant indigenous Fijian population, and by 1945, Indo-Fijians outnumbered indigenous Fijians for the first time.[46] By 1966, Indo-Fijians had become a 'clear majority'.[47]

Prior to independence, Indo-Fijians increased their representatives on the governing *Legislative Council* from one, in 1916, to an eventual twelve under the party system in 1966. Indo-Fijians had been campaigning for a common, rather than a communal, electoral roll since 1929.[48] In that year its three allocated representatives (out of a total of thirty-six) had walked out of the *Legislative Council* in protest at the refusal to vote in favour of a common roll.[49] Meller and Anthony observe that:

... over the following years common roll in the minds of European and Fijian members had become synonymous with an attempt at political domination by the Indians, and each proposal had been voted down.[50]

---

[38] ibid 25.   [39] ibid 7.   [40] ibid 31.
[41] ibid 31.   [42] Premdas (n 2) 11.
[43] Joseph Carens, 'Democracy and Respect for Difference: The Case of Fiji' (1992) 25 *UMJLR* 562.
[44] Premdas (n 2) 11.   [45] Howard (n 6) 36.
[46] Premdas (n 2) 11.   [47] ibid 22.
[48] In this quest, they were echoing a discussion that was already taking place in India in the context of its movement from British colony to independence. There is little evidence of a specific link between the movement in Fiji and the movement in the 'mother' country, rather a reflection of the similarity of the tone of the discussion in a period of transformation in a non-mono-cultural society. For more on the discussion in relation to India and how it pertained to India's own attitude to minority rights, see Joshua Castellino and Elvira Domínguez Redondo, *Minority Rights in Asia: A Comparative Legal Analysis* (Oxford: Oxford University Press, 2006) esp 58–103.
[49] Premdas (n 2) 22.
[50] Norman Meller and J. Anthony, *Fiji Goes to the Polls* (Honolulu: University of Hawaii Press, 1967) 15.

Criticism had been eroding indigenous Fijian privileges in the decade prior to independence. The influential Spate Report in the early 1960s criticized the traditional land tenure system, and called for individualization as epitomized by *galala* farmers as the required objective.[51] The extensive Burns Report of 1960 was severely critical of the Fijian administration that operated on the basis of nominations rather than elections. Burns called for elected representatives to the *Legislative Council* for Fijians, and in response, the 1963 *Legislative Council* elections were '... the first time the bulk of the people participated in selection of government representatives'.[52] By contrast Indo-Fijians had been electing rather than nominating representatives from the beginning.

Indigenous Fijians initially resisted independence, fearing the loss of power and Indo-Fijian dominance.[53] Yet constitutional change and independence were inevitable for Fiji, and in 1965 a constitutional conference was held in London with the participation of representatives of the three major ethnic groups, the indigenous Fijians, the Indo-Fijians, and the Europeans.[54] The 1966 election results, based on a communal roll that saw an alliance between the Fijian, European, various mixed groups, and a splinter Indian group, gave the Fijian-dominated *Alliance Party*, led by Kamasese Mara, an overwhelming victory over the *National Federation Party*, supported mainly by Indians. Resistance to independence was greatly reduced with the establishment of indigenous Fijian constitutional superiority in 1966.[55] Independence required a constitutional solution to be agreed between the two parties, and between August 1969 and March 1970, representatives of the *Alliance Party* and the *National Federation Party* negotiated an agreement.[56]

Under the terms of the 1970 Constitution, the *Alliance Party* conceded that common roll was a 'long term objective', with the future enactment of a Commission to re-examine the issue of common versus communal roll sometime between the first and second election following independence.[57] In the interim it was accepted that the communal system in place would continue.[58] Furthermore, full citizenship was granted to Indo-Fijians, and all citizens were to

[51] Howard (n 6) 57. *Galala* or independent farmers did not subscribe to the traditional form of landownership.

[52] Howard (n 6) 63.   [53] Premdas (n 2) 24.

[54] Carens (n 43) 567. On the disproportionate voice afforded the European group, see below, section 4.2.6.

[55] R.K. Vasil, 'Communalism and Constitution-making in Fiji' (1972) 45 *PA* 23.

[56] For more on the extent to which the ethnic divide in Fiji shaped the constitutional debate, see Yash Ghai and Jill Cottrell, 'A Tale of Three Constitutions: Ethnicity and Politics in Fiji' in Sujit Choudhry (ed), *Constitutional Design for Divided Societies; Integration or Accommodation?* (Oxford: Oxford University Press, 2008) 287–315.

[57] It is worth remembering that a similar discussion was also engaged upon in the context of the transition from British rule in multi-ethnic societies like Malaysia and India. For more, see Castellino and Domínguez Redondo (n 48) chs 2 and 3.

[58] Premdas (n 2) 25.

be called 'Fijians'. A *Bill of Rights* guaranteeing non-discrimination on grounds, *inter alia*, of race and place of origin, was enacted.[59] In return, a definite reference to the *Deed of Cession* in the Constitution was required, so that '... if there was a threat to their position through constitutional changes, they [the indigenous Fijians] would invoke the Deed';[60] the so-called 'paramountcy' requirement.[61] Furthermore, '... the 1970 Constitution did not allow Indians, by themselves, to form a majority government'.[62]

The negotiations established a bicameral parliament in which additional 'weightage' was allocated to indigenous Fijian interests. This was realized through the establishment of a lower house, a Senate, in which superior numbers of indigenous Fijians were represented. The Senate involved an amending procedure that entrenched protections for indigenous Fijian landownership and custom. This was achieved:

... by requiring a two-thirds majority in each chamber in order to alter the Constitution. Here, it must be noted that the Fijian *Great Council of Chiefs* had 8 out of 22 seats, that is, more than a third of the seats, and was thus capable of blocking any constitutional change without its consent.[63]

Land is considered '...the most significant triggering point of Fijian-Indian inter-group conflict'.[64] Crucially, the 1970 Constitution validated all Fijian claims to 83 per cent of the country's land and required a two-thirds majority of the *Grand Council of Chiefs* in the Senate to alter this provision.[65] Independence was proclaimed on 10 October 1970. On colonial rule, *Alliance Party* ideologue Ahmed Ali commented:

... it would be no exaggeration to conclude that the colonial regime failed to reconcile paramountcy for Fijians, over-representation of Europeans and promise of equality to Indians. Indeed, the three were and are incompatible'.[66]

In his address to the General Assembly of the United Nations in 1970, Prime Minister Mara stated:

Many speakers have commented on our peaceful transition to independence...But this is nothing new in the Pacific...We like to think that this is the Pacific Way, and that it underlines the case for a Pacific voice in this Assembly, both geographically and ideologically.[67]

---

[59] Constitution of Fiji 1970, c 4, ss 21–43. However 'individual rights were qualified by the collective rights of Fijians and were characterised by numerous restrictions and rules for their suspension'. Ghai and Cottrell in Choudhry (n 56) 293.

[60] Norton (n 13) 103.   [61] Ghai and Cottrell in Choudhry (n 56) 293.

[62] Ved Nanda, 'Ethnic Conflict in Fiji and International Human Rights Law' (1992) 25 *CILJ* 567.

[63] Premdas (n 2) 25.   [64] ibid 26.   [65] ibid 28.

[66] Quoted in Howard (n 6) 77.

[67] Quoted in ibid 129.

4.1.2 Post-independence

The collapse of independent Fiji's political institutions in 1987 occurred within one month of the loss of power by the ruling élite. The *Fiji Labour Party* emerged in the aftermath of the 1982 elections, and grew rapidly, to the surprise of observers used to categorizing Fijian politics as bipartisan and communal.[68] Its success was attributed to the fact that stability under *Alliance Party* rule was largely illusory; Mara's autocratic rule and system of patronage ignored the real needs of citizens across ethnic lines, and the presence of a strong, dynamic labour movement.[69] In 1987, the *Fijian Labour Party* won a hard-fought election, gaining twenty-eight seats to the *Alliance Party's* twenty-four.[70] It formed a coalition, non-communal government, with Timoci Bavadra, an indigenous Fijian commoner, as prime minister. This was followed immediately by a sustained, but unsuccessful, campaign of 'destabilization' of the new government, based on the accusation of Indian dominance of government.[71] It was organized around the *Taukei*, an extremist indigenous Fijian movement.[72] On the destabilization campaign, Sutherland remarks that '...here was Fijian elite racism at its Machiavellian worst'.[73] Nanda concurs that the *Taukei* Movement was 'racist and anti-Indian'.[74]

On 14 May 1987, Colonel Sitiveni Rabuka entered Parliament, took the government (whose membership was 95 per cent indigenous Fijian) hostage and declared the military to be in power.[75] Bavadra and the Labour coalition were evicted from office just thirty-three days after assuming power.[76] Rabuka claimed he acted '...to maintain order and prevent racial violence',[77] justifying military intervention on the basis of the need to protect indigenous rights and interests, especially landownership and political power. As a Methodist lay preacher, he stated he had the additional intent of establishing Fiji as a Christian State.[78] The *Great Council of Chiefs* met on 19 May '...to give its approval to the coup and to plans to establish a new racist regime'.[79] It was announced by the military that the 1970 Constitution was abrogated. Fiji '...was looking more and more like a military state'.[80]

On 25 September, following a series of attempts to reach an agreement culminating with the *Deuka Accord*, which would have seen power shared between the *Alliance Party* and a coalition of opposition parties, a second coup was launched.[81] One commentator wrote: 'It is deplorable that Colonel Rabuka staged the second coup when there was the possibility of a settlement of the

---

[68] ibid 146.   [69] ibid 146–7.   [70] ibid 223.
[71] Premdas (n 2) 62.   [72] Sutherland (n 26) 182.   [73] ibid.
[74] Nanda (n 62) 567.   [75] Premdas (n 2) 65.
[76] ibid 65.   [77] Nanda (n 62) 568.
[78] Joseph Bush, 'Defining Group Rights and Delineating Sovereignty' (1999) 14 *AUILR* 737.
[79] Howard (n 6) 276.   [80] ibid 278.
[81] ibid.

crisis created by the first coup'.[82] Rabuka declared Fiji a republic on 6 October 1987, and Mara was restored as prime minister in late 1987 with Rabuka's backing; '...the chiefly oligarchy had regained control of the country'.[83] Nanda also highlights the '...considerable overlapping party, tribal, regional, feudal, and family connections between the Alliance's Mara...and Rabuka'.[84] Thakur and Wood called it a 'camouflaged measure of intra-Fijian tribal and ruling élite protection'.[85] Ousted Prime Minister Bavadra described the new Mara regime as a 'military government in a civilian cloak'.[86] Premdas points out that the installation of a semi-civilian government under Mara laid the groundwork for a more permanent system of repression and human rights violations.[87]

The government abrogated the 1970 Constitution, and promulgated an amended version in 1990 by presidential decree that '...sought to ensure Fijian control over both the executive and the legislature'.[88] The 1970 Constitution had included a *Bill of Rights* based on the *European Convention on Human Rights* and the *Universal Declaration of Human Rights*. The 1990 Constitution retained the *Bill of Rights* in its chapter 2, but subject to a crucial section that gave '...carte blanche priority to the corporate interests of the indigenous Fijian people over all of the enumerated individual human rights'.[89] The 1990 Constitution was rejected in its draft form by a coalition of opposition groups. It stated that the document was:

...profoundly authoritarian, undemocratic, militaristic, racist and feudalistic. It would be divisive and sow the seeds of terrible violence. It would retard our social and economic development.[90]

It described the Constitution's electoral system as tainted with '...the same sinister motives of apartheid and the supremacy of one race to the exclusion of others'.[91]

In the wake of the second coup and the enactment of the new constitution, between 30,000 and 40,000 Indo-Fijians fled Fiji.[92] The 1990 Constitution did allow for a review to be conducted within seven years[93] and an independent

---

[82] Quoted in Nanda (n 62) 568.   [83] Howard (n 6) 341.

[84] Ramesh Thakur and Antony Wood, 'Fiji in Crisis' (1988) 43 *World Today* 207.

[85] ibid 567.   [86] Howard (n 6) 345.

[87] Premdas (n 2) 78.   [88] Bush (n 78) 737.

[89] ibid 738. Bush continues: 'not only does this section give blanket justification for the Parliament to contravene the Bill of Rights in the perceived interest of the indigenous people, but its language apparently mandates that Parliament do so'.

[90] Letter from the National Federation Party and the Fiji Labour Party Coalition to the Chairman and Members, Constitutional Advisory and Review Committee (6 January 1989), quoted in Nanda (n 62) 570.

[91] ibid.   [92] ibid 571.

[93] Iyer describes the review clause as an 'interesting twist' which the President included in the 1990 Constitution at the behest of the Indo-Fijians. Venkat Iyer, 'Restoration Constitutionalism in the South Pacific' (2006) 15 *PRLPJ* 54.

Constitution Review Commission was established in 1995.[94] The Commission's terms of reference emphasized the importance of considering internationally recognized principles and standards of individual and group rights.[95] It submitted its report in 1996, and following interpretation and implementation by a bipartisan parliamentary committee, Fiji's Constitution was successfully amended on 25 July 1997.[96] The amended document contained significant and far-reaching reforms that restored Fiji's constitutional order. The *Constitutional (Amendment) Act 1997* bears a striking resemblance to the abrogated Constitution of 1970.[97]

Elections in 1999 brought a multiracial government to power under Mahendra Chaudhry. On 19 May 2000, George Speight and members of his *Counter-Revolutionary Warfare Movement* stormed the Parliament, taking Prime Minister Chaudhry and his cabinet hostage and abrogating the Fijian Constitution.[98] Speight argued that the 1997 Constitution did not sufficiently protect indigenous Fijian interests. The coup again unleashed inter-ethnic violence:

> In the immediate aftermath of the attack, there was large-scale pillage and arson in Suva and intimidation of villagers by mobs who began running amok in the aftermath of any real attempt by the police to maintain law and order.[99]

Speight issued six decrees within a month, one of which purported to abolish the 1997 Constitution, leading to a declaration of a state of emergency.[100] Eventually the commander of the military forces, Bainimarama, assumed power as head of an *Interim Military Government* and imposed martial law. After five weeks he handed over power to an all-indigenous Fijian Interim Civilian Government headed by Laisenia Qarase. Qarase proclaimed the need for a new constitution under which indigenous Fijian interests would be better protected, including the reservation of the offices of prime minister and president for indigenous Fijians.[101]

Significantly, the *Interim Civilian Government* re-established the *Fijian High Court* and the *Court of Appeal*. This facilitated a challenge by an Indo-Fijian farmer, Chandrika Prasad, who had been forced off his land in the aftermath of Speight's coup by a mob which vandalized his homestead, butchered his cattle, damaged his crops, and issued death threats against him. The police failed to assist him, so he filed an action against the *Republic of Fiji* in the High Court.[102] The case was heralded as deciding whether 'minority rights survive' in Fiji.[103] His action called, *inter alia*, for the following declarations:

---

[94] Venkat Iyer, 'Courts and Constitutional Usurpers: Some Lessons from Fiji' (2005) 28 *DLJ* 47.
[95] Bush (n 78) 739.   [96] ibid 740.   [97] ibid 757.
[98] William Burke-White, 'Reframing Impunity: Applying Liberal International Law Theory to an analysis of Amnesty Legislation' (2001) 42 *HILJ* 497.
[99] Iyer (n 94) 48.   [100] ibid 48.   [101] ibid 49.
[102] ibid 50.
[103] 'Court Could Consign Fiji to *Apartheid*' *The Guardian* (19 February 2001) <http://www.guardian.co.uk/fiji/article/0,,439915,00.html> [last accessed 25 March 2009].

1. the attempted coup of 19 May 2000 by George Speight was unsuccessful;
2. the declaration of a state of emergency by the President was unconstitutional;
3. the purported revocation of the 1997 Constitution by the Interim Military Government was unconstitutional;
4. the 1997 Constitution still remained in force; and
5. the government formed following the May 1999 elections was still a legally constituted government.[104]

Gates J duly supported Prasad's action, holding that the attempted coup was unsuccessful, overruling the revocation of the 1997 Constitution, and declaring the 1999 government as still continuing to hold office. The decision was appealed, and the appellate hearings were conducted before five judges drawn from neighbouring Australia, New Zealand (who contributed two judges), Papua New Guinea, and Tonga.[105] Although disagreeing with some aspects of the High Court ruling, the appeal affirmed the central tenets of that judgment and the legitimacy of the 1997 Constitution. The *Prasad* cases arose as a result of substantial political and diplomatic pressure exerted by Fiji's neighbours, notably Australia and New Zealand.[106] The interim government's willingness to subject itself to independent judicial scrutiny was because it had not enjoyed full support from the military or the police, unlike the 1987 coups.[107]

The Appeal Court based its ruling on 'the modern shift towards insistence on basic human rights in a raft of international treaties'.[108] Counsel for Prasad had pointed out that:

... the explicitly racist nature of the political changes canvassed by the caretaker regime contravenes customary international law ... the relative disenfranchisement and subordination of any racial group, let alone one which comprises over 40% of Fiji's population, amounts to degrading treatment contrary to recognised international standards.[109]

The *Prasad* case represents the '... only time that a domestic court has pronounced that a coup is illegal and that the abrogation of a nation's constitution is legally ineffective'.[110]

The case did not result in the restoration of the deposed government. Fresh elections took place, with Qarase being returned and the deposed *Labour Party*, after a series of negotiations, settling for opposition status. *Prasad* succeeded

---

[104] *Prasad v The Republic of Fiji and anor* (2000), [2001] NZAR 21.
[105] *Republic of Fiji and anor v Prasad* (2001) NZAR 385.
[106] Iyer (n 94) 53.   [107] ibid 53.   [108] ibid 54.
[109] *Republic of Fiji v Prasad*, outline of submissions on behalf of the respondent, quoted in Iyer (n 94) 58. Indeed it could be suggested that this line of argument is in line with the famous opinion articulated by Judge Tanaka in the *South West African Case* where he stated: 'The norm of non-discrimination or non-separation on the basis of race has become a rule of customary international law. ... This principle [of equality before the law] has become an integral part of the constitutions of most of the civilized countries in the world'. See *South West Africa Case* (*Ethiopia v South Africa*; *Libya v South Africa*) Second Phase, (1966). *CJ Rep* 4, 293–99 (dissenting).
[110] George Williams, 'Republic of *Fiji v Prasad*' (2001) 2 *MJIL* 150.

in '...drawing Fiji back from the brink of chaos, anarchy and a further bout of ethnic cleansing which seemed inevitable in the immediate aftermath of the May 2000 events in Suva'.[111] The Qarase government sought to persuade domestic and international public opinion of its determination to return Fiji to the rule of law, and embarked on a swift trial of George Speight and ten others involved in the attempted coup:[112] an event attributed by authors such as Iyer to incessant international pressure from states such as Australia and New Zealand.[113] Charged with treason, Speight was convicted and received a mandatory death sentence, later commuted to life imprisonment.[114]

Despite the advances and guarantees for human rights in Fiji secured by the *Prasad* decision, the fragility of Fiji's political institutions was again exposed on 5 December 2006, when Bainimarama seized power as military commander.[115] The coup was triggered by Qarase's attempt to introduce legislation that would offer a pardon to those involved in the 2000 coup and the allocation of land.[116] Unlike previous coups, Bainimarama justified his actions on the need to forestall the government from continuing to adopt racist policies and programmes that appeal to indigenous Fijians.[117] The 2006 coup is therefore the first one to be purportedly justified, not by indigenous Fijian concerns, but by concern for the interests of other ethnic groups in the country.[118] Bainimarama was declared interim prime minister, and the military re-imposed a state of emergency,[119] with elections tentatively set for March 2009.[120]

Fiji's 'constitutional odyssey'[121] renders it difficult to judge the security of its human rights provisions. It remains impossible to differentiate political influence from legal safeguards, given the readiness of successive regimes and governments to abrogate the most fundamental rights. Currently, the 1997 Constitution remains the basic law of the state. The *Prasad* judgments seemed to cement the precarious position of the constitutional rights of Fiji's minority groups. Yet the 2006 coup has again illustrated the fact that Fiji's internal political mechanisms are disjointed. Concerted international pressure, in particular from Australia and New Zealand, has sent a strong message that constant upheaval, whatever the

---

[111] Iyer (n 94) 67.   [112] Iyer (n 93) 67.   [113] ibid 68.

[114] ibid 67–8.   [115] *The Guardian* (n 18).

[116] ibid.   [117] ibid.

[118] Citizens' Constitutional Forum, 'Submission to the Committee on the Elimination of Racial Discrimination concerning the Republic of the Fiji Islands' (2007) 6 <http://www.ccf.org.fj/confrence/CCF%20CERD%20Final%20AY.pdf> [last accessed 6 August 2008].

[119] 'Emergency Rule declared in Fiji' *BBC News* (7 September 2007) <http://news.bbc.co.uk/1/hi/world/asia-pacific/6981381.stm> [last accessed 6 August 2008].

[120] In January 2009, the Pacific Islands Forum issued a statement condemning Fiji's Interim Government for failing to prepare to hold elections in March. The statement noted that there was 'no clear timetable for the return of constitutional government to the people', and called on Fiji to hold elections by December 2009. See further Pacific Islands Forum Secretariat, 'Forum Leaders Special Retreat Communique on Fiji', Port Moresby, 27 January 2009, available at: http://www.forumsec.org.fj/pages.cfm/newsroom/press-statements/2009/forum-leaders-special-retreat-communique-on-fiji.html [last accessed 25 March 2009].

[121] Iyer (n 93) 41.

interests of the groups concerned, is unsustainable and is a major source of strife and imbalance in the region. These states argue that minority rights protection is crucial for the maintenance of stability in Fiji. However the reality remains that the efficacy of national and international legal rights for minorities will be determined by their ability to survive political machinations and élite manoeuvrings.

4.2 Identification of Minorities and Indigenous Peoples

The 1997 Fijian Constitution does not employ the term 'minority', instead, describing indigenous Fijians and Rotumans as 'people', and other ethnic groups, including the Indo-Fijians, as 'communities'.[122] The term 'minority' in the official language of the state of Fiji is clearly reserved for those diverse smaller groups who do not form part of the larger indigenous Fijian or Indo-Fijian groups. Thus the state has established two National Advisory Councils, one for the Indian community and one for Minority communities,[123] the latter safeguarding the interests of the smaller ethnic groups. Yet to some extent there is no 'majority' in Fiji, with every group having a claim to minority status.

The 1996 census of the population used eight categories to classify ethnic groups in Fiji: Chinese, European, Fijian, Indian, Part European, Rotuman, Pacific Islander, and All Other Ethnic Groups.[124] The most recent census, conducted in 2007, has issued only provisional population results, which show the following figures: Fijians: 473,983; Indians: 311,591; Others: 42,326.[125]

Unusually, ethnic conflict in Fiji has been the result of an indigenous group that has managed to acquire power,[126] with military coups overthrowing elected governments on the basis of 'indigenous rights'.[127] A Minority Rights Group International study describes the situation in Fiji as 'complex', whereby '...a numerically dominant indigenous community asserts that it is vulnerable and therefore demands a dominant role in government'.[128] Indo-Fijians similarly highlight their vulnerability, in relation to land and political rights. Meanwhile smaller minority groups face exclusion; but their plight is often ignored owing to the overriding focus, internally and externally, on the rights and interests of the two larger groups.[129]

---

[122] Constitution of Fiji, 1997. Although indigenous Fijians are also described as communities.

[123] Department of Multi-ethnic Affairs, <http://www.multiethnicaffairs.gov.fj/NAC.htm> [last accessed 25 March 2009].

[124] Committee on the Elimination of Racial Discrimination, State Report—Fiji (15 November 2002) CERD/C/429/Add.1 [19].

[125] Fiji Islands Bureau of Statistics, <http://www.statsfiji.gov.fj/> [last accessed 25 March 2009].

[126] Premdas (n 2) 6.   [127] Shameem (n 3) 661.

[128] Satendra Parasad, Jone Dakuvula, and Darryn Snell *Economic Development, Democracy and Ethnic Conflict in the Fiji Islands* (London: Minority Rights Group, 2001) 1.

[129] ibid.

4.2.1 Indigenous Fijians

Indigenous Fijians are the largest ethnic group in Fiji. They are not a homogenous group, and are divided into numerous communities, groups, and clans,[130] and by region, dialect, and social organization.[131] Indigenous Fijians from different regions have periodically laid claim to greater autonomy based on separate histories, languages, and economic conditions.[132] Ewins notes that being 'drafted' into what is referred to as the 'eastern confederacies' has not been accepted easily by western Fijians, who continue to '…have significant linguistic, political and cultural differences from eastern Fijians'.[133] In the aftermath of the 1990 Constitution, this western confederation labelled the eastern grouping 'an aggressive minority' that was seeking to 'use the power of government to colonize these people [Western Fijians] for their own benefit'.[134]

According to Basawaiya, the source of the indigenous Fijian claim to vulnerability is the annihilation of indigenous peoples in the Pacific region. He infers that the relative population success of the Fijian indigenous people relies on a robust defence of their rights:

Fiji has a population of 772,655 of which 394,999 (51.1%) are indigenous Fijians, the *I'Taukei*—while the Indo-Fijians comprise 336,59 (43.6%) with Chinese, Solomon Islanders, Rotumans, Europeans and people of mixed race making up the balance. It has been estimated that there are some 15 million indigenous people in the Pacific. By comparison, in Australia 250,000 out of a population of approximately 18 million are indigenous and in New Zealand, 350,000 out of a population of approximately 3.3 million are indigenous.[135]

The Fijian government has consistently argued that indigenous Fijians are the poorest group in the state. In its 2007 state report to the Committee on the Elimination of Racial Discrimination (CERD), Fiji cited international reports from 1997 in order to compare the incomes of indigenous Fijians as a group with other groups:

The 1997 UNDP Report and the 1996 Census clearly outline social and economic inequalities…the average weekly household incomes for Fijian households was 36% lower than that for the minorities, 20.3% lower than Indian households and 13% lower than the national average.[136]

---

[130] ibid 5.   [131] Premdas (n 2) 105.

[132] Prasad, Dakuvula, and Snell (n 128) 5.

[133] Roderick Ewins, 'Fiji's New Western Confederacy' (2000–2001) *Journal of South Pacific Law* <http://www.vanuatu.usp.ac.fj/journal_splaw/Special_Interest/Fiji_2000/Fiji_Ewins1.html> [last accessed 6 August 2008].

[134] Quoted in Premdas (n 2) 106.

[135] Nehla Basawaiya, 'Indigenous Renascence: Law, Culture and Society in the 21st Century: Status of Indigenous Rights in Fiji' (1997) 10 *STLR* 197.

[136] Committee on Elimination of Racial Discrimination, State Report—Fiji (2007) CERD/C/ FJI/17 [47].

A rural/urban divide exacerbates this gap, thus:

> ...a majority of Fijians live in rural areas, particularly in most remote places, where there is often difficulty of access to basic social services, including health, education, roads, water supplies, sanitation, electrification and so on. There are lower levels of income and standards in these areas.[137]

The state report predicts that figures will have changed since 1997 with the introduction of changes to land tenancy agreements.[138] The most recent UNDP report from 2007 asserts that socio-economic deprivation in Fiji cannot be categorized in terms of ethnicity, and points out instead that 'poverty is not concentrated in any particular sector of Fijian society but is an under-current across all communities'.[139] Nevertheless, as a group, indigenous Fijians perform poorly in certain areas, notably education and certain economic sectors.[140]

Despite these factors, Fijian society still provides Indigenous Fijians with certain important privileges. As outlined by *Minority Rights Group International*, they dominate several key areas:

> In addition to owning over 80 percent of Fiji's land, they make up over 99 percent of Fiji's military (FMF), 75 percent of Fiji's nurses, and hold the most senior positions in the justice system, military and police force. The focus of most recent policy initiatives has been on addressing indigenous Fijians' disadvantaged positions in business and education.[141]

4.2.2 Indo-Fijians

The Indo-Fijian community, constituting the second largest group in Fiji, is an equally diverse group. The majority of the community is Hindu, but Muslim, Christian, and Sikh minorities also form part of this community.[142] In fact the community can broadly be divided on the basis of the place of origin of the original immigrants, that is, whether they migrated from northern or southern India. During the inter-war years, Gujarati Indians arrived in Fiji and had come to rival Europeans for economic power by the 1960s.[143] Indo-Fijians identify themselves as members of the Gujarati community or as descendants of immigrants who arrived during the indenture period, and 'in some cases, the two groups have little regard for each other'.[144] The most recent UNDP report confirms this division, suggesting that Gujarati households are generally better off than most other Indo-Fijian households.[145]

---

[137] Ibid 46.   [138] ibid 50.
[139] United Nations Development Programme, 'Fiji Poverty Report' (21 February 2007) Executive Summary 2. Available at <http://www.undp.org.fj/_resources/main/files/fijipovertyreports/sum.pdf> [last accessed 6 August 2008].
[140] Prasad, Dakuvula, and Snell (n 128) 5.   [141] ibid.
[142] Coulter (n 1) 168.   [143] Prasad, Dakuvula, and Snell (n 128) 5.
[144] ibid.
[145] UNDP Report (n 139) ch 2—Income Distribution and Inequality in Fiji.

The indentured labourers that arrived in Fiji from India are generally said not to have reconstituted their caste divisions[146] in Fiji. Thus Indo-Fijian society has been described as 'egalitarian, belying its rigidly hierarchical roots in India'.[147] Grieco summarizes the reasons for this:

... it is generally viewed that the primary cause of caste disintegration in Fiji was the ritually polluting conditions of the voyage from India and the exploitative nature of life on the indenture plantations.[148]

She differentiates the descendants of indentured labourers from those that emanated from Gujarat, on the basis of the maintenance of caste differences. Thus:

... unlike the indentured laborers, the Gujarati immigrants represented a limited number of social groups that originated from specific towns and districts within a single state in India.[149]

As a consequence:

Because the Gujarati community was established through free, non-labor migration, it was possible to initiate and maintain family and caste-based migration chains within their migration streams. This allowed for the reestablishment of sub-caste group extensions in Fiji, which enabled the Gujarati community to continue caste-related behavior and maintain a level of caste consciousness that the descendants of the indentured immigrants could not. Indentured labor migration, by preventing the reestablishment of caste groups overseas, eliminated the structural basis for caste-related behavior, reducing it to individual or family custom. This established the caste-free culture experienced today by the descendants of the indentured immigrants.[150]

There appears to be a high degree of collective anxiety in the Indo-Fijian community since the 1987 coup,[151] epitomized by high levels of emigration. These anxieties revolve around security and human rights protections, access to fair political representation, and most specifically over issues concerning land rights. The coups unleashed high levels of violence against Indo-Fijians as an ethnic group, including 'systematic looting and burning of Indo-Fijians' homes, temples, and businesses in Suva and in neighbouring provinces', with the security forces often failing to intervene.[152]

---

[146] For a general overview of the question of caste in international human rights law as well as for its specific historical background and contemporary occurrence in India, see David Keane, *Caste-Based Discrimination in International Law* (Aldershot: Ashgate, 2007).

[147] K.A. Watson-Gegeo, 'The Study of Language Use in Oceania' (1986) 15 *ARA* 154.

[148] Elizabeth Grieco, 'The Effects of Migration on the Establishment of Networks: Caste Disintegration and Reformation among the Indians of Fiji' (1998) 32 (3) *IMR* 709.

[149] ibid 724.

[150] ibid 728. However, it is not simply a free/indentured migrational dichotomy. The Punjabi community of Fiji, while technically 'free' immigrants, has not maintained integral sub-caste groups, see ibid 730.

[151] Prasad, Dakuvula, and Snell (n 128) 5.   [152] ibid.

Whenever a government that could be said to be representative of Indo-Fijian interests has been elected into office, it has been violently removed within a very short period. Of Fiji's four contemporary coups, three have been motivated by the protection of indigenous Fijian interests over Indo-Fijian interests. The fourth and most recent 2006 coup appears to be an internecine dispute within the indigenous Fijian community, but it has its origins in the re-allocation of land and is inherently tied up with intra-community relations.

Emigration has had a significant impact on Indo-Fijian population numbers since the 1987 Rabuka coup. Compared with the previous 1986 census, indigenous Fijian numbers had increased in 1996 by 65,694 persons, while Indo-Fijian numbers registered a decrease, attributed to '...high international emigration and a lower rate of natural increase. The net population loss of Indians through emigration between the censuses was estimated at 58,300 persons'.[153] Premadas argues that the emigration of some 30,000 Indo-Fijian citizens between 1987 and 1990 was 'encouraged' by the government, and represented a 'pre-meditated tactic to drive Indians out of Fiji'.[154] The Prasad decision prevented large-scale flight in the aftermath of Speight's 2000 coup, effectively succeeding in '...drawing Fiji back form the brink of chaos, anarchy and a further bout of ethnic cleansing'.[155]

From a position of numerical dominance, Indo-Fijians are now the second-largest group in Fiji. *Minority Rights Group International* believes that it is difficult to make long-term projections about the emigration of Indo-Fijians, although '...many Indo-Fijian community organizations are talking of mass emigrations as the community's only option'.[156] The *Citizens' Constitutional Forum* states:

Indo-Fijians have been over-represented in emigration from Fiji throughout the independence period... the extent of this overrepresentation rose alarmingly after the 1987 coups and has only begun to reduce since the mid-1990s through a gradual increase in emigration by indigenous Fijians. This indicates that, besides exacerbating the overall problem of brain drain, Fiji's recent history of political instability has also disproportionately driven away Indo-Fijians... the current Government has taken no specific action to address this issue.[157]

If Indo-Fijian population numbers were again to surpass those of indigenous Fijians, it is likely a political crisis would be automatically triggered. Continuous low-level emigration operates almost as an internal check within the Indo-Fijian community to prevent further conflict. Vasil summarizes:

...there is an immense fear of majority rule among the Fijians who believe that it would inevitably lead to their dispossession in their own country. Added to this is the widely

---

[153] CERD State Report—Fiji (n 124) 20.   [154] Premdas (n 2) 82.
[155] Iyer (n 94) 67.   [156] Prasad, Dakuvula, and Snell (n 128) 6.
[157] Citizens' Constitutional Forum (n 118) 85.

held belief that Indians have a predominant share of economic and commercial power, and given equality to political rights, would take over the country.[158]

While indigenous Fijians own an estimated 83 per cent of the land, freehold ownership by the Indo-Fijian community is 1.7 per cent.[159] Crucially, indigenous Fijian hegemony in terms of landownership is not contested. Sharma, former head of the National Federation Party, summed up the Indo-Fijian position as consisting of a wide-spread recognition within the community for '... the rights of our Fijian brothers and for that reason our leaders agreed to entrenched land provisions in the 1970 constitution safeguarding those very rights'.[160] Indo-Fijians do not seek to contest indigenous Fijian claims to ownership of land.[161] Rather, the discord centres on the renewal of longer-term leases of the land, which are the cause of severe insecurity among Indo-Fijians.[162]

Ultimately Indo-Fijians believe that they are denied a fair share of state resources.[163] They point to unequal distribution of state-funded scholarships in education and the general imbalance within state-assisted programmes in favour of indigenous Fijians. In response, the government asserts that the Indo-Fijian community is fundamentally a wealthy one, whose commercial success has come at the expense of the indigenous Fijian community.[164] State programmes claim to seek to '... bridge the social and economic gap between the indigenous people and other ethnic communities'.[165] This can be interpreted to mean the reduction of the gap between indigenous Fijians and the more wealthy Indo-Fijians—a gap that appears to be largely illusory. In fact, according to the most recent UNDP report from 2007, Indo-Fijian households have a lower average income compared with indigenous Fijian households.[166]

4.2.3 Banabans

Banabans were shipped from their home, Banaba Island or 'Ocean Island' in the Gilbert Islands, to Rabi Island in Fiji, over 2,000 miles away, on 15 December 1945.[167] Their home had been progressively dug up when phosphate was discovered in the rock in 1900,[168] and, following further destruction from the invading

[158] Vasil (n 55) 22.   [159] Basawaiya (n 135) 199.
[160] Premdas (n 2) 105.   [161] Bush (n 78) 747.
[162] Carens (n 43) 602.   [163] Prasad, Dakuvula, and Snell (n 128) 5.
[164] ibid. 6.   [165] CERD State Report—Fiji (2007) (n 136) 56.
[166] See below, section 4.4.1.
[167] Martin Silverman, 'The Resettled Banaban (Ocean Island) Community in Fiji: A Preliminary Report' (1962) 3 (4) *CA* 429. Banaba was re-named Ocean Island after the British ship that first sighted it, the *Ocean*.
[168] This discovery did not take place on the island: 'The Banabans blame "the rock". A rock doorstop of unknown origin used to prop open a door in the Sydney office of the Pacific Islands Company. A particularly driven young geologist named Arthur Ellis had it analysed and found it to be over 80 percent pure phosphate of lime, far greater than any coming out of the other two known phosphate islands of Nauru and Christmas at that time. It took Ellis two months to trace the origin of this rock which had been brought back by a passing steamer from a tiny "unclaimed"

Japanese in World War II, they were re-located to an island they had never seen.[169] The plight of the Banabans is one of the worst examples of colonial exploitation in the Pacific Island Countries.[170] They claim that the decision to remove them to Rabi Island was '...an excuse to dispose of the Banabans who stood in the way of their [British] plans to continue phosphate mining of their homeland'.[171] The Banabans are divided between Fijian Banabans on Rabi Island and a small community that returned to Banaba and is governed by the Republic of Kiribati (formerly Gilbert Islands).[172]

Following litigation between the Banabans and the United Kingdom government, compensation was agreed in the 1970s under the *Banaban Settlement Act*.[173] The Act forms part of Fiji's 1997 Constitution and guarantees compensation regulated by a trust fund. Poor investments and management by the ruling Rabi Island Council in the 1980s jeopardized these funds and led to the dissolution of the Council in 1992. Correspondingly, the social well-being of the Banabans has shown a serious decline over recent years:

The community's marginal political influence means that Banabans barely feature in government policies and programmes—for example, the community was excluded from the 'positive discrimination' programmes in 1990 and from the Blueprint announced by the Qarase administration in late 2000.[174]

A report by journalist Gerard Hindmarsh, commissioned by UNESCO and published in 2002, describes the travails of a significantly displaced minority people, numbering just over 4,000 in population.[175] Life on Rabi is 'rudimentary' and 'basic', with many of the families that inhabit the island facing severe economic hardship, making them among the most underprivileged, in socio-economic terms, in Fiji.[176]

Belief in religion remains strong among the Rabi, with several Christian denominations proving to be a source of solidarity as well as, on occasion, the cause of some friction:

Methodists and Catholics make up the bulk of the Rabi population. Also represented in varying degrees are Mormons, Seven Day Adventists, Pentecostals, Assembly of God, Bahai and more lately a handful of Muslims. Some of these newer arrivals have sparked a strong response from the more traditional denomination churches.[177]

---

island called Banaba, way out on its own in the central Pacific. Arriving in May 1900, Ellis quickly established the lush island was almost all pure phosphate.' Gerard Hindmarsh, 'One Minority People: A Report on the Banabans' (UNESCO, Apia 2002) 15. Available at <http://www.banaban. info/UNESCO-v.3.PART1.pdf> [last accessed 6 August 2008].

[169] Silverman (n 167) 429.   [170] Prasad, Dakuvula, and Snell (n 128) 6.
[171] See 'Banabans: Their Story' available on the Abara Banaba website at <http://www. banaban.com/abarabanaba.html> [last accessed 6 August 2008].
[172] Abara Banaba, <http://www.banaban.com/histovie.htm> [last accessed August 2008].
[173] *Banaban Settlement Act* (c 123, amendment 8/96).
[174] Prasad, Dakuvula, and Snell (n 128) 6.   [175] Hindmarsh (n 168) 4.
[176] ibid 35.   [177] ibid 35.

Hindmarsh warns:

The outside world should not forget that the mood of Fiji these days is very much 'Fiji for the Fijians'. The Fijian Banabans are...discriminated against in much the same way as Fijian Indians are. Fewer school scholarships are made available, national banking credit and business encouragement are all restricted. Assistance is required.[178]

He goes on to elaborate what he believes is a pressing needs for urgent intervention:

Even the briefest visit to any school on Rabi leaves the impression of serious under-resourcing, with needs as basic as they get. The children of Tabiang Primary School for instance put up with a squalid pit toilet with barely a door. Their desks have had their legs sawn off because the school cannot afford any chairs, so they take their lessons on the floor. Teachers conveyed requests for sets of basic resources like readerbook sets...Compared to high schools elsewhere in Fiji, the resources given Rabi are sadly lacking, particularly technical, vocational and agricultural science, all subjects critical to advancing society here.[179]

4.2.4 Fiji-Chinese

In the 1996 census, Fiji-Chinese numbered just under 5,000.[180] They were free immigrants, with Chinese presence in the islands dating as far back as the nineteenth century.[181] The first Chinese arrivals are celebrated as consisting of two individuals called Luis and Saoo, who were on board the *Eliza* which was shipwrecked on Mocea Reef in 1808.[182] There are no recorded references to any other arrivals for several decades, but an 1875 description refers to a '...nucleus of a small Chinese business community'.[183] The early Chinese considered themselves to be temporary residents, constituting an 'expatriate minority' with strong ties to China.[184] In the 1960s, when Canada opened up its borders, an estimated 20 per cent of the Chinese population of Fiji migrated to Canada.[185] Greif describes a further population 'amputation' following independence, whereby some 20 per cent of the population left.[186]

Described in the post-independence period as '...miniscule in number with no logical racial allies',[187] the Fiji-Chinese nevertheless strengthened their socio-economic position to such an extent that by 1996, '...over 40 per cent of its economically active members were employed as legislators, professionals, senior officials, and technicians'.[188] The 1990s saw some 2,500 Chinese immigrants

---

[178] ibid 48.   [179] Hindmarsh (n 168) 56–7.
[180] Bessie Ng Kumlin Ali, 'Chinese in Fiji' (Suva, Fiji: Institute of Pacific Studies, University of the South Pacific, 2002) 19.
[181] Prasad, Dakuvula, and Snell (n 128) 6.
[182] Kumlin Ali (n 180) 11.   [183] ibid 2.
[184] Stuart Greif, 'Political Attitudes of the Overseas Chinese in Fiji' (1975) 15(11) *AS* 980.
[185] Kumlin Ali (n 180) 21.   [186] Greif (n 184) 971.
[187] ibid 980.
[188] Prasad, Dakuvula, and Snell (n 128) 7.

arriving in Fiji, with the community attracting adverse and at times racist commentary over its alleged support for such immigration.[189] There are presently about 6,000 Fiji-Chinese.[190] Stigmatization in the media over supposed links to organized crime has affected the community's traditionally strong standing.[191] Comments by political figures in the wake of criminal convictions of Fiji-Chinese have generated significant contempt requiring the public defence of the community by the Chinese embassy.[192]

In 1975, Fiji had become the first South Pacific Islands nation to establish relations with the government of the *People's Republic of China*, and an embassy was opened in Suva. This resulted in Taiwanese presence in Fiji being reduced to the status of a private business corporation in the form of the *East Asia Trade Centre*.[193] There was to be no official contact between Fiji and Taiwan. Many older residents maintained allegiance to the Kuo Min Tang government of Taiwan, a contact that had been established over many years, including the founding of the Fiji Chinese Primary School in 1936.[194] Taiwan continues to fund the salaries of the school's Chinese language teachers and equipment.

Commenting on the fact that after a century of residence in Fiji, Fiji-Chinese numbered only 4,939 persons, Ali states:

From the perspective of their hosts, both past and present, it is a resounding example of administrative success in controlling the number of Chinese. From the perspective of the Chinese, it is proof beyond doubt that their presence in Fiji has not always been welcome.

However, the situation is more complex, and underscored by strict immigration control and continuous emigration. Their relative success has been much resented, reflected in media 'scare tactics'.[195]

4.2.5 Rotumans

The island of Rotuma lies about 300 miles to the north of the Fiji group, on the western fringe of Polynesia.[196] Rotuma has been politically united with Fiji since

---

[189] ibid.

[190] Angela Gregory, 'Changing Fortunes in New Homeland' *New Zealand Herald* (10 December 2005) <http://www.nzherald.co.nz/section/2/story.cfm?c_id=2&ObjectID=10359275> [last accessed 22 January 2008].

[191] ibid. The article quotes the president of the Fiji Law Society, Graham Leung, who is of Chinese descent: 'New Chinese are unfairly stigmatised by the media, connections to prostitution, drugs, the underworld—some sort of seedy existence and a lifestyle of lounging about'.

[192] 'Embassy: We Do Not Condone Crime' *Fiji Times* (21 January 2008) <http://www.fijitimes.com/story.aspx?id=79194> [last accessed 6 August 2008].

[193] Kumlin Ali (n 180) 183.   [194] ibid 184.

[195] ibid 210. The author gives a further example of a February 1996 story in *The Daily Post* that some named Chinese restaurants were serving 'dog meat'. Perceived as an attack against the increasing number of Chinese restaurants in Suva, the issue was challenged in court.

[196] Alan Howard, 'Rotuma as a Hinterland Community' (1961) 70 *JPS* 272.

its annexation to the Crown in 1881, although Howard describes this union as anomalous:

The island's geographical location places it very near to the intersection of the conventional boundaries of Micronesia, Melanesia and Polynesia, and traces of influence from each of these areas can be found in the racial composition, language and culture of the people. The bulk of the evidence points to a Polynesian orientation, however, and it may be regarded as an anomaly of history that Rotuma should have become politically united with Fiji, instead of with islands like Samoa, Tonga, Futuna and Wallis, to which a large number of Rotumans can still trace their heritage. Nevertheless, the Rotumans have made a successful adjustment to these circumstances and have managed to become an integral part of the social, economic and political life of the Colony of Fiji.[197]

Emigration to Fiji has resulted in a significant population shift, so that there are now more Rotumans in Fiji than there are on the island of Rotuma. Thus:

Concordant with the changes that had taken place on the island was an intensified flow of people between Rotuma and Fiji, and a steady growth in the number of Rotumans who had settled in Fiji. Whereas the 1956 census revealed that two-thirds of Rotumans within the colony were resident in Rotuma, by 1986 more than two-thirds were living in Fiji… The population of Rotuma itself had actually declined during that period.[198]

Rotumans are identified as a separate group under the 1997 Constitution of Fiji, which calls them a 'people' alongside indigenous Fijians. In its report to the CERD, Fiji affirms their indigenous status declaring: 'As the indigenous communities of Fiji, Fijians and Rotumans have a special place in society'.[199] Rotumans are culturally and linguistically distinct from indigenous Fijians.[200] Ward provides a further explanation of this, stating that the Rotumans are ethnically distinct from indigenous Fijians, with a confirmed separate enumeration as an entity in the national census, and the treatment of their territory as a separate administrative province under Fijian administrative law.[201] A constitutional guarantee of a reserved seat in parliament and the appointment of a Rotuman senator institutionalize this separate status under Fijian law.[202]

The island of Rotuma has a history of religious strife between its Christian denominations. It was officially ceded to Britain in 1881 when hostility broke out between Wesleyan Methodists and Roman Catholics.[203] Differences on the basis of religion seem to have significantly alleviated since the 1960s and 1970s.

---

[197] ibid.
[198] Alan Howard and Jan Rensel, 'Contextualising Histories: Our Rotuman Experience' (2004) 29 (3/4) *PS* 21. The declination was from 2,993 to 2,588 despite a high birth rate.
[199] CERD State Report—Fiji (n 124) 52.
[200] Alan Howard and Jan Rensel, 'Rotuma' in Brij Lal and Tomasi Vakatora (eds), *Fiji in Transition (Fiji Constitution Review Commission Research Papers, Vol 1)* (Suva, Fiji: School of Social and Economic Development, University of South Pacific, 1997), reproduced online at <http://www.rotuma.net/os/howsel/28FijiConRpt.html> [last accessed 5 August 2008].
[201] R. Gerard Ward, 'The Population of Fiji', (1959) 49(3) *Geographical Rev* 338.
[202] Prasad, Dakuvula, and Snell (n 128) 7.   [203] ibid.

The question of independence, however, remains a pressing issue. In the wake of the 1987 Rabuka coup, the Rotuman Council issued a declaration of support for the new regime. Henry Gibson, a Rotuman 'sau' or spiritual leader, wrote to the Rotuman Council expressing his opposition to the Council's position and the need for independence.[204] Following the second coup in September 1987, Gibson declared Rotuma independent and wrote to Queen Elizabeth asking for recognition. This claim remained unrecognized and instead the dissidents were charged with sedition under Fijian law. The High Court of Fiji issued a decision ruling that '... for legal and other purposes Rotuma continues to be a part of the independent sovereign state of Fiji'.[205] Howard and Rensel note that sympathy for Gibson's movement persists. They highlight political complaints:

Politically, Rotumans express discontent on two levels. At the national level they have felt slighted by what they consider under-representation in the Legislature. The fact that they were given no seats in the lower house of Parliament in the original constitution was distressing, and the current demand for two seats, one representing the constituency on the island, the other Rotumans in Fiji, is generally seen as a necessary correction. From a socio-political as well as a demographic point of view this seems justified since the two constituencies face somewhat different circumstances; their interests only partially overlap... Quite apart from the independence issue it would seem to be worthwhile for Rotumans to consider ways to reconstitute a governing body that would enjoy popular support as well as authoritative legitimacy.[206]

This leads them to conclude that:

The termination of colonial rule, the coups, and the subsequent withdrawal of Fiji from the British Commonwealth, raise legitimate questions concerning the legacy of union. Rotumans have good reasons for wanting to preserve their unique cultural heritage. Many are apprehensive about being dominated, about being nothing more than a neglected minority in a multi-cultural state.[207]

4.2.6 Europeans

Europeans and part-Europeans have always had a relatively privileged position in Fiji,[208] although their political representation has been incrementally decreased. At the London Constitutional Conference in 1965 to establish the terms of Fiji's independence, there were three key ethnic groups represented: indigenous Fijians, Indo-Fijians, and Europeans.[209] Most commentators agree that the arrangement arrived at in London gave a '...strikingly disproportionate number of seats to the European population'.[210] The erosion of the

---

[204] Howard and Rensel (n 200).
[205] See *Mua v Attorney-General of Fiji* [2002] FJHC 147 (16 August 2002) 8. Another case that touches on this issue is *Duvuloco v Attorney-General of Fiji* [1994] FJHC 10 (27 January 1994).
[206] Howard and Rensel (n 200).   [207] ibid.
[208] Prasad, Dakuvula, and Snell (n 128) 7.   [209] Carens (n 43) 567.
[210] ibid 568.

constitutionally guaranteed political power far beyond population size has not resulted in disenfranchisement for the European minority. In the post-independence period, Europeans colluded with the *Alliance Party* to ensure the maintenance of their privileged position in Fijian society, and the arrangement was only broken in 1987 with the Alliance Party's electoral loss. European influence has waned, although it is difficult to assess their influence and role in contemporary institutions. They were removed from the indigenous Fijian voting roll in 1990.[211] In the 1997 Constitution they are mentioned only in the preamble.[212] Nonetheless, the Europeans continue to have the highest income of any group and also the highest emigration rate.[213]

4.2.7 Melanesians

Minority Rights Group International observes that the Melanesian communities, composed of Solomon Islanders and Ni-Vanuatu, are '...among the most excluded and vulnerable minority groups in Fiji'.[214] They were brought over as indentured labour in the early twentieth century and have continued to fare worst of all the groups in Fiji in almost all socio-economic indicators.[215] They were re-classified in 1990 into the 'Other' category having been identified closely in the past with indigenous Fijians.[216] This has significant repercussions in terms of access to affirmative action provisions. The policy has not changed and the 1997 Constitution does not group them with indigenous Fijians and Rotumans.

4.2.8 Tuvaluans

Tuvalu is a constitutional monarchy of three islands and six atolls 1,000 kilometres north of Fiji. A small Tuvaluan community is long-established in Fiji and suffers significant poverty and exclusion.[217]

A 2006 edition of *Pacific Magazine* reports the suggestion of an environmental expert that the entire population of Tuvalu, numbering some 9,000 people, be moved to Kioa, an island in Fiji.[218] Tuvalu is just three metres above sea level.

---

[211] Prasad, Dakuvula, and Snell (n 128) 7.

[212] The preamble states: '*Recalling* the events in our history that have made us what we are, especially the settlement of these islands by the ancestors of the indigenous Fijian and Rotuman people; the arrival of forebears of subsequent settlers, including Pacific Islanders, Europeans, Indians and Chinese...'

[213] Prasad, Dakuvula, and Snell (n 128) 7.   [214] ibid.

[215] ibid.   [216] ibid 8.   [217] ibid 8.

[218] 'Political Parties Cautious on Tuvalu-Kioa Plan' *Pacific Magazine* (21 February 2006) <http://www.pacificmagazine.net/news/2006/02/21/fiji-political-parties-cautious-on-tuvalu-kioa-plan> [last accessed 6 August 2008]. See further <http://www.tuvaluislands.com/news/archives/2006/2006–02-21.htm> [last accessed 25 March 2009] in which the former prime minister for Tuvalu said that his government was considering the idea of moving to Kioa but did not regard it as a priority; and *BBC news*, 'Tuvalu Struggles to Hold Back Tide', <http://news.bbc.co.uk/2/hi/science/nature/7203313.stm> [last accessed 25 March 2009].

The campaign to move the Tuvaluans to Kioa is based on the strong possibility that the islands will be swamped by rising sea levels, and is suggested as the only means of ensuring their cultural survival.[219] Thus although not attracting much attention in 'minority rights' literature, it could be argued that this group is one of the most vulnerable in real terms in Fiji's ethnic mix.

4.3 Rights of Minorities

Minority rights in Fiji constitute legal, sociological, and politically contested ground. Special measures are sources of animus between groups and suspicion surrounds affirmative action provisions. The primary source of minority rights is the 1997 Constitution and its non-discrimination and equality provisions. The departure point for constitutional protections is the document's 'Compact' outlined in its chapter 2, section 6:

The people of the Fiji Islands recognise that, within the framework of this Constitution and the other laws of the State, the conduct of government is based on following principles: (a) the rights of all individuals, communities and groups are fully respected; (b) the ownership of Fijian land according to Fijian custom, the ownership of freehold land, and the rights of landlords and tenants under leases of agricultural land are preserved; (c) all persons have the right to practise their religion freely and to retain their language, culture and traditions; (d) the rights of the Fijian and Rotuman people include their right to governance through their separate administrative systems (...)[220]

Affirmative action provisions are located within the controversial 'paramountcy' requirement, framed as follows:

(i) to the extent that the interests of different communities are seen to conflict, all the interested parties negotiate in good faith in an endeavour to reach agreement; (j) in those negotiations, the paramountcy of Fijian interests as a protective principle continues to apply, so as to ensure that the interests of the Fijian community are not subordinated to the interests of other communities; (k) affirmative action and social justice programs to secure effective equality of access to opportunities, amenities or services for the Fijian and Rotuman people, as well as for other communities (...)[221]

Fiji has not ratified the international covenants on civil and political rights and economic, social, and cultural rights.[222] It has ratified the *International Convention on the Elimination of Racial Discrimination 1969*[223] (ICERD), an

---

[219] ibid.   [220] c 2, s 6 Constitution of Fiji, 1997.

[221] c 2, s 6(i) Constitution of Fiji, 1997.

[222] Table of ratifications available at <http://www.unhchr.ch/tbs/doc.nsf/newhvstatusby country?OpenView&Start=1&Count=250&Expand=60#60> [last accessed 6 August 2008].

[223] An opposition member of Fiji's Parliament, Dr Ganesh Chand, has compiled government reports, concluding observations, and submissions to CERD in Ganesh Chand (ed), *Papers on Racial Discrimination* (Vols I and II) (Lautoka, Fiji: Fiji Institute of Applied Studies, 2005).

important source of minority rights provisions, and has reported under the Convention, most recently in 2002 and 2007.[224] Fiji has important reservations to ICERD which are discussed below. Fiji has also ratified the *Convention on the Elimination of Discrimination against Women 1979* and the *Convention on the Rights of the Child 1989*. In 1998, Fiji ratified *ILO Convention 169 on Indigenous and Tribal Peoples*.[225] This Convention applies to indigenous Fijians and Rotumans.

Minority rights issues in Fiji cannot be separated from crucial questions surrounding land. As the government acknowledges, '. . . land is central to the country's questions of politics, power, race and economics'.[226] Religion has divided the country's two largest ethnic groups and has caused fractures both between and within these and other minority groups. The constitution of the military, police, and judiciary has come under increasing focus and remains problematic. Human rights violations, particularly in the context of violence unleashed by political coups, have not been adequately addressed. Overarching policies informing legal and political developments such as 'paramountcy' and the 'Pacific Way' have further negative impacts upon minority rights safeguards. In the wake of the 1990 Constitution, the Fijian rulers were accused by several commentators of presiding over a form of *apartheid*.[227] While the 1997 Constitution has dispelled many barriers, the continued separation of Fiji's diverse communities is a cause for concern.

4.3.1 Land

As stated in its 2007 state report to CERD, 'Fiji's immediate land crisis centres on expiring agricultural leases on native land and terms and conditions for new leases'.[228] At the time of cession of Fiji to the British government, a 'remarkable' decision was made by the colonial government to prohibit further land sales by the native Fijians.[229] Consequently, indigenous Fijians were left with ownership of at least 83 per cent of the land that is leased on a long-term basis, ensuring the continuation of indigenous attachment to the land as well as economic benefit.[230] The Citizens' Constitutional Forum estimates that over 90 per cent of the land is in indigenous communal ownership.[231] In the 1940s the *Native Land Trusts*

---

[224] CERD State Report—Fiji (n 124) and CERD State Report—Fiji (2007) (n 136). In the absence of a state report, CERD has reviewed Fiji's compliance with the Convention, in 1996 and 2002—see further treaty-bodies database of the Organization of the High Commissioner for Human Rights available from <http://tb.ohchr.org/> [last accessed 6 August 2008].

[225] International Labour Organization, available from <http://www.ilo.org/ilolex/english/newratframeE.htm> [last accessed 6 August 2008].

[226] CERD State Report—Fiji (2007) (n 136) 99.

[227] See below, Section 4.4.2.   [228] CERD State Report—Fiji (2007) (n 136) 99.

[229] Basawaiya (n 135) 199.   [230] ibid.

[231] Citizens' Constitutional Forum (n 118) 2. This is significantly higher than the usual figure of 83 per cent.

Board (NLTB) was established by J.V.L. Sukuna,[232] which has centralized and controlled the system of land leases to Indo-Fijian farmers under the *Native Land Trusts Act* (NLTA).[233] Other instruments impacting on land include the *Fisheries Act*[234] and *Forest Decree*,[235] reserving customary fishing and gathering rights for indigenous Fijians.[236]

Extended families known as *mataqali* own indigenous land and individuals are prevented under the NLTA from selling their land, ostensibly for the benefit of future generations. As a result, indigenous Fijians '...own almost all the land in Fiji, but their rights to this land are actually less than other freehold landowners in society'.[237] Any leasing of the land outside the community must be approved by the NLTB. Indigenous Fijians' right to land is faced with 'tremendous conflict', and they have no individual right to sell or lease their own property.[238]

In 1967 the *Agricultural Land and Tenants' Act* (ALTA) was passed, enabling lessees to obtain a maximum thirty-year lease, and designed to give security of tenure to settler communities. The *International Work Group for Indigenous Affairs* write in their 2006 annual report on the indigenous world: '...the expiry of the agricultural leases under ALTA from 1997 on constitutes the most critical issue facing Fiji at the moment'.[239] It is not clear what will happen when leases expire, as there is no provision for renewal in the Act. The question facing the state is whether to extend the leases or hand the land back to indigenous owners.[240]

Not extending the leases will allow indigenous Fijians to re-occupy their lands. However:

...past trends and studies have shown that indigenous land owners are not as productive as the more experienced and better equipped Indian farmers, and this, in the context of Fiji's national economy, is of great concern to the government.[241]

The situation is exacerbated by the needs of dislocated Indo-Fijian farmers, including the identification of sites for their relocation and compensation for improvements made to the land during their tenure.[242] Extending the leases would bring stability to Fiji's economy but would also have the additional effect of antagonizing indigenous landowners who have turned in greater numbers to commercial farming, and as a result have been increasingly vociferous for the return of their lands at the end of the current leases.[243]

---

[232] Sukuna dominated the Great Council of Chiefs in the first half of the twentieth century. Basawaiya calls him a 'visionary', Basawaiya (n 135); Howard labels him a 'racist', Howard (n 6).
[233] Basawaiya (n 135) 200.
[234] c 158 (1 January 1942) as amended by *Fisheries Act (Amendment) Decree* No 46 of 1991.
[235] No 31 of 1992.   [236] Basawaiya (n 135) 201.
[237] Bush (n 78) 752.   [238] ibid 752–3.
[239] International Work Group for Indigenous Affairs, *Indigenous World 2006* (Copenhagen: Eks-Skolen Trykkeri, 2006) 251.
[240] ibid.   [241] ibid 251.   [242] ibid.
[243] ibid 251–2.

In its report to CERD, Fiji's government outlined that it envisages legally binding fifty-year leases to replace expiring leases, which will be rendered more attractive to indigenous landowners by improved rental rates.[244] Nevertheless, it exhibits strong support for indigenous rights in resolving the land question, as evident in the language used in the report. *Farming Assistance Schemes* (FAS) have been proposed seeking to benefit '... exited ALTA tenants and incoming replacement indigenous farmers'.[245] Under the scheme resettlement costs will be awarded both to the incoming landowners and the outgoing tenants, though it remains unclear how these costs are to be generated.[246] In addition, a Rehabilitation Grant will be given to each exited ALTA tenant who prefers not to be resettled.[247] The regulation of agricultural leases will be conducted under the NLTA and the ALTA's jurisdiction over leasing arrangements will be rescinded. This transfer of authority is symbolic of the re-orientation of Fiji's land policy towards indigenous farmers.

Figures given in the state report to CERD indicate a high level of transfer from Indo-Fijian tenants to indigenous Fijian landowners. The NLTB reported that between 1997 and 31 December 2004, a total of 5,506 leases had expired, with 1,127 being renewed to sitting tenants and 2,940 being leased to new incoming replacement landowners and new tenants.[248] Of the remaining cases still in negotiation, some 998 involve files that have been closed for various reasons, such as ineligibility or lack of information and feedback from affected farmers.[249] It would appear that almost as many files have been closed without any settlement as have been granted renewal status. Overall, to date, this suggests that around one in five leases are being renewed.

A total of 108 lots have been offered and resettled by former ALTA tenants.[250] Land purchase for the resettlement programme in the future will depend on the speed at which resettlement can take place, governed by the NTLB's own approach to lease renewal.[251] Nonetheless, the transition period could take several years.[252] The resettlement programme has been labelled 'slow', largely because of '... ex-ALTA tenants not being able to make up their minds and having their own individual preference regarding the resettlement estates'.[253]

The overall picture that emerges is one of profound change in rural Fiji. Indo-Fijian lessees who have been working land for thirty years under the terms of ALTA are being systematically moved off their farms. The NLTB has an interest in preserving land for use by indigenous Fijians, and it is unsurprising that a very low proportion of applications for lease renewals succeed. The alternative land being offered is not described in the state report to CERD, though it may

---

[244] CERD State Report—Fiji (2007) (n 136) 101–3.
[245] ibid 105.   [246] ibid 111.
[247] ibid 110. The figures involved are F$10,000 to an exiting ALTA tenant who is resettled; F$10,000 dollars to an incoming landowning/indigenous farmer; and F$28,000 to an exited ALTA tenant who agrees not to be resettled.
[248] ibid 121.   [249] ibid 126.   [250] ibid 131.
[251] ibid 134.   [252] ibid 139.   [253] ibid 138.

be inferred that it is inferior in quality. It may also be wholly unsuited to the type of farming formerly conducted by the lessee. The slow pace of availability of land for resettlement means that many Indo-Fijian farmers will be forced to give up their livelihood. They are then blamed for the slow rate of transition to alternative plots. In tandem with this process, incentives are being offered towards attracting Indo-Fijians to other means of livelihood or emigration.

It is clear that the mass transfer of land between Indo-Fijians and indigenous Fijians is extremely problematic, with Fiji's state report to CERD indicating the presence of refugee centres for displaced farmers.[254] The *Citizens' Constitutional Forum* has noted that '...growing squatter settlements are closely associated with the non-renewal of native leases resulting in mass evictions of Indo-Fijian farmers'.[255] It quotes the *National Advisory Council Cabinet Sub-Committee* Report on poverty (2002), entitled 'Poverty in Indo-Fijian and Minority Communities', which states:

Displaced farmers and those dependent on them, like cane cutters, are converging on the outskirts of town, overcrowding already overpopulated squatter areas, occupying marginal land (mangroves, swampy land, dumping areas), thus posing dangerous health and ecological problems, aggravating health related problems in poorly serviced squatter settlements.[256]

The effects of the expiry of land leases and forced evictions on Indo-Fijian families are profound:

The human costs are immense: break-up of family and community, social and cultural impoverishment, stress and emotional anguish and economic hardship. Hence suicides, family feuds, abuse of women and children are linked to internal displacement. Forced evictions are even more traumatic. Forceful occupation of homes has taken place when disagreement occurred between NLTB and landowners. Violations such as these traumatize women and children. There is a sense of powerlessness and loss of faith in the legal and political system. Children who are witness to evictions can become a generation filled with resentment for the establishment. Where homes and land have been taken over, the farmers are left without assets to begin a new life. Some are taken in by friends and relatives, thus increasing all-round impoverishment.[257]

In its 2008 Concluding Observations, CERD underlines the need for reform on the part of the Fijian state:

The Committee...encourages the State party to take appropriate and immediate measures to resolve the land rights issue, in a conciliatory and equitable manner, and

---

[254] ibid 67. This passage states that the Ministry of National Reconciliation and Unity is assisting in 'the resettlement of displaced farmers from the Girmit Centre in Lautoka (refugee centre for displaced farmers) (...)'.
[255] Citizens' Constitutional Forum (n 118) 58.
[256] K.J. Barr, 'Squatters in Fiji—The Need for an Attitudinal Change' (2007) *CCF Housing and Social Exclusion Policy* 18, quoted in Citizens' Constitutional Forum (n 118) 60.
[257] ibid.

to urgently put in place interim measures so as to prevent further deterioration of the economic situation of non-indigenous Fijians. It also strongly recommends that the State party consider reviewing its current land regime so as to make it more accessible to members of non-indigenous communities.[258]

4.3.2 Religion

The 1997 Constitution prescribes no state religion,[259] despite strong demands from some indigenous Fijians to declare Fiji a Christian state.[260] The preamble recognizes:

...the conversion of the indigenous inhabitants of these islands from heathenism to Christianity through the power of the name of Jesus Christ; the enduring influence of Christianity in these islands and its contribution, along with that of other faiths, to the spiritual life of Fiji.[261]

Under the 'Compact' in chapter 2, '...all persons have the right to practise their religion freely'.[262] Religious rights are expanded upon in chapter 4, section 35:

(1) Every person has the right to freedom of conscience, religion and belief.

(2) Every person has the right, either individually or in community with others, and both in public and in private, to manifest his or her religion or belief in worship, observance, practice or teaching.

(3) The right set out in subsection (2) extends to the right of religious communities or denominations to provide religious instruction as part of any education provided by them, whether or not they are in receipt of any financial assistance from the State.[263]

Freedom of religion in Fiji has been seriously threatened by the political upheavals, as best represented in the challenges posed by Rabuka's 1987 coup. Rabuka was a devout Methodist lay preacher, and imposed 'sabbatarianism' by decree once he had assumed power.[264] The *Economist* wrote in the wake of the *Sunday Observance Decree*:

...the Methodists are the ayatollahs of Pacific Christianity. After the coups the Methodist Sunday was enforced: no buses, no taxis, no sport, restaurants closed. Even taking a walk was frowned upon, except to church.[265]

---

[258] CERD Concluding Observations—Fiji (n 11) 22.

[259] c 1 s 5 states: 'religion and the State are separate', but acknowledges that 'worship and reverence of God are the source of good government and leadership'.

[260] Iyer (n 93) 56.

[261] Constitution of Fiji 1997, preamble.

[262] c 2 s 6(c), Constitution of Fiji 1997.

[263] c 4, s 35, Constitution of Fiji 1997.

[264] The decree, directed at all persons 'whether or not they profess the Christian faith', stated: 'Sunday shall be observed in the Republic of Fiji as a sacred day and a day of worship and thanksgiving to Christ the Lord'.

[265] 'Shameless in Fiji' *The Economist* (1 December 1990) 34, quoted in Nanda (n 62) 569.

Thakur and Wood described the '... unabashed assertion of indigenous Fijian hegemony, including the imposition of strict Methodist sabbatarianism on Fiji's non-Christian half and increased harassment of Fiji's Indians'.[266]

Heinz notes that Rabuka's coup claimed to be divinely inspired, and calls the decree a 'powerful symbol' which sought to turn a religious debate into a political conundrum.[267] The coups reasserted the colonial myth of Fiji as a paradise based on three values: land, chiefly rule, and conversion to Christianity.[268] The religious element migrated into the symbolic structure of the Methodist sabbath. While other Christian groups observed Sunday as a day of worship, '... it was Methodists and their tradition alone which prescribed Sabbath markings for Sundays', in particular conservative Methodists and *Taukei* nationalists.[269] The decree sought to attack the way of life of non-Christian Fijians:

... after 1970, when Fiji became a Commonwealth country under its own constitution, the Indian population began to raise its profile on Sunday. Public transportation, usually run by Indians, became more frequent, soccer became a major Indian sport, always played on Sunday.[270]

Sabbatarianism failed because of its socio-economic impracticalities. Opposition to the decree's relaxation took the form of extensive roadblocks, which Heinz terms '... a restaging of the 1987 military coups under the auspices of a religious symbol system'.[271] Judicial intervention was required, which 'tamed the Church and chased it out of politics and back to religion'.[272]

Attacks on religious places of worship pre-dated the 1987 coups:

In October 1991, arson and other attacks on Hindu shrines and temples and a priest revived memories of terrorist assaults on temples belonging to non-Christians in 1984.[273]

In the wake of George Speight's seizure of power in 2000, there was systematic burning and looting of Indo-Fijian property, including temples.[274] According to the *Citizens' Constitutional Forum*:

... a trend is clearly observable, in which young males from the majority indigenous Fijian community, who are overwhelmingly Christian, attack the places of worship of the minority Indo-Fijian community, who are overwhelmingly Hindu and Muslim. However, in the face of this trend, there has been little or no response from the leaders of the Christian churches in Fiji, or from indigenous Fijian chiefs—and the Christian-dominated Government appears to be ignoring the problem.[275]

---

[266] Thakur and Wood (n 84) 210.
[267] Donald Heinz, 'The Sabbath in Fiji as Guerilla Theatre' (1993) 61(3) *JAAR* 416 and 422.
[268] ibid 430. [269] ibid 428. [270] ibid 428.
[271] ibid 438. [272] ibid 439. [273] Nanda (n 62) 571.
[274] Prasad, Dakuvula, and Snell (n 128) 5.
[275] Citizens' Constitutional Forum (n 118) 99.

Fiji's 2007 CERD state report describes '...various incidents of sacrilege in Fiji, especially on Hindu temples'.[276] These offences are considered a felony under Fiji's Penal Code and perpetrators have been prosecuted '...in some cases'. The report considers that the motive for the attacks is not primarily one of racial or religious antipathy:

> Most of the offenders break into temples and places of worship not because of hatred of religion but with the intent to steal money and other valuables...There is a general perception this offence is racially motivated but it is not. The Christian places of worship have also been broken into in the past.[277]

The report gives a tabular breakdown of the total number of attacks on churches, mosques, and temples, with a clear rise in the number of these incidents from 21 in 2002 to 47 in 2004, the most recent year analysed. In 2004, thirty Hindu temples, fifteen churches, and two mosques were attacked.[278] Therefore Hindu temples are targeted disproportionately. Indo-Fijian victims have questioned whether the overriding motive is indeed money, highlighting destruction of sacred texts and statues.[279] A series of attacks in September 2006 led to an emergency meeting of Hindus, with the *National Federation Party* proposing the formation of vigilante and community groups to protect temples.[280]

4.3.3 Education

In the context of Fijian independence, the 1969 *Education Commission* had recommended using education as the foundation for the building of the new multiracial society.[281] The Commission emphasized three requirements: multiracial schools; special measures for improving indigenous Fijian education so that the gap between indigenous Fijian and other ethnic groups could be narrowed and eventually wiped out; and cross-cultural studies including cross-cultural language learning.[282] It expressed concern that many schools were independent of and unaided by the government.[283] It also noted '...a wide disparity...in

---

[276] CERD State Report—Fiji (2007) (n 136) 173.
[277] ibid 176.   [278] ibid 173.
[279] 'Call in Fiji to Make Penalty for Temple Attacks equivalent to Murder' *Radio New Zealand Intl* (13 September 2006) <http://www.rnzi.com/pages/news.php?op=read&id=26778> [last accessed 25 March 2009]. The article describes 'the latest of many such attacks during which a Hindu temple at Narare near Suva was broken into, statues and religious books were destroyed and inside set on fire, leaving only charred remains. The priest at the temple, Pundit Ram Gareeb, is questioning why the vandals would do all this when all they took was 11 US dollars in cash'.
[280] 'Hindus Called into Emergency Meeting after Further Temple Attacks in Fiji' *Radio New Zealand Int* (8 September 2006) <http://www.rnzi.com/pages/news.php?op=read&id=26858> [last accessed 25 March 2009]. Three temples were attacked in four days.
[281] Padmini Gaunder, *Education and Race Relations in Fiji: 1835–1998* (Lautoka, Fiji: Universal Printing Press, 1999) 138.
[282] ibid.   [283] ibid 131.

the educational development of [indigenous] Fijians by comparison with other races'.[284] However, despite this aspiration it became very clear from an early stage that the objective of multiracialism and integration was likely to fail.[285] As early as 1972, experts had already begun warning that claims that up to 65 per cent of schools in Fiji were multiracial were unfounded, with the majority of these mono-racial with no more than a handful of students from other ethnic groups.[286] Thus the vast majority of schools were racially separate. Throughout the 1980s, '...race relations loomed large in the background' of all surveys of Fijian education.[287]

The military coups had a clear polarizing effect in schools.[288] In their wake, a review on the economy by the Australian consultant E.K. Fisk counselled that education policy was one of the fundamental tenets for the establishment of an ethnic balance in Fiji.[289] An urgent need for reform was recognized in the late 1990s, beginning with the abolition of segregated schools on the grounds that they were anachronistic to the modern state.[290]

Gaunder writes that mono-racial schooling in Fiji came about not from any deliberate government policy but as a result of the Methodist Mission's emphasis on giving instruction in the mother tongue. The system became firmly entrenched:

...because the government refused to assume sole responsibility for education. Instead, it encouraged voluntary agencies, especially Indian committees, to establish and operate their own schools.[291]

Mono-racial schools thus persisted after independence because Fiji retained the voluntary school system. Initially the *Alliance Party* had proposed gradually taking over responsibility for schools, but this was shelved indefinitely in 1972 when free education became a major election issue.[292] As a result, nearly two decades after independence, most schools remained predominantly mono-racial with only a 'thin veneer of integration' while the aspiration of multiracialism gradually dissipated with the military coups of 1987.[293] This leads Gaunder to suggest:

Perhaps it was mainly due to this that the country also failed to become genuinely multiracial in the seventeen years after independence (1970–1987) because the foundation for such a society, which should have been an integrated school system, was never laid.[294]

---

[284] ibid 132. It could be argued that the debate in Fiji bears many similarities with the situation at independence in Malaysia. For more on this, also see Castellino and Domínguez Redondo (n 48) 165–73.

[285] Gaunder (n 281) 150.   [286] ibid.   [287] ibid 151.

[288] ibid 159.   [289] ibid 159.

[290] Prof Subramani, 'Preparing Education for the Twenty-first Century', Speech given at seminar on Management of Sangam Schools, Nadi (1997), quoted in ibid 164.

[291] ibid 8.

[292] ibid. The government sensed far greater electoral support for a policy of progressively reducing school fees than assuming control of voluntary schools.

[293] ibid 9.   [294] ibid 170.

The review of Fiji's 1990 Constitution that resulted in the 1997 document found that there was a duty not to discriminate on the part of all educational and training institutions wholly or partly funded by the state.[295] Schools were expressly required to admit students without discrimination on any ground prohibited by the Constitution. However, it was clear that this duty against discrimination took a distant second place behind the decision of schools to maintain their 'special character'.[296] This concept of a school's special character also finds protection under section 39(3) of the 1997 Constitution.

Gaunder concludes that while it may have been possible to envisage a government-run education system at the dawn of independence, taking over schools from voluntary agencies is now 'unimaginable'.[297] The only alternative that remains is to change the orientation of the schools, with reforms in curriculum and pedagogy, focusing on more diverse skills.[298] A residual challenge that must be addressed by the Fijian educational system is the consistent under-performance of indigenous Fijians at all levels. In its CERD report the government stresses that '. . . Fijians and Rotumans are lagging behind in many if not all areas of education, from primary to tertiary education'.[299] These differences, it points out, '. . . are not due to any innate differences in ability but usually the result of other variables that are not always easy to identify'.[300] Special assistance has been targeted at improving the poor conditions and lack of facilities in indigenous Fijian schools, resulting in some improvements.[301]

A 'damning' report by the *Fijian Teachers' Association* released in 2006 found that around 17,000 students dropped out of school each year in Fiji, the vast majority indigenous Fijians.[302] It found that parents were spending their income on customary and religious obligations before education, prompting the leader of the opposition to comment that racial segregation in Fiji would remain unless indigenous Fijians put education first.[303] The *Citizens' Constitutional Forum* also notes the view that indigenous Fijian families tend to give greater priority to social, cultural, and religious responsibilities, and this comes at the expense of their children's educational needs.[304] It does not endorse this view, instead counselling better management of affirmative action policies designed to benefit under-performing students:

---

[295] Shameem (n 3) 665.

[296] ibid. Although if the institution is in a position to admit students other than the category for whose benefit it was established, the admissions policy should not discriminate on any of the prohibited grounds.

[297] ibid 165.   [298] ibid 167–8.

[299] CERD State Report—Fiji (2007) (n 136) 371.

[300] ibid 193.   [301] ibid 203.

[302] 'Fiji Opposition Leader Says Racial Discrimination Will Remain Unless Education Given Priority' *Radio New Zealand International* (14 July 2006) available from <http://www.rnzi.com/pages/news.php?op=read&id=25421> [last accessed 25 March 2009].

[303] ibid. He added that there was 'too much pressure on families to spend their meagre incomes on the church'.

[304] Citizens' Constitutional Forum (n 118) 73.

It is undeniable that indigenous Fijian students continue to lag behind students from other communities in Fiji's education system, and affirmative action is needed to reduce this gap. However, the CCF believes that affirmative action programs in the education sector must change to be based on detailed and reliable information that identifies genuine needs, not suspicions and prejudices concerning ethnicity... there is also an urgent need for all affirmative action programs to be monitored and regularly evaluated.[305]

4.3.4 Language

The major languages spoken in Fiji are Fijian and Fiji Hindustani. Other languages spoken as first languages include Rotuman, Gilbertese, Tongan, Gujarati, Tamil, Telugu, and English. The colonial language, English, is the principal language of government, commerce, and education.[306] Cantonese and various other Chinese dialects as well as Malayalam are also listed as official languages.[307] Mugler writes that there is a 'hidden' linguistic diversity in Fiji, whose source is not the proliferation of languages spoken by small numbers of people, but rather the internal diversity of the two main 'vernaculars'.[308]

The Fijian language of today is not homogenous, consisting of one or two major dialect divisions, eastern and western, and approximately 300 'communalects' or varieties.[309] The majority Indo-Fijian language, Fiji Hindustani, has features from several Hindi dialects.[310] Other Indian languages have declined, with the exception of Gujarati, although Tamil and Telugu are still spoken.[311] Of the languages of the Pacific Islands, only the Kiribati language (or Gilbertese) is still used in Fiji today.[312] The only surviving North Malaitan dialect, brought over by labourers from the Solomon Islands, is called 'Wai' by its speakers and is on the verge of extinction.[313]

English dominates the print media, with two dailies and a number of monthly magazines.[314] The media broadcasts in the two major vernaculars, Fijian and Hindi, with radio, television, and print running in both languages.[315] Mugler points to a clouding of the meaning of the term 'vernacular', which translates as standard Fijian or Fijian-Hindi and ignores varieties within these languages to the detriment of Fiji's linguistic heritage.[316]

---

[305] ibid 77.
[306] Jeff Siegel, *Language Contact in a Plantation Environment: A Sociolinguistic History of Fiji* (Cambridge: Cambridge University Press, 1987) 4.
[307] France Mugler, 'Vernacular Language Teaching in Fiji' in France Mugler and John Lynch (eds), *Pacific Languages in Education* (Suva, Fiji: Institute of Pacific Studies, 1996) 275. However, the official languages of Fiji as recognized by the 1997 Constitution are Fijian (Bau), English, and Hindustani. Also see Francis Mangubhai and France Mugler, 'The Language Situation in Fiji' (2003) 4 *Current Issues in Language Planning* 367–456.
[308] Mugler (n 307) 278.   [309] ibid 25.   [310] ibid 185.
[311] ibid 205.   [312] ibid 215.   [313] ibid 217.
[314] ibid 273.   [315] CERD State Report—Fiji (2007) (n 136) 395.
[316] Mugler (n 307) 283–4.

4.3.5 Military and Police

Indigenous Fijians make up 99 per cent of Fiji's military.[317] In 1987 and 2000 the security forces failed to provide protection to members of the Indo-Fijian community, and in some cases were either tacitly or directly responsible for the violence and looting that broke out in the wake of the coups.[318] Fiji's CERD report documents that, since 1987, under 3 per cent of recruitment applications to Fiji's military were Indo-Fijians, with 5 per cent from other ethnic groups.[319] The government contends:

For the indigenous population, the 'soldiering' profession and its attributes is an attraction. However, for other communities, employment in the military is not necessarily appealing... The military headquarters asserts that its standards will not be compromised to cater for any political agenda given that the military will in the end become the nation's final guarantor for its survival.[320]

The composition of the police is approximately one-third Indo-Fijian and other minorities with two-thirds indigenous Fijian and Rotuman.[321] Current policy has been officially described as being 'quite adamant' in ensuring that there is no discrimination that can encroach on recruitment.[322] Of six executive positions in the Fiji police, two are held by indigenous Fijians, two by Indo-Fijians, one by an Australian and one by a 'part-European'.[323] CERD questioned the rationale given for the composition of the military and police in its 2008 Concluding Observations to Fiji's state report:

While noting the statistical information provided by the State party on the representation of the different ethnic communities in the military and police forces as well as the State party's explanation of this data, the Committee remains concerned about the lower levels of representation of Indo-Fijians in these forces and in the public administration in general (Articles 2(2) and 5(c)). The Committee recommends that the State party consider adopting measures to ensure that all ethnic groups are duly represented in State institutions and the public administration, including special measures aimed at achieving adequate representation of all communities, particularly in the military, taking into account its role during the recent political turmoil in the State party.[324]

4.3.6 Hate Speech

In its CERD report, the government notes that '... the Committee has recommended that Fiji should adopt all necessary measures to put an end to hate speech

---

[317] Prasad, Dakuvula, and Snell (n 128) 5. The military is governed by the *Royal Fiji Military Forces Act*, c 81 of 1985.
[318] Prasad, Dakuvula, and Snell (n 128) 5.
[319] CERD State Report—Fiji (2007) (n 136) 89.   [320] ibid 91.
[321] ibid 95.   [322] ibid 93.
[323] ibid 95. This is clearly an inappropriate description of ethnic origin.
[324] CERD Concluding Observations (n 11) 18.

and assertions of the supremacy of indigenous Fijians'.[325] The report observes that section 30 of the 1997 Constitution limits freedom of expression, including '...the right to be free from hate speech, whether directed against individuals or groups'. Hate speech is defined in the Constitution as an expression in whatever form that encourages, or has the effect of encouraging, discrimination on a ground prescribed by section 38 and applies also to Parliament.[326] The report states that the government is '...not aware of the number of prosecutions against any hate speech made either in public or in Parliament'.[327] Section 17 of the *Public Order Act*[328] sets out the crime of 'inciting racial antagonism'. The CERD report argues that what is 'acceptable' and what is 'unacceptable' in terms of the prohibition of hate speech depends on '...the way people live with each other in Fiji'.[329]

Fiji Human Rights Commission director Shaista Shameem has noted that those engaging in hate speech on weblogs cannot be protected by the freedom of expression provisions of the Constitution. She finds that hate speech is increasingly, and disturbingly, being expressed in weblogs.[330] In its 2008 Concluding Observations, CERD highlighted the absence of laws to the effect that committing offences for racial reasons constitutes an aggravating circumstance, recommending '...specific and unambiguous legislation prohibiting racist organizations' and amending its laws 'to the effect that racial motivation constitutes an aggravating circumstance for crimes'.[331]

4.4 Remedies

4.4.1 Affirmative Action/Special Measures

Fiji's 1990 Constitution enacted special measures for the protection of Fijian and Rotuman interests. The 1997 constitutional amendments kept the provisions for the protection of Fijian interests, but the other affirmative action provisions are now framed in neutral language and seek to protect disadvantaged citizens or groups.[332] The government is running an affirmative action project under the *Social Justice Act 2001*,[333] described in its report to CERD.[334] The

---

[325] CERD State Report—Fiji (2007) (n 136) 153.

[326] ibid 153–4.   [327] ibid 154.

[328] Ordinance 15 of 1969, Act 19 of 1976, amended by Public Order (Amendment) Decree No 48 of 1988.

[329] CERD State Report—Fiji (2007) (n 136) 167.

[330] Quoted in Citizens' Constitutional Forum (n 118) 25.

[331] CERD Concluding Observations (n 11) 20.

[332] Basawaiya (n 135) 205. These provisions are in c 5 of the 1997 Constitution.

[333] Act No 5 of 2001.

[334] Affirmative action under this act is defined as: 'State policies to assist groups or categories of persons who are disadvantaged so as to enable them to achieve equality of access with groups or categories who are not disadvantaged'.

main objective of the programme is to '...allow for equality of access to opportunities by addressing the social and economic inequalities that were reflected in the 1997 UNDP *Fiji Poverty Report* and the 1996 Census'.[335] The 1997 UNDP report, cited in the state submission to CERD, found that:

...average weekly household incomes for Fijian households was 36% lower than the national average. Average per capita income for Fijian households was 43.5% lower than minorities, 20.3% lower than for the Indian community and 15.5% lower than the national average.[336]

Furthermore, almost 70 per cent of Indo-Fijians were engaged in the money economy, compared with 47 per cent of indigenous Fijians.[337] There is an intention to broaden significantly the benefits of affirmative action to include increasingly non-indigenous Fijians, consistent with Fiji's constitution.[338] However, the report acknowledges that the current focus of these programmes is the indigenous Fijian community.

Consequently, of the twenty-nine programmes enumerated under the Act, seventeen benefit all communities irrespective of ethnicity; ten are specifically reserved for indigenous Fijians; and two are targeted at Indo-Fijian and minority communities.[339] The government accepts that '...there has been much controversy in recent years over affirmative action', but reasons that '...affirmative action has to involve issues of race'.[340] It insists that the programme '...should not be seen as a racial question, but as an issue of removing injustices and discrimination, and attaining fair and balanced development'.[341]

Yet this gap may be largely illusory. The most recent 2007 UNDP *Fiji Poverty Report* found that, on average, lower-income Indo-Fijian households are poorer than lower-income Fijian households.[342] The perception of Indo-Fijian wealth is attributed to inequality within, rather than between, the ethnic groups:

This supports what Stavenhuiter found from the 1977 HIES [Household Income and Expenditure Survey], that inequality within the major groups is greater than the differences between them. Indo-Fijian households are over-represented among the very poor and rich households.[343]

In the bottom ten per cent, Indo-Fijian households were fourteen per cent worse off than indigenous Fijian households. Thus:

...the higher average incomes for Indo-Fijian households reflect the high income of the highest income groups. Among the poor, Indo-Fijian households predominate.[344]

---

[335] CERD State Report—Fiji (2007) (n 136) 44.   [336] ibid 47.
[337] ibid 48.   [338] ibid 62.   [339] ibid 55.
[340] ibid 54.   [341] ibid 60.
[342] UNDP Report (n 139) c 2—Income Distribution and Inequality in Fiji.
[343] ibid 25.   [344] ibid 26.

In 2003, CERD warned:

The Committee further recommends that the State party guarantee that the special measures adopted to ensure the adequate development and protection of certain ethnic groups and their members in no case lead to the maintenance of unequal or separate rights for different ethnic groups after the objectives for which they were taken have been achieved (article 1, paragraph 4, and article 2, paragraph 2, of the Convention).[345]

The *Citizens' Constitutional Forum* has found that affirmative action provisions under the 1997 Constitution are in violation of the ICERD principles for the following reasons:

They are based on race rather than need. With far too few of the programs requiring a means test for eligibility, they do not target those who are genuinely disadvantaged. The majority of programs and the bulk of funds are targeted at one ethnic group alone, indigenous Fijians. This offends the principle of fairness. They are not informed by adequate research and analysis. They are not monitored and regularly evaluated for effectiveness and efficiency. This creates opportunities for abuse.[346]

The shadow report submitted by the group to CERD concludes:

The existence and perpetuation of these problems leads many to doubt the commitment of the current Government to genuine affirmative action. There is a suspicion that current programs are really only intended to maintain the political support of elements within the indigenous Fijian community.[347]

The report goes on to issue strong condemnation of the constitutional affirmative action policies, regarding them as 'making matters worse' rather than better in terms of achieving equality in Fiji.[348] In order to fulfil its Convention obligations and gain legitimacy for these programmes before all ethnic groups in Fiji, greater justifications are required from the government. Affirmative action programmes cannot be supported with general indications as to group under-achievement or under-performance in social and economic terms. The Forum calls for:

... specific, expert research and analysis, the results of which are open to public scrutiny and verification, to be limited to the achievement of specific objectives within a specific period of time, and to be closely monitored for effectiveness and efficiency. This is the only way that the programs can gain greater popular acceptance and legitimacy—or of course comply with the Convention.[349]

In its 2008 Concluding Observations, CERD echoed the concerns of the Forum in relation to special measures programmes, holding:

The Committee remains concerned, however, that the need for special measures, in sectors such as education and employment, may not be based on a realistic appraisal of the

---

[345] CERD Concluding Observations (n 11) 15.
[346] Citizens' Constitutional Forum (n 118) 28.
[347] ibid.   [348] ibid 38.   [349] ibid 38–9.

current situation of the different communities (article 2(2)). The Committee encourages the State party to engage in a data-gathering exercise to ensure that special measures are designed and implemented on the basis of need, and that their implementation is monitored and regularly evaluated. The Committee also reiterates the need to ensure that the special measures adopted in no case lead to the maintenance of unequal or separate rights for different ethnic groups after the objectives for which they were taken have been achieved.[350]

4.4.2 De-segregation

A United Nations-sponsored seminar to draw up a 'People's Strategy for Peace, Stability and Development in Fiji', found that segregation along ethnic lines is a serious concern.[351] The participants described how '...segregation along ethnic lines can be seen in the institutions, structures, policies, and practices of the state...[and] is a key obstacle to greater understanding between ethnic groups'.[352]

Many commentators have employed the term *apartheid* in describing the *de facto* separation of the two major ethnic groups in Fiji, particularly in the wake of the 1987 coups and 1990 Constitution. Thus Mauritius' then Foreign Minister, Paul Berenger, said at the UN *General Assembly* in November 1991:

Isn't it a paradox that at a time when apartheid is being dismantled at one end of the world, a constitution with racist attributes unfortunately continues to prevail in Fiji?[353]

According to Sutherland, the post-coup Mara government was '*apartheid*, Fiji-style'.[354] When responding to the proposed new constitution in 1990, the Western Confederacy, representing western indigenous Fijians, stated:

We conclude by reiterating that the pattern of government defined by the draft constitution is totally undemocratic. In West and Central Africa, it's called re-tribalization. In South Africa, of course, it's called apartheid![355]

Following George Speight's 2000 coup, then Australian foreign minister Alexander Downer described the situation as 'Pacific apartheid'.[356] Iyer writes:

---

[350] CERD Concluding Observations (n 11) 17.

[351] 'UN Seminar Highlights Concern in Fiji over Ethnic Segregation' *Radio New Zealand Intl* (9 April 2006) <http://www.rnzi.com/pages/news.php?op=read&id=23319> [last accessed 25 March 2009].

[352] UNDP, 'People's Strategy for Peace, Stability and Development in Fiji' (2006) 11, available from <http://www.undp.org/cpr/documents/prevention/integrate/country_app/fiji/fiji_report.pdf> [last accessed 25 March 2009].

[353] Quoted in Nanda (n 62) 577.

[354] Sutherland (n 26) 184.

[355] Quoted in ibid 190. The Fiji Labour Party coalition denounced the draft 1990 constitution's electoral system as tainted 'with the same sinister motives as *apartheid* and the supremacy of one race to the exclusion of others'. Quoted in Nanda (n 62) 570.

[356] 'Fiji Prime Minister Sacked' *BBC News* (27 May 2000) available at <http://news.bbc.co.uk/1/hi/world/asia-pacific/766221.stm>.

The indigenous Fijian and Indian populations have, for the most part, remained separate over the years, each adhering to its own culture, religion, language and social customs. The sole determinant of identity is ethnic affiliation, with de facto segregation featuring in almost all walks of life, including clubs, trade union and other voluntary organisations. One author ascribes this state of affairs to the history of British rule which, he says, is 'broadly speaking, one of benevolent apartheid'.[357]

Carens highlights the differences between the development of differential institutions in Fiji and the South African system. Fiji's separate institutions did not grow out of and perpetuate racial domination, especially by the European settlers; in a more positive sense, they were intended to preserve traditional values and the Fijian way of life against domination by European settlers.[358] Yet he finds that '... the dominant pattern was, and still is, one of "separateness" '.[359] The gulf between the two communities is described as being 'enormous', with differences in language, religion, culture, and occupation, and almost no intermarriage between the two groups.[360]

The 'People's Strategy for Peace, Stability and Development in Fiji' calls for specific measures to overcome segregation in Fiji, beyond constitutional rights protections:

It is critical to initiate a series of confidence-building measures. These can help create the necessary trust to address ethnic segregation and religious intolerance. Such measures are required between different ethnic groups, between religious groups, between political parties and between the state and the people.[361]

A number of examples of such measures are outlined in the document. Failure to heed the findings in the report could place Fiji in violation of Article 3 ICERD, which condemns racial segregation and apartheid. General Comment XIX clarifies that Article 3, although addressed at South Africa at the time of drafting, '... prohibits all forms of racial segregation in all countries'.[362] In the Summary Record of Fiji's 2003 report, January-Bardill, Rapporteur for Fiji, noted:

According to some NGOs, the Constitution was being used to entrench racial divisions rather than promote diversity, as it focused attention almost exclusively on indigenous Fijians. It did not contain a definition of racial discrimination, nor did it mention people of mixed race, who must have a place in Fijian society. The Constitution maintained an electoral system based on racial membership and provided for the supremacy of indigenous political power, with a reservation of communal and open seats in Parliament that was clearly discriminatory in effect, if not in intent. That cast doubt on the legitimacy of the political system, and could only jeopardize the reconciliation process. Critics of the

---

[357] Iyer (n 93) 51. [358] Carens (n 43) 594.
[359] ibid 563. [360] ibid 563–4. [361] UNDP (n 352) 11.
[362] See Michael Banton, *International Action against Racial Discrimination* (Oxford: Oxford University Press, 1996) 159–60 and 201–2.

political system considered that the Government continued to politicize culture, identity and ethnicity.[363]

The Citizens' Constitutional Forum report that '... the legacy of racial segregation is still being felt today',[364] and identify the political system guaranteed by the Constitution as the root cause of the separation of peoples in Fiji. They argue that:

The whole structure of Fiji's Constitution reflects this difficulty in balancing equal rights for all with the protection of indigenous Fijian culture. Segregation and separate rights are maintained through: the Fijian administration (a system of local, district, provincial and national institutions exclusively for the governance of indigenous Fijians); communal voting in national elections (46 of the 71 seats in Fiji's House of Representatives are reserved for members elected by voters of their own ethnicity, on separate electoral rolls); the reservation of 14 out of 32 Senate seats for nominees of the Great Council of Chiefs (Bose Levu Vakaturaga); appointment of the President and Vice-President by the Great Council of Chiefs (the chiefs have a policy of only appointing chiefs to these offices); and last but by no means least, the entrenchment of a system of collective, non-transferable indigenous Fijian land ownership, applying to approximately 90% of all land in Fiji.[365]

4.4.3 ICERD Reservations

Fiji has entered 'unusually extensive'[366] reservations to the ICERD, that have caused difficulty for the Committee. The development of a corpus of indigenous peoples' rights at the international level has questioned the use of reservations as a remedy for the protection of indigenous peoples' rights. CERD asked Fiji to clarify its position:

To the extent, if any, that any law relating to elections in Fiji may not fulfil the obligations referred to in article 5(c), that any law relating to the land in Fiji which prohibits or restricts the alienation of land by the indigenous inhabitant may not fulfil the obligations in article 5(d)(v), or that the school system of Fiji may not fulfil the obligations referred to in articles 2, 3 or 5(e)(v), the Government of Fiji reserves the right not to implement the aforementioned provisions of the Convention.[367]

Fiji's third report to CERD induced a wide-ranging discussion of its reservations, with the Committee urging the state to withdraw them or at least indicate their proposed duration.[368] In particular, the Committee questioned

---

[363] Committee for Elimination of Racial Discrimination, Summary Record—Fiji (2003) CERD/C/SR.1566 [16].

[364] Citizens' Constitutional Forum (n 118) 30.

[365] ibid 38.   [366] CERD Summary Record—Fiji (n 363) 29.

[367] Available at <http://treaties.un.org/Pages/ViewDetails.aspx?src=TREATY&id=319&chapter=4&lang=en#EndDec> [last accessed 25 March 2009]. The United Kingdom entered the reservations, which were subsequently confirmed by the independent government of Fiji.

[368] CERD/C/SR.553.

reservations concerning the electoral system under Article 5(c) and a declaration with respect to Article 4.[369] At the commencement of its fourth report, Fiji stated in relation to its reservations: '. . . the reservation and declarations will continue to provide some protection as a condition of the succession for Fiji in the considerable future'.[370] This merited a general call in the Committee to review the reservations,[371] and confusion about accepted reservations considered incompatible by some Committee members.[372]

In 1991 the Committee examined Fiji under its procedure dealing with overdue reports. The Rapporteur recalled that doubts had arisen as to the compatibility of Fiji's reservations with the Convention.[373] Another Committee member suggested Fiji be invited to withdraw the reservations, even though they had been accepted under Article 20. He expressed '. . . regret about the way in which the two-thirds rule on incompatibility operates, as it meant that the Fijian reservations that were contrary to the spirit of the convention had been accepted'.[374] In 1996, Fiji's attempt to renege on its commitments by means of the reservations was rebuffed, with the Committee holding that these were '. . . incompatible with the goal and purpose of the Convention'.[375] The summary records in 2003 reveal the Committee's opinion that the reservation to Article 5 '. . . could not be left in its current form'.[376] In its 2003 Concluding Observations:

The Committee notes with concern that the State party formulated, upon accession, declarations and reservations relating to articles 2, 3, 4, 5 and 6 of the Convention. The Committee suggests that the Fijian authorities review those reservations, which are inherited from colonial times, with a view to withdrawing them, taking into account paragraph 75 of the Durban Plan of Action. The State party should ensure that the specific protection and enhancement of indigenous Fijians' rights comply with international standards relating to the prohibition of racial discrimination.[377]

The 2007 report maintains the government's position,[378] analysing the rationale behind the reservations. They are justified on the principle of 'paramountcy' of indigenous Fijian interests.[379] The report acknowledges that at the time of ratification, international law on indigenous peoples had not evolved. It posits that the Committee may be suggesting that Fiji's concerns on indigenous rights could

---

[369] CERD/C/SR.553, paras12 and 18, quoted in Liesbeth Lijnzaad, 'Reservations to UN Human Rights Treaties: Ratify and Ruin?', (Dordrecht: Nijhoff, 1995), 158.

[370] CERC/C/89/Add.3, quoted in Liesbeth Lijnzaad, 'Reservations to UN Human Rights Treaties: Ratify and Ruin?' ibid 158.

[371] CERD/C/SR.629, para32 (Karasimeonov), ibid.

[372] CERD/C/SR.629, para 36 (Ingles), 42 (Shahi), 43 (Houshmand), cited in Lijnzaad, ibid.

[373] CERD/C/SR.925, para 64 (Wolfrum), ibid.

[374] CERD/C/SR.925, para 81 (Ferrerro Costa), ibid 158–9.

[375] CERD/C/SR.1165, para 9, cited in Iyer (n 94) 59.

[376] CERD Summary Record—Fiji (n 363) 15.

[377] CERD Concluding Observations (n 11) 12.

[378] CERD State Report—Fiji (2007) (n 136) 8: 'Fiji's policy thus far seems to either maintain these reservations or at least to not tamper with them'.

[379] ibid 11.

be addressed directly through new instruments governing indigenous rights, rather than being maintained indirectly through reservations to the ICERD.[380] This would amount to a justification for withdrawal owing to recent developments in human rights law rather than a challenge to Fiji's right to maintain its reservations.[381] The Committee's 2008 Concluding Observations appear to accept Fiji's analysis, calling for the withdrawal of its reservations because of the development of indigenous peoples' rights at the international level:

The Committee encourages the State Party to consider withdrawing its reservations and declarations. In particular, the Committee recommends the State party to reflect on the appropriateness of its reservation and declarations in light of the developments in international law in relation to indigenous peoples' rights.[382]

4.4.4 Institutions

Section 42 of the 1997 Constitution establishes the *Fiji Human Rights Commission* and outlines its duties and functions. Commission Director Shameem cites the *UN Declaration on the Rights of Persons belonging to National or Ethnic, Religious or Linguistic Minorities* as a relevant instrument taken into account by the Commission in its workings.[383] Additionally, the Commission ensures equal treatment and promotes equal opportunity for religious minorities and groups as part of its remit.[384]

The *Fiji Human Rights Commission* released a statement in January 2007 supporting the actions of the military in its takeover. As a result it was suspended from the international body that oversees human rights institutions, the *International Co-ordinating Committee*, which questioned its independence.[385] CERD expressed its concern that the *Fiji Human Rights Commission* does not meet the criteria set out in the *Paris Principles* relating to the status of national institutions for the promotion and protection of human rights,[386] and '...encourages the State party to take all necessary steps to ensure the independence of its national human rights institution, in accordance with the Paris Principles of 1993'.[387] However, according to the *Citizens' Constitutional Forum*, a generally critical body, the Commission '...acts independently of the government'.[388]

---

[380] ibid 17.   [381] ibid 18.
[382] CERD Concluding Observations (n 11) 9.
[383] Shameem (n 3) 667.
[384] ibid.
[385] 'Fiji Human Rights Commission suspended from International Body' *Radio New Zealand Intl* (2 April 2007) available from <http://www.rnzi.com/pages/news.php?op=read&id=31209> [last accessed 25 March 2009].
[386] United Nations General Assembly resolution A/RES/48/134, annex (20 December 1993).
[387] CERD Concluding Observations (n 11) 11.
[388] Citizens' Constitutional Forum (n 118) 106.

4.4.5 Peoples' Charter for Change and Progress

Fiji intends to finalize a *Peoples' Charter for Change and Progress* as a guide-line for future policies, through consultation and dialogue with various stake-holders, including civil society, as part of a 'road map' released by the Interim Administration in February 2007. The overall objective of the proposed Peoples' Charter, a draft version of which was published in April 2007, will be to '... rebuild Fiji into a non-racial, culturally vibrant and united, well governed, truly demo-cratic nation that seeks progress and prosperity through merit-based equality of opportunity and peace'..[389] A *National Council for Building a Better Fiji*, repre-sentative of Fiji society, will be constituted by the president, and supported by six national task teams on good governance, economic growth, public service reform, financial institution reform, access to land and land utilization, and social and community sectors.[390] In its 2008 Concluding Observations, CERD expressed concern that this process be inclusive and generate real dialogue with Fiji's ethnic groups and minorities:

The Committee recommends that the State party guarantee the participation of all ethnic communities in the elaboration of the draft Peoples' Charter for Change and Progress. It also expresses the hope that this process is in conformity with the Convention as well as with the Committee's recommendations. The Committee further encourages the State party to hold free and fair elections as soon as possible so as to form a government based on the 1997 Constitution which provides for power sharing between the ethnic commu-nities while ensuring that indigenous forms of governance are respected.[391]

Conclusion

Political stability has proven elusive in Fiji. Vigilance from its neighbours, Australia and New Zealand, has delivered a firm message that military con-trol of its legislative and executive organs is unacceptable. Furthermore the role of the courts as a defender of democracy in Fiji has been decisive. However population demographics are inextricably linked to a stable polity, and should Indo-Fijian numbers surpass those of indigenous Fijians, international oppro-brium may once again not be sufficient in preventing the dismantling of the constitutional order. Voluntary emigration unfortunately plays a role in the regulation of numbers, and will continue to do so with tacit state support until a more progressive order is constructed, possibly under the Peoples' Charter for Change and Progress.

---

[389] Fiji Government Press Release, 'Latest Development on Peoples' Charter for Change and Progress', (10 September 2007) available at <http://www.fiji.gov.fj/publish/page_10016.shtml> [last accessed 25 March 2009].
[390] ibid.   [391] CERD Concluding Observations (n 11) 10.

The primary impediment to achieving such an order and a true egalitarian state in Fiji is the monopolizing of minority status by the indigenous Fijian group. This is exacerbated by a perceived dichotomy involving indigenous Fijians and Indo-Fijians, to the detriment of 'other' groups, including Banabans, Rotumans, Fiji-Chinese, Melanesians, and Tuvaluans. The starting point for a fairer society is recognition of Fiji's diversity, and its complex matrix of entitlements and attainments that sees some groups more advanced than others in a variety of different spheres. However, no group is ahead of any other solely on the basis of race, ethnicity, or religion. As a result, a more nuanced understanding of legislative intervention is required. Affirmative action provisions must concentrate on lifting specific groups in specific areas, such as improved education for indigenous Fijians, or land access for Indo-Fijians, or commercial participation for Banabans.

Land remains the flashpoint in relations between the two dominant groups in Fiji. The 2007 state report to CERD is candid in its documentation of a movement of Indo-Fijians off the land they have tended for at least thirty years, to be replaced by indigenous Fijians. This project is enormously problematic, and the Report shows little awareness of the need for wide-ranging measures to offset the alienation and socio-economic destitution that such a policy is inevitably causing. Given that the issue of landownership is not contested, reciprocal acceptance of obligations towards Indo-Fijian farmers requires far greater engagement with their real needs, beyond the current policy of largely cosmetic compensation.

Separation exacerbates misplaced fears of control on the part of the indigenous Fijian group. To a certain extent, for the indigenous Fijians, the belief that their status was under threat was legitimate in a world climate hostile to the rights of indigenous peoples. This is changing, with growing acceptance of indigenous rights and the enactment of standards at the international level. Communities need to accept that domination of one by the other will not be countenanced by regional partners. They should focus instead on mutual recognition, co-existence, and solidarity through a range of policies, including education, protection for religious worship, greater participation in military and police, language rights, and monitoring of hate speech. As indicated in the chapter, none of these changes can be wrought easily. However, the task of a progressive state is to acknowledge the complexity of its problems.

5

Papua New Guinea

Introduction

Papua New Guinea (PNG) is the most ethnically fragmented society in the world,[1] and is described as 'a nation of minorities'.[2] There are approximately 840 distinct languages spoken, estimated to be around a quarter of the world's stock.[3] There is little detailed assessment of the total number of ethnic groups in PNG, but estimates are in the region of 5,000–7,000 separate groups,[4] in a total population of just over 5 million.[5] Larger units of measurement such as 'tribes' gives a figure of around 2,000 separate tribes.[6]

PNG comprises around half of the world's second-largest island, New Guinea, and about 600 smaller islands, sharing its western border with the Indonesian province of Irian Jaya/West Papua.[7] Administratively, it is divided into nineteen provinces in four main regions, each having different colonial, geographical, and cultural histories and characteristics: Papua (comprising Central, Gulf, Milne Bay, and Oro and Western Provinces); Mamose or New Guinea (comprising East Sepik, Sandaun, Madang, and Morobe); the Islands (Bougainville, New Ireland, Manus, and East and West New Britain); and the Highlands (Enga, Simbu, and the Eastern, Southern, and Western Highlands).[8]

PNG is an amalgamation of Papua, which had been ruled by Australia since 1906, and New Guinea, which had been a German colonial territory from 1884 to 1914, and had thenceforth been administered by Australia.[9] The post-colonial

---

[1] Benjamin Reilly, 'Democracy, Ethnic Fragmentation and Internal Conflict: Confused Theories, Faulty Data and the "Crucial Case" of Papua New Guinea' (2000) 25(3) *IS* 162–85 at 170.
[2] Minority Rights Group International, *World Directory of Minorities* (London: Minority Rights Group International, 1997) 682.
[3] Reilly (n 1) 170.   [4] ibid 175.
[5] National Statistical Office of Papua New Guinea, available at <http://www.nso.gov.pg/Pop_Soc_%20Stats/popsoc.htm> [last accessed 7 August 2008].
[6] Reilly (n 1) 175.
[7] Benjamin Reilly and Robert Phillpot, ' "Making Democracy Work" in Papua New Guinea: Social Capital and Provincial Development in an Ethnically Fragmented Society' (2002) 42(6) *AS* 906–27 at 908.
[8] ibid 910.
[9] Ben Reilly, 'Party Politics in Papua New Guinea: A Deviant Case?' (1999) 72(2) *PA* (1999) 225–46 at 226.

state was a '... rapid and fragile creation lacking any strong, nationwide basis of support'.[10] In 1975, 45 per cent of the government budget came in the form of an Australian grant, meaning PNG '... held the dubious distinction of being the most dependent independent country in the world'.[11]

Nevertheless, PNG is one of a select group of five developing countries that could be classified as 'stable' democracies;[12] one of four that can also be classified as 'established' democracies;[13] and one of the developing world's only 'consolidated' democracies, measured by three select criteria.[14] PNG also satisfies the more demanding 'two-turnover' test of consolidation.[15] Reilly writes that PNG, '... with its five post-independence elections, eight transitions of government and over thirty years of continuous democratic experience', sharply deviates from the comparative norm.[16] Power and Gaisorowski confirm that PNG is the developing world's *only* consolidated parliamentary democracy which features a 'multiparty' system.[17]

Despite PNG's impressive democratic history, the level of development remains low. It ranks 122 out of 162 countries on the United Nations Human Development Index.[18] Nearly 70 per cent of Papua New Guineans are illiterate; only 20 per cent of students reach secondary level and fewer than 1 per cent go on to university level; health services are grossly inadequate and

---

[10] Peter Fitzpatrick, *Law and State in Papua New Guinea* (London: Academic Press, 1980) 199.

[11] Mark Turner, *Papua New Guinea: The Challenge of Independence* (Harmondsworth: Penguin, 1990) 33, quoted in Deborah Gewertz and Frederick Errington, Emerging Class in Papua New Guinea: The Telling of Difference (Cambridge: Cambridge University Press, 1999) 3.

[12] Larry Diamond, Juan Linz, and Seymor Lipset, 'Introduction: What Makes a Democracy?' in Larry Diamond, Juan Linz, and Seymour Lipset (eds), *Politics in Developing Countries: Comparing Experiences with Democracy* (Boulder: Lynne Rienner, 1995) 35, quoted in Reilly (n 9) 228. The others are Venezuela, Costa Rica, India, and Botswana.

[13] Arend Lijphart, *Patterns of Democracy: Government Forms and Performance in 36 Countries* (New Haven, CT: Yale University Press, 1999), quoted in Reilly (n 9) 227. An 'established' democracy is a state with a population of over 250,000 which is democratic and has been continuously democratic for at least twenty years. The other developing states who qualify are India, Mauritius, and Trinidad and Tobago.

[14] Timothy Power and Mark Gasiorowski, 'Institutional Design and Democratic Consolidation in the Third World' (1997) 30(2) *Comparative Political Studies* 132–3, quoted in Reilly (n 9) 228. The criteria are: (1) the holding of a second election subsequent to democratic transition; (2) at least one alteration in executive power; and (3) twelve years of democratic experience. The other qualifying developing states are India, Jamaica, and Trinidad and Tobago.

[15] Samuel Huntington, *The Third Wave: Democratization in the Late Twentieth Century* (University of Oklahoma Press, Norman 1991) 266–7, quoted in Reilly (n 9) 228. The test is satisfied when the party or group that takes power in an initial election loses a subsequent election and turns over power to those election winners, and those election winners peacefully turn over power to the winners of a subsequent election.

[16] Reilly (n 9) 228.

[17] Power and Gasiorowski (n 14) 144, quoted in Reilly (n 9) 230. Of the other 'stable' developing world democracies, India and Botswana featured one-party dominant systems, Venezuela and Costa Rica featured two-party systems and only PNG had a multiparty system. It is thus an exception to the general conclusion in the studies that a one or two-party system is conducive to a stable democracy.

[18] Reilly and Phillpot (n 7) 910.

infant mortality rates are high; and life expectancy is five years below the average for middle-income countries.[19] There are serious underlying structural imbalances in the economy, high unemployment, a lack of growth in economic sectors other than mining, and a lack of physical and social infrastructure.[20] PNG's economic performance '...is especially poor in comparison with most developing countries in the Asia-Pacific region'.[21] It thus represents an '...unusual combination of democratic continuity with low levels of development and high levels of ethnic diversity'.[22] It has been stated that no other country in the world experiences greater challenges to achieving development and equity across the nation than PNG.[23]

UNDP reports that since the early 1990s, the number of people infected with HIV/AIDS has increased exponentially, with the result that PNG is judged to have a generalized HIV epidemic.[24] It is expected that the crisis may soon reach proportions comparable to a country like Uganda.[25] At the current rate of increase, by 2015 the number of recorded cases will reach half a million, accounting for approximately 7 per cent of the population—although these provisional projections are to be treated with 'the utmost caution', as they assume no change.[26] Police harassment of HIV workers represents a serious obstacle to PNG's goal of decreasing HIV incidence and stemming the worst AIDS epidemic in the Pacific Islands Countries.[27]

5.1 Historical Background

5.1.1 Pre-Independence

It takes only a thirty-metre drop in ocean level to join Australia and the island of New Guinea and for most of the last 120,000 years they formed a single ancient continent called Sunda, while Malaysia and Indonesia were merged to form a

---

[19] Heather White, 'Including Local Communities in the Negotiation of Mining Agreements: The Ok Tedi Example' (1995) 8 *TL* 307.

[20] ibid 307.

[21] Anne Booth, 'Development Challenges in a Poor Pacific Economy: The Case of Papua New Guinea' (1995) 68(2) *PA* 207–30 at 208.

[22] Reilly and Phillpot (n 7) 908.

[23] John Connell, *Papua New Guinea: The Struggle for Development* (London/New York: Routledge, 1997) 221.

[24] UNDP, 'Millennium Development Goals—Progress Report for Papua New Guinea 2004' (2004) 28, available at <http://www.undp.org.pg/documents/mdgs/National_MDG_Progress_Report_2004.pdf> [accessed 6 August 2008].

[25] For more on the HIV epidemic in Uganda and east Africa in general, see Frans Viljoen, *International Human Rights Law in Africa* (Oxford: Oxford University Press, 2007) 511.

[26] UNDP Progress Report (n 24) 29.

[27] Human Rights Watch, 'Still Making Their Own Rules: Ongoing Impunity for Police Beatings, Rape and Torture in Papua New Guinea', Vol 18(13) (2006) 2.

combined continent called the Sahul.[28] The sea reached present day levels only 10,000 years ago. There is a paucity of direct data on New Guinea prehistory,[29] and the earliest evidence of humans settling in the Sahul is contested. In New Guinea, human occupation goes back at least 40,000 years, with stone axes found raised on coral reefs on the Huon Peninsula dating from between 40,000 to 60,000 years ago.[30] Modern humans crossed the straits from the Sunda somewhere between 60,000 to 55,000 years ago and expanded through the Sahul to occupy widespread areas by at least 35,000 years ago.[31] The *Encyclopaedia of Papua New Guinea* states:

The settlement of both New Guinea and Australia was thus made within the Pleistocene period, the so-called Ice Age...New Guinea and Australia at this time were connected over the Torres Strait...whether Australia was colonized from New Guinea, New Guinea from Australia, or both independently, whether the crossings were made many times, few times, or once, we do not and probably will never know.[32]

According to Rynkiewich:

Melanesia was not settled by a few great waves of migration that, through mixing of people, resulted in today's diverse populations. That is, no group left Java or Taiwan and sailed all the way to Melanesia. Rather, Melanesia was settled slowly, over a 40,000 year period, by a nearly continuous stream of small groups of migrants.... Thus much of Melanesian culture and language and human biology developed in Melanesia itself.[33]

The earliest New Guineans were hunters and gatherers,[34] but patterns of life evolved which '...may well have been revolutionary in the history of Man'.[35] Archaeological research indicates that New Guineans were among the world's first agriculturists, growing bananas, vegetables, and possibly sugar cane 9,000 years ago, as well as domesticating pigs and developing drainage systems.[36] Archaeologists working at Kuk, near Mount Hagen, have found evidence of an extraordinarily complex system of agricultural drains that date back about 10,000 years, as well as elaborate ancient terraces on the mountainsides.[37]

Around 6,000 years ago a people originating in Taiwan began to move south and east into the Pacific islands, where they were able to overwhelm the local populations of hunters and gatherers.[38] The movement of these people, Austronesian speakers, was slow, taking 2,000 years to move from Taiwan to New Guinea. Even at the time of European colonization, Austronesian colonization

---

[28] Michael Rynkiewich, *Cultures and Languages of Papua New Guinea* (Goraka: The Melanesian Institute for Pastoral and Socio-economic Service, 2004) 17.

[29] Michael Ryan (ed), *Encyclopaedia of Papua and New Guinea* (Carlton: Melbourne University Press, 1972) Vol 2, 962.

[30] Rynkiewich (n 28) 17.   [31] ibid 17.

[32] Ryan (n 29) 962.   [33] Rynkiewich (n 28) 37.   [34] Ryan (n 29) 962.

[35] James Griffin, Hank Nelson, and Stewart Firth, *Papua New Guinea: A Political History* (Victoria: Heinemann Educational, 1979) 2.

[36] ibid.

[37] Sean Dorney, *Papua New Guinea* (New South Wales: Random House, 1990) 25.

[38] Rynkiewich (n 28) 37.

continued.[39] Before the coming of Europeans, Indonesian traders also made frequent contact and possibly reached east New Guinea, while the Chinese apparently knew of New Guinea at the time of Marco Polo.[40] Yet the Europeans were the foreigners whose interest in PNG was responsible for its transformation.[41] Although Europeans were a force for change, the process was slow and fitful.[42] Thus it has been argued that '... prehistory continues up to the present day and archaeology passes directly over into the ethnographic study of living peoples'.[43]

Joao de Barros, the seventeenth century Portuguese chronicler, wrote in his *Decadas da Asia* that in 1526, Jorge de Meneses was blown off course on his route to the Moluccas and awaited a change of wind on islands inhabited by people called 'Papuas'.[44] On the meaning of the word 'Papua', the Portuguese chronicler Diogo do Couto remarked that it meant 'people of dark skin pigmentation in the language of the natives'.[45] It is not certain that de Meneses did arrive in New Guinea, although a strip of coastline as opposed to 'islands' was shown on contemporary Portuguese charts. The Portuguese knew indirectly of New Guinea before de Meneses' accident of navigation, and 'islands of *papoia*' are named in a chart dating from between 1513 and 1520, although this appears to be a result of confused information. The land of the 'Papuas' in these uncertain early accounts may well have been offshore islands rather than New Guinea proper.[46]

By the second quarter of the nineteenth century, following further Portuguese, Spanish, Dutch, British, and French expeditions, the general outline of New Guinea was quite well-known to Europeans, and the major islands offshore had been charted.[47] Europeans most often made first contact with Austronesian speakers.[48] Some PNG communities first encountered Europeans 450 years ago, while others only made contact after the Second World War.[49] From the first Portuguese landings in the sixteenth century to the establishment of the British colony of New South Wales in Australia in the late eighteenth century, '... Europeans and Papua New Guineans met rarely and in total ignorance of each other, with no idea of the other's language, customs, gestures and intentions'.[50] The first anthropologist to live in New Guinea, the Russian aristocrat Nicolai Mikluho-Maclay, spent a year among the people of the southern Madang district from 1871–1872, and recounted in his diary: '... why in fact have I come and bothered these people?'[51] He protested when Germany, a new power seeking influence, annexed New Guinea in 1884.

The 'Oceanic equivalent of the Scramble for Africa'[52] began with Australian colonists, fearing Germany as an immediate neighbour, forcing Britain to

---

[39] ibid 38.   [40] Griffin, Nelson, and Firth (n 35) 2.   [41] ibid 2.
[42] Ryan (n 29) 969.   [43] ibid 969.   [44] ibid 246.
[45] ibid 247.   [46] ibid.   [47] ibid 256.
[48] Rynkiewich (n 28) 39.   [49] Griffin, Nelson, and Firth (n 35) 2.
[50] ibid.   [51] ibid 5.
[52] James Boutilier, 'Papua New Guinea's Century: Reflections on Imperialism, Accommodation and Historical Consciousness', in Deborah Gewertz and Edward Schieffelin (eds), *History and Ethnohistory in Papua New Guinea* (Sydney: Oceania Monographs, 1985) 7–26 at 7.

proclaim a British protectorate in Papua in the same year.[53] An official wrote of the proclamation ceremony at Port Moresby: 'The natives, who are beginning to get accustomed to seeing the flag hoisted, were apathetic, and only a few stragglers turned up'.[54] The German 'treaty' was signed when '... ten men from the Bogadjim area ... put their marks on a piece of paper shown to them by Germans who came in a steamship'.[55] From 1884, the people of eastern New Guinea and its offshore islands lived in British and German protectorates, though most were not aware of the fact.[56] Griffin, Nelson, and Firth summarize:

South-eastern New Guinea and its islands south of 8°S latitude became first the Protectorate of British New Guinea, then in 1888 the Crown colony of British New Guinea, and in 1906 passed into Australia's control as the Territory of Papua. The borders of the German possession changed a number of times. In 1884 it consisted of north-east mainland New Guinea (Kaiser Wilhelmsland) and New Britain, New Ireland, New Hanover, Manus and other islands that have since been called the Bismarck Archipelago. The islands of Buka and Bougainville in the Solomons Group were added in 1886 and remain as part of Papua New Guinea in 1979, but the Shortlands Islands, Choiseul and Ysabel were German only from 1886 until 1899.[57]

In 1914, at the request of Britain, Australia took German New Guinea by conquest.[58] Hudson notes that Australian strategic concern in PNG was of a 'negative kind', in that it was not focused on building up PNG as a base for military or naval operations, but rather to deprive a potential enemy of a base for use against Australia.[59] Although there was clear economic interest, the principal aim was to prevent the territory becoming a potential base for an aggressive occupier by instead taking over its possession.[60] As a result, Australian effort in terms of 'money, men and planning' was minimal, and its policy was characterized by indifference. Significant change came in the 1940s, when coherent foreign policies on colonial questions were developed by the *Minister for External Affairs*.[61] For example, Papua received an Australian grant-in-aid of just AUS$90,000 in 1939, which had risen to AUS$6 million in 1948 and AUS$110 million by 1968, two-thirds of the territory's revenue.[62] Australian colonial rule of PNG can be categorized as falling into three distinct periods:

... the rather sleepy, poor decades to 1945; the years from 1945 to the early 1960s when real efforts at last were made to transform the condition of indigenous society; a final decade when, to a large degree now free of old security fears and, anyway, feeling both domestic and international pressures, Australian governments moved away from the imperial role even faster than most New Guinean opinion actively sought.[63]

---

[53] Griffin, Nelson, and Firth (n 35) 7–8.   [54] ibid 9.
[55] ibid 7.   [56] ibid 9.   [57] ibid 9.
[58] W.J. Hudson, *New Guinea Empire: Australia's Colonial Experience* (Melbourne: Cassell Australia, 1974) viii.
[59] ibid.   [60] ibid.   [61] ibid ix.
[62] ibid.   [63] ibid x.

Australia initially administered New Guinea under the very light trammel of a 'C' class mandate supervised by the League of Nations, enshrined in Article 22 of the League of Nations Covenant.[64] The award to Australia of the New Guinea mandate was confirmed in 1920, and Article 2 of the mandate confirmed that the Commonwealth of Australia could apply its laws to the territory.[65] The Minister for External Affairs, R.G. Casey, stated in a radio address:

...the Commonwealth of Australia is responsible to the League of Nations for the welfare and advancement of a native territory the size of England and Scotland, containing about half a million natives, mostly of stone-age mentality. We do not own the Mandated Territory of New Guinea; we have it in our keeping as a trust from the rest of the world. We have accepted the responsibility of looking after this legacy, as an advanced nation looking after a backward race, not for our own interests, but strictly in the humanitarian interests of the natives themselves.[66]

In 1946, under the United Nations international trusteeship system, Australia submitted a trusteeship agreement for New Guinea following consultation with New Zealand, the United States, Britain, and France, which was '...couched in terms more favourable to Australia than the old mandate'.[67] The agreement was approved by the General Assembly on 13 December 1946. It resulted in the administration of New Guinea '...as if it were an integral part of Australia' (Article 4), and the only concession to international reservations on the agreement was a native bill of rights inserted as Article 8.[68] That provision held in Article 8(2):

a. [Australia] will take into consideration the customs and usages of the inhabitants of New Guinea and respect the rights and safeguard the interests both present and future of the indigenous inhabitants of the Territory; and in particular ensure that no rights over native land in favour of any person not an indigenous inhabitant of New Guinea may be created or transferred except with the consent of the competent public authority;

b. promote...the educational and cultural advancement of the inhabitants;

c. assure to the inhabitants...a progressively increasing share in the administrative and other services of the Territory;

d. guarantee...freedom of conscience and worship and freedom of religious teaching.[69]

---

[64] ibid 68. Clause 6 of art 22 read: 'There are territories, such as South West Africa and certain of the Pacific islands, which, owing to the sparseness of their population, or their small size, or their remoteness from the centres of civilization, or their geographical contiguity to the territory of the Mandatory, and other circumstances, can be best administered under the laws of the Mandatory as integral portions of its territory subject to the safeguards above mentioned in the interests of the indigenous population'.

[65] Mandate for the German Possessions in the Pacific Ocean Situated South of the Equator Other Than German Samoa and Nauru, reprinted in ibid 70–1.

[66] R.G. Casey, *Australia's Place in the World* (Melbourne, 1931) 38, quoted in Hudson (n 58) 72.

[67] ibid 79.

[68] 'Trusteeship Agreement for the Territory of New Guinea', reproduced in ibid 79–81.

[69] ibid 81.

Australia was one of nine states which abstained from voting in favour of the 1960 *UN Declaration on the Granting of Independence to Colonial Countries and Peoples*, adopted under Resolution 1514 (XV) of 14 December 1960. The Declaration's implementation was supervised by a committee, which viewed Papua and New Guinea as one dependent territory, although the UN Trusteeship Council was continuing to supervise New Guinea separately.[70] The Trusteeship Council sent periodic missions to New Guinea to examine the situation and report back, and in 1962, a delegation led by Hugh Foot, a British UN diplomat, issued three recommendations: a full economic survey by the World Bank; a new programme of university and higher education; and immediate preparations for the election of a representative Parliament.[71]

5.1.2 Post-Independence

Independence came in a rush,[72] and, for many, it came too soon.[73] The post-colonial PNG state is a '... recent, rapid and fragile creation lacking any strong nationwide basis of support'.[74] Prior to independence, the *Constitutional Planning Committee*, established in 1972, engaged in an extensive consultation process with the ancillary aim of dispelling doubts and fears as to PNG's ability to self-govern.[75] The recommendations of the Committee were 'overtly political', and the resulting constitution, a 'strange document',[76] was seen to be a political charter as well as a legislative framework.[77] It was adopted by the *Constituent Assembly* on 15 August 1975, and the Australian Parliament duly passed the *Papua New Guinea Independence Act 1975*.[78] The Constitutional Planning Committee's final report expressed a clear desire to make a complete break from colonial rule, and establish new political, economic, and social conditions based on traditional values.[79] The report stated:

The process of colonisation has been a huge tidal wave. It has covered our land, submerging the natural life of our people. It leaves much dirt and some useful soil, as it subsides. The time of independence is our time of freedom and liberation. We must rebuild our society, not on the scattered good soil the tidal wave of colonisation has deposited, but on the solid foundations of our ancestral land.[80]

---

[70] ibid 84.

[71] Report of the United Nations Visiting Mission to the Trust Territories of Nauru and New Guinea: Report on New Guinea, United Nations Trusteeship Council, UN doc T/1597 (New York 1962) 41–3, reproduced in ibid 87–9.

[72] Dorney (n 37) 48.

[73] John Goldring, *The Constitution of Papua New Guinea* (Sydney: The Law Book Company, 1978) 28.

[74] Fitzpatrick (n 10) 199.   [75] Goldring (n 73) 28–9.

[76] ibid 274.   [77] ibid 29.   [78] Act No 98 of 1975.

[79] Donald Chalmers and Abdul Paliwala, *An Introduction to the Law in Papua New Guinea* (Sydney: The Law Book Company, 1984) 107.

[80] Constitutional Planning Committee of Papua New Guinea, Final Report, ch 2 [98], quoted in Chalmers and Paliwala (n 79) 107.

The Constitution is autochthonous or home-grown, in that it did not arise from an Australian Act of Parliament. The *House of Assembly* thus reconstituted itself into a *Constituent Assembly* to enact the Constitution.[81] It is distinctive in that it contains a full statement of non-justiciable 'National Goals and Directive Principles' under section 25. Goldring states:

What is unusual about the Papua New Guinea Constitution is the degree of detail with which the political aims are set out and also the fact that, to some extent, at least, those political aims are made enforceable.[82]

The five 'National goals' consist of: integral human development, equality and participation, national sovereignty and self-reliance, conservation of national resources and the environment, and the use of Papua New Guinean forms of social, political, and economic organization. The National goals 'pervade the whole Constitution'.[83]

The Constitution has been labelled as representing a '... transmutation of the legal system from one clearly rooted within the common law tradition to one which is rooted firmly in the customs, values and traditions of the people'.[84] Dissatisfaction with the application of 'imposed' colonial rules in official courts was translated into a system of village courts, enacted under the *Village Courts Regulation 1974*,[85] so that by Independence Day a considerable number of village courts applying traditional or customary rules of dispute resolution were in operation.[86] The legislation ensured recognition that customary law should be an integral part of the legal system of Papua New Guinea.[87] Functionally, the village courts resolved small disputes and extended to relatively serious criminal offences, despite technically limited jurisdiction. The establishment of the village courts was one of the first examples of 'Papua New Guinean ways' becoming part of the governmental structure of the state.[88] The Constitutional Planning Committee had stressed the use of 'Papua New Guinean ways' in its final report as a National Goal.[89] In practice, the operation of customary rules is fascinating, given the sheer multiplicity of customs. Goldring explains:

There are over 700 language groups in the country, and if each of these does not have a totally separate body of rules, there are differences between the customs of each group, some of which may be significant; and if in some groups the customs are a fairly settled body of norms, in others they are flexible to the extent that the way in which disputes arising out of similar fact situations will be determined in different ways according to a variety of circumstances.[90]

---

[81] ibid 108.   [82] Goldring (n 73) 29.
[83] ibid 33.   [84] ibid 150.
[85] *Village Courts Regulation 1974* (c 44), now governed by *Village Courts Act*, No 37 of 1989.
[86] Goldring (n 73) 151.   [87] ibid.
[88] ibid 152.   [89] ibid.   [90] ibid 153.

Barnett, legal adviser to the government at the Constitution's drafting stage, stresses the flexible and transitory nature of customary norms:

> There are few if any *rules* of custom. Rather there are acceptable, less acceptable and unacceptable ways of doing things...A custom could be described as a guiding norm around which people plan their behaviour and anticipate that of others, and it is one of many things to which they refer in situations of dispute. To record native customs as rules to be applied inflexibly would not only miss the point but would fossilize customs which will rapidly become less and less acceptable as a guide to behaviour as people's attitudes change. Even the act of recording customs as a mere guide to court decisions can have the same effect.[91]

The Constitution makes custom part of the 'underlying law' in Schedule 2, thereby institutionalizing it. Schedule 1 to the Constitution defines 'custom' as:

> ...the customs and usages of the indigenous inhabitants of the country existing in relation to the matter in question at the time when and the place in relation to which the matter arises, regardless of whether or not the custom or usage has existed from time immemorial.[92]

Nevertheless the rules of common law prevail under Schedule 2.2(1)(c), unless '...in their application to any particular matter they are inconsistent with custom'. Thus the common law applies *prima facie* unless a customary norm is raised that shows it does not. Schedule 2 specifically charges the courts with developing the underlying or customary law in its Part 3. The courts are required to fulfil the constitutional direction by finding the underlying law in the customary rules of the country.[93]

This can be said to conflict with the nature of customary norms; according to Goldring 'the mere fact that the "rule" was given the status of law would mean that it would lose its character as a flexible means of settlement of disputes'.[94] However he concedes:

> ...the customs of the people of Papua New Guinea may be preferable as a source of the norms which, it seems inevitably, must form the basis of the legal system; those norms reflect far more accurately than any norms derived from western society the needs, wishes and aspirations of the people of Papua New Guinea.[95]

The apparent contradiction between flexible custom and inflexible positive law has been over-emphasized. The constitutional arrangement cleverly entrenches the flexible nature of customary norms, and in the direction to the courts to develop or 'find' the existing customary law, ensures its future role as an evolving primary source of law in the state.

---

[91] T.E. Barnett, 'Law and Justice Melanesian style', in A.I. Clunies-Ross and J. Langmore (eds), *Alternative Strategies for Papua New Guinea* (Melbourne: Oxford University Press, 1973), quoted in Goldring (n 73) 153.
[92] Constitution of Papua New Guinea, Sch1(1).
[93] Goldring (n 73) 162.   [94] ibid 165.   [95] ibid 167.

The first human rights legislation in PNG was inspired by an English missionary and member of the Houses of Assembly, Percy Chatterton, who recalls how he 'roughed out the sort of thing I had in mind on a single sheet of foolscap. It came back from the lawyers on 24 sheets'.[96] The result of his efforts was the *Human Rights Act 1971*, reproduced and modified as 'Basic Rights' in Part III.3 of the Constitution. These are enforceable and justiciable and are thereby distinguished from the National Goals and Directive Principles.[97] Indeed section 57 empowers the courts to enforce the Basic Rights on the application of a person or 'on its own initiative', a 'most unusual provision'.[98] Under section 55(3)(1), all citizens have the same rights, privileges, obligations, and duties 'irrespective of race, tribe, place of origin, political opinion, colour, creed, religion or sex'. Section 55(3)(2) states that subsection 1 '...does not prevent the making of laws for the special benefit, welfare protection or advancement of...members of under-privileged or less advanced groups or residents of less advanced areas'.[99]

PNG remained heavily dependent on Australia from independence, during which it enjoyed what became known as a 'unique' relationship.[100] At independence, Australian aid constituted 40 per cent of PNG's budget.[101] Attempts to reduce this by 5 per cent annually failed, with the result that modest reductions led to a crisis in the mid-1980s, wherein Australian demands were for aid to be linked to specific projects rather than given as a grant of the national budget.[102] Despite strong opposition from PNG, negotiations established the link between Australian aid and projects, and Australian-based companies or Australian components of transnational corporations became more actively involved in the PNG economy.[103] This involvement stretched to the commercial and transport sectors as well as plantations and mining. Similarly New Zealand has a strategic interest in PNG, and has exported a range of manufactured goods as well as forming a significant section of the expatriate population.[104]

PNG joined other Pacific Island Countries in opposing French nuclear testing on Mururoa Atoll and supporting moves to have the region declared a nuclear-free zone.[105] In 1980 combat troops from PNG became involved in Vanuatu in assisting the state suppress rebel attempts to overthrow the government.[106] The intervention was subject to a Supreme Court challenge and labelled a 'fiasco'.[107] Apart from these incidents, there is little engagement with other states in the PIC region.[108]

---

[96] Quoted in ibid 213.   [97] ibid.
[98] ibid.   [99] Constitution of Papua New Guinea, s 55(3)(1) and (2).
[100] John Waiko, *A Short History of Papua New Guinea* (Oxford: Oxford University Press, 1993) 195.
[101] ibid 196.   [102] ibid.   [103] ibid.
[104] ibid 197.   [105] ibid 197.   [106] ibid 197–8.
[107] Eric Kwa, 'Treaty Law Making in Papua New Guinea: After Two Decades, *Yumi Stap We?*' (1997) 25 *MLJ* 43–64 at 59.
[108] Waiko (n 100) 198.

PNG's relationship with Indonesia is dominated by the existence in Irian Jaya of a Melanesian population opposed to the Indonesian presence. This opposition often took the form of armed conflict, and a guerrilla movement known as the *Organisasi Papua Merdeka* formed in opposition to the colonial border between PNG and Irian Jaya, often crossing into PNG to avoid Indonesian troops.[109] A series of border incidents throughout the 1980s threatened to escalate, but the two states responded by re-affirming the border, and accepting guarantees for the safe return of refugees.[110] In this period Indonesia had no financial investment in PNG, and did not supply aid.[111]

Rapid expansion of the Japanese economy in the 1960s and 1970s and its consequent need for raw materials led to Japan becoming a major buyer of PNG copper. However the 1974 world recession had a strong effect on the Japanese economy, and its recovery in the 1980s saw a change in policy from purchase of raw materials to direct investment via transnational corporations, with Japan establishing several major timber and fishing projects and investigating copper exploration.[112] Other large Asian states and economies, notably China, Hong Kong, South Korea, and the Philippines, have sent trade missions to PNG.[113]

The United States of America has maintained a high profile in Port Moresby through its embassy.[114] While direct trade between the two states is negligible, transnational corporations have shown interest in the potential of PNG's natural resources, in particular in its copper and oil.[115] The United States of America has also provided military training and is involved in several aid projects through government and private agencies.[116] The European Union is increasingly a source of exports.[117]

PNG began by expounding a 'universalist' foreign policy, which shifted to a more targeted policy of 'selective engagement', including stronger links with Japan, China, and Korea, as well as consolidation of strong bonds with Australia, and greater engagement with regional organizations such as ASEAN.[118] The aim was to move further into the western cash economy model. In 1985, 80 per cent of the population was still engaged in subsistence agriculture supplemented by hunting, fishing and gathering, and small amounts of cash produced by selling excess fish and produce.[119] Exploitation of natural resources was the most important means of generating a western cash economy, and mining of copper and gold provided 25 per cent of internal revenue.[120] The crucial mining and petroleum sectors have traditionally contributed about a quarter of PNG's total gross domestic product.[121] Mining projects in Bougainville and Ok Tedi have

---

[109] ibid.   [110] ibid 199–200.   [111] ibid 200.
[112] ibid 201.   [113] ibid 200.   [114] ibid 202.
[115] ibid.   [116] ibid.   [117] ibid.
[118] ibid 204.   [119] ibid 205.   [120] ibid 204.
[121] Mark Tacon, 'Papua New Guinea in 2000: Taking the Bull by the Horns' (2000) 41(1) *AS* 143–7 at 144.

caused serious environmental degradation and social disruption.[122] According to Waiko:

... nowadays, the most important single distinction between traditional society and the modern state concerns land resource use. The basic social unit is the land group... The different concepts of ownership of land and water and the use of resources have been one of the reasons for the disputes between the villagers and the state in recent years. Amongst the most publicised and tragic of these are the forestry resource exploitation in the Golgol area, illegal transnational fishing in the 200 kilometres of the territorial zones, Ok Tedi mining activity and, the most disruptive of all, the Bougainville Copper Limited mine at Panguna. In each of these projects transnational corporations have aggressively exploited the Papua New Guinea élite's acceptance of the modern state's concept of land and resource use to the detriment of villagers.[123]

The secessionist movement in Bougainville, '... perhaps the most convulsive event that PNG has ever encountered since its independence',[124] was fuelled by the failure to adequately negotiate mining contracts in consultation with landowners. Bougainville has the world's biggest copper mines, and in 1964, *Bougainville Copper Limited* was commissioned to exploit the deposits, an agreement that was re-negotiated by the then newly independent government in 1974. Mine-side landowners were unhappy with the amount of compensation and the pace of development, and the leader of the landowners, Francis Ona, issued demands for AUS$11.5 million compensation for environmental and social damage, the closure of the mines on ancestral lands, and a referendum for Bougainvillians to decide whether to secede from PNG.[125] The claims were ignored, and rebel landowners perpetrated substantial damage to the mines, leading to the declaration of a state of emergency on 26 June 1989. This was met with an armed resistance as disaffected groups polarized around the newly created *Bougainville Revolutionary Army* in response, culminating in a full-scale civil war.[126] Failed ceasefire agreements led to the proclamation of the island as a republic with an interim government in May 1990, a proclamation that was rejected by the government of PNG. A nascent peace agreement was reached in 1997.[127] The civil war claimed several thousand lives,[128] and was the most serious conflict in the Pacific Island Countries since the Second World War.[129]

---

[122] Waiko (n 100) 205.   [123] ibid 237–8.

[124] M. Rafiqul Islam, 'The Bougainville Secession Crisis in Papua New Guinea' (1990) 18 *MLJ* 31–7 at 31.

[125] ibid 31.   [126] ibid.

[127] For general reading about the Bougainville Accord, see Edward Wolfers, 'Joint Creation: The Bougainville Peace Agreement and Beyond' available from Conciliation Resources <http://www.c-r.org/our-work/accord/png-bougainville/joint-creation.php> [accessed 4 July 2008]. For more on the peace agreements in the Pacific Islands, see Graham Hassall, *Peace Agreements in the Pacific Islands*, Regional Workshop on Conflict Prevention and Peace-building in the Pacific (Nadi: Pacific Islands Forum Secretariat, United Nations DPA, 2005).

[128] Reilly (n 1) 176.   [129] Connell (n 23) 315.

The *UN Observer Mission in Bougainville* (UNOMB) formally closed down its activities in June 2005.[130] Bougainville held elections and formed an autonomous Bougainville government, completing the political role of the United Nations in the peace process.[131] The success of the Bougainville peace process was secured through:

...consistent and cooperative efforts of the Papua New Guinea Government and the Bougainville parties to the peace agreements and the strong support of the neighbouring States and donor countries. UNOMB and its predecessor have also played a significant role in facilitating those efforts. They have set an example of how a small United Nations team can work efficiently and effectively.[132]

5.2 Identification of Minorities and Indigenous Peoples

The remarkable complexity in identifying minorities and indigenous groups in PNG is evident from the introductory comments of the *Historical Atlas of Ethnic and Linguistic Groups in Papua New Guinea*:

Tribal units in Papua New Guinea are vexing categories and seldom fit into neatly defined, named boxes...ever since systematic documentation of, and research on, the cultures of Papua New Guinea began, different people have tended to call the same group by different names. In other cases, already defined ethnic groups underwent re-classification in a later period and were identified as being only a sub-group of a larger tribal unit. In order to come to terms with the voluminous, and often contradictory and transitory data on tribal groups, we decided it was necessary not only to produce one map but five for each map section, each map displaying the knowledge of the distribution of ethnic groups during one specific historical period.[133]

The summary records of the Committee on the Elimination of Racial Discrimination on PNG describe how '...the majority of the population was Melanesian, with a minority of Europeans, Asians, Chinese, Indians and Africans'.[134] No dialogue between PNG and the Committee has taken place since 1984, and the Committee's request to the state party to provide information on the demographic composition of the population has been ignored.[135] Minority Rights Group International has a relatively imprecise listing of regional differences in its *World Directory of Minorities*, including '...distinctions between

---

[130] Report of the Secretary-General on the United Nations Observer Mission to Bougainville (28 March 2005) UN doc S/2005/204 [10].

[131] ibid 18.   [132] ibid 19.

[133] Meinhard Schuster in Jurg Wassmann (ed), *Historical Atlas of Ethnic and Linguistic Groups in Papua New Guinea* (Basel: Institute of Ethnology, University of Basel, 1995) viii.

[134] Committee on the Elimination of Racial Discrimination, Summary Record—Papua New Guinea (16 March 2005) CERD/C/SR.1695 [4].

[135] Committee on the Elimination of Racial Discrimination, Concluding Observations—Papua New Guinea (21 March 2003) CERD/C/62/CO/12 [1].

highlanders and other Papua New Guineans, based on social and physical characteristics and on the late development of much of the highlands'.[136] The Highlands, where almost half the population lives, are the site of PNG's 'most fluid, aggressive and competitive micro-societies'.[137] Ethnic identity, a 'notoriously slippery concept', is considered '... both a salient feature of traditional society and also a reaction to colonial rule, modernization and independence'.[138] According to Levine:

> ... if ethnic communities are understood to be groups possessing a distinctive language, custom and memories—traits that give its members a sense of unity and cause them to distinguish themselves (and be distinguished by) others—then Papua New Guinea may have more than one thousand such ethnic groups within its borders.[139]

Reilly and Phillpot stress the definitional difficulties:

> In fact, in terms of ethnopolitical units, 1,000 is almost certainly too low an estimate: some scholars, for example, claim that Papua New Guinea has more than 10,000 microsocieties. Whatever the real figure (which depends to a large extent on how an 'ethnic group' is defined), there is also a great deal of regional variation in Papua New Guinea's ethnic structure. In the lowlands, the coastal plains and deltas of the south and north coasts, for example, the population of separate ethnolinguistic units can range from a few hundred to perhaps 10,000 speakers. By contrast, in the Highlands, Papua New Guinea's most populous region, language groups may number up to 150,000 or more members.[140]

Since the nineteenth century large numbers of anthropologists have travelled to PNG to conduct specialized ethnographic study, and it was only following independence in 1975 that there was a recognized need for the localization of anthropological research.[141] The 'decolonization' of anthropology in PNG has illustrated a gap between the approach of PNG researchers and external researchers, leading to the conclusion that Papua New Guineans' anthropology is in some ways different from the anthropology of foreigners.[142] The substantial body of writing by foreign anthropologists has been criticized and often rejected by Papua New Guinean writers since the late 1970s.[143] Thus Talyaga wrote in 1974, '... don't let the world know what we are not'; while Kasaipwalova labelled the

---

[136] Minority Rights Group International, 'World Directory of Minorities and Indigenous Peoples', Papua New Guinea Overview, available at <http://www.minorityrights.org/?lid=4763> [last accessed 25 March 2009].

[137] Reilly and Phillpot (n 7) 909.   [138] ibid 917.

[139] Stephen Levine, 'Culture and Conflict in Fiji, Papua New Guinea, Vanuatu and the Federated States of Micronesia', in Michael Brown and Sumit Ganguly (eds), *Government Policies and Ethnic Relations in the Asia-Pacific* (Cambridge, MA: Massachusetts Institute of Technology Press, 1997) 479, quoted in Reilly and Phillpot (n 7) 909.

[140] Reilly and Phillpot (n 7) 909. The authors also point to the 'retribalization' and 'neotribalization' processes, in which group affiliation is formed as a means of accessing public goods or as a response to armed conflict between groups.

[141] Louise Morauta, 'Indigenous Anthropology in Papua New Guinea' (1979) 20 (3) *CA* 561.

[142] ibid.   [143] ibid.

findings of foreign anthropologists 'half-truths' and 'empty masks'.[144] There was a need, according to indigenous anthropologists, for research in one's own small community of origin; Enos states, for example: '...although I am a Niuginean, I am at the same time a stranger, an outsider in other cultures but my own, no matter how hard I try'.[145] In a similar vein, Donigi writes:

Foreigners who come to my country do so with a pre-conceived idea about my history which was written by a foreigner. They then promote this idea as truth and are not prepared to listen to what I have to say. They change the burden of proof and place it on me to prove the contrary to what has been written by a foreigner. Why do I have to bear the burden of proof?[146]

While Papua New Guineans stress the need for localized research, cultural unity over diversity is also emphasized, in line with Michael Somare's[147] dictum that:

...for all the infinite variety of forms and styles, we believe that we share some very fundamental, basic attitudes to life that will enable us to make a modern State with a distinct identity and culture of our own.[148]

The concept includes common cultural themes based around the concept of the 'Melanesian way', and the state's motto is 'unity in diversity'; former Prime Minister Paias Wingti stated that '...this diversity is slowly strangling our nationhood'.[149] Thus diversity for Papua New Guinean anthropologists, or knowledge of specific cultures, has as its aim the identification of the common space for inter-cultural exchange. A distinction has been posited wherein foreign anthropologists are most interested in cultural diversity while Papua New Guineans are keen to find ways of understanding cultural unity.[150]

There are no reliable figures on the total number of politically relevant ethnic groups in PNG.[151] The government of PNG has not provided any official survey of the peoples of the state. Its overdue report to the Committee on the Elimination of Racial Discrimination, to which it submitted just once over twenty-five years ago, would be an opportunity for the state to engage in a process of identification of ethnic and linguistic groups in the state in accordance with is obligations under Article 9 of the Convention.[152]

---

[144] Quoted in ibid 563.   [145] Quoted in ibid.

[146] Peter Donigi, *Indigenous or Aboriginal Rights to Property: A Papua New Guinea Perspective* (Utrecht: International Books, 1994) 17.

[147] Michael Somare was prime minister of PNG from independence in 1975 until 1980, and 1982 to 1985. He was re-elected prime minister at the 2002 and 2007 elections and is current leader of the National Alliance Party. See further <http://www.pm.gov.pg> [last accessed 25 March 2009].

[148] Quoted in Morauta (n 141) 564.   [149] Reilly and Phillpot (n 7) 927.

[150] Morauta (n 141) 564.   [151] Reilly and Phillpot (n 7) 918.

[152] CERD, 'Information on the Demographic Composition of the Population', UN doc A/9018 (1973) General Comment 4. The General Comment invites states parties to include in their reports 'relevant information on the demographic composition of the population referred to in the provisions of Article 1 of the Convention'.

Currently, anthropologists are divided between national and non-national researchers, and while there are areas of concordance, contradictions within the voluminous data on PNG's ethnic groups are rife. Localized studies from a national and international perspective exist, but no authoritative overview has emerged. The challenge for the PNG government is to report to the Committee on the Elimination of Racial Discrimination, providing the treaty-body with a coherent and balanced account of the state's ethnic and linguistic groups.

Differentiating ethnic and linguistic groups is a process that is complex and difficult, and lies in the realm of anthropology rather than law. Identification of regional differences on the basis of administrative domain remains the only effective means of assessing minority and indigenous rights. In this sense, until greater knowledge of specific ethnic and linguistic groups is compiled, the less-developed regions of PNG can be considered to be its minorities. The 2004 UNDP report notes that '... virtually all socio-economic and other indices indicate that disparities in PNG at the provincial and sub-provincial level are very large by any standard'.[153] The assessment of the state's compliance with the Millennium Development Goals by UNDP takes place at the sub-national, provincial, and district levels, using a composite index. By this standard, '... differences in the degree of poverty between provinces are very high indeed with the highest levels in the provinces of the Northern Coastal Region and in Gulf Province'.[154] The four lowest ranking provinces are Southern Highlands, West Sepik, Gulf, and Enga. Consequently:

... the most obvious, cost effective and easiest way of making progress towards achieving the MDGs and, in the process closing the millennium gaps within the country, is to concentrate on the low achievers amongst the provinces.[155]

It is submitted that legal remedies aimed at *de facto* equality must target low-performing regions. According to Connell:

Many areas of the country, some with quite large populations, have few physical resources and are handicapped by their isolation. Between the coasts and the highlands, thinly populated areas of mountains and swamp were and are largely ignored, as development efforts focused on relatively large, accessible and nucleated populations... Poorer regions have been poorly served by national political and economic decisions, and did not 'catch-up'; their interests had few effective advocates. Regional, provincial and district inequalities—of income and human development—are likely to have increased further... [providing] a disturbing picture of regional imbalance.[156]

Finally, PNG hosts up to 10,000 mainly West Papuan refugees.[157] Some cases date back to the 1960s, generated in the context of the Indonesia annexation

---

[153] UNDP Progress Report (n 24) 38.   [154] ibid 10.

[155] ibid 41.   [156] Connell (n 23) 222–3.

[157] United Nations High Commissioner for Refugees, 'Papua New Guinea: Country Operations Plan for 2007', available at <http://www.unhcr.org/cgi-bin/texis/vtx/refworld/rwmain?docid=452f50342> [accessed 5 July 2008].

of the province of Irian Jaya in 1962. The largest influx of refugees occurred between 1984 and 1986.[158] The conspicuous absence of international and national NGOs working on refugee issues,[159] and the failure to establish legal provisions or regulations for establishing the procedure and criteria for the determination of refugee status, make this a particularly intractable problem. In 2001, PNG and Australia signed a memorandum of understanding under which PNG agreed to host a group of 225 mainly Afghan asylum seekers and to consider hosting further groups of asylum seekers, as part of the Australian policy termed the 'Pacific Solution' under which asylum seekers are processed at offshore centres.[160] The processing facility in PNG was closed in 2003, although the Australian government announced that it would be available for reactivation on short notice.[161]

5.3 Rights of Minorities

5.3.1 Land and Mining

Land occupies a 'complex social, economic, cultural, religious, psychological and therefore legal role in Papua New Guinea society'.[162] Between 95 and 96 per cent of the land in PNG is 'customary' land belonging to indigenous tribes under customary or traditional title, and held in group ownership.[163] There are various types of landowning groups, which may be formed on the basis of lineage, geography, or participation in common activities. Tribes, the largest customary social organization, are too large and diffuse and exercise no control over land rights. Instead, land rights are vested in a subset of the tribe, such as the clan, which exercises a management role and governs hunting areas, croplands, and the defence of the land from neighbouring landowning groups. Sub-clans determine rights of *usus* among clan members, including leases. Some rights are also invested at the level of the family or the individual, (e.g. intensive use of a particular plot for gardening). However, as with the larger sets and subsets of traditional landowners, rights generally accrue on the basis of function and do not equate to ownership.[164]

---

[158] See further Rosemary Preston, 'Refugees in Papua New Guinea: Government Response and Assistance, 1984–1988' (1992) 26 (3) *IMR* 843–76. Preston describes the policy developed at this time as one of 'minimal assistance so as not to jeopardize national security by antagonizing Indonesia"'. See 843.

[159] UNHCR (n 157).

[160] Savitri Taylor, 'The Pacific Solution or a Pacific Nightmare? The Difference between Burden Shifting and Responsibility Sharing' (2005) 6 *APLPJ* 1–43 at 7.

[161] ibid 13.

[162] Michael Trebilcock and Jack Knetsh, 'Land Policy and Economic Development in Papua New Guinea (1981) 9 *MLJ* 102–15 at 102.

[163] Katherine Dixon, 'Working with Mixed Commons/Anticommons Property: Mobilizing Customary Land in Papua New Guinea the Melanesian Way' (2007) 31 *HELR* 219–77 at 220.

[164] Dixon (n 163) 226.

Zorn describes the customary system as 'much more sophisticated' than English common law principles of landownership.[165] Private citizens' land rights are protected by section 53(1) of the *Papua New Guinea Constitution*, as part of its basic human rights provisions, under which possession cannot be taken compulsorily of any property except in certain specified circumstances. These circumstances are where the land is acquired for a 'public purpose' (e.g. health, education, roads, defence), or for a purpose that is reasonably justifiable in a democratic society and described in an organic law or act of parliament.[166] Chalmers, writing in 1975, predicted difficulties in any attempt to apply the term 'reasonably justifiable' in a logical manner.[167] Muroa explains:

> ... where a minority group has refused 'unreasonably' to give up their land or interests therein to the government for development programs beneficial to the public at large, the government can invoke the power of compulsory acquisition and take the land in the interest of the public and compensate the landowners.[168]

According to Connell:

> Few countries in the world are endowed with mineral resources on anything like the same scale as Papua New Guinea. Copper, gold and oil are abundant; no country in the Asia-Pacific region has been so transformed by recent mineral exploitation. Mining has brought great wealth and new conflicts over resources, localised environmental degradation and political problems of unparalleled severity. Its impact has been much more than merely economic.[169]

In its preparations for independence, the *Constitutional Planning Committee* showed an acute awareness of the impact of foreign investment and produced a well-worked basis for its control to be included in the Constitution.[170] This was rejected without substantial debate, and the first national government inherited broad, discretionary legal powers over the conditions under which resources can be extracted, emphasizing returns to the state through revenue.[171] Serious disputes over the allocation and distribution of benefits are an inescapable dimension of resource development in PNG.[172]

---

[165] Jean Zorn, 'Fighting Over Land' (1976) 4 *MLJ* 7–36 at 8.

[166] George Muroa, 'The Extent of Constitutional Protection of Land Rights in Papua New Guinea' (1999) 26 *MLJ* 85–114 at 88.

[167] Donald Chalmers, 'Human Rights and what is Reasonably Justifiable in a Democratic Society' (1975) 1 *MLJ* 92–102 at 93.

[168] George Muroa, 'Recognition of Indigenous Land Rights: A Papua New Guinean Experience' (1994) 22 *MLJ* 81–102 at 84.

[169] Connell (n 23) 121.

[170] Fitzpatrick (n 10) 209.

[171] ibid 215 and 218.

[172] Don Gardner, 'Continuity and Identity: Mineral Development, Land Tenure and "Ownership" Among the Northern Mountain Ok' in Alan Rumsey and James Welner (eds), *Mining and Indigenous Lifeworlds in Australia and Papua New Guinea* (Oxon: Sean Kingston Publishing, 2004) 101–24 at 101.

Mining and petroleum projects have caused widespread tension in the interpretation of customary land rights. Peter Donigi, writing in 1994, listed fifteen projects, including the Bougainville and Ok Tedi mines, and assessed whether customary landowners had any interest in the mines. In the majority of cases landowners either had no direct interest or had a small minority shareholding.[173] The most successful was the Lihir prospect, a gold deposit on Lihir island, in which landowners had negotiated a 20 per cent interest in the project.[174] At common law, gold and silver found in the soil belonged to the Crown by royal prerogative and was deemed not to form *partes soli*. Following independence, the *Mining Act 1977* [175] amalgamated the laws of the country to restate the basic principle of state ownership of all gold and materials.[176] Donigi argues:

... the provision of the mining and petroleum legislations which vests ownership of gold, minerals and petroleum under customary land or land other than state land, in the state, is unconstitutional... The mining and petroleum legislations are not only unconstitutional but are also contrary to international law as regards the rights of 'peoples'.[177]

5.3.2 Language

PNG has about one-fifth of the world's languages, and there are 852 known languages spoken in the state—more than in the whole of Africa.[178] One-third of the languages are related, belonging to the Austronesian language family group. The other languages, many of which are unrelated, belong to the Non-Austronesian language family group. Very small communities have languages spoken by about 15 per cent of the country's population.[179] The multiplicity of languages at the micro level has led to a degree of integration at the national level, with English the language of official communication, and *Tok Pisin* and *Hiri Motu* the neutral *lingua francas*.[180]

The *Summer Institute of Linguistics* (SIL), an international non-governmental organization working in PNG since 1956, is engaged in a process of documenting and archiving Papua New Guinea's languages in conjunction with the *Department of Education*.[181] It also lists endangered languages, extinct languages

---

[173] Donigi (n 146) app 14, 125–8.   [174] ibid app 14, 127.
[175] *Mining (Safety) Act 1977*, No 45 of 1977. See also *Mining Act 1992*, No 20 of 1992; *Mining (Ok Tedi Agreement) Act* 1976, c 363 of 1976.
[176] R.W. James, *Land Tenure in Papua New Guinea* (Port Moresby, 1985) 17.
[177] Donigi (n 146) 34.
[178] Reilly and Phillpot (n 7) 908.
[179] Naihuwo Ahai, 'Literacy in an Emergent Society: Papua New Guinea' (Summer Institute of Linguistics Working Papers, 2005) available at <http://www.sil.org/silewp/2005/silewp2005-002. pdf> [last accessed 5 August 2008].
[180] Reilly (n 1) 179.
[181] Summer Institute of Linguistics, Papua New Guinea, available at <http://www.png languages.org> [last accessed 7 August 2008].

such as Arabaga and Aribwatsa, and language maps of PNG's regions and provinces.[182]

The PNG Constitution states that everyone has the right to literacy in a vernacular, a national *lingua franca* (Tok Pisin or Hiri Motu), and English. The Constitution does not specify how to do this, other than to encourage government departments and NGOs to be active in programmes aiming to improve literacy.[183] Until 1989, the government made no serious effort to make the general populace literate in the languages of PNG. In more recent years governmental policy has shifted towards the use of vernacular languages in education. In its 'National Language and Literacy Policy', the government aims to encourage *tok ples* [vernacular] preparatory classes for children before they enter grade one of community schools, and continue the use and maintenance of *tok ples* once they enter community schools.[184]

Robert Litteral charts the development of linguistic policy in PNG, and traces the emergence of the focus on vernacular languages to 1980, when the provincial government of North Solomons introduced the *Viles Tok Ples Skuls* (Village Vernacular Schools) programme in two languages with SIL assistance. The programme was the '…simple beginning of the post-independence move towards vernacular education which by 1993 had grown to over 250 languages'.[185] The aim is indigenous development, with the government's role that of an enabler rather than a provider. Policy, accountability and implementation lies with the communities that receive the education, making the communities active producers of education.[186]

5.3.3 Intellectual Property Rights

In 1992, PNG signed the *Convention on Biological Diversity*,[187] which raises the issue of cultural property rights, including the protection of indigenous knowledge about medicinal resources and ownership rights to plant cultivars.[188] Article 8(j) of the Convention requires states parties to '…respect, preserve and maintain knowledge, innovations and practices of indigenous and local communities embodying traditional lifestyles relevant for the conservation

---

[182] ibid.   [183] Ahai (n 179).

[184] National Language and Literacy Policy of Papua New Guinea, reproduced in Robert Litteral, 'Language Development in Papua New Guinea' (Summer Institute of Linguistics Working Papers, 1999) Annex, available at <http://www.sil.org/silewp/1999/002/SILEWP1999-002.html> [last accessed 5 August 2008].

[185] ibid.   [186] ibid.

[187] Convention on Biological Diversity, adopted at the Earth Summit, Rio de Janeiro, Brazil (June 1992), entered into force December 1993.

[188] Leslie Harroun, 'Intellectual Property Rights in Papua New Guinea' in Kathy Whimp and Mark Busse (eds), *Protection of Intellectual, Biological and Cultural Property in Papua New Guinea* (Port Moresby: Asia Pacific Press, 2000) 29–46 at 40.

and sustainable use of biological diversity'. PNG has yet to incorporate the Convention into domestic policies or legislation.[189]

Scientific and industrial demand for access to PNG's genetic resources is increasing, and the value of medicinal and industrial applications is likely to grow in the coming decades.[190] Indeed, the last fifteen years has seen '...an unprecedented interest in bioprospecting in Papua New Guinea'.[191] PNG and other island countries in the Pacific region need to formulate policies to govern sustainable biodiversity prospecting, with the *Convention on Biological Diversity* providing 'an international legal justification and a framework for the country to establish sovereign rights over its genetic resources'.[192] Under Article 3 of the Convention, rights of biodiversity are the sovereign rights of the states. These rights can only exist '...if they are built on the rights of the communities that have conserved and protected biodiversity within national territories'.[193]

Brendan Tobin sketches an initial phase of protection for PNG, based on his experience of negotiations in Peru on behalf of the Aguarunas to the *International Collaborative Biodiversity Group*.[194] The proposal uses intellectual property regimes as a means of ensuring that prior informed consent becomes a condition for commercial use of traditional knowledge.[195]

The following elements are needed to safeguard indigenous and local community collective knowledge:

(1) ensure recognition of the collective nature of knowledge;
(2) ensure that control of the use of knowledge remains firmly in the hands of indigenous peoples, even where such information is found within the so-called public domain;
(3) ensure that the exercise of the rights by any community or group does not infringe the rights of other communities or groups;
(4) avoid creating monopolistic rights over knowledge;
(5) ensure equitable benefit-sharing within and among communities;
(6) assist in the revaluation of indigenous knowledge; and
(7) establish a presumption that the use of resources over which there exists knowledge, in particular regarding medicinal plants, implies use of that knowledge.[196]

An approach that incorporates both *sui generis* regimes and modification of existing intellectual property rights regimes may prove most appropriate and

---

[189] ibid 42.

[190] R.N. Kambuou, 'Plant Genetic Resources of Papua New Guinea: Some Thoughts on Intellectual Property Rights' in Whimp and Busse (n 188) 127.

[191] Lohi Matainaho, 'Genetic, Biochemical and Medicinal Resources: How Much Can We Own, Protect and Receive Credit For?' in Whimp and Busse (n 188)136.

[192] Kambuou (n 190) 127–8.   [193] ibid 132.

[194] Brendan Tobin, 'The Search for an Interim Solution', in Whimp and Busse (n 188) 169–82.

[195] ibid 170.   [196] ibid 171–2.

effective.[197] Commercial systems of control, including a 'certificate of origin' scheme, would limit the possibility of commercial reward for unapproved use and thereby induce users to seek the prior informed consent of the communities affected.[198] A blend of national and international measures will be necessary to ensure comprehensive and effective protection.[199]

5.3.4 Religion

A vast majority of the inhabitants of PNG see themselves as Christian, and the preamble of the constitution sets out the goal of handing down to future generations the 'Christian principles' that the people claim for themselves today, as well as the 'noble traditions' of their ancestors.[200] At the national level, Christianity has been installed as a 'traditionalized state religion', absorbed into each local area's interpretation of its own tradition, and a part of contemporary identity.[201] Yet, according to Barker, there have been few appraisals of Christianity as it is currently experienced and practised in Pacific societies.[202] The general growth of smaller denominations that arrived after the larger churches is treated even more rarely.[203] Literature on Melanesia, taken as a whole, contains no works in which the adoption of different forms of Christianity is examined using an approach based on the anthropology of religion.[204]

Christianity in PNG is divided largely between Catholics and fundamentalist Seventh Day Adventists (SDA),[205] with the denominations co-existing peacefully.[206] The SDA is enjoying increasing success.[207] The growth in the numbers of Adventists is curious, given that conversion requires stricter discipline, including giving up one's social prestige, the keeping of pigs, consumption of different types of meat, and the enjoyment of tea, coffee, beer, betel nut, and tobacco.[208] Catholics claim that conversion is largely for material motives, with Adventists promising money and clothing to adherents; while Adventists claim

---

[197] ibid 173.   [198] ibid 181–2.   [199] ibid 182.

[200] Holger Jebens, *Pathways to Heaven: Contesting Mainline and Fundamentalist Christianity in Papua New Guinea* (New York: Berghahn Books, 2005) 1.

[201] ibid xv. In West Papua, Christianity is a key vehicle for the expression of Papuan identity and indigenous spirituality in opposition to the Indonesian state and Islam.

[202] John Barker, 'Introduction: Ethnographic Perspectives on Christianity in Oceanic Societies' in J. Barker (ed), *Christianity in Oceania: Ethnographic Perspectives* (Lanham: ASAO Monographs 12, 1990) quoted in ibid 208.

[203] Jebens (n 200) 214.   [204] ibid 217.

[205] ibid 230. 'Fundamentalism' being understood as groups or movements seeking to undo the process of modernity in its different aspects by linking particular ideas with transcendent origins and thus strengthening them religiously.

[206] ibid 241.

[207] ibid 145. Other denominations are increasingly competing with one another throughout Papua New Guinea (246).

[208] ibid 146.

a theological foundation underpinning their growing numbers, with converts essentially representing a criticism of Catholicism.[209]

Traditional religion, like traditional culture, was subject to processes of colonization and 'missionization', the latter term generally meaning the process of acceptance of Christianity, first triggered by white, then by indigenous religious functionaries.[210] The process of 'missionization' seems to go much deeper than colonization, since at first sight the traditional religion appears to have '...not merely been changed but completely eradicated and replaced by Christianity'.[211] Jebens argues that traditional religion has nevertheless maintained its influence through transformation and adaptation, and members of Christian denominations are actively adopting these practices '...in order ultimately to win back their lost autonomy and claim their identity'.[212]

The initial impression that 'missionization' had eradicated the role of traditional religion is misleading.[213] The view that indigenous peoples in Papua New Guinea are only Christian 'on the surface' could be considered equally misleading. There is a growing argument that Melanesian Christianity needs far greater study as a complex subject in which traditional and Christian beliefs are simultaneously held. Citing the work of anthropologist Joel Robbins, Jebens writes:

It is precisely by taking indigenous ideas and practices seriously, as well as by stating a simultaneity of traditional and Christian morality, that Robbins refutes not only the allegation of 'indigenous superficiality', but also the opposite yet equally obsolete claim that Christianity 'spells the dissolution of everything indigenous'.[214]

There are approximately 15,000 Baha'i living in all provinces of PNG and about 2,000 Muslims.[215] The Constitution protects freedom of religion and the practice of religion is generally free, although some incidents of religious discrimination have been reported. The *Islamic Human Rights Commission* issued an 'urgent alert' following comments by the PNG Home Affairs minister in 2000, who stated:

We don't want Muslims to come to this country. We already have the Melanesian religion and Christianity. We will come up with an amendment to the constitution or come up with a separate legislation that will set up measures to control the emergence of different religions.[216]

5.3.5 Education

The level of educational development in PNG remains low. Before educational reforms in 1992, there were only four national high schools in PNG.[217] A 1995

---

[209] ibid 173–4.   [210] ibid 75.   [211] ibid 91.
[212] ibid 202–3.   [213] ibid 219.   [214] ibid, Preface, xiii-xiv.
[215] CERD Summary Record (n 134) 4.
[216] Islamic Human Rights Commission, 'Urgent Alert: Papua New Guinea' (28 September 2000) available at <http://www.ihrc.org.uk/show.php?id=134> [last accessed 7 August 2008].
[217] UNDP Progress Report (n 24) 16.

article describes how up to 70 per cent of Papua New Guineans are illiterate; only 20 per cent of students go past the sixth grade; only 3 per cent complete the tenth grade; and fewer than 1 per cent go on to university level.[218] In 1994, schools closed two months early for Christmas because the government could not afford to complete the school year.[219] These stark figures have been improving more recently. Over 90 per cent of Papua New Guineans enter primary school at some stage.[220] UNDP's regional *Millennium Development Goals Report 2007* in Asia and the Pacific states that 58 per cent of children enrolled in primary school reach fifth grade.[221]

As is the case elsewhere, there is a strong inverse correlation between education and poverty in PNG.[222] Differences in enrolment and retention at the provincial level are extreme. The provinces of the Highlands Region, most notably Southern Highlands and Enga, drag down the national indices.[223] UNDP points to:

…a very significant gap between the relatively high educational performance in matrilineal societies and the much lower performance in most patrilineal societies, particularly those in the Highlands region. This applies particularly to girls' education.[224]

The report notes that the government considers the global target of universal primary education by 2015 as unrealistic. Consequently the target has been tailored, and is now an enrolment rate of 85 per cent and retention rate of 70 per cent by 2015, with youth literacy to increase by 70 per cent in the same period.[225] The report highlights the significant impact a regional approach to educational reform would have:

Achieving further substantial improvements in education and literacy in the next 11 years in provinces that already have a reasonable education and literacy record, especially those in the Islands Regions, may not be easy and will certainly be costly. However, it would be significantly less difficult and costly to improve the extremely low enrolment and retention rates in provinces like Southern Highlands and Enga. The same applies to the youth (15–24) and adult (over 15) literacy rates. Since the populations of these low achieving provinces are relatively large, even moderate improvements will have a significant impact on the national average education and literacy indices for PNG.[226]

---

[218] White (n 19) 307.   [219] ibid 307.
[220] UNDP Progress Report (n 24) 16.
[221] UNDP, 'Regional Millennium Development Goals Report—Progress 2007 (Asia and the Pacific)' (pt 1) 10, available at <http://www.mdgasiapacific.org/node/160> [last accessed 5 August 2008].
[222] UNDP Progress Report (n 24) 11.   [223] ibid 14.
[224] ibid 15.   [225] ibid.
[226] ibid.

5.4 Remedies

5.4.1 Land and Mining

Customary land is not considered 'property' and is therefore inalienable,[227] with a prohibition on the sale of land by traditional landowners except to the state or other customary landowning groups. All dealings in customary land are subject to state oversight, and there is inevitable tension between the state's need to reconcile economic development with the protection of indigenous interests.[228] The *Constitution of Papua New Guinea*, which recognizes customary law as part of the underlying law of the state, provides overarching legal protection, interpreted as requiring consent of the clan in order to affect a significant change in land use.[229] Economic theorists have claimed that the customary land tenure system is a severe impediment to development activities in PNG.[230]

Dixon highlights two aspects of the 'anti-commons' nature of indigenous land rights; first, that there is no practical hierarchy of use-rights within customary landowning groups such that would invest in one owner the right to determine the ultimate use of a resource; and second, the existence of an effective veto power that accords to each member of the customary landowning group.[231] Although the veto can be mollified by hierarchies within clans that can effectively vest decision-making in the hands of the clan leaders, Dixon cites the case of the *Tolai* people, who responded to irresponsible profit-making decisions by their leaders by re-instituting new customary law requiring that land not be sold without the express agreement of all affected members.[232] This veto power of all members has been recognized in the land courts, which were established shortly after PNG gained independence in 1975. The courts have developed a significant body of customary land law through arbitration of disputes.[233]

Under the Constitution, customary land may only be sold among tribes or to the State. The *Land Act 1996*[234] requires that all commercial dealings with respect to customary land be subject to state oversight and approval. As a result, '... absolute exclusionary power over commercial land use lies with the State itself'.[235] Indeed, the state has the option of compulsory acquisition available to it, although this only applies in emergency conditions. The scheme generally employed is termed 'lease-lease-back' and codified by the Land Act 1996, in which the state customary landowners lease their land to the state, usually for a period of 99 years, which in turn sub-leases the land to an individual or business

---

[227] James notes that 'The broad division unalienated and alienated, carries the implication of the contrast of unwritten and written laws'. James (n 176) 21.

[228] Dixon (n 163) 221.   [229] ibid 231.

[230] ibid 253.   [231] ibid 246.   [232] ibid 248–9.

[233] Robert Cooter, quoted in ibid 255.   [234] No 45 of 1996.

[235] Dixon (n 163) 255.

seeking to use or develop it. The land reverts to the indigenous landowners at the expiry of the lease.[236]

There are critical problems associated with the lease-lease-back scheme. Crucially, '. . . the Papua New Guinea government is effectively the only formal avenue available to customary landowning groups for mobilizing customary land'.[237] State inefficiency means that, in practice, there is a severe backlog of applications in the Department of Lands. The opening up of customary land is extremely limited, with state intervention functionally operating as an exclusionary veto in land management.[238] Because of bureaucratic incompetence by a 'disorganized, underfunded, volatile and often corrupt' government,[239] informal markets in customary land have developed, involving direct negotiations between customary landowning groups and non-indigenous developers. Cooter describes '. . . substantial black or grey market activity in land', although he acknowledges that '. . . documenting its extent is impossible'.[240] As a solution, Dixon recommends that commercial land use determinations should be made by customary landowners rather than by the government. She argues:

As a first step, this might mean eliminating the lease-lease-back programme and lifting the Land Act's ban on direct dealings in land with non-indigenous citizens. Although this prohibition on direct dealings was implemented to protect customary landowners from unscrupulous investors, the informal economy that has developed around customary land demonstrates that this blanket prohibition is unnecessary... Lifting this ban would effectively help formalize the informal economy currently in place by rendering direct dealings enforceable in the land courts... The rights of indigenous people to control their land and resources are also recognised under international law.[241]

Similarly, Donigi notes that traditional or indigenous landowners in PNG:

. . . have not conveyed, assigned, transferred or done any act which can be interpreted to amount to a termination of their rights to the sub-soil resources under their land... so as to justify the declaration of the vesting of ownership in the state in the mining and petroleum legislations.[242]

The Bougainville Copper project and Ok Tedi mining project illustrate the difficulties involved when the landowners are excised from the process. In Bougainville, force was used to compel the local people to sell their land to the administration.[243] Consultation did not take place before allowing the mining company to occupy the land. Subsequent explanations were inadequate and biased, emphasizing benefits and concealing negative effects. Compensation payments made were 'grossly unfair' compared with the profits accrued to the company. When the landowners stood up to the government, brute force was

---

[236] ibid 256–7.   [237] ibid 257.   [238] ibid 258.
[239] ibid 275.   [240] Robert Cooter, quoted in ibid 264.
[241] ibid 273–4.   [242] Donigi (n 146) 39.
[243] Muroa (n 168) 97.

used to subjugate people.[244] Muroa concludes that the actions of the government 'could be described as giving a "lie" to its role as a protector of indigenous
peoples' rights and interests in land'.[245] He underlines the fact that compulsory acquisition ought to be governed strictly by constitutional provisions.[246] As
Connell summarizes, 'A localised dispute over services and compensation payments for environmental damage had become a national and regional political
nightmare', in which mining no longer played a significant part, despite its role
as the catalyst of the crisis.[247]

The Ok Tedi mine, owned 52 per cent by the mining company *Broken Hill
Proprietary Company*, 18 per cent by Toronto-based *Metal Mining Corporation*
and 30 per cent by the national government of PNG,[248] created nearly 5,000
jobs, and contributed 3.3 per cent of the state's total internal revenue in 1991.[249]
Yet in 1994, local landowners filed suits against *Broken Hill* and *Ok Tedi Mining
Limited*, claiming compensation and exemplary damages of up to four billion
Australian dollars, the largest compensatory action in Australian history.[250]
Because of difficulties in constructing a plant to treat waste from the mine
(attributed by mining companies to frequent landslides), waste was dumped in
the river system without first being treated.[251]

The mine was governed by an act of parliament, the *Mining (Ok Tedi Sixth
Supplemental Agreement) Act 1986*,[252] which allowed for the suspension of
the requirement for the construction of disposal facilities and a tailings dam
pending the outcome of a detailed environmental study to be carried out by
the company. In the meantime, the company was allowed to continue dump-
ing waste into the Fly River system.[253] Eventually the state decided to allow the
company to continue dumping directly into the river system, with the government and the company then being committed to compensate the people living
the length of the Fly River.[254] The decision was described as one of 'political
expediency' according to the *Times of Papua New Guinea*, '... forgoing the welfare and health of thousands of Western (Fly River) people and the environment
of the nation to boost its financial capacity in a trying time'.[255]

Several NGOs, including the *Australian Conservation Foundation*, charted
the resulting destruction, including a 50–80 per cent decline in fish stock and
threats to subsistence staples such as crustaceans, turtles, and crocodiles, as
well as gardens and sago palms growing along the riverbanks and swamps.[256]
It is estimated that the ecology of the river system will be disrupted for at least

---

[244] ibid.   [245] ibid.   [246] ibid 100.
[247] Connell (n 23) 140.   [248] White (n 19) 308.
[249] ibid 309.   [250] ibid 305.
[251] Lawrence Kalinoe and M.J. Kuwimb, 'Customary Landowners' Right to Sue for
Compensation in Papua New Guinea and the Ok Tedi Dispute' (1997) 25 *MLJ* 65–86 at 67.
[252] No 27 of 1986. Also see *Mining (Ok Tedi Seventh Supplemental Agreement) Act 1986*,
c 363(g) of 1986.
[253] Kalinoe and Kuwimb (n 251) 68.   [254] ibid.
[255] Quoted in ibid.   [256] ibid 69.

fifty years.[257] Consequently the majority owner of the mine was sued in the Victorian Supreme Court, with villagers claiming compensation for discharging poisonous material into the Ok Tedi-Fly River systems and destroying the villagers' subsistence way of life.[258] A total settlement package of AUS$550 million was reached.[259] According to White, local communities '...should be involved in the negotiation of mining agreements', and the Ok Tedi disputes '...exemplifies the problems that may arise between indigenous populations and the owners of major natural resource exploitation projects in developing countries'.[260] She quotes the *Australian Conservation Foundation* to the effect that:

The absence of informed community participation in the decision to mine at Ok Tedi and in the management of the mine, means that this operation has failed to reflect the needs of the local population.[261]

At the core of government minerals policy has been the concept of 'resource rent', which has the aim of channelling benefits to the government and minimizing its diversion to other channels.[262] The legal framework for access to minerals was based on the principle that all minerals are the property of the state, denying mineral ownership to landowners.[263] The emergence of landowners and a greater concern for environmental issues has led to new demands, requiring recognition of local ownership of mineral resources.[264] Mining remains the most important sector in the economy and the future development of the national economy appears to hinge on its success or failure.[265]

5.4.2 Human Rights Monitoring

The *Ombudsman Commission* of PNG can inquire into government policy that may be contrary to the goals and principles set out in the Constitution.[266] It has the power to investigate basic violations of rights, but has focused on official corruption where it plays a critical monitoring role.[267] The Commission's human rights desk, established in May 2005, has only one member of staff, Patrick Niebo.[268] *Human Rights Watch* reports, in the context of police beatings and torture, that the human rights desk staff member can visit correctional facilities, but does not have the power to follow up on these visits. In the continued absence of an independent human rights commission, *Human Rights Watch* recommends that the government must allocate additional resources for the Ombudsman Commission to take on human rights cases.[269]

---

[257] White (n 19) 312.   [258] Kalinoe and Kuwimb (n 251) 70.
[259] ibid 70.   [260] White (n 19) 305.
[261] Australian Conservation Foundation, quoted in ibid 316.
[262] Connell (n 23) 141.   [263] ibid 142.
[264] ibid 143.   [265] ibid 165.
[266] Fitzpatrick (n 10) 205.   [267] HRW (n 27) 44.
[268] ibid 44.   [269] ibid 4.

Writing in relation to the prospect of an international supervisory mechanism on human rights in PNG in 1980, Brunton states: 'Papua New Guinea is unlikely to accede to proposals that human rights issues arising within its territory should be reviewed by any international agency'.[270] Proposals to establish international supervisory bodies in the state would be interpreted as 'unwarranted interference', underlined by the view that the constitutional human rights provisions provide adequate protection for the individual. Furthermore, there would be resentment to external supervision by countries 'with human rights records inferior to that of Papua New Guinea'.[271]

Brunton compares the Pacific region with Europe, concluding that while European states could ratify international treaties and then ignore their *de facto* provisions, states within the Pacific region tend not to be interested in taking the first step of engaging with international instruments and mechanisms. In fact states in the region go further than unwillingness to ratify human rights instruments—they often refuse publicly to acknowledge that there are international standards according to which the world will judge their acts in the first place.[272] He warns:

Many of the Asian Pacific nations, including Papua New Guinea, are not parties to all the international treaties and conventions on human rights. This matter is basic. Nations must acknowledge publicly that they are bound by the rule of law in these matters. There is no room for equivocation.[273]

PNG has signed three of the UN human rights treaties, the *Convention on the Rights of the Child*, the *Convention on the Elimination of Discrimination against Women*, and the *International Convention on the Elimination of All Forms of Racial Discrimination*.[274] Against these ratifications the government has submitted just two reports to the monitoring bodies: to the Committee on the Elimination of Racial Discrimination (CERD), nearly twenty-five years ago,[275] and more recently to the Committee on the Rights of the Child (CRC). Kwa describes the difficulties PNG experienced when it ratified the *Convention on the Rights of the Child*:

Papua New Guinea ratified the Convention on the Rights of the Child 1989 on 1 March 1993. Under Article 44 of the Convention, member countries are required to submit a country report within two years of ratification. For this purpose, a Joint Working Committee was initiated by DFA in 1996, with members from the DFA, Department of Education, Department of Home Affairs, Youth and Religion, Attorney-General's Department, the Child Welfare Office and the Department of Health. The initiative in

[270] Brian Brunton, 'Human Rights in Papua New Guinea and the Prospects for International Supervision' (1980) 8 *MLJ* 143–57 at 155.
[271] ibid 155–6.   [272] ibid 156.   [273] ibid.
[274] United Nations High Commissioner for Human Rights, Status of Ratifications, available at <http://www.unhchr.ch/tbs/doc.nsf/newhvstatusbycountry?OpenView&Start=1&Count=250& Expand=134#134> [last accessed 7 August 2008].
[275] CERD Summary Record (n 134) [1].

fact never got off the ground. The Department of Home Affairs, Youth and Religion is planning to resurrect the Joint Working Group. This is only one example of the many initiatives involving various Departments which have stalled over the years.[276]

The government eventually submitted a report to the CRC in 2003,[277] and the CRC issued its Concluding Observations in 2004.[278] While welcoming the state report, the Committee emphasized the importance of reporting and the need to produce reports regularly and within the prescribed time period of five years.[279] CERD is considering the situation of PNG in the continued absence of a state report. In its most recent summary record from 2005, one member noted that the submission of a report to the CRC '. . . showed that it was capable of submitting a report'.[280] In the Summary Records, the country Rapporteur is quoted:

> It could thus be concluded that Papua New Guinea was a country in distress. It was cru-
> cial that it should resume the process of dialogue with the Committee. She accordingly
> suggested that a representative of the Committee might be authorized to travel to New
> York to meet a representative of the State party in order to encourage it to cooperate with
> the Committee, and, if it so wished, to seek technical assistance from OHCHR in the
> preparation of a report.[281]

5.4.3 Aid Reform

PNG is dependent on foreign aid for delivery of the majority of its public services.[282] In 2005, foreign aid amounted to 22 per cent of the national budget, with Australian aid representing around 81 per cent of international grant aid. Australian aid to PNG is governed by an international treaty, under which Australia delivers around AUS$300 million per annum, which represents a 60 per cent decline in real terms since PNG gained independence.[283] Other donors include the European Union, Japan, New Zealand, and the UN agencies. The World Bank and Asian Development Bank have provided assistance.

Reviews of aid programmes have questioned their effect in PNG. Hnanguie points out that since 1978, over 60 per cent of the World Bank and Asian Development Bank's projects were deemed to have failed. He attributes this to poor economic management and coordination by the PNG government.[284] Although consistent with poor aid effectiveness across the Pacific region, the

---

[276] Kwa (n 107) 58 fn 41.

[277] CRC/C/28/Add.20, State Report—Papua New Guinea (21 July 2003).

[278] Committee on the Elimination of Racial Discrimination, Concluding Observations—Papua New Guinea (26 February 2004) CRC/C/15/Add.229.

[279] ibid 68.   [280] CERD Summary Record (n 134) 12 (Mr de Gouttes).

[281] ibid 10.

[282] Danielle Heinecke, Brian Dollery, and Euan Fleming, 'The Samaritan's Dilemma: The Effectiveness of Australian Foreign Aid to Papua New Guinea' (2008) 62(1) *AJIA* 53–71 at 54.

[283] ibid 55.

[284] C. Hnanguie, Department of Finance: Economic Briefing Papers, 'The Future of Foreign Aid in Papua New Guinea After 25 Years of Successes or Failures?' (2005) available at <http://www.pngbuai.com> [last accessed 25 March 2009], quoted in ibid 58.

literature paints '... a bleak picture' of aid effectiveness in PNG, with aid acting as a disincentive to engage in public sector reform by funding too large a proportion of the PNG government's core service delivery responsibilities.[285] In their analysis of Australian aid to PNG, which has seen a 'steady poisoning' of the relationship between the two states over the lack of accountability for aid, Hanecke, Dollery, and Fleming state:

Australian aid... has operated on the assumption of 'trickle-down', with around 89 percent directly supporting national expenditure responsibilities and primarily delivered through national institutions. Often national institutions, which are the primary negotiators of aid, have targeted assistance for their own needs. For example, in the education sector, 94 percent of funding has supported national functions. Provincial and local level governments have historically only benefited through goods and services flowing from the national level.[286]

The authors highlight a new sub-national initiative for Australian aid, which directs a small percentage of aid expenditure to support reform in the provinces, bypassing the national government. Three pilot provinces will receive aid directly in their own budget framework, 'a move in the right direction'.[287]

Conclusion

There is extreme diversity in PNG, to the extent that technical assessments of its ethnic and linguistic groups have failed to come up with any reliable description. As a consequence, legal intervention in the form of rights-based tools cannot at present isolate individual ethnic or linguistic groups. Evidently, nomenclature of the past mingles with that of the present, and national and international anthropologists disagree as to format and degree of classification, rendering the identification of minority and indigenous groups confused and difficult. There is tension between national and international researchers, and an evident lack of consensus. Donigi's comments on the need for national researchers to 'prove' the contrary to what was written in the past by foreign anthropologists should be a serious cause for concern within the discipline.

The legal approach that is required is evidently a provincial or sub-provincial one. UNDP has identified gross imbalance in development between PNG's provinces, with the highest levels of development found in the Northern Coastal Region and in Gulf Province, and lowest ranking provinces being Southern Highlands, West Sepik, Gulf, and Enga. These lower-ranking provinces require urgent and more focused intervention. In terms of education, the significantly lower attendance and literacy levels in the underdeveloped provinces illustrate the need for a greater devolution of state resources to bring these areas into

---

[285] ibid 59.   [286] ibid 67.   [287] ibid.

line with the rest of the state. The example of the move towards reforming Australian aid packages with a greater regional and provincial investment correlates with UNDP analysis, that inequality in PNG is provincial.

From a national perspective, the customary ownership of land enjoys constitutional protection. Yet increasingly indigenous peoples are debarred from effective consultation in the development of their resources. While constitutional and legislative safeguards are important, the disputes over mining in Bougainville and Ok Tedi illustrate the fact that the PNG state, as a guardian of customary interest, has often failed in its role. The reality of black or grey markets is relevant. International standards stress the need for effective participation of indigenous peoples in decisions that affect them.

The current system appears to act as a bar against indigenous control over their resources. The state's constitutional history indicates that the intention is to provide PNG's ethnic and linguistic groups with the best possible levels of protection from exploitation. Ironically, this system is resulting in higher degrees of exploitation than would have taken place had the peoples concerned been afforded the means of negotiation.

Finally, PNG's legal system is a fascinating amalgamation of customary and common law. The land courts and various dispute resolution mechanisms are generating a corpus of customary law that will be of interest to national and international jurists. It remains a remarkable experiment in alternative legal resolution, and one which demands greater interest from the international community. The constitutional decree that the courts must find the underlying customary law is challenging. In tandem with resource development, the state must focus on effective participation, language protection, education development, and an overall higher degree of equality between the provinces. The courts should unearth the underlying law that can assist in balancing the need for development with the protection of the extraordinary ethnic, linguistic, and environmental heritage of the state.

Conclusion

In the Pacific, legal discourse has been largely restricted to the domestic rather than the international sphere owing to the inherently local nature of the issues covered by regulation. However comparative law can offer significant insights into legal conundrums. Material that takes a comparative approach usually examines how effectively legal systems in two or more settings operate, and draws inferences that may be applicable across jurisdictions. Australia and New Zealand have benefitted from such analyses, usually in comparison with common law jurisdictions such as the United States of America, the United Kingdom, and South Africa. In addition both states have eminent jurists that have published widely on various aspects of their domestic and international law.

There is scant knowledge as to the difficulties that exist in the legal infrastructure of the smaller, more numerous states that make up the Pacific. As we have sought to demonstrate in this volume, the Pacific states present models of law that are of particular interest to those who are designing legal policy or seeking to operate within these policies. The story of the peopling of the Pacific is in itself a fascinating one, and the evolution of law in this region can provide an important insight into the values of these states and their populations. The extent to which law can operate meaningfully against a backdrop of complex layers of identities, and contested territories and versions of history, is a persistent challenge. The following section sets out the findings of each of the chapters, with a view to understanding the general and particular challenges facing countries in the Pacific region.

The Pacific region is composed of the peoples of Polynesia, Melanesia, and Micronesia, terms coined by European explorers to delineate perceived ethnic markers. Debates around the origin of these peoples have occurred across many disciplines, notably biology, anthropology, archaeology, genetics, and linguistics. There is a paucity of reliable historical data, and contemporary accounts draw on technological advancements, particularly in genetics, to establish coherent narratives of Pacific migrations. Importantly, genetic research is pointing towards a complex admixture in which no overall theory is prevailing. The terms 'Polynesian', 'Melanesian', and 'Micronesian' are increasingly redundant, and remain useful only in the sense that they describe geographic regions rather than ethnic groups. It may be concluded that there is no 'Polynesian' people, but a sub-region, Polynesia, which can be marked on a map. The only characteristic common to all 'Melanesians' is their difference from each other. 'Micronesians' present a study in the technology of voyage rather than any coherent population group. All three geographic regions were almost certainly populated from Asia and display a remarkable array of diversity.

The diversity of the Pacific region has attracted generations of scholars, particularly anthropologists. A lively debate in anthropology has seen strong differences arise in how peoples should be studied, with indigenous anthropologists challenging the position of external researchers who had, until the 1960s, a monopoly in defining the diverse groups of their fields of research. Hence many states do not know the extent of their diversity, as nomenclature and identifying characteristics are constantly being changed and revised, by both external and internal researchers. It is interesting to see a process of identification of groups occurring in a reformed global climate, where greater sensitivity as to the complexity of diversity is being displayed. Contemporary anthropology is more attuned to the need for localized knowledge, and cooperation is growing between international and domestic researchers in order to advance the process of understanding the region's astounding array of ethnic and linguistic groups.

From an international perspective, the Pacific needs to engage further with the human rights regime. There is evidence of growing interest, emanating from the University of the South Pacific, LAWASIA, and other civic institutions, in moving towards a regional body of human rights protection. The debate has focused on the functions of this body and experts in the region agree that the primary focus of any regional body must be the engagement of the Pacific Island Countries in the international human rights system. The low levels of ratification of treaties and poor fulfilment of monitoring requirements means the region lags behind others, in congruity with low levels of socio-economic development. Human rights protection is essential for states to improve their standards, a fact not always acknowledged at governmental level. Therefore a regional body is desirable, perhaps necessary, with the aim of fostering greater participation in the international human rights system and working towards a binding regional charter that would apply to all states in the region. The first aim is paramount, for unless there is engagement in the international system, no effective regional system can be enacted without the danger of watering-down existing international protections.

Australia is emerging from a particularly challenging epoch in its relations with its minorities and indigenous peoples. The hope of reconciliation raised after the *Mabo* case was diminished as Australia embarked on active denial of the rights of indigenous Australians under John Howard. Aspirations for a treaty between the Howard government and the communities recognizing indigenous peoples as the first occupants of the land dissipated as the government retracted existing rights, which were already inadequate. Kevin Rudd's government has begun to revise the most disastrous aspects of the relationship with an apology to aboriginal nations for genocide, but the challenges ahead are manifold.

Sporadic bouts of violence against new immigrants continue, especially Asians and Muslims, and the previous government's harsh refugee policy needs urgent reform. The fundamental question at stake in Australia appears to be one of 'national identity'; what it consists of, how it is configured, and how it can be expressed in a modern multicultural society, dependent on regional neighbours.

The key to reconciliation between Australian settlers and the indigenous peoples lies in a resolution of the land rights issues. The *zero-sum* nature of that discourse has had an inordinate impact on the neglect of important social empowerment schemes. Meanwhile aboriginal life expectancy is twenty years lower than that of other Australians, and indigenous communities are over-represented in an array of social problems besetting the state. The viability of some of these communities are threatened by the disappearance of aboriginal languages, and the general difficulty of maintaining livelihoods in an ever more urbanized and modern society.

Although similar in many respects to Australia, New Zealand approaches indigenous and minority rights issues very differently. The fundamental cause for that difference is the ratification of the historic *Treaty of Waitangi* signed on 6 February 1840, at the Bay of Islands, New Zealand. The Treaty is considered a founding document for the state of New Zealand and is an agreement, in Maori and English, between the British Crown and about 540 Maori *rangatira* (chiefs). It set the tone for the settlement of New Zealand territories while recognizing and gaining the consent of the indigenous Maori community. As demonstrated, despite numerous problems of interpretation and subterfuge that have beset the Maori since the arrival of the first settlers, the Treaty established a relationship that allowed reconciliation to be pursued with clearly defined objectives.

In addition, New Zealand differs from Australia in the relative size and homogeneity of the Maori population, which accounts for close to 15 per cent of the total population of the state, along with a further 6.5 per cent Pacific Islanders. By comparison, Australia has significantly smaller numbers of indigenous people. The process of reconciliation, so wanting in Australia, is being advanced in New Zealand by the *Waitangi Tribunal* which was established specifically to address a range of issues concerning the settlement of New Zealand and its impact on the indigenous population. The Tribunal is not an unqualified success, and is making relatively slow progress—however it remains a positive institution.

The fundamental issue of land return or compensation is at the forefront of the negotiated settlement between the government and the Maori (with a governmental fiscal envelope of NZ$ 1,000 million), and many land claims remain outstanding with the reconciliation process expected to terminate by 2020. A recent move that arrested progress was the passage by the *New Zealand Parliament of the Foreshore and Seabed Act 2004* which denied Maori title to the foreshore and seabed. This galvanized Maori opposition, with the political party launched in its wake holding 4 of the 7 seats reserved for the Maori electorate in Parliament. Beyond land rights issues, Maori continue to face lower life expectancy and higher rates of unemployment, although the direction of the statistics would indicate the situation is improving.

It is easy to conceive of New Zealand as being bicultural, consisting of white settlers and the Maori. An overt policy accommodating the Maori has not been beneficial to other minorities. Pacific Islanders, numerically significant and sharing much of the 'indigenous' ethos of the Maori, have not benefited from similar targeted policies. To some extent, they, along with new migrant populations, have fallen victim to the perceived bicultural structure of the state of New Zealand. Pacific Islanders are disproportionately represented in unemployment statistics and are a higher proportion of the urban poor.

The social fabric of New Zealand has changed dramatically over the last two decades with Asian immigration. This has led to a degree of angst among the population, especially among unemployed youth who see newcomers as unfair competition for limited jobs. The fact that the government has been actively recruiting immigrants with particular qualifications means that often they go straight into good jobs. As a result there is some level of discontent reported towards Asian and particularly Muslim immigrants.

The case studies on Fiji and Papua New Guinea examine questions of conflicting identities in societies that have not always been stable, and where fundamental questions remain about the role and efficacy of law. After a period of significant strife, stability returned to Fiji in 2006 when the *Fijian Labour Party* took its place in a power sharing system with the ethnic Fijian *Soqosoqo Duavata ni Lewenivanua* party, along the principles of consociationalism established and applied in contexts such as Northern Ireland, Cyprus, and Lebanon. While this is a welcome development, the underlying tensions between indigenous Fijians and Indo-Fijians have not dissipated. The decline of the sugar industry can be viewed as exacerbating the deterioration in relations.

The land rights regime is fundamental to an understanding of the deeper issues and tensions underlying contemporary Fijian society. The failure to renew the leases of Indo-Fijian tenant farmers has increased the number of Indo-Fijians living in poverty. More recently tensions have been growing at the acquisition of wealth by recent immigrants from the Chinese mainland and other islanders. The draft *Peoples Charter for Change and Progress* offers an opportunity for the engagement of all interest groups in the construction of a more equitable and stable society. In the meantime stability in Fiji is reliant on vigilance from its neighbours, notably Australia and New Zealand.

Papua New Guinea is the most linguistically diverse state in the world, with over 840 languages in use. In comparison to other states in the region, Papua New Guinea is in the process of building a relatively coherent system of autonomy for the Bougainville minority in fulfilment of the conditions laid out for the implementation of the *Endeavour Peace Agreement*. This comprehensive agreement was signed by the government and the Bougainville Revolutionary Army in 2001. The Agreement set down a timetable for autonomy for the island, and in more recent years this saw the election of former rebel Joseph Kabui as President in the June 2005 elections. The threat of conflict is present in the state, in disputes between groups over land and property rights, and tensions attendant to large-scale migrations from the highlands to coastal areas in search of better economic prospects and development. The situation is further complicated by the flow of refugees from the Irian Jaya conflict in Indonesia, whose arrival has the tendency to inflame contests for resources.

There is an intriguing contrast between extreme ethnic and linguistic diversity in Papua New Guinea and its political success, as it counts itself the developing world's only consolidated democracy with a multiparty system. While ethnic conflict is present, it is not common, and PNG's myriad groups form a growing nation that seeks 'unity in diversity'. Problems stem from over-reliance on aid, in particular from Australia, and unequal distribution of resources between PNG's regions. In addition, United Nations Development Programme and other organizations point to growing socio-economic disparity between these regions. PNG is a battleground for the promotion of indigenous rights, as contests over control of the environment, land, resources, and traditional knowledge engage the concept of indigenous consent in decisions that affect them. The courts will play a crucial role in these future contests, as they follow the constitutional direction to 'find' the customary law that will allow an indigenous resolution to conflicts of rights.

In a comparative study of this nature we believe it is important to assess the intricate details of each legal system selected as case studies. The primary motivation for this lies in unearthing the specific sets of circumstances in which law has developed, and the nuances of the conflicts it has emerged to protect. However, it is equally important in a comparative context to be able to examine the primary issues that have arisen across the models examined. While there are several themes that have emerged from this study, not least the impact of the historical and contemporary movement of peoples, we have chosen to focus on four cross-cutting themes that arise in each of the case studies, to try and provide an insight into the manner in which the different states have addressed them. The themes selected are: (*a*) Land and Resources; (*b*) Political Participation; (*c*) Language, Education, and Religion; and (*d*) Customary Law.

The decision to focus on land and resources is evident from the substantive content of each of the chapters presented here. Irrespective of the models of governance adopted, the question of contested territory and resources is the main cause for conflict (physical or other) in the region. We have selected the issue of political participation in the belief that it remains the most fundamental of remedies if societies are to become inclusive. To us, each case demonstrated the extent to which the failure to consult and gain the consent of populations invalidated certain acts. Thus any remedy that would redress an imbalance in the legal system would necessarily have to begin with an attempt to include the various constituents of society. The issues of language, education, and religion are selected as being endogamous to the notion of minority or indigenous identity. The extent to which a state can provide protection for the promotion of identity is likely to be a benchmark against which its minority and indigenous protection can be measured. The need for such protections are likely to have ever greater salience as the peopling of the Pacific continues. The role of customary law has never been resolved, and continues to pose fundamental conflicts within law. In the more established states of Australia and New Zealand, these questions are subsumed within a common law regime with a colonial heritage. Yet In Fiji and Papua New Guinea, attempts to consolidate 'customary law' provide clear models of the dangers or difficulties inherent in such a process, as well as its potential success.

(a) Land and Resources

In Australia, the issue of indigenous sovereignty remains contested with the courts having played an ambiguous role. While initially upholding indigenous dispossession, the courts became a vehicle for eventual gains as symbolized by the *Mabo* judgment. The justiciability of indigenous sovereignty is under debate, and the adverse reaction to *Mabo* illustrates the vulnerability of judge-made law to political vagaries. It is difficult to escape the conclusion that indigenous activism in Australia suffers for lack of an institutional legal benchmark on title to territory, whether treaty-based or constitutional.

This is emphasized when contrasted with New Zealand, where land issues are filtered through the founding *Treaty of Waitangi*. The government of New Zealand has acknowledged the *prima facie* role of the Waitangi Tribunal in overseeing territorial disputes of this nature, and the Tribunal holds a macro function as the constitutional underpinning of Maori claims as well as a micro function in resolving detailed, individual cases. There are difficulties in its operation, such as the backlog of claims, the scale of compensation, and the skewing of rights towards better-organized, centralized tribes. However unlike Australia, the Treaty and Tribunal provide an immovable framework for the resolution of these problems. Waitangi acts as a benchmark from which a national discussion can take place, and below which no legislative act can fall. Allied with a strong Maori activist movement, the extensive case-law of the Tribunal is proving an impressive source of land rights jurisprudence.

Fiji is a curious instance of indigenous hegemony over title to territory. The claim of 'paramountcy' has been enforced to the extent that indigenous majority landownership, nearing 90 per cent, is uncontested by half of the state's inhabitants. Pointing to the example of the decimation of indigenous numbers in Australia and New Zealand as justification for an aggressive policy of indigenous Fijian land control, successive governments have reinforced the conviction that indigenous survival is premised on exclusive land title. Indo-Fijians were granted access to land, and the precarious balance was offset by rising socio-economic standards among that community. The current wave of dispossession of Indo-Fijian farmers, in line with repeated indigenous Fijian aims since independence, threatens the cohesion of the islands. Repeated coups add menace to the land question, and it remains difficult to engage in an open debate on rights and entitlements. There is also a lack of urgency on the part of the government to implement effective compensation for Indo-Fijian farmers.

In Papua New Guinea, the notion of customary landownership is enshrined in the constitution. Embarking on a remarkable project since independence, the courts are entrusted with seeking out the customary law of the state, in order to resolve questions of land disputes among the many ethnic and linguistic groups. The constitutional provisions were designed to protect what were considered to be vulnerable groups from dominant exploitative third parties. They were premised on the notion that the state was in the strongest position to negotiate with developers, and to exact proper compensation for use of PNG's resources. The flourishing black or grey market on land, in which the state is being bypassed by indigenous groups, is evidence that the government is not fulfilling its constitutional promise. Similarly the disjunction between the centre and the regions means that benefits from the land in the regions are too often absorbed by the state and disproportionately re-allocated from the centre. As indigenous rights grow and take root at the international level, the state needs to take greater account of the ability of indigenous peoples to decide how to exploit their resources. The Ok Tedi and Bougainville mines disputes starkly illustrate the need for effective consultation and a far greater input from the groups concerned. Failing this the state can be accused of paternalism, albeit motivated by an original altruistic motive.

Non-indigenous groups in the Pacific region are often ignored in the greater clash between indigenous and settler groups over land and resources. New migrants from Asia and other Pacific Islands are marginalized in a perceived continuing post-colonial rivalry over title to territory. These smaller groups must find a voice in a more nuanced discussion around sharing of resources and a movement towards *de facto* equality.

(b) Political Participation

Indigenous participation in Australian society has been stunted by the historical view of Aboriginals and Torres Strait Islanders as subjects rather than objects of law. While the question of indigenous self-governance remains open, currently participation broadly takes the form of indigenous involvement in decisions which affect them. Progress made in the 1970s towards nationwide indigenous representation was stalled in 2005, a reflection of a retrograde viewpoint that indigenous peoples in the state could not take responsibility for their own advancement. The move ignores the fact that indigenous governance is a reality in Australia, with the only relevant question being how the government chooses to recognize this. Commentators have highlighted the need to side-step issues of self-determination and sovereignty, to focus on potential remedies for governance under the existing federalist polity. Nevertheless self-determination and sovereignty remain powerful tools for rooting all such strategic claims to governance.

New Zealand offers a contrasting model in which indigenous participation is cemented in the Waitangi Tribunal and its rulings. The appointment of a Maori Chair of the Tribunal was a key turning point, confirming the dynamic nature of the institution, promoting confidence, and contributing to the extension of its mandate to cover violations post-1840. Effective participation in New Zealand is now evident, illustrated by the breadth and impact of its rulings in diverse areas, notably land, environmental, and customary rights.

Fiji presents a study in political manipulation by a ruling oligarchy, to the detriment of those outside its narrow interest range. The exclusion of the large Indo-Fijian minority, once a majority, is fixed through constitutional manipulation. Military coups have acted as a check against any attempt towards egalitarianism and a common roll, to the point where rival groups, notably but not exclusively the Indo-Fijians, have accepted their disproportionate share of power. Reconciliation is being policed by Australia and New Zealand, and cautious optimism surrounds initiatives such as the *Peoples Charter for Change and Progress*. Yet Fiji appears to be a society in which separation of peoples is accepted, with various spheres of domination mapped out for the two largest groups: indigenous Fijians dominate the military for example; while Indo-Fijians dominate the commercial sector. Such exclusive delineations are unsustainable in the long-term, and compromise is required if Fiji is to emerge as a model of pluralist participation. The 1997 Constitution remains an imperfect framework for Fiji's institutions. While it does not guarantee fair and full participation, the highly discriminatory 1990 Constitution serves as a warning that further reform may prompt a fall-back to more repressive means of control. There is benefit to all groups in supporting the 1997 Constitution, and the courts need to be vigilant, as illustrated in the *Prasad* judgment. Institutional reform will only follow a broader reconciliation between Fiji's communities.

Papua New Guinea's constitution, progressive and unique, has overseen a successful multiparty electoral system. Difficulties are evident, particularly in the focus of electoral representatives, who often fail to benefit anyone beyond their own narrow interest group. Yet PNG's difficulties do not lie in its levels of participation, but rather in the drastic need for development that benefits communities in all of its regions.

(c) Language, Education, and Religion

The threat to indigenous culture in Australia is represented by the disappearance of many aboriginal languages; of an estimated 200 languages, only 20 remain in active use. Educational initiatives need to stem from indigenous groups themselves, who have a stated interest in combining knowledge of their traditions, customs, and history with formal achievements for greater integration into the mainstream educational system.

In New Zealand the Waitangi Tribunal has engaged with language and education questions in its case-law, and in the *Mokai School* decision, the claimants emphasized: 'This isn't really just about education. This is about who we are. Our identity. This is about our whole being, our wairua, our tinana, our tikanga, our kawa...And it is time for us to stand up, as we are doing, and reclaim that'. While there have been significant provisions within the educational system for Maori knowledge, the overtly bicultural nature of the state is reflected in the failure to reflect the increasingly multicultural ethos of the state with regard to other minorities.

Fiji has historically had a troubled relationship with the creation of educational systems. Originally seen as the means by which community integration would be fostered, this hope foundered through lack of government oversight in education. The under-achievement in education by indigenous Fijians has been cause for extensive concern and numerous affirmative action provisions. Generally, the goal of an integrated education system is preferable, but commentators are sceptical as to whether this is achievable in the Fijian context. The present policy focuses on raising standards in indigenous Fijian schools, with the issue of religious education accused of distracting students from achieving success. By contrast, linguistic rights appear generally secure, although there is considerably less linguistic diversity in the state.

Papua New Guinea suffers from abysmal rates of literacy, which are disproportionately low in the outlying regions. Policies protecting linguistic rights are precarious, and largely conducted by non-governmental bodies, in particular the Summer Institute of Linguistics. Given that Papua New Guinea represents the world's linguistic heritage, far greater domestic and international support for this crucial civil society work is needed.

Fiji and Papua New Guinea, like the states across the region, are largely Christian, although there are significant religious minorities. Little is known as to the exact nature of Pacific Christianity, with gaps in particular on the co-existence of traditional notions of spirituality alongside formal Christian teachings. Anthropologists have conducted some investigation, but leading writers consider this to be inadequate. Fiji's Hindu and Muslim populations need greater protection for their temples and mosques, and a spate of attacks, questionably attributed to motives of larceny, underline the vulnerability felt by the Indo-Fijian population in the state. The 'religious' conflict is clearly a manifestation of the wider conflict between the indigenous and Indo-Fijians. The government has indicated an unwillingness to accept that such attacks are racially and religiously motivated, despite clear evidence. Religious tolerance is an essential feature of any stable society, and the extent to which it becomes a priority in Fiji will probably reflect the enhanced possibility of peace and mutual co-existence between the communities.

(d) Customary Law

The issue of the role of customary law and its potential as a *sui generis* system of governance arises in a range of countries across the Pacific. Of the four states under review only Papua New Guinea has established a formal requirement for seeking out the customary law of the state, placing this obligation on the courts through a constitutional provision. In this regard, common law applies until the courts have established a customary provision to the contrary. The resultant view is that the privilege of common law is considered temporary. The difficult nature of customary law has been analysed in the context of the four case studies, with advocates generally emphasizing the dangers inherent in the codification of customary law. Customary law is, by its nature, transient, flexible, and changing, and an evolving source of rights and obligations. Any attempt to integrate customary law into existing systems would need to take account of its fluidity and be aware of the perennial vigilance required on the part of adjudicators. Yet Papua New Guinea represents an example of how such an ostensibly complicated system can be tackled, and the dynamic nature of conflict resolution in the state, whether over land, resources, or related issues, is an example for other states in the region that may increasingly seek to unearth customary law rules. Such a regime will inevitably be problematic and all customary law provisions ought to be underscored by minimum human rights standards, so that decisions of customary courts could not conflict with international protections.

*

The book has sought to characterize the Pacific as a region of important minority and indigenous rights progression. The four case studies have highlighted the need for specialization, in the sense that each state in the study has its own problems generated by the history of engagement between its indigenous, settler, and migrant peoples. The influence of Europe has waned and Asian powers are establishing their dominance in the region. The change in ethos is reflected in the manner in which the communities engage in the global economy, especially since the newer migrant populations share kinship with the rising economic superpowers. The question of how all groups can engage in the future state-building process is vital.

The colonial period swept away thousands of years of settlement, law, and custom, and the imposition of common law standards have too often ignored the pre-colonial achievements of the Pacific peoples. Independence in the Pacific Islands has not led to wide-scale reform, with many governments continuing the exploitative system constructed by the colonists through inherited social, legal, and political machinery. Enhanced regional cooperation would assist in enacting common standards for development. The protection of indigenous and minority communities and their advancement in terms of equality with established groups is crucial if the region is to fulfil its potential and move closer to the harmonious ideal, so often portrayed as symbolic of Pacific culture.

As a final analysis, we would like to pose five questions and offer some thoughts designed to generate further debate:

a. What is the object and purpose of minority and indigenous rights law in the Pacific states?
b. What are the tensions between minority and indigenous rights law and human rights law?
c. What is the role for law in the creation of standards for minority and indigenous protection and promotion?
d. In what way could it be asserted that global minority and indigenous rights principles have been applied in the region?
e. What can the Pacific teach the world about minority and indigenous rights protection?

First, the object and purpose of minority and indigenous rights law as applied in domestic regimes ought to be the realization of the rights of every single individual and community. Our rationale for a focus on minority and indigenous peoples lies in assessing the impact of law and rights realization against individuals and groups that are excluded. The underlying premise of human rights is to provide a vehicle through which the rights and inherent dignity of every human being are realized. Yet minorities and indigenous peoples lag behind majorities in nearly every domestic context. In the Pacific, this fundamental principle of human rights protection is best seen in New Zealand, and not always coherently applied elsewhere. In Australia, indigenous peoples have historically been excluded and there appears to have been a conscious decision under the Howard regime to dismiss the question of indigenous rights as additional, unearned entitlements. In Fiji, the notion of 'indigenous' and 'minority' have seen a continuing clash between the two largest groups in the state while the notion of paramountcy over land rights has raised difficult questions. In Papua New Guinea, the difficulty in identification of specific groups in a state of such diversity has meant that indigenous rights and customary law are generally applied.

On the other hand, our study of the states in this region has demonstrated examples of where human rights and indigenous and minority rights could clash. In other regions and contexts, this question would usually involve the extent to which cultural practices, engaged upon as vestiges of minority or indigenous identity, conflict with human rights principles (often in the specific context of women's rights). However in the Pacific region, the conflicts lie much deeper to the extent to which a system of laws, even based on human rights, can be imposed upon societies with ancient traditions and systems. Could human rights law be a new panacea for socio-legal issues in the manner that common law sought to be? If so, could it not be considered equally colonial in guise and might it not further undermine the cultural rights of indigenous peoples that may prefer to return to their customs and traditions?

These questions are particularly relevant since human rights law may provide avenues towards achieving the realization of cultural law through mechanisms of restorative justice. It is questions such as these that led Kingsbury to argue that a basis for indigenous rights was the existence of a *sui generis* category of law. While not advocating this position, this volume has demonstrated that tensions exist when well-meaning attempts are made to 'shoehorn' indigenous peoples and minorities into systems that are not designed with their particular nuances in mind.

This conclusion links to the third question about the efficacy of law as a vehicle for the promotion and protection of indigenous and minority rights in the Pacific. While the book has assessed alternative means of protection, a pragmatic analysis must accept the existence of human rights law and the established common law systems. Customary legal models may be unearthed and may subsequently be regarded as adequate for attempting to understand other analogous situations. Such work assumes that law is an important vehicle in addressing societal injustices. However, law is only one part of this equation and other measures through education and inclusion can be more appropriate. Law is a means through which society can establish just parameters, offering the quest for social justice a strong grounding in the design of future protection and adequate remedies for past violations.

The final question of what the Pacific states can teach the rest of the world is an important one. The two outstanding examples of the particularities of the Pacific relevant beyond its geographic parameters are the reconciliation process in New Zealand, arguably the most progressive of its type anywhere in the world, and the attempt in Papua New Guinea to arrive at a stable understanding of the notion of customary law and how it can play a role in contemporary society. Both of these examples address questions that are relevant across the globe.

In many societies, including Australia, the questions over reconciliation are in their infancy. In other parts of the world fledgling attempts at reconciliation have foundered on the shores of political uncertainty. If South Africa is a model for Truth and Reconciliation processes, New Zealand provides an equally compelling model of a specific body created by statute with the power to address individual and collective grievances, make awards, and address concrete policy recommendations to the government of the day. The Waitangi Tribunal is testimony to the maturity of New Zealand's desire to address this controversial issue. The fact that its findings are widely accepted both by the public and the government is an indicator of the nature of commitment required for such processes to be real. It continues to face difficulties, but this is a manifestation of the scale of its mandate.

The discussion of customary law in Papua New Guinea, and to a lesser extent in New Zealand, Fiji, and Australia, is a particularly rich one that many Asian and African states are yet to embark upon. Unlike Papua New Guinea, most states appear to have accepted the efficacy of colonial law, seeking to modify it to the exigencies of the post-colonial state. Yet colonial law was not imposed in a vacuum and this inevitably brings customary legal systems (traditional law) into direct conflict with it. The significant advantages of the existence of codified national law, although based on older colonial models, means that it is inevitable that it will trump more amorphous traditional legal systems. Yet such law could deny the very basis of indigenous identities, calling into question the extent to which 'self-determination' has been truly achieved. Papua New Guinea's solution is to charge the courts with finding customary law, accepting that common law is to apply in the interim by default. It is a fascinating constitutional project that should engender lessons for other states wrestling with similar conflicts. Overall in taking on the role of customary law with all its attendant difficulties, each of the Pacific States examined in this book provide an insight that may be useful in other contexts.

A final word needs to be reserved for emphasizing the importance of every part of the globe in the context of the study of law in general, and the focus on human rights in particular. Pacific Island Countries may be on the periphery on physical world maps but they ought not to be neglected for this reason. Their geographic isolation and limited possibilities for participation in the global economy mean it is even more important that the international community engages in human rights issues that arise in these states, as in other parts of the world. The continued movement of peoples is creating heightened tensions that need to be addressed. The Pacific states provide an example of how law has to struggle to ensure that the 'old' indigenous groups, and the 'new' minorities, can see their rights realized alongside majoritarian and other dominant populations.

Bibliography

'Australian Government Response to the UNCERD Request for Information under Article 9(1) of the ICERD' (9 July 1999)

[editorial] 'Australia Ships out Afghan Refugees' *BBC Asia Pacific Desk* (3 September 2001) <http://news.bbc.co.uk/1/hi/world/asia-pacific/1522723.stm> [last accessed 25 March 2009]

[editorial] 'Call in Fiji to Make Penalty for Temple Attacks equivalent to Murder' *Radio New Zealand Intl* (13 September 2006) transcript available at: <http://www.rnzi.com/pages/news.php?op=read&id=26778> [last accessed 25 March 2009]

[editorial] 'CoAG: A Black Hole of Government Approach' *National Indigenous Times* (10 November 2005) available at <http://www.nit.com.au/Opinion/story.aspx?id=7223> [last accessed 25 March 2009]

[editorial] 'Court Could Consign Fiji to *Apartheid*' *The Guardian* (19 February 2001) available at <http://www.guardian.co.uk/fiji/article/0,,439915,00.html>

[editorial] 'Embassy: We Do Not Condone Crime' *Fiji Times* (21 January 2008) available at <http://www.fijitimes.com/story.aspx?id=79194> [last accessed 25 March 2009]

[editorial] 'Emergency Rule declared in Fiji' *BBC News* (7 September 2007) available at <http://news.bbc.co.uk/1/hi/world/asia-pacific/6981381.stm> [last accessed 25 March 2009]

[editorial] 'Fiji Human Rights Commission suspended from International Body' *Radio New Zealand Intl* (2 April 2007) available from <http://www.rnzi.com/pages/news.php?op=read&id=31209> [last accessed 25 March 2009]

[editorial] 'Fiji Opposition Leader Says Racial Discrimination Will Remain Unless Education Given Priority' *Radio New Zealand Intl* (14 July 2006) transcript available at <http://www.rnzi.com/pages/news.php?op=read&id=25421> [last accessed 25 March 2009]

[editorial] 'Fiji Prime Minister Sacked' *BBC News* (27 May 2000) available at <http://news.bbc.co.uk/1/hi/world/asia-pacific/766221.stm> [last accessed 25 March 2009]

[editorial] 'Fiji's History of Coups', *The Guardian* (5 December 2006) available at <http://www.guardian.co.uk/world/2006/dec/05/fiji.travel1> [last accessed 25 March 2009]

[editorial] 'Hindus Called into Emergency Meeting after Further Temple Attacks in Fiji' *Radio New Zealand Intl* (8 September 2006) transcript available at <http://www.rnzi.com/pages/news.php?op=read&id=26858> [last accessed 25 March 2009]

[editorial] Review Article in (1998) *21(3) UNSWLJ* (1998) 947–50

[editorial] 'Shameless in Fiji' *The Economist* (1 December 1990) 34

[editorial] 'The Biodiversity Convention: The Concerns of Indigenous Peoples' [1996] AILR 84

[editorial] 'Thunderous applause in Sydney for Rudd's speech', *Australian Associated Press, Sydney Morning Herald* (13 February 2008)

[editorial] 'UN Seminar Highlights Concern in Fiji over Ethnic Segregation' *Radio New Zealand Intl* (9 April 2006). Full interview available at <http://www.rnzi.com/pages/news.php?op=read&id=23319> [last accessed 28 June 2009]

[editors] *Historical Records of Australia* vol VII, July 1813—December 1815, Library Committee of Commonwealth Parliament, 1916

[editors] 'Instructions to Governor Philip', *HRNSW* (23 April 1787) Vol 1 (2) 52

[various editors] *Rangahaua Whanui National Overview* [Research report published in three volumes in 1997, Wellington]

Abel, S., *Shaping the News: Waitangi Day on Television* (Auckland: Auckland University Press, 1997)

Ahai, N., 'Literacy in an Emergent Society: Papua New Guinea' (Summer Institute of Linguistics Working Papers, 2005) available at <http://www.sil.org/silewp/2005/silewp2005-002.pdf> [last accessed 5 August 2008]

Aiers, D.P., Foreign and Commonwealth Office South West Pacific Department, 'Discussions on Fiji at the United Nations' FCO 58/493 (5 January 1970)

Alexandrowicz, C.H., *The European-African Confrontation* (Leiden: A.W. Sijthoff, 1973)

Alfred, T., *Peace, Power, Righteousness: An Indigenous Manifesto* (New York: Oxford University Press, 1999)

Alston, P., and Crawford, J. (eds), *The Future of UN Human Rights Treaty-monitoring* (Cambridge: Cambridge University Press, 2000)

Alves, D., *The Maori and the Crown: An Indigenous People's Struggle for Self-Determination* (Westport, Connecticut/London: Greenwood Press, 1999)

Angelo, A.H., and Townsend, A., 'Pitcairn: A Contemporary Comment' (2003) *1 NZJPIL* 233–51

Aroney N., *Freedom of Speech in the Constitution* (Australia: The Centre for Independence Studies, Policy Monograph 40, 1998)

Asher, G., 'Planning for Maori Land and Traditional Maori Uses' (1982) *65 TPQ*

Attwood B., *Telling the Truth about Aboriginal History* (Crow's Nest, NSW: Allen & Unwin, 2005)

Attwood B., and Markus, A., *The Struggle for Aboriginal Rights: A Documentary History* (St. Leonards, NSW: Allen & Unwin, 1999)

Attwood B., and Markus A., *The 1967 Referendum: Race, Power and the Australian Constitution* (Canberra: Aboriginal Studies Press, 2007)

Baleinakorodawa, P., 'Minority Rights in Fiji' (Citizens' Constitutional Forum, 2007) <http://www.ccf.org.fj/confrence/GROUP%20AND%20MINORITY%20RIGHTS.pdf> [last accessed 6 August 2008]

Ballara, A., *Iwi: The Dynamics of Maori Tribal Organisation from c. 1769 to c. 1945* (Wellington: Victoria University Press, 1998)

Bann, P., 'Customary Adoption in Torres Strait Islands; Towards Legal Recognition *3(66) ALB* (1994) 8

Banner, S., 'Conquest by Contract: Wealth Transfer and Land Market Structure in Colonial New Zealand' (2000) *34 LSR* 47–71

Banton, M., *International Action Against Racial Discrimination* (Oxford: Oxford University Press, 1996)

Barker, A., *What Happened When: A Chronology of Australia from 1788* (St. Leonard's NSW: Allen & Unwin 2000)

Barker, J. (ed), *Christianity in Oceania: Ethnographic Perspectives* (Lanham: ASAO Monographs 12, 1990)

Barkin, J.S., and Cronin, B., 'The State & the Nation: Changing Norms and the Rules of Sovereignty in International Relations' 48(1) *Intl Organization* 107–30

Barnard, M., *A History of Australia* (New York: Frederick A. Praeger, 1963)

Barnett, T.E., 'Law and Justice Melanesian style', in A.I. Clunies-Ross, and J. Langmore (eds), *Alternative Strategies for Papua New Guinea* (Melbourne, 1973) 153

Barnsey, H., 'Protecting the Environment: A Trans-Tasman Synergy' (2003) 28 *NZIR*

Barr, K.J., 'Squatters in Fiji—The Need for an Attitudinal Change' (2007) *CCF Housing and Social Exclusion Policy* 18

Barsh, R.L., 'Indigenous Peoples in the 1990s: From Object to Subject in International Law?' in 7 *HHRJ* (1994) 33–62

Barume, A.K., 'Indigenous Battling for Land Rights: The Case of the Ogiek of Kenya' in J. Castellino and N. Walsh (eds), *International Law & Indigenous Peoples* 365–91 (Leiden/Boston: Martinus Nijhoff, 2005)

Basawaiya, N., 'Indigenous Renascence: Law, Culture and Society in the 21st Century: Status of Indigenous Rights in Fiji' (1997) 10 *STLR* 197

Beaglehole, J.C. (ed), *The Journals of Captain James Cook* (Cambridge: Cambridge University Press, 1974)

Bekker, P., 'Recent Developments at the World Court: ICJ Dismisses New Zealand's Request to Reopen Nuclear Tests Case' (1995) *ASILN*

Belgrave, M. (ed), *The Recognition of Aboriginal Tenure in New Zealand, 1840–1860* (WAI 45/G4) (Wellington: Waitangi Tribunal, 1987)

Belich, J., *Making Peoples: A History of the New Zealanders from Polynesian Settlement to the End of the Nineteenth Century* (Auckland: Penguin Books, 1996)

Bello, J., 'International Decision: New Zealand Challenge to Underground Testing by France in South Pacific', (1996) 90 *AJIL* 280–6

Belshaw, C.S., *Island Administration In The South West Pacific: Government And Reconstruction In New Caledonia, The New Hebrides, And The British Solomon Islands* (London: Royal Institute Of International Affairs, 1950)

Beltran, J. *et al*, *Indigenous & Traditional Peoples and protected Areas: Guidelines and Case Studies* (WCPA and IUCN, Gland Publishers, 2000)

Berman, A., '1998 and Beyond in New Caledonia: At Freedom's Gate?' (1998) 7(1) *PRLPJ* 1–76

Berman, A., 'Future Kanak Independence in New Caledonia: Illusion or Reality?' (1998) 34 *SJIL* 287–346

Berman, A., 'The Noumea Accords: Emancipation or Colonial Harness?' (2001) 36 *TILJ* 277–97

Bhikhu Parekh, *Rethinking Multiculturalism: Cultural Diversity and Political Theory* (Basingstoke: Palgrave Macmillan, 2006)

Billson, B., 'Australia and New Zealand: A Shared Purpose in the Pacific' (2006) 31 *NZIR*

Binney, J., 'The Native Land Court and the Maori Communities, 1865–1890' in Judith Binney, Judith Basset, and Erik Olssen (eds), *The People and the Land* (Wellington: Allen & Unwin, 1990) 143–64

Blackstone, W., 1 *Commentaries on the Laws of England* (London: Legal Classics Library, 1983)

Blank, P., 'The Pacific: A Mediterranean in the Making?' (1999) 89 (2) *OC* 265–77

Boast, R.P., 'The Treaty of Waitangi; A Framework for Resource Management Law' (1989) 19 *VUWLR* 1–68

Bobroff, K.H., 'Retelling Allotment; Indian Property Rights and the Myth of Common Ownership' in 54 *VLR* (2001) 1571

Booking, T., 'The Waitangi Tribunal and New Zealand History' (2006) 68 *The Historian*. Also see the official website of the Waitangi Tribunal available at <http://www. waitangi-tribunal.govt.nz/> [last accessed 6 August 2008]

Booth, A., 'Development Challenges in a Poor Pacific Economy: The Case of Papua New Guinea' (1995) 68(2) *PA* 207–30

Borrie, W.D., *Immigration to New Zealand: 1854–1938* (Canberra: Highland Press, 1991)

Bourassa, S.C., and Strong, A.L., 'Restitution of Property to Indigenous People: The New Zealand Experience' (Working Paper No 7, Auckland: Real Estate Research Unit, University of Auckland, 1998)

Bourassa S.C., and Strong, A.L., 'Restitution of Fishing Rights to Maori: Representation, Social Justice and Community Development' (August 2000) 41 (2) *APV* 155–75

Bourassa, S.C., and Strong, A.L., 'Restitution of Land to New Zealand Maori: The Role of Social Structure' (2002) 75 (2) *PA* 227–60

Boutilier, J., 'Papua New Guinea's Century: Reflections on Imperialism, Accommodation and Historical Consciousness' in Deborah Gewertz and Edward Schieffelin (eds), *History and Ethnohistory in Papua New Guinea* (Sydney: Oceania Monographs, 1985) 7–26

Bravo, K.E., 'Balancing indigenous Rights to Land and the Demands of Economic Development: Lessons from the United States and Australia' in 30 *Columbia J of L & Social Problems* (1996–1997) 529–86

Brett, J., *The Australian Liberals and the Moral Middle Class: From Alfred Deakin to John Howard* (Cambridge: Cambridge University Press, 2003)

Bringing Them Hope: The Report available at <http://www.austlii.edu.au/au/special/ rsjproject/rsjlibrary/hreoc/stolen/stolen62.html>

Brookfield, F. M., 'Sovereignty: The Treaty, the Courts and the Tribunal' [1989] *NZ Rec L Rev* 292–8

Brookfield, F. M., 'The Treaty of Waitangi, the Constitution and the Future' (1995) 8 *BRNZS* 4–20

Broome, R., *Aboriginal Australians* (2nd edn. Sydney: Allen & Unwin, 1994)

Broome, R., *Aboriginal Australians: Black Responses to White Dominance, 1788–2001* (Crow's Nest, NSW: Allen & Unwin 2002)

Brown, K., and Care, J.C., 'Conflict in Melanesia: Customary Law and the Rights of Women' (1998) 24 *CLB* 1334–55

Brownlie, I., *Treaties and Indigenous Peoples* (Oxford: Clarendon Press, 1992)

Brunton, B., 'Human Rights in Papua New Guinea and the Prospects for International Supervision' (1980) 8 *MLJ* 143–57

Buchheit, L.C., *Secession: The Legitimacy of Self-Determination* (New Haven: Yale University Press 1978)

Buddle, T., *The Maori King Movement in New Zealand* (Auckland: 'New Zealander' Office, 1860) (reprinted by AMS Press, New York 1979)

Burke-White, W., 'Reframing Impunity: Applying Liberal International Law Theory to an analysis of Amnesty Legislation' (2001) 42 *HILJ* 497

Busby, J., *The Pre-emption Land Question* (Auckland: Richardson and Sansom Publishers, 1859)

Buschmann, R., 'Oceans of World History: Delineating Aquacentric Notions in the Global Past' (2004) 2 (1) *HC* 1–10

Bush, J., 'Defining Group Rights and Delineating Sovereignty' (1999) 14 *AUILR* 737

Byers, M., *Custom, Power and the Power of Rules: International Relations and Customary International Law* (Cambridge: Cambridge University Press, 1999)

Cain, T.N., 'Convergence or Clash—The Recognition of Customary Law and Practice in Sentencing Decisions of the Courts of the Pacific Island Region' (2001) 2 *MJIL* 48–68

Caldwell, J.L., 'Judicial Sovereignty' 11 *NZLJ* (1984) 357–9

Campbell, I.C., *A History of the Pacific Islands* (Christchurch: University of Canterbury Press, 1989)

Capotorti, F., UN doc E/CN.4/Sub.2/384/Add.1–7 (1977)

Care, J.C., 'Bedrock and Steel Blues: Finding the Law Applicable in Vanuatu' (1998) 24 *CLB* 594–612

Carens, J., 'Democracy and Respect for Difference: The Case of Fiji' (1992) 25 *UMJLR* 562

Carol, A., *Maori Sovereignty: The Pakeha Perspective* (Auckland: Hodder Moa Beckett, 1995)

Casey, R.G., *Australia's Place in the World* (Melbourne, 1931)

Cassese, A., *Self-Determination of Peoples, A Legal Reappraisal* (Cambridge: Cambridge University Press, 1995)

Castellino, J., 'National Identity & the International Law of Self-determination: The Stratification of the Western Saharan "Self"' in Stephen Tierney (ed), *Accommodating National Identity: New Approaches in International and Domestic Law* (The Hague: Kluwer Law International, 2000) 257–84

Castellino, J., 'Affirmative Action for the Protection of Linguistic Rights: An Analysis of International Human Rights Legal Standards in the Context of the Irish Language' (2004) 25 *DULJ* 1–43

Castellino, J., 'Conceptual Difficulties and the Right to Indigenous Self-Determination' in Nazila Ghanea, and Alexandra Xanthaki (eds), *Minorities, Peoples and Self-Determination: Essays in Honour of Patrick Thornberry* (Leiden/Boston: Martinus Nijhoff, 2005) 55–74

Castellino, J., 'A Re-Examination of the International Convention for the Elimination of All Forms of Racial Discrimination' (2006) 2 *RIDH* 1–29

Castellino, J., 'Drink Ban for Australian Aboriginals: Paternalistic Determinations for a 'Sub-Human Race'?' 25 July 2007, *American Chronicle* available at <http://www.americanchronicle.com/articles/30579> [last accessed 2 April 2008]

Castellino, J., 'Territorial Integrity and the "Right" To Self-determination: An Examination of the Conceptual Tools' in 33(2) *BJIL* (2008) 1–65

Castellino, J., and Allen, S., *Title to Territory in International Law: An Inter-temporal Analysis* (Dartmouth: Ashgate, 2003)

Castellino, J., and Gilbert, J., 'Self-determination, Indigenous Peoples and Minorities' (2003) 3 *MQLJ* [Special Issue: Self-determination] 155–78

Castellino, J., and Walsh, N. (eds), *International Law and Indigenous Peoples* (Leiden/Boston: Martinus Nijhoff, 2005)

Castellino, J., and Domínguez Redondo, E., *Minority Rights in Asia: A Comparative Legal Analysis* (Oxford: Oxford University Press, 2006)

CERD—*Concluding Observations*, New Zealand, UN doc CERD/C/NZL/CO/17 (15 August 2007)

Challis, A.D., *Motueka: An Archaeological Survey* (Auckland: Longman Paul, 1978)

Chalmers, D., 'Human Rights and what is Reasonably Justifiable in a Democratic Society' (1975) 1 *MLJ* 92–102

Chalmers D., and Paliwala, A., *An Introduction to the Law in Papua New Guinea* (Sydney: The Law Book Company, 1984)

Chamerovzow, L.A., *The New Zealand Question and the Rights of Aborigines* (London: T.C. Newby, 1848)

Chand, G. (ed), *Papers on Racial Discrimination* (Vols I and II) (Lautoka, Fiji: Fiji Institute of Applied Studies, 2005)

Chanwai, K., and Richardson, B., 'Re-working Indigenous Customary Rights? The Case of Introduced Species' (1998) 2 *NZJEL* 157–86

Charney, J., 'The Persistent Objector Rule and the Development of Customary International Law' (1985) 56 *BYIL* 1

Charters, C., and Erueti, A., 'Report from the Inside: The CERD Committee's review of the Foreshore and Seabed Act 2004' (2005) 36 *VUWLR* 257–90

Chowdry, M., and Mitchell, M., 'Responding to Historic Wrongs: Practical and Theoretical Problems' in 27(2) *OJLS* (2007) 339–54

Clark, C.M.H., *A History of Australia: From the Earliest Times to the Age of Macquarie* (Melbourne: Melbourne University Press, 1962)

Clark, R.S., 'Humanitarian Intervention: Help to Your Friends and State Practice' (1983) 13 *GJICL* 211–16

Clarke, F.G., *The History of Australia* (Westport, CT: Greenwood Press, 2002)

Clarke, P., *Where the Ancestors Walked: Australia as an Aboriginal Landscape* (Crow's Nest, NSW: Allen & Unwin, 2003)

Coates, K.S., and McHugh, P.G. (eds), *Living Relationships Kokiri Ngatahi: The Treaty of Waitangi in the New Millennium* (Wellington: Victoria University Press, 1998)

Cocks, D., *People policy: Population Choices* (Sydney: University of New South Wales Press, 1996)

Colebatch, H.K., *Beyond the Policy Cycle: The Policy Process in Australia* (Sydney: Allen & Unwin, 2006)

Connell, J., *Papua New Guinea: The Struggle for Development* (London/New York: Routledge, 1997)

Connolly, W., *The Ethos of Pluralization* (Minneapolis: University of Minnesota Press, 1995)

Cornell, S., Goodswimmer, C., and Jorgensen, M., 'In Pursuit of Capable Governance: a Report to the Lheidli T'enneh First Nation' (Arizona: Native Nations Institute for Leadership, 2004) available at <http://www.fngovernance.org/pdf/LTReportFinal.pdf> [last accessed 25 March 2009]

Coulter, J., *The Drama of Fiji: A Contemporary History* (Tokyo: Charles Tuttle, 1967)

Cowdery, N., *Getting Justice Wrong: Myths, Media and Crime* (St. Leonard's, Allen & Unwin, 2001)

Cowlishaw, G., *Rednecks, Eggheads, and Blackfellas: A Study of Racial Power and Intimacy in Australia* (Sydney: Allen & Unwin, 1999)

Crengle, D.L., *Indigenous Peoples and Sustainability: Cases and Actions* (Washington: IUCN Inter-Commission Task Force on Indigenous Peoples, 1997) 339–52

Crocombe, R., *The South Pacific: An Introduction* (Auckland: Longman Paul, 1987)

Crowley, T., *Beach-la-Mar to Bislama: The Emergence of a National Language in Vanuatu* (Oxford: Clarendon Press, 1990)

Cunneen, C., *Conflict, Politics and Crime: Aboriginal Communities and the Police* (Crow's Nest, NSW: Allen & Unwin, 2001)

Curthoys, A., *Freedom Ride: A Freedom Rider Remembers* (Sydney: Allen & Unwin, 2002)

Custos, D., 'New Caledonia, a Case of Shared Sovereignty within the French Republic: Appearance or Reality?' (2007) 13(1) *EPL* 97–132

Dafler, J.R., 'Social Darwinism and the Language of Racial Oppression: Australia's Stolen Generations' *A Review of General Semantics*, Vol 62, (2005)

Darcy, S., *Collective Responsibility and Accountability under International Law* (Leiden: Brill NV, 2007)

David, K., 'Self-Determination and Constitutional Change' (2000–2003) 9 *AULR* 235–47

Davis, M., 'Indigenous Peoples and Intellectual Property Rights' (Research Paper No 20, Australian Parliamentary Library, 1997)

Davis, M., 'Law, Anthropology, and the Recognition of Indigenous Cultural Systems' in (2001) *Law and Anthropology* 11, 306

Deklin, T., 'Strogim Hiumen Raits: A Proposal for a Regional Human Rights Charter and Commission for the Pacific' (1992) 20 *MLR* 93–106

Derrick, R., *A History of Fiji* (Suva, Fiji: Printing and Stationery Department, 1946)

Diamond, J.M., *Guns, Germs and Steel: The Fates of Human Societies* (New York: W.W. Norton, 1997)

Diamond, L., Linz J., and Lipset, S., 'Introduction: What Makes a Democracy?' in Larry Diamond, Juan Linz, and Seymour Lipset (eds), *Politics in Developing Countries: Comparing Experiences with Democracy* (Boulder: Lynne Rienner, 1995) 35

Dixon, K., 'Working with Mixed Commons/Anticommons Property: Mobilizing Customary Land in Papua New Guinea the Melanesian Way' (2007) 31 *HELR* 219–77

Docker, J., and Fischer, G., *Race, Colour and Identity in Australia and New Zealand* (NSW: University of New South Wales Press, 2000)

Dodson, M., 'Statement on Behalf of the Northern Land Council' in The Australian Contribution: UN Working Group on Indigenous Populations (Geneva: Xth session, July 1992 at 35)

Dodson, M., 'From Lore to Law: Indigenous Rights and Australian Legal Systems' (February 1995) *ALB* 2.

Dodson, M., and Strelein, L., 'Australia's Nation-Building: Renegotiating the Relationship between Indigenous Peoples and the State' (2001) 24 *UNSWLJ* 826–40

Domínguez Redondo, E., 'Vulnerability and the Principle of Non-Discrimination' presented at the *EU-China Experts Network Meeting*, Beijing, 9 November 2003. Hard copy available with the author

Donigi, P., *Indigenous or Aboriginal Rights to Property: A Papua New Guinea Perspective* (Utrecht: International Books, 1994)

Dorney, S., *Papua New Guinea* (NSW: Random House, 1990)

Dorsett S., 'Civilisation and Cultivation: Colonial Policy and Indigenous Peoples in Canada and Australia' in 4(2) *GLR* (1995) 214–38

Douglas, B.C., Kearney, M.S., and Leatherman, S.P. (eds), *Sea-Level Rise: History & Consequences* (San Diego: Academic Press, 2001)

Dugdale, S., 'Chronicles Of Evasion: Negotiating Pakeha New Zealand Identity' in Docker, J., and Fischer, G. (eds) *Race, Colour and Identity in Australia and New Zealand* (NSW: University of New South Wales Press, 2000) 190–202

Dunne, J., Interview with Rt Hon Helen Clark, Prime Minister (Breakfast Show TRN 3ZB) (14 March 2005)

Durie, M.H., *Te Mana Kawanatanga: The Politics of Maori Self-Determination* (Auckland: Oxford University Press, 1998)

Eastwood, E., and Miller, F., 'Asia' in *State of the World's Minorities 2008* (London: Minority Rights Group International, 2008) 127

Edgeworth, B., 'Tenure, Allodialism, and Indigenous Rights at Common Law: English, United States, and Australian Law Compared After Mabo v. Queensland' in 23 *AALR* (1994) 397

Ehrlich, C.E., 'Democratic Alternatives to Ethnic Conflict: Consociationalism and Neo-Separatism' (2000–2001) 26 *BJIL* 447

Evatt, E., *Review of the Aboriginal and Torres Strait Islander Heritage Protection Act 1984*, (Canberra: Commonwealth of Australia, 1996)

Evison, H.C., *The Long Dispute: Maori Land Rights and European Colonisation in Southern New Zealand* (Christchurch: Canterbury University Press, 1997)

Ewins, R., 'Fiji's New Western Confederacy' (2000–2001) *JSPL* <http://www.vanuatu.usp.ac.fj/journal_splaw/Special_Interest/Fiji_2000/Fiji_Ewins1.html> [last accessed 6 August 2008]

Farran, S., 'Family Law and French Law in Vanuatu: An Opportunity Missed' (2004) 35 *VUWLR* 367–84

Faulstich, P., ' "You Read 'im This Country": Landscape, Self and Art in an Aboriginal Community' in P. Dark, and R. Rose (eds), *Artistic Heritage in a Changing Pacific* (Bathurst: Crawford House Press, 1993)

Fenton, F.D., *Important Judgements Delivered in the Compensation Court and the Native Land Court 1866–1879* (Auckland: Native Land Court, 1879)

Finnigan, R.A., 'Indian treaty Analysis and Off-reservation Fishing Rights: A Case Study (1975) 51 *WLR* 61

Firth, S., *Australia in International Politics: An Introduction to Australian Foreign Policy* (Crow's Nest, NSW: Allen & Unwin, 2005)

Fitzpatrick, P., *Law and State in Papua New Guinea* (London: Academic Press, 1980)

Forsyth, M., 'Beyond Case Law: Kastom and Courts in Vanuatu' (2004) 35 *VUWLR*

Foster, J.B., *Naked Imperialism: The US Pursuit of Global Dominance* (New York: Monthly Review Press, 2006)

Fraenkel, J., 'Minority Rights in Fiji and the Solomon Islands' UN doc E/CN.4/Sub.2/AC.5/2003/WP.5

Gani, A., 'Some Empirical Evidence on the Determinants of immigration from Fiji to New Zealand' (1998) 32 *NZEP*

Gann, L.H., and Duignan, P. (eds), *Colonialism in Africa 1870–1960* (Cambridge: Cambridge University Press, 1969–75)

Gann, L.H., and Duignan, P. (eds), *The Rulers of British Africa 1879–1914* (London: Croom Helm, 1978)

Ganz, B., 'Indigenous peoples and Land Tenure: An Issue of Human Rights and Environmental Protection' in 9 *GIELR* (1996) 173

Gardiner, W., *Return to Sender: What Really Happened at the Fiscal Envelope Hui* (Auckland; Reed Consumer Books, 1996)

Gardner, D., 'Continuity and Identity: Mineral Development, Land Tenure and "Ownership" Among the Northern Mountain Ok' in Alan Rumsey, and James Welner (eds), *Mining and Indigenous Lifeworlds in Australia and Papua New Guinea* (Oxon: Sean Kingston Publishing, 2004) 101–24

Gaunder, P., *Education and Race Relations in Fiji: 1835–1998* (Lautoka, Fiji: Universal Printing Press, 1999)

Gewertz, D., and Errington, F., *Emerging Class in Papua New Guinea: The Telling of Difference* (Cambridge: Cambridge University Press, 1999)

Ghai, Y., and Cottrell, J., 'A Tale of Three Constitutions: Ethnicity and Politics in Fiji' in Sujit Choudhry (ed), *Constitutional Design for Divided Societies; Integration or Accommodation?* (Oxford: Oxford University Press, 2008) 287–315

Gibbons, A., 'The Peopling of the Pacific' (2001) Science, Vol 229 No 5509, 1735–7

Gibson, J., 'Sheepskin Effects and the Returns to Education in New Zealand; Do They Differ by Ethnic Groups?' (2000) 34 *NZEP*

Gibson, M.T., 'The Supreme Court & Freedom of Expression From 1791 to 1917' (1986) 55 *FOLR* 263

Gille, B., and Sage, Y.L., 'The Territory of French Polynesia' (1993) 23 (1) *VUWLR* 1–14

Gilling, B.D., 'Engine of Destruction? An Introduction to the History of the Maori Land Court' (1994) *24 VUWLR* 115–39

Gillion, K., 'Fiji's Indian Migrants: A History to the End of Indenture in 1920', (Melbourne: Oxford University Press, 1962)

Giraud-Kinley, C., 'The Effectiveness of International Law: Sustainable Development in the South Pacific Region' (1999) 12 *GIELR* 125–76

Glass, A., 'Multiculturalism, Law and the Right of Culture' (2001) 24 *UNSWLJ* 862

Goldflam, R., 'Noble Salvage: Aboriginal Heritage Protection and the Evatt Review' [1997] *ABL* 2; 3(88) 2

Goldring, J., *The Constitution of Papua New Guinea* (Sydney: The Law Book Company, 1978)

Golvan, C., 'Aboriginal Art and the Copyright: The Case for Johnny Bulun Bulun' in *10 EIPR* (1989) 346

Golvan, C., 'Aboriginal Art and the Protection of Indigenous Cultural Rights' (1992) 7 *EIPR* 227

Graham, D., *Trick or Treaty?* (Wellington: Institute of Policy Studies, Victoria University of Wellington, 1997)

Gray, S., 'Aboriginal Designs and Copyright' (1992) 66 *LIJ* 46–9

Gray, S., 'Wheeling, Dealing and Destruction; Aboriginal Art and the Land Post-Mabo' (1993) 63 *ALB* 10

Greenwood, G., *Australia; a Social and Political History* (London: Angus and Robertson, 1955)

Greer, P., 'Aboriginal Women and Domestic Violence in New South Wales' in Julie Stubbs (ed), *Women, Male Violence and the Law* (Sydney: Institute of Criminology, 1994)

Gregory, A., 'Changing Fortunes in New Homeland' *New Zealand Herald* (10 December 2005)

Greif, S., 'Political Attitudes of the Overseas Chinese in Fiji' (1975) 15(11) *AS* 980

Grey, A.H., *Aotearoa & New Zealand: A Historical Geography* (Canterbury: Canterbury University Press, 1994)

Grieco, E., 'The Effects of Migration on the Establishment of Networks: Caste Dis-integration and Reformation among the Indians of Fiji' (1998) 32 (3) *IMR* 709

Griffin, J., Nelson H., and Firth, S., *Papua New Guinea: A Political History* (Victoria: Heinemann Educational, 1979)

Griffiths, J., 'What is Legal Pluralism?' (1986) 24 *JLP* 1–38

Grove, R., *Ecology, Climate and Empire* (Cambridge: White Horse Press, 1977) 3

Halperin, M.H., and Scheffer, D.J., with Small, P.L., *Self-Determination in the New World Order* (Washington DC: Brookings Institute Press, 1992)

Hannum, H., *Autonomy, Sovereignty and Self-determination: The Accommodation of Conflicting Rights* (Philadelphia: University of Pennsylvania Press, 1990)

Hanson, F., 'Promoting a Pacific Pacific: A Functional Proposal for Regional Security in the Pacific Islands' (2003) 4 *MJIL* 254 -98

Harel, A., and Parchomovsky, G., 'On Hate & Equality' (1999) 109(3) *YLJ* 507–9

Harris, B., 'Constitutional Mechanisms for the Protection of Group Rights' (1991) 2 *SLR* (1991) 49

Harris, H., *Its Coming Yet . . . An Aboriginal Treaty Within Australia between Australians* (Canberra: Barossa Vintage Books, 1979)

Harris, M., ' ". . . Another Box of Tjuringas Under the Bed": The Appropriation of Aboriginal Cultural Property to Benefit Non-Indigenous Interests' in J. Castellino and N. Walsh (eds), *International Law and Indigenous Peoples* (Leiden/Boston: Martinus Nijhoff, 2005) 133–57

Harroun, L., 'Intellectual Property Rights in Papua New Guinea' in Kathy Whimp and Mark Busse (eds), *Protection of Intellectual, Biological and Cultural Property in Papua New Guinea* (Port Moresby: Asia Pacific Press, 2000) 29–46

Hassall, G., *Peace Agreements in the Pacific Islands,* Regional Workshop on Conflict Prevention and Peace-building in the Pacific (Nadi: Pacific Islands Forum Secretariat, United Nations DPA, 2005)

Hawke, A., 'New Zealand and Australia: Three Years Later' (2006) 31 *NZIR*

Hawke, G., 'New Zealand and Australia: Moving Together or Drifting Apart?' (2002) 27 *NZIR*

Heinecke, D., Dollery, B., and Fleming, E., 'The Samaritan's Dilemma: The Effectiveness of Australian Foreign Aid to Papua New Guinea' (2008) 62(1) *AJIA* 53–71

Heinz, D., 'The Sabbath in Fiji as Guerilla Theatre'(1993) 61(3) *JAAR* 416

Heraclides, A., *The Self-Determination of Minorities in International Politics* (London: Cass, 1991).

Hinde, G.W., McMorland, D.W., and Sim, P.B.A., *Land Law* (Wellington: Lexis Nexis, 1978)

Hindmarsh, G., 'One Minority People: A Report on the Banabans' (Apia: UNESCO, 2002) 15.

Hoadley, S., 'Immigration Policy: A Steady Convergence' (2003) 28 *NZIR*

Howard, A., 'Rotuma as a Hinterland Community' (1961) 70 *JPS*

Howard, A., and Rensel, J., 'Rotuma' in Brij Lal and Tomasi Vakatora (eds), *Fiji in Transition (Fiji Constitution Review Commission Research Papers, Vol 1)* (Suva, Fji: School of Social and Economic Development, University of South Pacific, 1997)

Howard, A., and Rensel, J., 'Contextualising Histories: Our Rotuman Experience' (2004) 29 (3/4) *PS* 21

Howard, M., *Fiji: Race and Politics in an Island State* (Vancouver: University of British Columbia Press, 1991)

Howe, K.R., *Nature, Culture and History: The 'Knowing' of Oceania* (Honolulu: University of Hawaii Press, 2000)

Howitt, R., *Rethinking Resource Management: Justice, Sustainability and Indigenous Peoples* (London/New York: Routledge, 2001)

Howitt, R., 'Scales of Coexistence: Tackling the Tension Between Legal and Cultural Landscapes in Post-Mabo Australia' in *6 MQLJ* (2006) 49–64.

Hudson, W.J., *New Guinea Empire: Australia's Colonial Experience* (Melbourne: Cassell Australia, 1974)

Huggins, J., 'The 1967 Referendum: Thirty Years On' (1997) 1997/1 *Australian Aboriginal Studies* 3–4

Huntington, S., *The Third Wave: Democratization in the Late Twentieth Century* (Norman: University of Oklahoma Press, 1991)

Irene-Daes, E., *Protection of the Heritage of Indigenous Peoples* (1997) Sub-Commission on Prevention of Discrimination and Protection of Minorities and President of the Working Group on Indigenous Populations, Geneva, 49th Session, E/CN.4/Sub.2/1997/28

Iyer, V., 'Courts and Constitutional Usurpers: Some Lessons from Fiji' (2005) 28 *DLJ* 47

Iyer, V., 'Restoration Constitutionalism in the South Pacific' (2006) 15 *PRLPJ* 54

Jackson, M., *The Maori and the Criminal Justice System: He Whaipaanga Hou—A New Perspective* (Study Series 18, Policy and Research Division) (Auckland: Department of Justice, 1988)

Jackson, R., *The Global Covenant: Human Conduct in a World of States* (Oxford: Oxford University Press, 2003)

Jalal, P.I., 'Pacific Culture and Human Rights: Why Pacific Island Countries Should Ratify International Human Rights Treaties' (2006) Pacific Regional Rights Resource Team (RRRT/UNDP)

James, R.W., *Land Tenure in Papua New Guinea* (Port Moresby, 1985)

Jansz, W., 'Uncultivated, Savage, Cruel, 1606' in Tim Flannery (ed), *The Explorers*, (New York: Grove Press, 1999) 17

Jebens, H., *Pathways to Heaven: Contesting Mainline and Fundamentalist Christianity in Papua New Guinea* (New York: Berghahn Books, 2005) 1

Jennings, I., *The Approach to Self-Governance* (Cambridge: Cambridge University Press, 1956)

Jennings, R., and Watts, A. (eds), *Oppenheim's International Law: Volume 1 Peace* (9th edn. London: Longman, 1992)

Johns, F., 'Portrait of the Artist as a White Man: The International Law of Human Rights and Aboriginal Culture' in 16 *AYIL* (1995) 173–97

Kalinoe L., and Kuwimb, M.J., 'Customary Landowners' Right to Sue for Compensation in Papua New Guinea and the Ok Tedi Dispute' (1997) 25 *MLJ* 65–86

Kambuou, R.N., 'Plant Genetic Resources of Papua New Guinea: Some Thoughts on Intellectual Property Rights' in Kathy Whimp, and Mark Busse (eds), *Protection of Intellectual, Biological and Cultural Property in Papua New Guinea* (Port Moreseby: Asia Pacific Press, 2000) 127

Karsten, P., *Between Law and Custom: 'High' and 'Low' Legal Cultures in the Lands of the British Diaspora: The United States, Canada, Australia and New Zealand, 1600–1900* (Cambridge: Cambridge University Press, 2002)

Keane, D., *Caste-Based Discrimination in International Law* (Aldershot: Ashgate, 2007)

Keith, A.B., *The Dominions as Sovereign States: Their Constitutions and Governments* (London: Macmillan & Co, 1938).

Kelley, T., and Slaney, D., 'A Comparison of Environmental Legislation and Regulation in New Zealand and the United States' (2006) 69 *JEH* 20–2

Kelsey, J., 'World Trade and Small Nations in the South Pacific Region' (2005) 14 *KJLPP* 247–89

Kemp R., Stanton, M., & Blainey, G. (eds), *Speaking for Australia: Parliamentary Speeches That Shaped Our Nation* (Crow's Nest, NSW: Allen & Unwin, 2004)

Kenderdine, S., 'Statutory separateness; Maori Issues in the Planning process and the Social Responsibility of Industry' (1985) *NZLJ* 249

Keyes, T., 'Indigenous Rights Sidelined Again: The Federal Environment Protection and Biodiversity Conservation Bill (1999) 4 *ILB* 22, 14–15

Kingsbury, B., 'Reconciling Five Competing Conceptual Structures of indigenous Claims in International & Comparative Law' (2001) 34 *NYUJILP* 189–250

Kinnane, S., 'Indigenous Sustainability: Rights, Obligations, and a Collective Commitment to Country' in J. Castellino and N. Walsh (eds), *International Law and Indigenous Peoples* (Leiden/Boston: Martinus Nijhoff, 2005) 159–94

Kooiman, J., *Governing as Governance* (London: Sage, 2003)

Koskenniemi, M., 'National Self-Determination Today: Problems of Legal Theory and Practice' (1994) 43 *ICLQ* 857

Kostovicova, D., *Kosovo: The Politics of Identity and Space* (London/New York: Routledge, 2005)

Kretzmer, D., *The Occupation of Justice: The Supreme Court of Israel and the Occupied Territories* (Albany: State University of New York Press, 2002)

Krygier, M., *Between Fear and Hope: Hybrid Thoughts on Public Values* (Sydney: ABC Books, 1997)

Kwa, E., 'Treaty Law Making in Papua New Guinea: After Two Decades, *Yumi Stap We?*' (1997) 25 *MLJ* 43–64

Kymlicka, W., *Multicultural Citizenship: A Liberal Theory of Minority Rights* (Oxford: Oxford University Press, 1995)

Kymlicka, W., 'Theorizing Indigenous Rights' in 49 *UTLJ* (1999) 281–292

Kymlicka, W., *Multicultural Odysseys: Navigating the New International Politics of Diversity* (Oxford: Oxford University Press, 2007)

Lauren, P.G., 'A Very Special Moment in History: New Zealand's Role in the Evolution of International Human Rights' (1998) *NZIR* 1–19

Lawrence, D., *Kakadu: The making of a National Park* (Carlton South, Victoria: Miegunyah Press, 2000)

Lawrey, A., 'Contemporary Efforts to Guarantee Indigenous Rights under International Law' (1990) 23 *VJTL* 703

Legg, M., 'Indigenous Australians and International Law: Racial Discrimination, Genocide and Reparations', in 20 *BBJKIL* (2002) 387

Lenzerini, F., (ed), *Reparations for Indigenous Peoples: International & Comparative Perspectives* (Oxford: Oxford University Press, 2008)

Levey, G.B., 'The Political Theories of Australian Multiculturalism' (2001) 24 *UNSWLJ* 869

Levine, S., 'Culture and Conflict in Fiji, Papua New Guinea, Vanuatu and the Federated States of Micronesia', in Michael Brown and Sumit Ganguly (eds), *Government Policies and Ethnic Relations in the Asia-Pacific* (Cambridge, MA: Massachusetts Institute of Technology Press, 1997) 479

Lijnzaad, L., *Reservations to UN Human Rights Treaties: Ratify and Ruin?* (Dordrecht: Nijhoff, 1995)

Lijphart, A., *Patterns of Democracy: Government Forms and Performance in 36 Countries* (New Haven, CT: Yale University Press, 1999)

Litteral, R., 'Language Development in Papua New Guinea' (Summer Institute of Linguistics Working Papers, 1999) Annex, available at <http://www.sil.org/silewp/1999/002/SILEWP1999–002.html> [last accessed 5 August 2008]

Lola, N., 'Exploring Disallowed Territory: Introducing The Multicultural Subject Into New Zealand Literature' in Docker and Fischer 203–17

Lyons G., 'The Portland Case: Onus and another v Alcoa of Australia Ltd' [1981] *ALB* 14 1(1) 9

Maddison, S., Denniss, R., and Hamilton, C., 'Silencing Dissent: NGOs and Australian Democracy' Canberra: The Australian Institute, Discussion Paper No 65, June 2004, available at <http://www.tai.org.au> [last accessed 1 August 2008]

Maddox, M., *God under Howard: The Rise of the Religious Right in Australian Politics* (Crow's Nest, NSW: Allen & Unwin 2005)

Malezer, L.,'Permanent Forum on Indigenous Issues: Welcome to the Family of the UN' in J. Castellino and N. Walsh (eds), *International Law & Indigenous Peoples* (Leiden/Boston: Martinus Nijhoff, 2005) 67–88

Mangubhai, F., and Mugler, F., 'The Language Situation in Fiji' (2003) 4 *Current Issues in Language Planning* 367–456

Manus, P., 'Indigenous Peoples' Environmental Rights: Evolving Common Law Perspectives in Canada, Australia and the United States' (2008) 33 *BCEALR* 1–86

Marais, J.S., *The Colonization of New Zealand* (Oxford: Oxford University Press, 1927)

Marks, G., 'Avoiding the International Spotlight: Australia, Indigenous Rights and the United Nations Treaty Bodies' (2002) 2(1) *HRLR* 19–57

Marks, K., 'A £160m apology to the Maoris for shameful history of injustice' *The Independent Newspaper* (26 July 2008) 19

Markus, A., *Australian Race Relations* (St. Leonard's: Allen & Unwin, 1994)

Marotta, V., 'The Ambivalence Of Borders: The Bicultural And The Multicultural' in John Docker and Gerhard Fischer, *Race, Colour and Identity in Australia and New Zealand* (NSW: University of New South Wales Press, 2000) 177–90

Marr, C., *Public Works Takings of Maori Land, 1840–1981* (1997) [Report for the Treaty of Waitangi Policy Unit](Rangahaua Whanui National Theme G) (Wellington: Waitangi Tribunal)

Matainaho, L., 'Genetic, Biochemical and Medicinal Resources: How Much Can We Own, Protect and Receive Credit For?' in Kathy Whimp, and Mark Busse (eds), *Protection of Intellectual, Biological and Cultural Property in Papua New Guinea* (Port Moresby: Asia Pacific Press, 2000) 136

Mattoo-Smith, E., Robins, J.H., and Green, R.C., 'Origins and Disperals of Pacific Peoples: Evidence from mtDNA Phylogenies of the Pacific Rat (2004) Vol 101 No 25, *PNASUSA* 9167–72

McElhatton, E., 'Australia and New Zealand: Like minded Defense Partner?' (2006) 31 *NZIR*

McGinty, J.S., 'New Zealand's Forgotten Promises: The Treaty of Waitangi' (1992) *VJTL* 681

McHugh, P. , 'Aboriginal Servitudes and the Land Transfer Act' (1986) 16 *VUWLR* 313

McHugh, P., *The Maori Magna Carta: New Zealand Law and the Treaty of Waitangi* (Auckland: Oxford University Press, 1991)

McKinnon, M., *Immigrants and Citizens. New Zealanders and Asian Immigration in Historical Context* (Wellington: The Printing Press, 1996)

McLay, G. (ed), *Treaty Settlements; The Unfinished Business* (Wellington: NZ Institute of Advanced Legal Studies, 1995)

McLean, D., 'Australia and New Zealand: Two Hearts Not Beating as One' (2001) 26 *NZIR*

McNamara, L., *Regulating Racism: Racial Vilification Laws in Australia* (Sydney: Sydney Institute of Criminology Monograph Series No 16, 2002)

McNeil, K., 'A Question of Title: Has the Common Law Been Misapplied to Dispossess the Aboriginals?' 16 *Monash U L Rev* (1990) 91

McRae, H., Nettheim, G., and Beacroft, L., *Aboriginal Legal Issues: Commentary and Materials* (Sydney: Law Book Company of Australasia, 1991)

Meller, N., and Anthony, J., *Fiji Goes to the Polls* (Honolulu: University of Hawaii Press, 1967)

Meyerson, D., 'Multiculturalism, Religion and Equality' (2001) *Acta Juridica* 104

Miller, J., *Early Victorian New Zealand; A Study of Racial Tension and Social Attitudes 1839–1852* (Oxford/London/New York/Wellington: Oxford University Press, 1958)

Monin, P., 'The Maori Economy of Hauraki 1840–1880' (1995) 29 *NZJH* 197–210

Moore, S. G., and Lemos, M. C., 'Indigenous Policy in Brazil: The Development of Decree 1775 & the Proposed Raposa/Serra do Sol Reserve, Roraima, Brazil' (1999) 21(2) *HRQ* 444–63

Moran, A., *Australia: Nation, Belonging, and Globalization* (New York: Routledge, 2004)

Morauta, L., 'Indigenous Anthropology in Papua New Guinea' (1979) 20 (3) *CA* 561

Morphy, H., 'Now you Understand: An Analysis of the Way Yolngu Have Used Sacred Knowledge to Retain their Autonomy' in M. Langton and N. Peterson (eds), *Aborigines, Land and Land Rights* (1983) 110

Mortensen, R., 'Comity and Jurisdictional Restraint in Vanuatu' (2002) 33 *VUWLR* 95–116

Mugler, F., 'Vernacular Language Teaching in Fiji' in Mugler, F. and Lynch, J., (eds), *Pacific Languages in Education* (Suva, Fiji: Institute of Pacific Studies, 1996) 275

Mulgan, R., *Democracy and Power in New Zealand: A Study of New Zealand Politics* (Auckland: Oxford University Press, 1989)

Mulgan, R., *Maori, Pakeha and Democracy* (Auckland: Oxford University Press, 1989)

Mulvaney, J., and Kamminga, J., *Prehistory of Australia* 1–2 (Smithsonian, 1999)

Muroa, G., 'Recognition of Indigenous Land Rights: A Papua New Guinean Experience' (1994) 22 *MLJ* 81–102

Muroa, G., 'The Extent of Constitutional Protection of Land Rights in Papua New Guinea' (1999) 26 *MLJ* 85–114

Nanda, V., 'Ethnic Conflict in Fiji and International Human Rights Law' (1992) 25 *CILJ* 567

Neill R., *White out: How Politics Is Killing Black Australia* (St. Leonard's, NSW: Allen & Unwin, 2002).

Nettheim G., ' "The Consent of the Natives": Mabo and Indigenous Political Rights' in 15 *SYLR* (1993) 223–46

Nettheim, G., 'Indigenous Australians and the Constitution' (1999) 74 *Reform* 29

Nettheim, G., 'Reconciliation and the Constitution' (1999) 22 *UNSWLJ* 625

Nettheim, G., 'Indigenous Australian Constitutions' (2001) 24 (3) *UNSWLJ* (2001) 840–9

Ng, B., and Ali, K., *Chinese in Fiji* (Suva, Fiji: Institute of Pacific Studies, University of the South Pacific, 2002)

Nollkaemper, A., 'Internationally Wrongful Acts in Domestic Courts' (2007) 101 *AJIL* 760–99

Norton, R., *Race and Politics in Fiji* (St Lucia: University of Queensland Press, 1977)

Nugent, M., *Botany Bay: Where Histories Meet* (Crow's Nest, NSW: Allen & Unwin, 2005)

Núñez Astrain, L., *The Basques: Their Struggle for Independence* (Cardiff: Welsh Academic Press, 1997) Stephens, M. (translator)

Nunn, P., 'Recent Environmental Changes on Pacific Islands' (1990) 156 (2) *GJ* 125–40

O'Bryan, K., 'The Appropriation of Indigenous Ecological Knowledge: Recent Australian Developments' in 1 *MQJICEL* (2004) 29–48

O'Connor, P.S., 'Keeping New Zealand White, 1908–1920' (1986) 2 *NZJH* 41–65

Ogle, L., 'The Environment Protection and Biodiversity Conservation Act 1999 (Cth): How Workable is it?' in 17 *EPLJ* (2000) 468

Olowu, D., 'The United Nations Human Rights Treaty System and the Challenges of Commitment and Compliance in the South Pacific' (2006) 7 *MJIL* 155–84

Opeskin, B.R., and Rothwell, D.R. (eds), *International Law & Australian Federalism* (Melbourne: Melbourne University Press, 1997)

Oppenheimer, S., 'The Express Train from Taiwan to Polynesia: On the Congruence of Proxy Lines of Evidence' (2004) 36(4) *WA*

Orange, C., *The Treaty of Waitangi* (Wellington: Allen & Unwin, 1987)

Orlow, D., 'Of Nations Small: The Small State in International Law' (1995) 9 *TICLJ*

Osaghae, E., 'Federalism in Comparative Perspective' in 16 *Politeia* (1997) 1

Otto, D., 'A Question of Law or Politics? Indigenous Claims to Sovereignty in Australia' (1995) 21 *SJILC* 65–103

Palat, R., 'Pacific Century: Myth or Reality?' (1996) 25 (3) *Theory and Society* 303–47

Palmer, K.A., *The Planning System and the Recognition of Maori Tribal Plans* (Ministry of the Environment: RMLR Working Paper No 28, 1988)

Parasad, S., Dakuvula, J., and Snell, D., *Economic Development, Democracy and Ethnic Conflict in the Fiji Islands* (London: Minority Rights Group, 2001)

Parkinson, P., 'Strangers in the House: The Maori Language in Government and the Maori Language in Parliament 1865–1900' (2001) 32 *VUWLR*, Monograph 1–60

Paterson, D., 'New Impulses in the Interaction of Law and Religion: A South Pacific Perspective' (2003) *BYULR* 593–623

Patterson, J., 'Maori Environmental Values' in 16 *Environmental Ethics* (1994) 397

Pearson, N., *Our Right to Take Responsibility* (Cairns, Queensland: Noel Pearson and Associates, 2000)

Pike, D., *Paradise of Dissent: South Australia, 1829–1857* (Melbourne: Melbourne University Press, 1957)

Pocock, J.G.A., 'Law, Sovereignty and History in a Divided Culture: The Case of New Zealand and the Treaty of Waitangi' (1998) 43 *MGLJ* 481

Poirier, R., and Ostergren, D., 'Evicting People from Nature: Indigenous Land Rights and National Parks in Australia, Russia and the United States' (2002) 42 *National Resources J* 331–52

Posey, D.A., and Dutfield, G., *Beyond Intellectual Property: Toward Traditional Resource Rights for Indigenous Peoples and Local Communities* (Ottawa: International Development Research Centre, 1996)

Povinelli, E.A. (ed), *The Cunning of Recognition* (Durham/London: Duke University Press, 2002)

Peebles, D., *Pacific Regional Order* (Canberra: Australian National University, 2005)

Powles, G., 'Duties of Individuals: Some Implications for the Pacific Including "Duties" in "Human Rights" Documents' (1992) 22 (3) *VUWLR*, 49

Powles, G., 'Changing Pacific Island Constitutions: Methods and Philosophies' (1992) 22 *VUWLR* 63–83

Power, T., and Gasiorowski, M., 'Institutional Design and Democratic Consolidation in the Third World' (1997) 30(2) *Comparative Political Studies* 132

Premdas, R., *Ethnic Conflict and Development: The Case of Fiji* (United Nations Research in Ethnic Relations Series) (Aldershot: Ashgate, 1995)

Preston, R., 'Refugees in Papua New Guinea: Government Response and Assistance, 1984–1988' (1992) 26 (3) *IMR* 843–76

Pritchard, S., 'Special Measures' in Race Discrimination Commissioner (ed), *Racial Discrimination Act: A Review* (1995) 183

Pritchard, S., 'Native Title from the Perspective of International Standards' in 18 *AYIL* (1997) 127–74 at 130–6

Pritchard, S., 'Constitutional Developments in Northern Territory' (1998) 4(15) *ILB*

RAFI (Rural Advancement Foundation International), *Patents, Indigenous Peoples, and Human Genetic Diversity* (Ottawa, Canada: RAFI Communiqué, May 1993)

Rafiqul Islam, M., 'The Bougainville Secession Crisis in Papua New Guinea' (1990) 18 *MLJ* 31–7

Ranney, A., and Penniman, H.R., *Democracy in the Islands: The Micronesian Plebiscites of 1983* (Washington DC: American Enterprise Institute for Public Policy Research, 1985)

Rees, N., 'Police Questioning of Aborigines and Islanders: The Bonner Bill' in *ALB* (1981) 1, available at <http://www.austlii.edu.au/au/journals/AboriginalLB/1981/5.html> [last accessed 31 March 2008]

Reilly, A., 'A Constitutional Framework for Indigenous Governance' in 28 *Sydney L Rev* (2006) 403–35

Reilly, B., 'Party Politics in Papua New Guinea: A Deviant Case?' (1999) 72(2) *PA* 225–46

Reilly, B., 'Democracy, Ethnic Fragmentation and Internal Conflict: Confused Theories, Faulty Data and the "Crucial Case" of Papua New Guinea' (2000) 25(3) *IS* 162–85

Reilly, B., and Phillpot, R., ' "Making Democracy Work" in Papua New Guinea: Social Capital and Provincial Development in an Ethnically Fragmented Society' (2002) 42(6) *AS* 906–27

Reynolds, H., *The Laws of the Land* (2nd edn. Sydney: Penguin Australia, 1992)

Reynolds, H., *Aboriginal Society: Reflections on Race, State and Nation* (Crow's Nest, NSW: Allen & Unwin, 1996)

Reynolds, H., *Aboriginal Sovereignty* (Sydney: Allen & Unwin, 1996)

Reynolds, H., 'The Law of the Land' available at <http://www.austlii.edu.au/au/journals/AboriginalLB/1987/57.html> [last accessed 2 April 2008]

Rodman, M.C., *Masters of Tradition: Consequences of Customary Land Tenure in Longana, Vanuatu* (Vancouver: University Of British Columbia Press, 1987)

Rodrigues, M.G.M., 'Indigenous Rights in Democratic Brazil' (2002) 24(2) *HRQ* 487–512

Ryan, M. (ed), *Encyclopaedia of Papua and New Guinea* (Carlton: Melbourne University Press, 1972)

Rynkiewich, M., *Cultures and Languages of Papua New Guinea* (Goroka: The Melanesian Institute for Pastoral and Socio-economic Service, 2004)

Sadurski, W., '*Gerhardy v Brown* v the Concept of Discrimination; Reflections on the Landmark Case that Wasn't' (1986) *11 SYLR* 5

Schabas, W.A., *Genocide: The Crime of Crimes* (Cambridge: Cambridge University Press, 2002)

Schmidhauser, J.R., 'The Struggle for Cultural Survival: The Fishing Rights of the Treaty Tribes of the Pacific Northwest' (1976) *52 NDL* 30

Schuster, M., in Jurg Wassmann (ed), *Historical Atlas of Ethnic and Linguistic Groups in Papua New Guinea* (Basel: Institute of Ethnology, University of Basel, 1995)

Segal, G., *Rethinking the Pacific* (Oxford: Clarendon Press, 1990)

Senate Standing Committee on Constitutional and Legal Affairs, 'Two Hundred Years later: A Report on the Feasibility of a Compact or 'Makarrata' between the Commonwealth and Aboriginal People' (Canberra, 1983)

Shameem, S., 'New Impulses in the Interaction of Law and Religion' (2003) *BYULR* 661

Sharp, N., *No Ordinary Judgment* (Canberra: Aboriginal Studies Press, 1996)

Sharp, N., *Saltwater People: The Waves of Memory* (Crow's Nest, NSW: Allen & Unwin, 2002)

Shelton, D., 'Reparations for Indigenous Peoples: The Present Value of Past Wrongs' in Federico Lenzerini (ed), *Reparations for Indigenous Peoples: International & Comparative Perspectives* (Oxford: Oxford University Press, 2008) 1–19

Shergold, P., Secretary, Department of the PM and Cabinet quoted in DIMIS, *New Arrangements in Indigenous Affairs (2005)* available at <www.oipc.gov.au/About_oipc/new_arrangements.asp>

Sibley, C.G., 'Political Attitudes and the Ideology of Equality: Differentiating Support for Liberal and Conservative Political Parties in New Zealand' (2007) 36 *NZJP*

Siegel, J., *Language Contact in a Plantation Environment: A Sociolinguistic History of Fiji* (Cambridge: Cambridge University Press, 1987)

Silverman, M., 'The Resettled Banaban (Ocean Island) Community in Fiji: A Preliminary Report' (1962) 3 (4) *CA* 429

Simpson, T., 'Claims of Indigenous Peoples to Cultural Property in Canada, Australia, and New Zealand' (1994–1995) 18 *HICLR* 195–221

Sinclair, K., *The Origins of the Maori Wars* (Wellington: New Zealand University Press, 1957)

Sinclair, K., *A History of New Zealand* (Harmondsworth: Penguin Books, 1959)

Smandych, R., Lincoln R., and Wilson P., 'Towards a Cross-Cultural Theory of Aboriginal Culture: A Comparative Study of the Problem of Aboriginal Overrepresentation in the Criminal Justice Systems of Canada and Australia' in 3 *ICJR* (1993) 1–24

Spate, O.H.K., ' "South Sea" to "Pacific Ocean": A Note on Nomenclature' (1977) 12 (4) *JPH* 205–11

Strang, H., *Homicides in Australia 1990–1991* (Canberra: Australian Institute of Criminology, 1992)

Strelein, L., 'From *Mabo* to *Yorta Yorta*: Native Title Law in Australia' (2005) 19 *WUJLP* 225–72 at 228

Stubbs, J., and Tolmie, J., 'Falling Short of the Challenge? A Comparative Assessment of the Australian Use of Expert Evidence on the Battered Woman Syndrome' (1999) 23 *MULR* 709–48

Sutherland, W., *Beyond the Politics of Race: An Alternative History of Fiji to 1992* (Canberra: Australian National University, 1992)

Sutton, P., 'Archaeology and Linguistics: Aboriginal Australia in Global Perspective' 72 *Oceania* (2001)

Tacon, M., 'Papua New Guinea in 2000: Taking the Bull by the Horns' (2000) 41(1) *AS* 143–7

Taiaiake, A., *Peace, Power, Righteousness: An Indigenous Manifesto* (1999)

Tamihere, J., 'Te Take Maori: Maori Perspectives of Legislation and its interpretation with an Emphasis on Planning Law' (1985) 5 *AULR* 137

Tarte, S., and Kabutaulaka, T.T., 'Rethinking Security in the South Pacific: Fiji and the Solomon Islands' in Bruce Vaughn (ed), *The Unravelling of Island Asia? Governmental, Communal and Regional Instability* (Westport, CT: Praeger, 2002) 61–82

Taylor, S., 'The Pacific Solution or a Pacific Nightmare? The Difference between Burden Shifting and Responsibility Sharing' (2005) 6 *APLPJ* 1–43

Techera, E.J., 'Protected Area Management in Vanuatu' (2005) 2 *MJICEL* 107–19

Tench, W., *Sydney's First Four Years* (Botany Bay, NSW: Angus & Robertson, 1961)

Terrell, J., Hunt, T., and Gosden, C., 'The Dimensions of Social Life in the Pacific: Human Diversity and the Myth of the Primitive Isolate' (1997) 28 (2) *CA* 155

Thakur, R., and Wood, A., 'Fiji in Crisis' (1988) 43 *World Today* 207

Thomas, N., *Marquesan Societies: Inequality and Political Transformation in Eastern Polynesia* (Oxford: Clarendon Press, 1990)

Thompson, A.S., *The Story of New Zealand* (London: John Murray, 1859)

Thompson E., *Fair Enough: Egalitarianism in Australia* (Sydney, NSW: University of New South Wales Press, 1994)

Thomson, B., *The Fijians: A Study in the Decay of Custom* (London: Dawsons, 1908, reprinted *Fiji Times*, Suva, Fiji, 1981)

Thornberrry, P., *International Law and the Rights of Minorities* (Oxford: Clarendon Press, 1991)

Thornberry, P., *Indigenous Peoples and Human Rights* (Manchester: Manchester University Press, 2002)

Tickner, R., 'Government response to the final report of the RCIADIC' in *Aboriginal and Islander Health Worker Journal* (1992) 16–19

Tierney, S., *Accommodating National Identity* (Leiden: Martinus Nijhoff, 1999).

Tobin, B., 'The Search for an Interim Solution', in Kathy Whimp and Mark Busse (eds), *Protection of Intellectual, Biological and Cultural Property in Papua New Guinea* (Port Moresby: Asia Pacific Press, 2000) 169–82

Trebilcock, M., and Knetsh, J., 'Land Policy and Economic Development in Papua New Guinea (1981) 9 *MLJ* 102–15

Triggs, G., 'Australia's Indigenous Peoples and International Law: Validity of the Native Title Amendment Act 1998 (Cth)' in 23 *MULR* (1999) 372–415

Tuffin, K., 'Racist Discourses in New Zealand and Australia: Reviewing the Last 20 Years' (2008) 2(2) *SPPC* 591–607

Tully, J., 'The Struggles of Indigenous Peoples for and of Freedom' in Duncan Ivison, Paul Patton, and Will Sanders (eds), *Political Theory and the Rights of Indigenous Peoples* (Cambridge: Cambridge University Press, 2002) 36–59

Turnbull, C., *A Concise History of Australia* (London: Thames & Hudson, 1965)

Turner, M., *Papua New Guinea: The Challenge of Independence* (Harmondsworth: Penguin, 1990)

Unwin, G., 'Australia, New Zealand and the South Pacific' (2006) 31 *NZIR*

Upson-Hooper, K., 'Slaying the Leviathan: Critical Jurisprudence and the Treaty of Waitangi' (1998) 28 *VUWLR* 683

Van Dyke, J., 'Prospects for the Development of Inter-governmental Human Rights Bodies in Asia and the Pacific' (1988) 16 *MLR* 28–33

Vanstone, Senator Amanda, 'Minister Announces New Indigenous Representation Arrangements' Press Release (20 June 2005)

Vasil, R.K., 'Communalism and Constitution-making in Fiji' (1972) 45 *PA* 23

Viljoen, F., *International Human Rights Law in Africa* (Oxford: Oxford University Press, 2007)

Voigt, A., and Drury, N., *Wisdom from the Earth* (Boston: Shambhala Publishers, 1997)

Vrachnas, J., *et al*, *Migration and Refugee law: Principles and Practice in Australia* (Cambridge: Cambridge University Press, 2005)

Waiko, J., *A Short History of Papua New Guinea* (Oxford: Oxford University Press, 1993)

Waldron J., 'Superseding historic Injustice' in 103 *Ethics* (1992) 4

Waldron, J., 'Redressing Historical Injustice' in Lukas H. Meyer (ed), *Justice in Time: Responding to Historical Injustice* (Baden-Baden: Nomos Verlagsgesellschaft, 2004) 55–77

Waldron, W., 'Indigeneity? First Peoples and Last Occupancy' (2003) 1 *NZJPIL* 56–82

Ward, A., *National Overview*, Vol II, 255–78

Ward, R.G., 'The Population of Fiji', (1959) 49(3) *GR* 338

Watanabe, A., 'Japan, the United States, and the Pacific since 1945: An Overview' (1989) 16 *Ecology L Q* 9–21

Watson-Gegeo, K.A., 'The Study of Language Use in Oceania' (1986) 15 *ARA* 154

Way, F., and Beckett, S., 'Governance Structures for Indigenous Australians On and Off Native Title Lands' *Discussion Paper 4—Land-Holding and Governance Structures under Australian Land Rights Legislation* (University of New South Wales and Murdoch University, unspecified date) available at *Indigenous Law Resources: Reconciliation and Social Justice Library* at <http://www.austlii.edu.au/au/other/IndigLRes/1998/3/4. html> [last accessed 27 January 2009]

Weisbrodt, D., 'Comment on the ALRC Discussion Paper: Customary Law' (1981) 2 *ALB* 1(1), 3

West, P., and Brechin S. (eds), *Resident Peoples and National Parks* (Arizona: University of Arizona Press, 1991)

Westermark, G.D., 'Reflections on Customary Law: The Mirror of Pacific Kastom' (1993–1994) 17 *LSF* 269–73

Wheatley, S., *Democracy, Minorities and International Law* (Cambridge: Cambridge University Press, 2005)

Whelan, A., 'Wilsonian Self-Determination and the Versailles Settlement' (1994) 43 *ICLQ* 99–115

White, H., 'Including Local Communities in the Negotiation of Mining Agreements: The Ok Tedi Example' (1995) 8 *TL* 307

Wickliffe, C., 'Human Rights Education in the Pacific' (1999) 3 *JSPL*

Wilde, R., 'NGO Proposals for an Asia-Pacific Human Rights System' (1999) 1 *YHRDLJ* 137–42

Wiessner, S., 'Rights and Status of Indigenous Peoples: a Global Comparative and International Legal Analysis' in 12 *HHRJ* (Spring 1999) 57–128

Williams, G., 'Republic of *Fiji v Prasad*' (2001) in 2 *MJIL* 150

Williams, J.R., 'The Land Question in Fiji', FCO 24/1143, 5 October 1971

Wippman, D., 'Powersharing as a Response to Cultural Dominance' (1996) 90 *ASILP* 206

Wolfers, E., 'Joint Creation: The Bougainville Peace Agreement and Beyond' available from Conciliation Resources <http://www.c-r.org/our-work/accord/png-bougainville/joint-creation.php> [accessed 4 July 2008]

World Conservation Union, Javier Beltran (ed), *Indigenous & Traditional Peoples and protected Areas: Guidelines and Case Studies* (Gland, Switzerland: IUCN Gland, Switzerland and Cambridge, UK and WWF International, 2000)

Xanthaki, A., 'Multiculturalism and Extremism: International Law Perspectives' in Rehman, J., and Breau, S. (eds), *Religion, Human Rights Law and International Law* (The Hague: Martinus Nijhoff Publishers, 2007) 443–64

Yael, T., 'A Note on Multiculturalism and Cultural Dominance' (1996) 90 *ASILP* 200

Yildiz, K., *The Kurds in Iraq: The Past, Present and Future* (London: Pluto Press, 2004)

Zorn, J., 'Fighting Over Land' (1976) 4 *MLJ* 7–36

Index